The *Hellraiser* Films
and Their Legacy

ALSO OF INTEREST BY
PAUL KANE AND MARIE O'REGAN

Voices in the Dark: Interviews with Horror Writers, Directors and Actors (McFarland, 2011)

The *Hellraiser* Films and Their Legacy

PAUL KANE

Foreword by Doug Bradley

McFarland & Company, Inc., Publishers
Jefferson, North Carolina, and London

All the photographs and images used in this book are from private collections and picture libraries and are used solely for the advertising, promotion, publicity and review of the specific motion pictures they illustrate. They have not been reproduced for advertising or poster purposes, nor to create the appearance of a specially licensed or authorized publication. Grateful acknowledgment is made to the following for the use of their material. All rights reserved. While every effort has been made to trace and acknowledge all creators and copyright holders, the author apologizes for any errors or omissions and, if informed, will be glad to make corrections in any subsequent editions.

Clive Barker, Gary J. Tunnicliffe, Doug Bradley, Randy Falk (NECA), Stephen Lane (The Prop Store of London), Les Edwards, Phil and Sarah Stokes (Revelations), Marc Calma and Kacey Rodriguez, David A. Magitis, Eric Gross, Shelly Berggren, David Robinson, Eric Horton, Mark Thompson (Checker Books), Gabrielle White (Random House), Dan Cope, Nathan Green, David Stoner (Silva Screen), Rita Eisenstein (Starlog Group), Ian Frost and Dan Forbes.

The present work is a reprint of the illustrated case bound edition of The *Hellraiser Films and Their Legacy*, *first published in 2006 by McFarland.*

LIBRARY OF CONGRESS CATALOGUING-IN-PUBLICATION DATA

Kane, Paul, 1973–
The Hellraiser films and their legacy / Paul Kane ; foreword by Doug Bradley.
    p.   cm.
Includes bibliographical references and index.

ISBN 978-0-7864-7717-3
softcover : acid free paper ∞

1. Hellraiser films—History and criticism.   I. Title.
PN1995.9.H42K36   2013   791.43'67 — dc22   2006029845

BRITISH LIBRARY CATALOGUING DATA ARE AVAILABLE

© 2006 Paul Kane. All rights reserved

No part of this book may be reproduced or transmitted in any form or by any means, electronic or mechanical, including photocopying or recording, or by any information storage and retrieval system, without permission in writing from the publisher.

On the cover: Doug Bradley as the Lead Cenobite (Pinhead) in *Hellraiser* (New World Pictures/Photofest)

Manufactured in the United States of America

*McFarland & Company, Inc., Publishers
Box 611, Jefferson, North Carolina 28640
www.mcfarlandpub.com*

For Eric Popplewell and Shelley Baker: tutors and friends.
You pulled back the magician's curtain and allowed me to look behind.
With huge respect and thanks.

Acknowledgments

This book couldn't have been written without the help and support of so many people: My mum and dad, and the rest of my family, Clive Barker, Kurt Adam, Doug Bradley, Stephen Jones, Michael Marshall Smith, Kim Newman, Peter Atkins, Gary J. Tunnicliffe, David Robinson, Randy Falk, Les & Val Edwards, Frazer Lee, Shelly Berggren, John B. Ford, Simon Clark, Russell Blackwood, Shannon Larratt, Alec Worley, Joseph O'Regan, Bob Keen, Mark Thompson, Eric Gross, Yoram Allon, Max Lichtor, Allan Bryce, Constance Taylor, Nathan Green, Dan Cope, Peter E. Keighrey, Rita Eisenstein, Ken Patterson, Eric Horton, Christopher Fowler, Martin Roberts and Helen Hopley, Marc Calma, Lee Glasby and Claire Wood-Glasby, David Stoner, Peggy J. Shumate, Gabrielle White, Kevin Knott, Judith A. and Scott Richard, Ken Snyder, Phil and Sarah Stokes, David Bamford, Dan Forbes, Caroline Noonan at HarperCollins UK, Peter London at HarperCollins US, Ian Frost, Neil Gaiman, Ed Martinez, Tim Lawes, Stephen Lane, David A. Magitis, and, of course, Marie O'Regan, who has been my anchor while writing this book and who persuaded me to do it in the first place. A big thank you to everyone.

Table of Contents

Acknowledgments   vi
Foreword by Doug Bradley   1
Preface   5

1. The Road to Hell   9
2. Opening the Box   27
3. Demons to Some   40
4. Such Sights to Show You   45
5. No Limits   51
6. To Hell and Back   53
7. Opening Doors   66
8. The Doctor Is In   77
9. The Devil You Know?   84
10. The Sweet Suffering   92
11. Earthbound   95
12. Completing the Pattern, Solving the Puzzle, Turning the Key   114
13. Pinhead Unbound   126
14. What Started in Hell   130
15. Production Hell   132
16. Open the Gates, Lay Low the Ramparts   144
17. A Distinct Sense of Déjà Vu   155
18. A Bloodline Cursed to the End of Time   157
19. Dante's Footsteps   159
20. A World Full of Riddles   167
21. Welcome to Hell   173
22. Hide and Seek   175

23. All Problems Solved	181
24. Hellbound Hearts	187
25. Sought After?	189
26. Deader Certainty	191
27. Fear Is Where We Go to Learn	199
28. Deader, Like Me?	203
29. Hell of a World	204
30. Welcome to the Party	210
31. World in Action	215
32. No More Souls	217
33. Comics from Hell	219
34. Further Explorations	224
Chapter Notes	229
Bibliography	237
Index	243

Foreword

by Doug Bradley

It is, as I write this, exactly nineteen years to the month since the cameras were rolling at Cricklewood Production Village in North London on a largely unheralded, British-made, American-produced horror film whose darkly enigmatic subject matter provides the inspiration for this book. In the intervening time, I have been pretty thoroughly cross-examined about that same subject matter — in print, on radio and TV, in person at conventions and, latterly, increasingly via email — and in particular, of course, about the role of those mysterious leather-clad theologians of the Order of The Gash and their unceasing explorations in the higher reaches of pleasure.

In a question and answer session more than ten years ago, I recall being asked, "Do you think the ending of *Hellbound* suggests that there is no possibility of Heaven, only the certainty of Hell?" I didn't have an answer then, and I'm not sure I do now. More than likely I turned the proposition back on the questioner to buy thinking time: "Wow, that's a great question. I'm not sure. What do you think?" Or I may have fled to The Last Resort, what might be called, with thanks to the United States Constitution, the Actor's Fifth. "Hey, come on, guys. It's just a movie, you know."

More recently, I've found myself approached on film sets with the query, "What do you think, Doug? Are we allowed to do this?" "What do you mean, allowed to do it?" "Well, is it right? Does it fit the mythology?" In those situations, I feel like some kind of representative for the Union of Cenobites and Assorted Soul Tearers. "Hold on, I'll just consult my manual. Now look: page 42, clause 3, paragraph E, section (i) clearly states...." In fact, my answer tends to be: if it feels right, do it. It's more a question of ideas being good or bad, exciting or dull, original or hackneyed, rather than right or wrong. Besides, if something is going to have the temerity to claim the name of mythology for itself, it cannot be finished or immutable: it must be fluid, constantly changing and modifying, and have the ability to be one thing today and something quite different tomorrow.

I have good reason for taking this approach. Towards the end of filming *Hell on Earth* I sat in the bar of the Howard Johnson hotel in High Point, North Carolina, listening to a fellow cast member outline his idea for the fourth film. I don't remember the details, but it somehow involved the Lament Configuration and, by extension, Pinhead being fired into outer space to rid the earth of its power. It would somehow find its way onto a space station and.... Well, I think I nodded politely while feeling that he should possibly spend less time in the bar. Pinhead in space? Don't be ridiculous. And look what happened next. I don't *think*, by the way, that I ever recounted that story to Clive Barker.

I think I know Clive well enough to assert that if you give him a rule book, his first instinct will be to torch it: tell him what he can't do and he'll gleefully roll up his sleeves and dive right in. Catch him in a mischievous mood, and he'll be the first to say, "Look, this is an entertainment I dreamed up to enliven a drab Tuesday afternoon in February. It's not that big of a deal." Or, as he once said to an audience when sharing a stage with me at a Fangoria convention, "It's just a guy with a bunch of nails banged into his head. Get over it."

But this is Clive Barker, so it's not quite that easy, is it? As with all his work, the ideas in his *divertissement* of a dysfunctional family and the nasty secret in its attic, his *sonata* for puzzle box, hooks and chains, linger in the mind long after the film has finished: fascinating and frightening, delighting and disturbing. And it has continued to do that for millions of

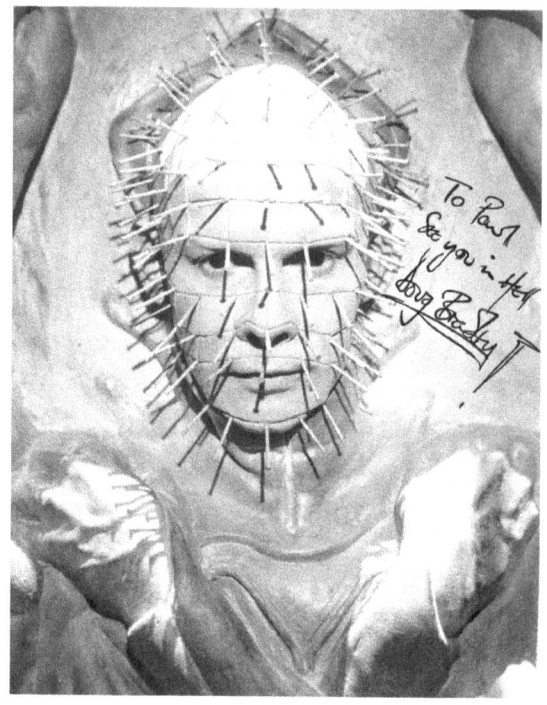

Hellraiser III: Hell on Earth still (photograph credit Keith Payne).

Paul Kane with Doug Bradley at the British Fantasy Society Open Night 2 September 2005 (copyright Paul Kane).

people around the planet across nearly two decades, eight (to date) films and numerous comic strips, graphic novels and who knows what other manifestations.

But this is why we come to horror films after all, isn't it? Not just to hide behind our hands and the sofa cushions, to squirm at the gore and jump at the shocks. For me, the ideas and the imagery in a horror film have always been as important as anything else. And it's the nature of those ideas that draws us in, the deeper, darker — dare I say it — more profound ideas than you're going to find in, say, the average Richard Curtis movie. In the — God help us all — nearly forty years that I've known him, it is that realm that Clive has been restlessly and relentlessly roaming. Paul Kane has, wisely or otherwise, chosen to follow in the great man's footsteps, to reach down into the reeking heart of this mythology and see what he comes up with. I'll leave it to you to find out exactly what that might be, but I can assure you that he has left few, if any, stones unturned in his pursuit. It would be, perhaps, facile of me to say that he has such sights to show you, but the simple fact is, he has.

Doug Bradley
London, Fall 2006

PREFACE

Welcome to Hell.

By opening this book you have entered into an agreement. The contents are only for those with a craving, a passion to learn about the *Hellraiser* mythos, primarily the cinematic interpretations, but also its intrusion into other artistic and cultural forms. If you are not ready to witness such sights, then this book may not be for your eyes. But if you come with me I guarantee an experience that will stay with you for eternity.

And as with most legends it all began with one person: a storyteller.

"I have seen the future of Horror and his name is Clive Barker." It is perhaps appropriate that with these almost prophetic words of praise from the one-man American horror factory that is Stephen King, audiences were introduced to the shocking yet spectacular cinematic vision of Clive Barker. For there they were in big white letters preceding the trailer to the very first *Hellraiser* movie, unleashed upon an unsuspecting public in 1987. I say it was appropriate because these two masters of the macabre have much in common. Both are, of course, best-selling novelists. Both stamp their own inimitable signature on anything they produce — so much so that readers soon spotted the connection between King and his literary alter ego, Richard Bachman. But, more significantly, both have also written and directed movies in their time.

However, while King's attempt at filmmaking resulted in a critical and box office failure (*Maximum Overdrive*, 1986),[1] Barker's first commercially released film went on to become one of the most distinctive and chilling pieces of celluloid since *Night of the Living Dead* (George A. Romero, 1968) or *The Exorcist* (William Friedkin, 1973), spawning a franchise which is still active today. At the time of this writing there have been seven motion picture sequels (taking in a variety of genres from science fiction and historical to murder mystery and serial killer), a number of spin-off comics, and even been talk of a TV production. Horror and film fans regularly cite the original movie as among their favorites,[2] and it groomed a legion of devoted fans worldwide eager to taste more of the pleasures on offer. The British Film Institute's *Companion to Horror* acknowledged its contribution to the continuing redefining of the genre in the late twentieth century[3] and its far-reaching stylistic legacy can be detected in films such as *Cube* (Vincenzo Natali, 1997), *Event Horizon* (Paul W.S. Anderson, 1997), *Dark City* (Alex Proyas, 1998), *The Cell* (Tarsem Singh, 2000), *The Matrix Reloaded/Revolutions* (The Wachowski Brothers, 2003), *Hellboy* (Guillermo del Toro, 2004) and *White Noise* (Geoffrey Sax, 2005), as well as in TV series such as *The X-Files*, *Buffy the Vampire Slayer* (most notably in the silent Gentlemen of "Hush"), *Star Trek: The Next Generation* (who could fail to notice the similarities between the Borg and their Cenobite counterparts?) and *Farscape* (the character of Scorpius). The

Clive Barker at the Forbidden Planet signing for *Weaveworld* in London, 1987 (courtesy Forbidden Planet; photograph credit Dick Jude).

series' figurehead was even immortalized on that most reliable gauge of public opinion, *The Simpsons* (in a 1994 Halloween special).

But what makes its conception even more remarkable is the fact that the first movie was shot in the director's native England. Admittedly, funding came from the U.S., but this was still an achievement at a time when the UK's cinematic contributions to the horror scene could be listed on the back of a small tombstone. In the days when Hammer's productions were a distant memory, Barker was one of the few talents attempting to revitalize the industry on British shores, as recognized in Steve Chibnall and Julian Petley's *British Horror Cinema*, which called him "One of Britain's undoubted horror auteurs."[4]

Because of his involvement at every stage of the film, from writing the novella on which it was based to providing demon drawings and hand painting special effects onto film cells, there certainly *is* a case for *Hellraiser* being not only one of the landmark horror films of all time, but also a true auteur movie.[5] The titles don't just say *Hellraiser*, they say *Clive Barker's Hellraiser*. Barker would be the first to admit that he approached the venture knowing relatively little about directing, and that the support of experts like cinematographer Robin Vidgeon and make-up effects man Bob Keen was invaluable, but the film sits very neatly within his canon of work as a whole. The look is pure Barker, as are the themes and the ambitious scope, something that ensuing writers and directors picked up on then extended even further.

As so often happens, nobody who worked on the movie could comprehend just how much of a phenomenon *Hellraiser* would become, though most did realize they were creating something more cerebral than its contemporaries. To quote Keen: "I think we thought it was going to be a good film, an original film. But I don't think we thought it would be as big—you couldn't possibly imagine ... I think we thought it would be a stepping stone to other projects, but it really caught the imagination of the audience."[6]

And there can be no doubt that much of this has to do with the central character of Pinhead himself. Unwittingly, Barker—with the help of Keen, partner Geoff Portass, and actor Doug Bradley—gave the genre and popular culture one of its enduring icons. A figure that could so easily have been presented as a disgusting mess was turned into something outlandish and transfixing, elegant and even beautiful, in its own way. Viewers embraced Pinhead, ensuring that he would be the one constant factor throughout the history of the film series, and that he would develop during the course of that time on screen. We would discover his background, see him run amok on earth, toy with the lives of key individuals, and finally return full circle. It would also mean fame for the man who played him, having his image plastered twenty feet high on billboard posters.

Barker, too, was catapulted to celebrity status because of *Hellraiser*, as his appearances on chat shows and TV programs testified—allowing him, like his champion King, to reach a much wider audience and readership. Although he limited his involvement after the first movie—to executive producer, occasional consultant, a name at the beginning, "Clive Barker Presents"—and concentrated more on his books and painting than directing, the originator of this series has returned to its themes time and time again, so much so that a current cinematic project (at the time of this writing) revolves around the Cenobite-esque Tortured Souls, and a novella in his new fiction collection, *Scarlet Gospels*, features Pinhead, albeit recounting his demise. Barker's presence is perpetually felt and his bloody fingerprints will always be on the screen, in spite of the fact that he had to give up the cinematic rights to the characters to get the first installment made. In essence, it was Barker's own deal with the Devil.

Not a bad price to pay, some might argue, for it has secured his place in history. But it is the history of *Hellraiser* in its entirety that this book is about. And now that the introductions—and warnings—are over and done with, the examination can at last begin.

Time to play.

1

THE ROAD TO HELL

The road to Hell, they say, is paved with good intentions. But in Clive Barker's universe it is paved only with desire, torture, suffering, and exquisite pleasure.

Clive Barker was born in Liverpool on October 5, 1952, to a father who worked in industrial relations and a mother who was a schoolteacher. From an early age, there were incidents and events that informed his later work. For instance, he attributes his own fear of—and fascination with—blood to a distressing caesarean birth: "There was a series of traumatic first impressions of the world, which I believe have become a *leitmotif* of terror for me. A lot of noise. Panicked voices ... I think the first few minutes of my life were just horrible."[1] Most significantly, with regards to *Hellraiser*, Barker's grandfather was a ship's cook who brought him back exotic presents from the Far East. One of these just happened to be a puzzle box that Barker spent hours trying to solve.

As a child, Barker was also obsessed by a book on anatomy by Andreas Vesalius, *De Humani Corporis Fabrica* (1543). Its pages depicted skinless figures in delightfully graceful poses. "They're very meticulous, neoclassical," Barker once commented, "...and these are very beautiful etchings in which you get flayed men and women standing in classical poses or leaning against pillars. The whole atmosphere of these pictures is cool and elegant and beautiful."[2] This contrast between the repugnant and the resplendent would infuse many of his pieces in years to come.

Barker lived on Oakdale Road, near Penny Lane, in an ordinary house with four bedrooms—his was at the top of the stairs—and, yet, extraordinary, forbidden things occurred inside. Here he read such landmark horror books as *Frankenstein* (Mary Shelley, 1818), *Dr. Jekyll and Mr. Hyde* (Robert Louis Stevenson, 1886) and *Dracula* (Bram Stoker, 1897) and devoured the works of M.R. James, Arthur Machen, and Edgar Allan Poe, who became a particular favorite. Indeed, the first horror book he ever read was *Tales of Mystery and Imagination* which had a lurid front cover featuring a skull, a red sky and an old dark house. He also began to stretch his imagination, particularly through art—a quality he picked up from his parents, who were both decent artists.

But it was at Quarry Bank School that this talent started to seep out in various ways, particularly via the plays he wrote and organized. His art teacher at the time, Alan Plent, has mentioned seeing Barker walking through the corridors with a mock severed head to promote a play he'd written.[3] His reaction against the mundane, official plays that were being performed at the school, these productions also brought him to the attention of friends and collaborators like Peter Atkins and Pinhead-to-be Doug Bradley. This group, led with passion and verve by Barker, formed the nucleus of Hydra Theatre, and would finally evolve into his fringe theatre group, the Dog Company.

After leaving Liverpool University with a BA (Hons) in English literature, Barker and the Company went on tours giving performances of plays like *Dog* (1978), *Nightlives* (1979) and *The History of the Devil* (1980), all penned by Barker and following the tradition of Grand Guignol theatre (see Chapter 4). The latter clearly displays a certain fixation with all things hellish and biblical, though here Lucifer stands trial to decide whether he is eligible to return to heaven. Doug Bradley actually played the Devil in the original production, but his portrayal was very different from the Cenobites of *Hellraiser*. In truth, some of the dialogue spoken when he is being cross-examined displays more of a connection to Frank's character than anything. Here he talks about his travels to distant regions on earth after he was cast out: "I was a student of the world, sir, and something of a sybarite. I wanted to taste every pleasure. I'd been a while in Athens and I'd heard of these towns on the very edge of the civilized world."[4]

Page from *De Humani Corporis Fabrica* by Andreas Vesalius (1543).

It was around this time that Barker began to write short stories to amuse his friends in the Dog Company, now based firmly in London. These stories grew into the first volumes of his popular *Books of Blood*, published in England by Sphere in 1984. Intelligent, yet uncompromising in their graphic nature, these stories also contained many of the seeds for *Hellraiser*. In the first story, for instance — "The Midnight Meat Train"— we are witness to the results of brutal killing: "It filled every one of his senses: the smell of opened entrails, the sight of the bodies, the feel of fluid on the floor under his fingers, the sound of the straps creaking beneath the weight of the corpses, even the air, tasting salty with blood."[5] Not a far cry from the slaughterhouse created by the Cenobites at the opening, or even by Frank and Julia.

Then there are the notions of existence and love beyond death rendered in "The Forbidden" (later filmed as *Candyman*, Bernard Rose, 1992). Here a woman searching for the roots of an urban myth about a hook-handed killer discovers that her fate is inexorably linked to his, and that her love for this fiend overwhelms what he might actually be — definitely a common motif in Barker's stories.

The characters in *Books of Blood* very often fall in love with monsters in spite of, or more commonly *because* of, their physical appearance. The children in "Skins of the Fathers," for example, are the result of communion between the town's women and what can only be described as creatures beyond our understanding, although the real monsters turn out to be human (a theme Barker explored more fully in his book *Cabal*, filmed as *Nightbreed*). On a different tack, it is the base urge rather than emotion that is highlighted in "The Age of Desire," where a scientist's experiments imbue his subject with pure, unadulterated lust pushed way beyond its limits.

Also relevant is the way Barker approaches "the flesh" and its malleability in stories like "Jacqueline Ess: Her Will and Testament" and "Confessions of a Pornographer's Shroud." As Michael A. Morrison points out in his study, "Monsters, Miracles and Revelations," "In his [Barker's] tales the easy mutability of the human form opens up the possibility of rebirth, at least for those willing to face his myriad marvels, mysteries, and monsters."[6]

Finally, we have the appearance of demons bound by the laws of Hell in "The Yattering and Jack" and "Hell's Event." In the former their breakage forces the nuisance demon Yattering to become a slave to his victim; in the latter, failure to win a race means that the Earth is "safe" for another 100 years. Their summoning is also depicted by way of the solving of a knot-puzzle in "The Inhuman Condition." This last idea is an extremely close precursor to the one in *Hellraiser* — simply exchanging rope for the puzzle box — and also dwells on the obsessive tendencies of its solver:

> And still the knots. Sometimes he would wake in the middle of the night and feel the cord moving beneath his pillow. Its presence was comforting, its eagerness was not, waking, as it did, a similar eagerness in him. He wanted to touch the remaining knots and examine the puzzles they offered. But he knew that to do so was tempting capitulation: to his own fascination; to their hunger for release.[7]

Running parallel to these fixations are the doorways that open up, revealing other realities that exist alongside our own — much like the city shown to the prisoner as part of the story "In the Flesh."

Even more telling, though, was Barker's first full-length, and arguably only, horror novel, *The Damnation Game* (1985). In this, Barker reworks a favorite story of his, the Faustian fable (see Chapter 2) through the eyes of Marty Strauss. Paroled from prison, this character has already paid a high price to feed his gambling addiction. But when Marty is hired as a bodyguard to rich businessman Joseph Whitehead, he discovers his boss has made an even more dangerous bargain with the deadly Mamoulian, the embodiment of our own guilt and desire. The power of love is again touched on as Marty falls for Whitehead's

CLIVE BARKER'S
Books of Blood
VOLUMES 1-3

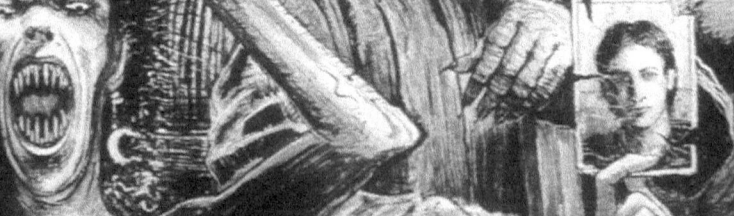

'I have seen the future of horror...
and his name is Clive Barker' STEPHEN KING

daughter, Carys, but it is that central relationship between Mamoulian — to all intents and purposes the Devil figure, even though we discover he is nothing of the kind — and his victim that is of interest to students of the *Hellraiser* saga.

What's more, there can be no denying that both *The Books of Blood* and *The Damnation Game* have a definite cinematic quality to them. In fact, Barker's short story "Son of Celluloid" relies inherently upon cinematic inspirations and icons. This is probably why fellow Liverpudlian and horror author Ramsey Campbell drew the comparison in a letter to Sphere about Barker: "He's the first writer to write horror fiction in Technicolor — the first to take the gruesome horror movie and make it work as prose."[8] The author has made no secret of his love of cinema in all its forms, and it was an early encounter at age fourteen with Hitchcock's *Psycho* that showed him how this medium could be used to its full advantage. After sneaking in to see it with a friend, Barker caught the ending, where Mother Bates's skeleton is found in the basement. Once he'd got over his initial fright, he waited around for it to play again and observed the reaction of four girls watching: "I remember thinking quite distinctly, 'I am in control this time, because I know what's going to happen. And these poor creatures in front of us don't.'"[9] Renaissance man that he is, it could only have been a matter of time before he turned his attentions to horror films himself. And that time was fast approaching.

Speaking in an interview with *Fangoria* in 1986 after the *Books of Blood* had been released in the U.S., Barker revealed that he had recently returned from Hollywood, where he had been pitching story and novel ideas to studios like Columbia and Paramount. He also told the magazine he'd written one original screenplay for a movie called *Underworld* (a.k.a. *Transmutations*), and had been working on another for a film based on one of his shorts, *Rawhead Rex*.[10] Barker's association with the director of both these films, George Pavlou, began in 1982 when the pair met at a dinner party. At that time London International Film School graduate Pavlou had only helmed a few TV commercials and short films, and had served as second unit director on the British-based episodes of *Hart to Hart*. Understandably he was keen to direct a feature of his own, and asked Barker to write a synopsis. This Barker did, once again pre-empting the themes of *Nightbreed*, that of monsters living in a clandestine community.

The twist here was the film noir/horror cross fertilization — or as Barker succinctly put it, "Gangsters vs. Mutants"[11] and this eventually attracted financing (under £1 million) from U.K. producers Green Man in 1984, who also optioned five of Barker's stories from the *Books of Blood*. Unfortunately, the money was only available if they started straight away, *without* a full script. Filming on *Underworld* began in 1985 at Limehouse Studios (who were co-producing the film), with Barker on hand during principal photography to do the necessary rewrites. But as shooting went on, James Caplan was hired to redraft the screenplay. Caplan cut out over half of Barker's dialogue and replaced it with clichéd gangster speak. The result was a disjointed story, doomed right from the start.

While the set designs by Len Huntingford (lit by Sidney Macartney's cinematography) are impressive, and notable British actors Denholm Elliott and Stephen Berkoff deliver entertainingly hammish performances, the rest of the cast are wooden in the extreme. Pavlou's visuals are more MTV than Dario Argento or David Cronenberg, as he claimed, and it was later discovered that the producers had come up with funding by telling potential backers that it would be an hour and a half rock video! The real tragedy, though, was

Opposite: **Books of Blood** front cover (courtesy Clive Barker/Sphere).

a missing scene Barker scripted in which Elliott's Dr. Savary, who has been using hypodermic needles on people throughout the film, has his face punctured by dozens of them, a familiar image to *Hellraiser* fans. Instead, Savary gets set alight because it was the much cheaper option.

After filming was completed, there followed a long battle to try to secure a distributor. Finally a deal was struck with Empire Pictures from the U.S., Charles Band's company. Empire trimmed the movie by almost ten minutes to make the pace faster and renamed it *Transmutations*. They gave it a limited release, with no promotion whatsoever, so it died at the box office. The film appeared, with the cut footage restored, on Vestron Video the following year.

But worse was yet to come. In spite of this catastrophe, Green Man ploughed ahead with a version of *Rawhead Rex*, one of Barker's most popular short stories. And although he hated what they had done with *Underworld*, the writer listened to what his producers had to say. "When Kevin Attew (of Green Man) asked me to write the script for *Rawhead Rex*, we had a couple of exchanges that went something like, 'We know we fucked up the first one because we didn't concede the fact that it was a horror movie.'"[12] After being assured that they'd leave the horror in this time, and that he would be given a greater amount of control over the project, Barker produced a first draft screenplay.

The location had to be shifted from England to Ireland for funding reasons, and the lead character—originally an ad executive—was turned into an American university professor visiting to research pre–Christian burial sites with his family. *The Winds of War* actor David Dukes was drafted in to play the lead, while Kelly Piper, whose previous roles had included a nurse in *Maniac* (William Lustig, 1980) and a prostitute in *Vice Squad* (Gary Sherman, 1982), signed on as his wife. Meanwhile, the crucial job of creature effects was given to Peter Litten's Coast to Coast company, who would have to commute from their studio in Britain. The seven-week shoot began in County Wicklow, Ireland, in February 1986. However, once filming commenced, Barker wasn't even allowed on set and alterations were again made without his say. As the budget dwindled from $3 to $2 million, fears rose that this film would turn out like the last.

If judged as a straight piece of horror entertainment, *Rawhead Rex* isn't the worst movie you'll ever see. There are even some resemblances between the early parts of John Landis's seminal *An American Werewolf in London* (1981) and *Rex*, certainly when it comes to the rural setting and the sense of outsiders invading a tight-knit community. The film cleverly draws on the opposites of Pagan and Christian standpoints for its central conflict, which can also be extended to the ideas about unbridled desire and rage versus goodness and faith. This is complemented by solid performances from Piper and the late Dukes, whose outbursts after his son is murdered are emotionally draining to watch.

What fetters the movie is the Rawhead creature itself, which deviates quite markedly from Barker's original vision of a ten-foot phallus on legs (see Les Edwards' graphic novel adaptation for a better idea of what Rex *should* have looked like). This is crucial for the payoff to work, where we discover that Rex is scared of women, more specifically female genitalia. It explains the creature's adverse reaction to pregnant females throughout the story and film, and, more importantly, how he is defeated. The loss of this subtext drags the movie down to the level of a simple monster-on-the-loose flick, which is, sadly, how Attew viewed the concept: "It's *Jaws* on land ... purely an updated '50s B movie."[13] In all honesty, Litten's Rex looks like some kind of weird gigantic monkey with a punk haircut.[14] Working with very little to go on, and with only six weeks of preproduction afforded to him, he came up with a one-piece suit for the gigantic German commercials actor, Heinrich von Buneau—which he had originally intended to be a twenty-piece prosthetic—and an animatronic head with fifteen facial movements and glowing red eyes for close-ups. With the right lighting setups and editing, they might have worked, but, unlike the shark in Spielberg's classic or even the Alien in Ridley Scott's 1979 classic of the same name, Rex spends far too much time on-screen and in the unforgiving light of day. Buneau's inexperience playing monsters is obvious in his lumbering performance, while the mechanical head looks just that: clunky and, at times, faintly ridiculous.

Quite rightly, Barker disassociated himself from both *Underworld* and *Rawhead Rex*. There was no more contact between himself and George Pavlou and Green Man unknowingly let their options lapse on the other four stories from *Books of Blood*. This didn't stop them trying to develop another couple of projects based on the tales, but Barker involved his lawyers and the producers soon backed down.

It is interesting, though, that without these experiences he wouldn't have had the major impetus to direct. If they had taught him one thing it was this: To see a satisfactory adaptation of his work, he'd have to make one himself. And it is ironic that a line David Dukes utters in *Rawhead* should show him the way. "Go to Hell," he says. "Just go right to Hell!"

In the same 1986 interview with *Fangoria*, Barker also stated: "I want to direct. I directed in theatre, and I like working with actors, I like community projects. So, we're putting a project together from a novella I wrote called 'The Hellbound Heart.' ... I did a screenplay from it which I hope to be directing this year. We're going to call the movie *Hellraiser*."[15] Obviously the author would find film directing a little different from plays, but his theater experiences still stood him in good stead. It is at this point that we must also consider the art house shorts he shot in the 1970s, made with many of those same friends. Actually, Barker's first films were naive experiments with a friend from his early teens, Phil Rimmer. He'd already written short plays with Rimmer—*Voodoo & Inferno* (1967)—about crazed Germans and, naturally, Hell. Then they progressed on to stop-motion efforts with a Super 8 millimeter camera influenced greatly by Barker's hero, effects

Rawhead Rex as depicted by artist Les Edwards was much closer to the original concept than its cinematic counterpart (courtesy Les Edwards).

man Ray Harryhausen. One of these involved an Action Man (the UK equivalent of a G.I. Joe doll), some plasticine and lots of worms from the garden. The setting was a slime-covered graveyard constructed in Barker's bedroom and the directors held lamps close enough to make the scenery bubble.

In 1973, the pair made a version of Oscar Wilde's *Salome*, itself a biblical tale which recounts another bargain. The legend of Salome revolves around King Herod's stepdaughter, who falls in love with the pious Jokanaan (John the Baptist) but is rejected. In exchange for his severed head, she dances for Herod. The group filmed on 8mm stock in the cellar of a florist's shop in Liverpool. They had a single handheld light and the sets were wallpaper turned over with patterns painted on it. Anne Taylor took the title role, while Doug Bradley — who had played a blind Jokanaan in a previous stage version — was granted his first cinematic encounter with make-up, playing King Herod. The whole thing was developed in Rimmer's house, then edited by hand.

Displaying definite expressionist and surrealist tendencies, as one would expect after the group's exposure to film societies in the area, the movie also boasts some unique visual parallels with *Hellraiser*. We pass through a doorway, for instance, and a strange light sheen gives the frame an unreal quality. Taylor very closely resembles Kirsty with her long, dark hair, white smock and black-stained eyes. Then there are the requisite candles (present in both Kirsty's dream sequence and at Frank's puzzle-solving near the beginning). And the resemblance between Herod and the bearded Keeper of the Box is uncanny.[16] But most intriguing is the first cinematic use of a kiss as a betrayal, in addition to Taylor's scratching of a cheek, which Kirsty recreates when Uncle Frank is pretending to be her father.

Yet more similarities abound in a second short, *The Forbidden* (1975–78). This is probably not that surprising, as it was based loosely on Christopher Marlowe's *Doctor Faustus*, Barker's preferred reworking of the Faust myth. Funded by £600 from Merseyside Arts, this time the footage was shot in negative on 16mm black and white stock, but stood for quite a while before being put together. The first thing to say is that *The Forbidden* plays very heavily on an obsession with puzzles and games. The opening shots are bare feet on a chessboard floor, while the odd symbols painted on paper and put together like a jigsaw puzzle recall the sides of the Lament Configuration box itself. Hand animated birds flutter behind a grid, trapped like the birds at

Cenobite concept sketch for *Hellraiser* (courtesy Clive Barker).

Cenobite concept sketch for *Hellraiser* (courtesy Clive Barker).

the pet shop where Kirsty works. And there is a gridded piece of wood with nails at each intersection.

Talking about this, Doug Bradley recalls:

> Clive had built what he called his nail board ... and spent endless hours playing with what happened if a light was swung around in front of it to see the way the shadows of the nails moved and what happened if it was top lit and so forth. Of course, when I saw the first illustrations for this gentleman [Pinhead] it rang a bell with me — that here was actually Clive putting the ideas that he'd been playing around with, with the nail board, in *The Forbidden*. Now ten to fifteen years later or whatever, here he'd actually put the image over a human's face, which is typical of the way he works.[17]

But undoubtedly the most recognizable factors are the Angels at the end — robed figures who inflict pain — and the figure of Faust himself once he is skinned. Peter Atkins played him in full make-up, actually strips of paint that were peeled back revealing new layers of flesh and muscle. When viewed in negative and for the amount of money available, the results are shockingly effective and would prove to be Barker's first ventures into making less look like more. Owing much to those Vesalius pictures, Faust's character is a distinct antecedent to skinless Frank Cotton in *Hellraiser*, and those torturing him can only be equated to the Cenobites.

These same preoccupations would resurface when Barker wrote *The Hellbound Heart* novella almost a decade later. Originally published in 1987 as part of the *Night Visions 3* anthology — alongside stories by Ramsey Campbell and Lisa Tuttle — the tale is prefixed by a quote from John Donne's *Love's Deitie* ("I long to talk with some old lover's ghost, Who died before the god of love was born.") and differs from the finished *Hellraiser* in a number of ways.

First, we are provided with more explanation about the puzzle box itself: created by a Frenchman called Lemarchand, a "maker of singing birds."[18] Later this would form the genesis of the fourth movie in the series. Second, the Cenobites are given a definite back history: referred to as "the order of the Gash," hinted at in the diaries of Bolingbroke and Gilles de Rais.[19] They are more conversational and far less imposing than their cinematic counterparts. During the hospital confrontation with Kirsty, one muses, "We'd better go.... Leave them to their patchwork, eh? Such depressing places."[20] The figure we would come to call Pinhead is here

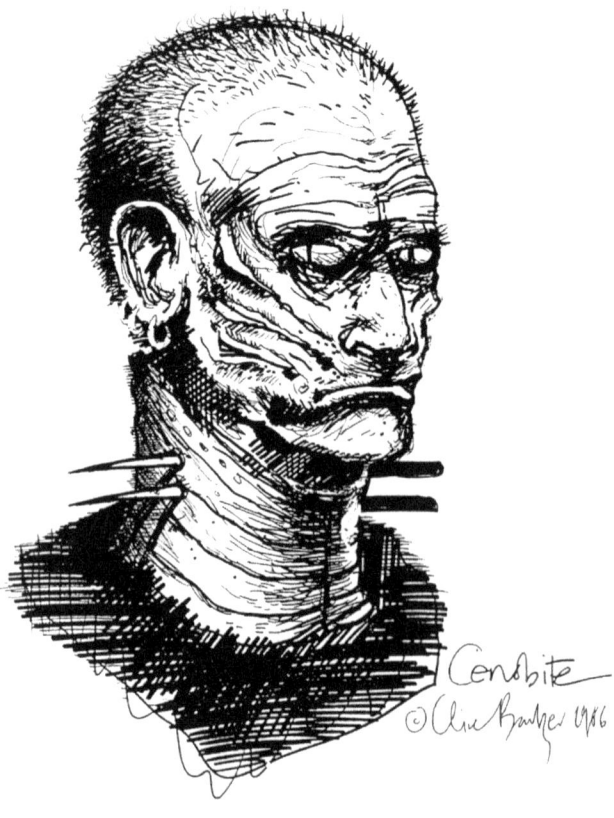

Cenobite concept sketch for *Hellraiser* (courtesy Clive Barker).

Night Visions, the original anthology featuring *The Hellbound Heart* (Arrow Books).

asexual, bordering on female: "Its voice, unlike that of its companion, was light and breathy — the voice of an excited girl."[21] And the Engineer creature, in the film a fleshy, noisy mass with rows of teeth, hovers at the edge of the action and only intervenes to whisk a dying Julia off at the end and then pass the box back to Kirsty. Their lines are not quite as polished, either. Compare, "Maybe we won't tear your soul apart" with the immortal tagline everyone knows from the film.

The female protagonist, Kirsty, is the friend, not the daughter, of Rory Cotton (renamed Larry in the film), a fact which holds great significance when exploring the relationship between these two characters, as well as the family dynamics we will come to later. She is also, to quote Barker, "A total loser. You can live with someone like that for the length of a novella. You can't for a movie."[22] Even her body works against her as Frank is chasing her through the house at the climax: "Swallowing the breath her cry had been mounted upon had brought an unwelcome side-effect: hiccups. The first of them, so unexpected she had no time to subdue it, sounded gun-crack loud."[23]

Also, Frank appears to Julia the first time through a gap in the wall: a more traditional shade haunting the upstairs "damp room," able to maintain his substance only for a short time. And he is brought back not simply by the blood, but by route of leaving his spilled seed on the floor. The murder weapon of choice for Julia in this novella is a knife, and Frank uses bandages to cover his regenerating skin, a homage to the Mummy films Barker so admired when he was growing up (this image would be adopted by a skinless Julia in *Hellbound: Hellraiser II*). Most of the changes made to the story at script level can be understood perfectly from a visual point of view. It makes for better cinema to have Pinhead speaking with a deep, booming voice, or to have Julia wielding a hammer and being splattered with blood, or even a skinless Frank walking around in his far less clichéd shirt and suit.

As is to be expected in a work of prose, Barker delves deeper into character backgrounds and motivations. We learn exactly how Frank came to be in possession of the box, for instance. While smuggling heroin in Düsseldorf he'd come across the legend again, which led him to a German called Kircher, who in turn could get him the box. "The price? Small favors, here and there. Nothing exceptional. Frank did the favors, washed his hands, and claimed his payment."[24] Not only that, Frank's experiences *after* he has opened the box are much more internalized. We're given passages about how the Cenobites heighten his senses: his touch, sight, sound, everything magnified to make the best use of his suffering. "It seemed he could suddenly feel the collision of the dust motes with his skin. Every drawn breath chafed his lips; every blink, his eyes. Bile burned the back of his throat, and a morsel of yesterday's beef that had lodged between his teeth sent spasms through his system as it exuded a droplet of gravy upon his tongue."[25] And, of course, his true feelings about Julia are made more explicit: "He remembered her as a trite, preening woman, whose upbringing had curbed her capacity for passion."[26] We even find out more about Julia's victims, something which had to be achieved with the shorthand of dress and dialogue in the film.

The basic story line remains the same from *The Hellbound Heart* to *Hellraiser*, however, and regardless of the fact that Barker claims he never wrote it with a movie in mind, the novella has a very resolute three-act structure. It is set in a limited — even claustrophobic — handful of locations, with the *ordinary* house on Lodovico Street playing host to much of the gruesome action. And there is only a quartet of characters at the very kernel of the story: Rory, Julia, Frank and Kirsty. Whether he did it consciously or not, in *The Hellbound Heart* Barker fashioned the ideal template for a low-budget horror movie. Now all he needed was a way to get that movie made.

At first, Barker thought about shooting the project with his friends on Super 8 or 16mm. Then, by chance, he was introduced to Christopher Figg through an old Dog Company friend, Oliver Parker. Figg, an assistant director on pictures such as *The Dresser* (Peter Yates, 1983) and *A Passage to India* (David Lean, 1984), was now interested in producing a horror film. Still very inexperienced, Figg joined forces with Barker and they were given some start-up money by Oliver's brother. Next they put together a package containing a number of Barker's conceptual drawings and a draft version of the script. Armed with these they flew out to L.A. to find backers. New World Pictures, founded by B-movie director Roger Corman (famous for his Poe adaptations in the 1960s) offered them a $4.2 million budget; not an inconsiderable amount for a first time director with hardly any footage under his belt. Suddenly *Hellraiser* was about to become a reality.

Work began gathering cast and crew, and with the help of his fellow producers, David Saunders and Christopher Webster, Figg assembled a technical dream team for Barker. To start with, there was the director of photography, Robin Vidgeon, with twenty years of experience. Vidgeon had worked as an assistant cameraman on films like *Rollerball* (Norman Jewison, 1975) and *Raiders of the Lost Ark* (Steven Spielberg, 1981), and, like Barker, was a fan of the Italian horror films of Dario Argento. This explains why some of the lighting set-ups very closely resemble scenes from *Suspiria* (1977) and *Inferno* (1980).

Then came production designer Mike Buchanan, responsible for the film's décor and set construction. He secured the location house in the suburban district of Dollis Hill, North London, where most of the filming would occur (it was rumored someone had gassed themselves in the garage) and the stage at Cricklewood's Production Village — only a few minutes away — which would double for the opening bazaar and attic room. In charge of special effects were Bob Keen, Geoff Portass and Image Animation. Keen came fresh from triumphs on such movies as *Return of the Jedi* (Richard Marquand, 1983) and *Highlander* (Russell Mulcahy, 1986), although it was his first time as effects supervisor.

In terms of casting (with the aid of casting director Sheila Trezise), young German-born actor Sean Chapman was chosen to play the part of Frank Cotton. Chapman had made his screen debut in *Leidenschaftliche Blümchen* (André Farwagi, 1978) and *Scum* (Alan Clarke, 1979) and landed TV work in the aborted *Dr. Who* spin-off, *K-9 and Company* (1981), before appearing in the ill-fated *Underworld*. His look was totally right: dark, brooding and charming. And his initiation into the world of *Hellraiser* was to hang upside down from chains for a test shoot until he threw up, footage of which was used in the flashback sequence where skinless Frank recounts his tale.

Meanwhile, British actress Clare Higgins came on board as Julia, having had a little experience of wayward women roles playing parts like Stella in *A Streetcar Named Desire* onstage. Higgins had also carved a name for herself in various BBC television serials—*Pride and Prejudice* (1979), *The Citadel* (1983)—and debuted on the big screen in Hugh Brody's feature film *1919* (1985). The attraction for her was plain: "I've done all the nice parts, but I love playing Julia because she's so evil. There's a great range to the part: I go from being bored and domestic to being absolutely vile...."[27]

Fresh-faced American actress Ashley Laurence became involved with the film after she got a phone call from a friend who was PA-ing at New World, and who was also in her teenage drama workshop. Barker and Figg had auditioned a number of actresses for the role of Kirsty, but couldn't find one they wanted. So when they traveled from New York to Los Angeles, Laurence had a chance to impress them. Recalling her first encounter with Barker, Laurence says: "I didn't know what the script was about. I didn't know anything.

I met him [Clive Barker] and he was really enthusiastic and he was really communicative, and he said to me, 'Okay, your Uncle Frank is in your father's skin and he wants to kill you and have sex with you. Tell me how you feel about that.'"[28]

Barker, too, has warm memories of Laurence's audition, claiming she could outscream Fay Wray,[29] and didn't mind looking grimy. It also helped that she resembled Jessica Harper, star of Argento's *Suspiria*, who also spent much of that movie in a state of perpetual disarray. Moreover, both Barker and Figg recognized a feistiness about the cinematic newcomer, something that would translate well in her scenes with Frank, Julia and the Cenobites. Here was someone who, unlike her literary counterpart, *would* fight back, who would carry on the tradition of the tough female heroine from horror films of the late '70s and early '80s, typified by Sigourney Weaver's Ripley.

The most famous member of the cast, and a real coup for the production, was well-known U.S. actor Andrew Robinson. In the two years before *Hellraiser*, audiences had seen him starring alongside Cher in the moving film *Mask* (Peter Bogdanovich, 1985), and opposite Sylvester Stallone in the action movie *Cobra* (George P. Cosmatos, 1986). But he was probably still best known at that time for his debut role in *Dirty Harry* (Don Siegel, 1971) as the lunatic rifleman Scorpio. Robinson took a huge gamble flying over to star in this film; not only was it in the horror genre, with everything that implied, it was also being directed by a novice. Fortunately, after reading the script he was very impressed and liked the idea of being able to play both the mild-mannered Larry *and* his demented brother Frank.

His presence added extra credibility to what was already becoming much more than the average shocker, and he improvised some classic moments in the film (Frank readjusting his eye; his last line, the shortest verse in the Bible: "Jesus wept"). Speaking about the film as part of an electronic press kit for New World, Robinson said, "I think the movie is unique within the genre. I think the images, especially the images of horror, are unlike anything anybody has seen. I think it'll be a bizarrely fascinating film. There's no middle ground. They [the audience] will either loathe it or go out of their minds about it. But at least they'll have a reaction to it."[30]

When it came to roles for the Cenobites, the director selected actors who were closer to him. Bedfordshire born Simon Bamford had been attending North London's Mountview Theatre School when he met Barker for the first time: "I met Clive through a friend of mine who I was sharing a house with at the time. Clive was doing one of his horror plays and this friend was making some specialist props for him. That's how I got introduced to him. We became good friends and then he asked me to join his company."[31] He played with the Dog Company for about a year and a half before they disbanded, and then went on to do other theater work. He rang up out of the blue to see what Barker was working on and it just so happened that his call coincided with this project. Barker told Bamford about *Hellraiser* and offered him the Butterball role there and then.

Nicholas Vince was also a Mountview student and used to live around the corner from Barker, who saw the actor in some of his drama school shows and liked his performances. "He and I met up at a party over a cup of coffee and said, 'We must work together sometime.' And it took us six years!"[32] That turned out to be as the Chatterer Cenobite. For the Female Cenobite, Barker enrolled his cousin, Grace Kirby, whose only previous film role had been as a French teacher in *Heavenly Pursuits* (Charles Gormley, 1985).

But when it came to the part of Lead Cenobite, Barker turned to his old school friend and a Dog Company player, Doug Bradley, although he gave him the option of playing one of the removal men with the mattress. "It seems odd to me now, but I very nearly settled for the latter. This was going to be my first movie, so why would I want to be buried in latex? Who would be any the wiser? Much better to make the briefest of appearances and be seen."[33] After much deliberation, and assuming he'd drawn the short straw, Bradley plumped for the Cenobite and let Oliver Parker have the other part.

The requirements for skinless Frank were a little more exact. They needed an actor who was thin enough to wear the muscle-coated bodysuit. Step forward Oliver Smith, who had starred in the *Jesus of Nazareth* miniseries (1977). As with the Cenobite roles, the actor also had to be comfortable spending up to six hours in make-up getting ready before the cameras even started rolling: "The main body was prefabricated around my form, so I got into that for each morning's work. So the head was done bit by bit each morning.... Bob Keen and Cliff Wallace [the personal creator] whacked on several sections of thin rubber. It was a grueling process, glue and gunge."[34] And those cameras actually began rolling towards the end of 1986 when *Hellraiser* was made over a nine to ten week period (seven weeks initially, extended by New World), under Barker's tongue-in-cheek alternative title *Sadomasochists from Beyond the Grave*.[35]

Most of the cast remember the shoot with affection, especially Barker. Speaking about it in the introduction of *The Hellraiser Chronicles*, he comments: "I think back to the making of *Hellraiser* with unalloyed fondness.... The cast treated my ineptitudes kindly, and the crew were no less forgiving."[36] It was certainly a steep learning curve for someone who admitted that when he first started out he "didn't know the difference between a 10-millimeter lens and a 35-millimeter lens. If you'd shown me a plate of spaghetti and said that was a lens, I might have believed you."[37] Luckily, as he remarks, the cast and crew were supportive, and showing his efforts to the producers was a major incentive to get things right.

On a set visit, Tim Pulleine of *Films and Filming* had this to report about the director firsthand.

> Certainly Barker, affable and unassuming behind his designer stubble, seems very much at ease on the set as he rehearses and blocks out part of a scene between Oliver Smith and one of his intended victims. "Keep squirting to the last minute," he cheerfully adjures the make-up man who has been spraying a glistening substance onto Smith's cranium to make him look more awful than ever.[38]

Undoubtedly, the fact that cast and crew were all living in close proximity to each other, some in the location house itself, gave the shoot a communal feel that harked back to the days of the Dog Company. Perhaps this accounts for why Barker relaxed into his stride so quickly. He knew how to deal with actors, he knew how to tell stories visually; all that was lacking was the technical expertise, which he picked up as the production progressed.

Most crucially there was this underlying ethos to spur him on: "The force of imagination behind these things is finally more important, I believe, than knowing the rules, because somebody else will help you with the rules. That's what technicians are there for, to say no, no, you can't possibly do that, it'll be out of focus. And that's fine — you learn as you go along."[39]

Obviously, no production is all plain sailing, particularly a first time one. Bradley had trouble hitting his marks the first time in make-up because he couldn't see through his black contact lenses, and he was also frightened of tripping over Pinhead's skirts. He had a difficult moment on a wooden support that was being raised into the air above Kirsty, and tumbled off. There were reports of some tension between Robinson and Barker over how to play certain scenes, possibly not helped by the new director finding his feet,[40] so much so that

Barker described his job as being 50 percent diplomat. They had to rush a shoot in a Chinese restaurant between Kirsty and Larry because the man who was supposed to let them in was late, the consequence of which is one of the flattest scenes in the whole film. The Engineer creature, that Barker actually spent evenings with the special effects team helping to construct, proved cumbersome to maneuver — in fact, if you watch the scene closely where it runs down the hallway, you can see the men operating it and pushing it from behind. Additionally, there was little time and money to effectively destroy the house for the denouement. Handfuls of dust and a few bits of wood falling from the roof have to stand in for this. But, taking everything into consideration, it was a much easier shoot than some (*The Exorcist* comes to mind). There was also nothing like the misfortune that would plague Barker on his next movie as director (see Chapter 11).

When filming wrapped, the editors proved no less considerate: Richard Marden, who had worked with John Schlesinger and David Lean, and an uncredited Tony Randel. Marden, who started out in the business as sound editor on *The Vicious Circle* in 1957 (Gerald Thomas) and was responsible for editing such diverse films as *Bedazzled* (Stanley Donen, 1967) and *Half Moon Street* (Bob Swaim, 1986), was apparently the "soul of tact" when Barker sat in on the process.

Finally, the importance of Christopher Young's music cannot be underestimated. Barker originally wanted the electronic band "Coil" because he claimed their music made his "bowels churn," although unit publicist Stephen Jones tactfully suggested that cinema management might prefer it if he said "spine chill" instead.[41] However, the idea was rejected by New World and it was actually Randel who brought New Jersey native Young into the *Hellraiser* stable. No stranger to working in the science fiction and horror fields, Young had provided the music for movies like *Godzilla* (Koji Hashimoto and R.J. Kizer, 1985) and *A Nightmare on Elm Street Part 2: Freddy's Revenge* (Jack Sholder, 1985). Strangely, his compositions would mark *Hellraiser* out as distinct from

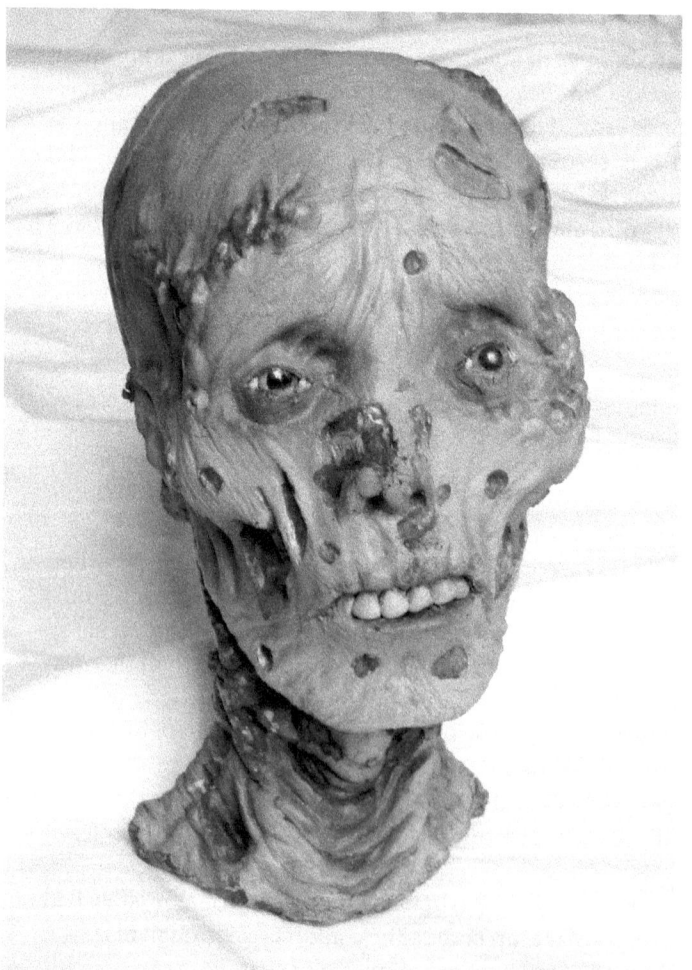

Original Frank make-up reference head (courtesy Phil and Sarah Stokes of the Revelations Web site www.clivebarker.info).

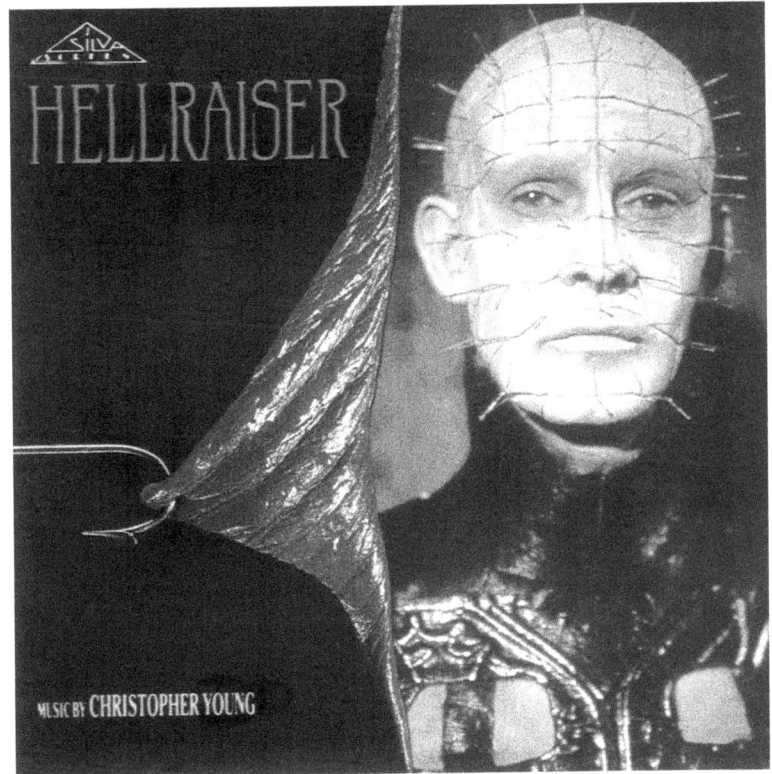

Above: Clive Barker on set (photograph credit Tom Collins). *Right: Hellraiser* soundtrack by Christopher Young (cover courtesy Silva Screen).

such fare, in particular the slasher flicks of the *Nightmare* series, which was into its third installment by 1987. From the very opening bars of the movie the majestic signature tune speaks of deadly elegance, a much more classy horror film. And who can imagine Frank's resurrection sequence without the celebratory waltz?

Barker has said in retrospect about the musician, "In a sense he made a larger mark on the movie than practically anyone else associated with it, because his score elevates the picture with its scale, majesty, complexity and emotional richness. Chris is an old style composer, and a little crazy I think — and he'd probably admit to that. An extraordinary talent."[42] High praise, but then Young did give the director a crash course on spotting and scoring, continuing his involvement in the project at every level. Barker even pitched in with the people at New World's publicity, marketing and distribution departments — unaware as he was at that time of the significance of a really excellent marketing campaign (it can make or break the picture, as he discovered later in his career). From the beginning, Barker was the driving force behind this project. And he was there right at the end when, upon its general release, *Hellraiser* recouped its production costs in just three days.

2

OPENING THE BOX

Deals with the Devil

> Faustus, ah Faustus! Poetry, perversity, farce and damnation! What more could I ask for? I adored its rapid changes of tone, its sheer theatricality.
> — Clive Barker, "Keeping Company with Cannibal Witches,"
> *Daily Telegraph*, January 6, 1990.

As befits a story based around the Faustian myth, the overriding theme of *Hellraiser* is the bargain, or pact. The tale originates from fifteenth and sixteenth century Germany where a Dr. Georgius Faust of Helmstadt encouraged the rumor that he had sold his soul to the devil in exchange for magical powers. This was transcribed as *Historia von Johann Fausten* (1587), and translated into English as *The Historie of the Damnable Life, and Deserved Death of Doctor John Faustus*. Around the same time, Christopher Marlowe reworked the story as *The Tragical History of the Life and Death of Doctor Faustus*, in which a scholar trades his soul to the demon Mephistopheles for knowledge and is sucked into the pits of Hell. In Barker's own words, "It tells of a shaman who touches an inner darkness—a forbidden place that promises dangerous knowledge—and is snatched off by the very forces he's hoped to control."[1] But in Johann Wolfgang Goethe's nineteenth century verse drama, *Faust*, the main protagonist escapes his damnation by cheating the demon Mephisto. *Hellraiser*'s story of Frank Cotton and the Cenobites, therefore, is a skilful conjunction of the last two. Although, this being Barker, there is no escape for long.

The very first scene depicts a deal in the process of being struck. Frank is asked, "What's your pleasure?" by the merchant. The pleasure Frank seeks is not magical powers or knowledge, but the ultimate in sexual and hedonistic experiences. Frank is the quintessential thrill-seeker who has been constantly searching his whole life for something "more." The small ivory ornament of a man and woman coupling and the photographs he leaves behind all point to his particular weakness for pleasures of the flesh. Unfortunately, "It's never enough." And his brother's line about Frank never being one to kick cash out of bed denotes that he has always been willing to pay for his enjoyment. Later, Frank confesses to Julia, "I thought I'd gone to the limits. I hadn't. The Cenobites gave me an experience beyond limits. Pain and pleasure, indivisible." Frank strikes a deal for the box, hands over his cash, expecting his version of pure pleasure. It isn't until later that he discovers not everyone's idea of "pleasures of the flesh" are the same.

Desire and gratification are at the heart of the next deal we see, too; indeed, they intertwine with this theme throughout the film. In the attic flashback scene where Julia remembers her own sexual brush with Frank, two critical bargains are made. Just before they make love, Julia asks Frank, "What about Larry?" to which he replies, "Forget him." This is the price *she* must pay for his favors. Incidentally, it must be pointed out here that the sex scene in the finished movie isn't the original one Barker scripted and filmed. In this version, the act is longer and much more passionate, as this screenplay extract shows:

> Their love-making is not straight-forward: there is an element of erotic perversity in the way FRANK licks at her face, almost like an animal, his hold too tight to be loving. The sequence escalates into a series of strange details from their locked bodies. Nails digging into palms; sweat rivulets running down their torsos. And once in a while we see their faces. JULIA watching FRANK, mesmerized and amused by his intensity.[2]

Barker wanted there to be no doubt in the viewers' minds that she'd never experienced anything like this before; so intense it has stayed with her all these years. Interestingly, though, it was New World who forced the director to cut back on the sex and introduce the switchblade element — where Frank cuts the strap of Julia's chemise. "I lost the situation I'd written," explained Barker in a later interview, "which was they fuck like crazy. I wanted to motivate her with this incredibly raunchy sex scene, they said, 'sorry, we simply can't use this material because you can't mix sex with violence'.... I could only hint at that."[3] The idea was that Julia feels excited and alive rather than in danger — this is no rape — and that's an important distinction when it comes to the second bargain the lovers make.

Julia and Frank. Hellraiser still (photograph credit: Tom Collins).

After the deed is done and he is about to walk away, she implores him: "Please, I'll do anything you want." This bargaining chip doesn't work the first time, but Frank will hold her to the promise when he is the one who needs her. Essentially, he uses her longing to make good his escape and swindle the demons. The deal is simple: in exchange for luring and killing men to feed him, Frank will stay with Julia this time, or so he has her believe. If she'd felt overtly threatened the first time they'd met, there would be no way she'd *want* to bring Frank back.

A scene was actually shot of Julia and Larry's wedding, which would have illustrated a further pact. Barker chose not to include this in the finished cut of the movie (it actually turns up in *Hellbound*), perhaps for running time purposes or because it was already quite obvious that the deal Julia made with Frank was always of greater import. The symbolism of Frank and Julia having sex atop her wedding dress, Julia's fist crushing the material, and her flashback occurring just as Larry is hauling the matrimonial bed up the stairs, is enough. It makes a mockery of the legal and religious contract between Larry and his wife. Regardless of this, it would have presented a nice contrast to later parallel scenes where Julia and Frank exchange twisted wedding vows. In the first of these Frank asks if she'll spill more blood for him and Julia replies, "I will." In the next, Frank swears to Julia, "We belong to each other now. For better, for worse. Like love, only real." Theirs is the only wedding that counts in *Hellraiser*— a warped bonding of a skinless man and a murderess. But just as pleasure and pain are indivisible for the Cenobites, so, too, are love and desire for Julia and Frank. This is something Frank substantiates when he kills Julia at the end. "Nothing personal, babe," he sneers.

Cracks are apparent, though, in Larry and Julia's union from the second they open the door to the house on Lodovico Street. Barker highlights this in the screenplay.

> We see the pair on the doorstep. LARRY is an American in his early forties, an attractive man who has lost his edge in recent years. He looks harassed; he smirks too much. A little, but significant, corner of him is utterly defeated. JULIA, his wife, is English: and looks perhaps ten years his junior. She is beautiful, but her face betrays a barely buried unhappiness. Life has disappointed her, too, of late: and LARRY has been a major part of their disappointment.[4]

Thanks to the adroit acting of Robinson and Higgins, this *is* conveyed to the viewer. When Larry mentions the difficulties they had in Brooklyn and states unconvincingly, "We can make it work here," it only confirms our suspicions. And when Julia agrees to Larry's "So?" with a "Why not?" we realize that instead of strengthening their covenant they are heading for its complete dissolution. Furthermore, because Julia has stolen a picture of Frank we also know that he will be the principal cause of this annulment. Her powerful attraction to Frank means that any deal they made will always have priority, though both deals have serious repercussions. Her pact with Larry has left her trapped in a loveless marriage. Her pact with Frank might lead to transient sexual fulfillment, but it also forces her to kill and initiates her own death.

An unfilmed scene from the novella has a bleeding Julia wearing her wedding dress at the end, further emphasizing the hideous mistakes she has made and her wish to turn back the clock:

> And there, in the middle of this domestic wasteland, sat a bride. By some extraordinary act of will, Julia had managed to put her wedding dress on, and secure her veil upon her head. Now she sat in the dirt, the dress besmirched. But she looked radiant nevertheless; more beautiful, indeed, for the fact of the ruin that surrounded her.[5]

More hopeful is the alliance between Kirsty and her new boyfriend, Steve (played by Robert Hines). The pair meet at her father's housewarming dinner party and we sense immediately the first blossoming of young love. The eye contact and laughter is genuine, as opposed to Julia's false smiles when placating Larry or luring her male victims to the house. There is a hint of sex when Steve wants to pour more wine and Kirsty insists she won't be able to stand up. "So lie down," says Steve with a grin. But compared with the animal passions of Julia and Frank this is all very tame, and when the couple kiss for the first time in the underpass we definitely feel there is potential for a real relationship. However, this shot then pulls back and dissolves to a scene with Larry and Julia in bed — a cynical extrapolation of how the romance might culminate. Barker himself has wickedly said of this, "We cut to Julia and Larry and what marriage actually is: someone lying snoring and farting on one side of the bed while the other one has a good smoke and curses the moment they ever got married."[6]

We can't help but contrast this with a more innocent, or naïve, pre-wedding Julia. "I'm very happy," she affirms, talking about her impending nuptials, and it seems as if she really means it. What would have happened if Frank hadn't come along is certainly cause for speculation. Would she have been a different person without his corrupting influence? Even though she denies any feelings for Larry, she still initially resists the idea of killing him for his skin.

There are signs that Kirsty and Steve's association could last, nonetheless. They don't yet share a bed, for one thing; when they wake from a nightmare about Larry dying, they are shown in two single beds. Steve comes to visit her at the pet store where she is working, and worries when he can't find her at the hospital, enough to follow her to Lodovico Street. Here he attempts to rescue Kirsty, although it is she who ends up rescuing him. To all intents and purposes the dynamics of the relationship switch after their first date. Steve is the one who initiates the kiss after the party, but at the end Kirsty is definitely the one in control. There is a danger here that Steve might become just as weak and ineffectual as Larry, but it does at least suggest that Kirsty will not be forced into any deals like the one Julia makes with Frank. She has a mind of her own and is strong enough to use it; she won't be manipulated by anyone — apart, perhaps, from her father, for reasons we will come to later.

One last thing to mention about the relationships between these couples is the significance of the kisses traded. Of them all, only Kirsty and Steve's is genuine and seals what could potentially be a good partnership. But, as in *Salome*, the rest mark betrayal, deception, or even impending death. We do not see Frank and Julia kiss at all until the very end, and this is only so Frank can feed himself. The kiss Julia gives Larry is to distract him from investigating the Damp Room, then she shuns his attentions. And the one she shares with her first victim, angrily instigated by him and over in seconds, signals that his end is not far away.

The final pacts to be made involve Kirsty. Inadvertently, she opens the puzzle box in the hospital, thus unconsciously striking the same deal Frank made at the start. The Cenobites are summoned and verify what she has done. "The box. You opened it. We came," says their leader. It doesn't matter that she has done this in ignorance; her curiosity was the catalyst, just as Frank's desire was his undoing. When Kirsty tells them to "Go to Hell!" the female Cenobite confirms her worst fears: "We can't. Not alone." The box has been opened and Kirsty must live up to her end of the bargain. Swiftly, she counters this with a deal of her own, offering them something they crave even more than her: Frank. The lead

Cenobite barters from a position of weakness now, in spite of his apparent dominance of the situation. He argues that no one has ever escaped them, but all evidence points to the contrary. We have seen Frank, he *has* escaped them. The lead Cenobite is forced to contradict himself seconds later, then reluctantly agrees to this new bargain. But they also close their end of the deal with a threat. If Kirsty deceives them they will tear her soul apart!

Just like the pact between Julia and Frank, this one is wholly unstable—and it is the Cenobites who ultimately double-cross Kirsty. She fulfils her promise and delivers Frank, but that is not enough. They want to take Kirsty back as well, their hunger for her just as great as Frank's for survival or Julia's lust. As a result, Kirsty is perfectly within her rights to send them back. They have the one soul as agreed, and so the puzzle box now complies.

Cotton Family Values

The second major theme running through *Hellraiser* is that of the family, or, more correctly, an undermining of the traditional family unit. *Hellraiser* was by no means the first horror movie to do this, and we can trace the concept back to genre films of the 1960s and '70s. In earlier U.S. and UK horror films the moral supremacy of the nuclear family and all it stood for tended to be asserted. Heterosexual couples and stable family units fought against threats from the outside, like the overtly supernatural vampire, mummy or werewolf. This can be seen in the Universal and RKO movies of the '30s and '40s, and also in certain Hammer productions from the 1950s. By this time, though, American horror films were also considering the danger from within, fueled largely by the fear of communism, classic examples being *Invaders from Mars* (William Cameron Menzies, 1953) and *Invasion of the Body Snatchers* (Don Siegel, 1956). Hitchcock's *Psycho* (1960) completely internalized the threat, fixing the attention firmly on the mother-son relationship and its effect on Norman Bates (Anthony Perkins). As we've already seen, *Psycho* was the first adult horror film Clive Barker ever saw and it had a huge impact on him.

Other U.S. horror movies that challenged the family's stabilizing role included *Rosemary's Baby* (Roman Polanski, 1968) and *Night of the Living Dead*, while *The Texas Chainsaw Massacre* (Tobe Hooper, 1974) remains the epitome of dysfunctional family life: a cannibalistic clan who butcher and eat passersby. Similarly, the stalk and slash films of the late '70s and '80s depicted killers who had uneven upbringings: Jason from the *Friday the 13th* series had a psychotic mother, Michael Myers from *Halloween* (John Carpenter, 1978) was put in a secure psychiatric facility when he was young for killing his sister. Or else they targeted weak families, as Freddy Krueger does in *Nightmare on Elm Street* (Wes Craven, 1984). For a British equivalent, one could go back to Michael Powell's *Peeping Tom* (1960), in which a father's experiments on his son turn him into a voyeuristic murderer.

Because of the commercial sense of casting American *and* British actors, and thanks to Barker's broad international outlook, *Hellraiser* could claim a lineage to both U.K. and U.S. "family horror" films. But, at its very core, it is a British film with a British writer/director. If anything, the film's bland domestic setting, the suburban environment against which such an extraordinary story plays out, has its origins in the black and white Kitchen Sink or British New Wave dramas of the late 1950s and 1960s, typified by films like *Look Back in Anger* (Tony Richardson, 1958) and *A Taste of Honey* (Tony Richardson, 1961)—a realism which helps immensely when it comes to suspension of disbelief. At the very least, the saga of the Cottons, on one level, is pure British soap opera in the *Eastenders* mold.

But there is a massive difference. *Hellraiser* scratched beneath the veneer, in much the same way David Lynch did with small town America in *Blue Velvet* (1986). Barker's film is a metaphor for what really goes on behind the net curtains in certain British households, and not just because of its S&M overtones. This concentration on verisimilitude, on human and family situations, could also be the reason *Hellraiser* has been dubbed "Ibsen with monsters."[7]

The relationships between family members are key to the understanding of *Hellraiser* and how it subverts conventional roles. The four primary characters are all introduced to us by way of their position in this family. Julia and Larry are man and wife; Kirsty is Larry's daughter and Julia's stepdaughter (we discover the real matriarch has passed away when the removal men comment that Kirsty has her mother's looks. "Her mother's dead," snaps Larry), while Frank is the black sheep brother and Kirsty's uncle. As a primary player in this story, Frank states his affiliation every time he encounters a new character. "I'm Frank," he tells Julia when he turns up just before the wedding, "*Brother* Frank." Later, when Kirsty comes across him in the attic, he says: "Kirsty, it's Frank. It's Uncle Frank."

Barker then deliberately contorts the roles so that they often result in uncomfortable and disturbing viewing. Julia is Larry's wife, yet there are times when she acts more like his mother. When he cuts his hand he seeks Julia out. "You know me and blood," he says, looking like he's about to faint. Julia immediately adopts the position of caring parent, holding his arm up, preparing to rush him to the hospital and comforting him by saying, "It's all right." Here is another reason their marriage is on a collision course for disaster. In true Greek tragedy form, Larry is fulfilling some subconscious Oedipal desire to sleep with his mother (or a figure who represents his mother). But this situation is fundamentally wrong and Julia knows it. As stated earlier, she uses her sexuality to divert Larry when he is about to investigate the attic room, but cannot go through with the act itself: for one thing her *real* lover is watching close by.

Conversely, there are moments when Julia becomes the child and Larry the parent, the most obvious example being when he thinks she is ill, after she has committed the first murder, though this could just as easily translate as subservience. His throwaway joke of, "Wanna cookie, little girl?" is disquieting, especially when one scrutinizes his relationship with Kirsty in more detail.

Kirsty is introduced via a telephone conversation with her father, and the contrast between his body language with Julia and now is incredibly revealing. Larry's face lights up; there is pure delight in his voice. Kirsty, not Julia, is the great love of his life. When she arrives to help them move in, the kiss they share is full on the lips, not a general peck on the cheek: there is not a hint of betrayal here. Larry's jealousy of Steve is apparent at the dinner party, and then the pair have an intimate Chinese meal together to discuss Julia. It is evident that the affection he has for Kirsty is mutual. Kirsty has a severe Elektra complex (the female version of Oedipus) when it comes to her father. Her dislike of Julia stems from this love, tinged with jealousy itself. Kirsty's own body language is responsive in the scenes she shares with Larry, and she phones him in the middle of the night just to check that he is unharmed.

The original character of Kirsty from Barker's novella is a friend who adores Rory/Larry. Barker might have altered the character's relationship to Larry — at New World's suggestion, it should be stressed — but he was still writing and directing it from that standpoint, which is where the incestuous overtones creep in. The genuine feeling of love and adoration the original character of Kirsty had for Rory/Larry remains. This is not to imply that anything sexual has occurred or ever would occur between them. Theirs is a different kind of love, with Larry transferring his devotion for his late wife onto Kirsty, while Kirsty is happy to play the archetypal Freudian Daddy's Girl.

In stark contrast, Frank's blatantly lustful feelings for Kirsty are all too evident from their first rendezvous. After establishing he is Uncle Frank, he comments about how beautiful she's grown. Their clinch is akin to a rape stance. Frank pins her against the wall and growls, "Some things have to be endured. And that's what makes the pleasure so sweet." Yes, he is referring to his time with the Cenobites, but also of the forbidden delight the pair of them could experience if only she'd stop struggling. Near the end, he stalks Kirsty through the house, holding up that most transparent of phallic symbols from many a slasher film: the knife. His aim? Penetration. For Frank, as we have seen, there is no difference between love and desire. What he sees when he looks at Kirsty is not his niece, but another potential sexual conquest.

The fascinating thing is Frank's use of the phrase, "Come to Daddy." This not only foreshadows Frank's "borrowing" of his brother's skin, providing a clue to his real identity, it also suggests that some part of him actually wants what Larry has: Julia as his partner, Kirsty as his daughter. In one scene Frank, Julia and Kirsty create the three corners of a dysfunctional family triangle, literally, in long shot. "Stay with us," says Frank. "We can all be happy here.... Come to Daddy." In this family unit, Kirsty would experience not the deep platonic love she shared with her father, but a more physical level of incestuous love. Little wonder she declines his offer.

"Come to Daddy." Uncle Frank as sculpted by Ian Frost (courtesy Ian Frost).

Julia's relationship with Kirsty is also intriguing. She is the archetypal evil stepmother from fairytale lore, and this is referenced in *Hellbound: Hellraiser II*, where Julia says, "They didn't tell you, did they? They changed the rules of the fairy tale. I'm no longer just the wicked stepmother. Now I'm the Evil Queen." Kirsty resents Julia for taking her own place as the woman of the household, but if we look at it from the other angle Julia has more than just one reason to hate Kirsty. She is her love rival not only for Larry's affections—which she insists she doesn't require anyway—but also Frank's. Both men are attracted to Kirsty in different ways, and Julia can't help but be resentful of her younger, apparently more attractive, adversary.

Anyone outside of this "family unit" isn't utilized much in *Hellraiser*. This explains why Steve, as an outsider, is allowed to participate only in the very last sequence of the film. Even then he is virtually relegated to the role of spectator while Kirsty battles it out with the Engineer. Equally, the Cenobites, regardless of their undeniable screen presence, appear only very briefly, although it could be argued that they form a family unit of their own, with the lead Cenobite as father, Female Cenobite as mother, and Chatterer and Butterball as the two siblings—mirroring Frank and Larry.

Secrets and Masks

Another important motif in the film is that of masks. Gary Hoppenstand notes in his essay "The Secret Self" that Barker's characters often hide their true natures: Mamoulian from *The Damnation Game* might appear to be all powerful, but his use of these supernatural abilities is simply a smokescreen for who he really is, weak and vulnerable; the central hero Boone from *Cabal* (and *Nightbreed*) has a dark, bloodthirsty side, which forces him to hide away and seek the town of Midian—yet he is also in his heart a leader; the ape in "New Murders in the Rue Morgue" pretends to be human,[8] a homage to Poe, one of Barker's favorite authors as he was growing up. Barker has expressed a particular admiration for the stories *The Fall of the House of Usher* (1839), about another fated family cursed by evil, and *The Masque of Red Death* (1842), where a deadly plague disguised as one of the guests at a masquerade ball infiltrates a sealed off Abbey:

> The mask which concealed the visage was made so nearly to resemble the countenance of a stiffened corpse that the closest scrutiny must have had difficulty in detecting the cheat. And yet all this might have been endured, if not approved, by the mad revelers around. But the mummer had gone so far as to assume the type of the Red Death. His vesture was dabbled in blood—and his broad brow, with all the features of the face, was besprinkled with the scarlet horror.[9]

Just as the Red Death did, most of the characters in *Hellraiser* wear masks, too. Sometimes they are corporeal, other times less so. Frank's face is stripped from him at the beginning; in fact, it becomes a puzzle in itself that the lead Cenobite has to put together. When he returns without his skin, Frank takes the drastic measure of stealing his brother's face. This he uses to deceive Kirsty, gain her trust, and play out the role of her father, albeit briefly. He also fools the Cenobites, who must hear from his own lips that he is Frank. When he confesses, they strip this second mask away from him accordingly.

The mask Julia wears at the beginning is the face of a happily married woman. She wears another mask when she preys on her female victims, sexually alluring and available, with sunglasses to cover her eyes. The more she kills, the more she turns into a Lady Macbeth figure who can wash the blood off her hands but carries the mark of it nonetheless. Julia is able to conceal these crimes from her husband behind a façade of innocence, but her half-smile as she remembers the murders betrays her.

Larry wears the mask of a man who fundamentally believes—or should that be hopes?—Julia still loves him, but has his doubts. His nice guy act also cloaks a subconscious undercurrent of rampant emotion which he can release only by watching boxing on television. He would love to be in the ring himself, but unlike his brother he has repressed these feelings to the point where he is a pale shadow of a man. The scene between Larry and Julia when they are watching the boxing match is therefore laced with ironic black comedy. When Larry comments that she used to hate this kind of thing and asks if it's upsetting her, Julia replies coolly, "I've seen worse." Both are hiding their secret selves from each other, but, in fine theatrical tradition, Barker has revealed them to the audience for their fullest effect.

Kirsty barely disguises her feelings about Julia, so her one true mask is that of vulnerability she displays with Steve. She allows him to dominate the relationship at first, hiding, or even subduing, her true fiery nature — which forces him to become more like her father, and thus more attractive in her eyes. It isn't long afterwards that her true character surfaces, more in keeping with a horror heroine who doesn't need a man to fight on her behalf.

Lastly, the box and its keeper wear their own masks. Camouflaged as a trinket, the Lament Configuration is really a doorway to another very dangerous dimension, just as the carpet in *Weaveworld* (1987), the dream sea Quiddity in *The Great and Secret Show* (1989) and the lighthouse in *Abarat* (2002) are portals to other places. Essentially, though, it is more than that. It is Pandora's Box by any other name.

There are various versions of the Pandora legend. One Greek version says that Pandora was created by the gods and taken as a wife by the titan Epimetheus. Pandora had a sealed vase, which Epimetheus opened, causing all the troubles, weariness and illnesses of mankind to escape. In a Roman retelling it was Pandora herself who opened the box — brought by Mercury — and once all the evils had escaped the only thing left inside was hope. In the first, we can exchange Epimetheus for Frank, while in the second, Pandora herself becomes Kirsty. But one thing remains a constant: the disguise of the innocent-looking vessel.

The keeper in *Hellraiser* (Frank Baker), who initially appears as a derelict, is also much more than he seems. He goes from being a character who seemingly has no power, except that of unnerving people when he eats bugs or stares at them, to one who obviously has a great deal. At the end, he is the one who retrieves the box from the flames, simultaneously transforming into a winged skeletal creature. Beyond the human flesh, he is obviously a demon himself. Crucially, he is the "person" who returns the box so it can be purchased by the next Frank Cotton who comes along, literally completing the circular narrative. Without him, there would be no *Hellraiser* story.

Heaven or Hell

To conclude, we have the religious aspects of the movie. Though not particularly religious himself, Barker has always said that, "The Bible is a source of inspiration constantly for me and remains a significant source of inspiration ... biblical stories have a kind of ... primal quality to them."[10] This has been especially true when constructing his own mythologies, including *Hellraiser*'s, as we shall see later on, but also when considering the eternal struggle of good versus evil.

Filmically, in this respect *Hellraiser* shares its roots with movies like *The Exorcist* and *The Omen* (Richard Donner, 1976), which also address this question through the device of demonic interjection. But the lines between notions of good and evil in *Hellraiser* are far less distinct. In *The Exorcist* the evil is quite obviously the demon that has taken control of the child Regan, while at the other end of the scale are the priests attempting to free her soul. Karras may well be losing his faith but there is no question as to his intentions, nor

The cover of Clive Barker's *Abarat*, featuring Barker's own artwork (© HarperCollins and Clive Barker, used by permission).

which side he fights on. Likewise, Damien has — indirectly — committed murders, manipulated events and positioned himself to take over the empire of his "father." Gregory Peck's politician Thorn and David Warner's photographer Jennings may not be the most religious people, but during the course of the film they seek out those who are — like the monks in Italy, or Leo McKern's Exorcist. The polarization between good and evil, between who should win and who should lose, is extremely clear-cut; and in religious terms it comes down to the simple conflict between God and the Devil.

Ashley Laurence publicity shot (photograph credit: Tom Collins).

At the outset of *Hellraiser* Kirsty might appear to be on the side of Heaven as she occupies a contrary position to the Cenobites. The first time we see her, she is virtually in soft focus, her face bathed in light like an angel. During the Argentoesque dream sequence, too, with white feathers floating around her, Kirsty resembles the Madonna from a painting by an Italian master. Even her name is Christ-like. Kirsty also wears a white T-shirt throughout the film, in line with the basic iconographic symbolism of color clothing schemes.[11] This follows if we also examine Julia's choice of outfits: she begins with white blouses, then switches to orange, then finally to dark blue, thus reflecting her journey through passion to the dark side.

However, Kirsty does not adhere to the moral codes of a Heavenly heroine, or even a heroine from previous horror films. Most noticeably, she does not remain virginal. Whether or not anything happened after her kiss with Steve, it is still insinuated that she has slept with him. In slasher films this is usually the grounds for punishment by the killer, as Carol Clover elucidates in her groundbreaking book, *Men, Women and Chainsaws*. The Final Girl, as she calls the Stalk and Slash heroine, is usually a "spunky enquirer into the terrible place,"[12] but never sexually active. Secondly, when Kirsty first arrives at the house on Lodovico Street, she sees statues of saints and Christ on the doorstep, cast out ready for Hell to enter. Her reaction is simply to smile, shrug, and walk in through the door. Such ignorance of the portent leads to terrible heartache later. Perhaps this is why the statue that falls out and scares Kirsty as she is being chased by Frank *has* to be Christ — in retaliation for her apathy? But given this, Kirsty still turns her back on the power of faith and uses her own mettle instead.

There was even a deleted scene where an evangelist spoke to Kirsty directly through the radio to warn her, which would have highlighted her rejection yet further:

INT: KIRSTY'S ROOM. NIGHT
Music from the radio: a love song. The radio is badly tuned: the song sounds tinny. It fades, then comes back into focus again. We move around the room, over an unfinished puzzle, left on the bed; over a few pictures of LARRY, set lovingly beside the bed, and finally, onto KIRSTY, who is drying her hair after a shower.

> The radio channel slips. The radio whines. Then, an evangelist's voice on the air-waves.
> EVANGELIST: The Devil is watching you. That's the message I came here tonight to bring you. The Devil is watching you and he sees the corruption in your hearts. He hears you! He sees you! Every night, every day.
> KIRSTY has got up now and is trying to change channels, but the controls defeat her. She gets more and more annoyed.
> KIRSTY: C'mon, damn you. C'mon.
> EVANGELIST: The Devil knows your soul.
> KIRSTY: No he doesn't! Damn thing!
> Eventually she pulls the back off the radio. The batteries fall out.
> KIRSTY (to herself): Nice going.
> Thunder.[13]

In addition, Kirsty swears, she fights dirty, and to save herself she negotiates with the Cenobites, offering up Frank. Because Frank is such a morally bankrupt character, we can forgive this behavior, but it blurs the line between right and wrong even more. If there hadn't been a scapegoat around to give the demons, would she have offered up an innocent? Possibly not, but Kirsty's strong streak of self-preservation is what makes her such a tough heroine in the first place, and her complexity is what makes her an enduring screen champion.

By the same token, Julia, for all the terrible things she does, has a compassionate side — evidenced by her response to Larry after he cuts himself. The act of kindness can be viewed as pity, of course, for an inferior person, or — more logically — it can be seen as a natural reaction to anybody in pain. Remember, this is before she has the motivation to kill for "love." When she first enters the house and climbs the stairs, she, too, sees the statue of Christ on the windowsill. Another warning, this time for her not to go any further, up the stairs and down the road to damnation. But she gives the effigy a cold stare and carries on, and will regret it just as Kirsty does.

Larry's religious beliefs are just as indistinct. It's unclear whether he gets rid of all the religious artifacts simply to please Julia, or for his own benefit. Has the death of his previous wife shaken any faith he might have had in the Lord? He does choose Sunday for them to move in, indicating that he cares little for religious tradition. In *The Hellbound Heart* it says, "It was the Lord's Day up this end of the city. Even if the owners of these well-dressed houses and well-pressed children were no longer believers, they still observed the Sabbath."[14] All except Larry and his clan. But perhaps there's another explanation. A man so apathetic about everything else, his family, pleasing his wife, the state of his marriage, might also be lackluster when it comes to believing in something spiritual.

Like Julia, Frank is another contradiction in terms. On the surface he's everything reprehensible and amoral about the human race. Selfish, lecherous and downright vicious: the *true* villain of the piece. So one has to ask why he allows the religious artifacts to remain in the house while he conducts his transaction with the Cenobites. Is it for protection in case things go horribly wrong — in which case, they offer none at all. Or is it because he believed they might well be angelic beings, come to provide him with pleasure: if they are, then they have more in common with the angels from *The Forbidden* than with any biblical text. Frank realizes all too late that Hell is not the place he thought it would be. By seeking to escape, therefore, he seeks to redeem himself. He is, quite literally, born again. Either that or he's resurrected, which has the same religious connotations. A shame then that his base nature comes to the fore again as the film progresses. Despite this he still plays the martyr when the Cenobites catch up with him. Strung out with arms wide in a re-creation of the crucifixion, he recites a line from the Bible: "Jesus wept." It doesn't save him, just as his victims who called out "Christ!" before their death were shown no mercy.

It might sound odd, but the Cenobites are even more ambiguous from a religious standpoint. They are demons, true, but not in the typical sense of the word. They do not seek to bring about chaos; rather, theirs is an order of discipline. They have to follow codes insomuch as they can only take back people who have opened the box, generally those who have been searching for them in the first place, with the right frame of mind. As Pinhead says, they are, indeed, "Angels to some, demons to others." Theirs is a religion in itself, and the Hell they come from contains none of the reported fires or pits; its corridors are gray stone, just like a church or monastery (the very name itself, Cenobite, is derived from the term coe'nobite, which means member of a monastic community). And as actor Doug Bradley recalls, "There was this stuff that was filmed for *Hellraiser* and I don't know whether it exists, but it was certainly filmed. Clive ... had us in these little monkish cells with the walls covered in taboo fetishist quasi-religious iconic things, pacing backwards and forwards."[15]

The arrival of the Cenobites in this realm is heralded by the chiming of a bell, similar to the one we hear on the Sunday as Larry and Julia move into Lodovico Street. And when they are gathered together only three are generally shown in a shot at a time — A trinity: a darker Father, Son, and Holy Ghost, with Pinhead's crown of nails replacing the thorns. Like Kirsty, they are also bathed in light when we see them properly for the first time in the hospital. The Cenobites are not merely evil for evil's sake, rampant creatures causing devastation and destruction like the monsters from so many B movie horror flicks. They only practice their trade on those who deserve and desire their attentions.

3
DEMONS TO SOME

There can be no denying the Cenobites' contribution to making *Hellraiser* a milestone of the genre. Their total screen time is approximately seven minutes, but their impact is out of all proportion to this. Yet their introduction — or lack thereof — may certainly have something to do with the phenomenon. At the start of the film we are only granted extremely quick flashes of them: the Female Cenobite in close-up, Pinhead's hands as he picks up pieces of Frank's face, a shot of him standing up with the nails in his head visible. Then they are gone. After this sudden sensory overload, we are deprived: all is quiet, and the camera is free to pull back and away from the room where we just encountered them. Just as the box does with Frank and Kirsty, this piques the audience's curiosity and forces them to ask questions about exactly who these strange beings are. How can it not? We know they must be integral to the story, but why?

When we do finally see the Cenobites properly, it is the look of them that captivates. At the time, audiences had never seen characters like these. They were totally original, a tricky thing to accomplish in a cliché-driven genre like horror. The closest precursors are actually from a different, though obviously related, genre: science fiction. They are the members of the Spice Guild in David Lynch's adaptation of Frank Herbert's sprawling epic, *Dune* (1984). The entourage who bring on the monstrously mutated Guild Navigator at the very beginning of the film for a meeting with the Emperor are dressed in long leather or PVC robes and have pus-ridden sores. The look of the bald Bene Gesserit witches also resembles that of the Female Cenobite, and Baron Harkonnen's playthings have open bloodstained wounds. Whether or not this influenced former Dog Company costume designer Jane Wildgoose is open to speculation, but there were other very real and traceable lines of origin.

When he first came down to London, Barker found himself illustrating a couple of centerfolds for some S&M magazines, which later were investigated by Scotland Yard for their content. The magazines were burned, which Barker found to be "the ultimate compliment."[1] His interest in the taboos of society has always been great, and when researching the Cenobites he definitely returned to this hunting ground. One magazine in particular proved invaluable: *Piercing Fans International Quarterly*, which showed people with hooks inserted in their flesh, bodies dangling from chains — following the heritage of men like Fakir Musafar, the human pincushion who warranted a feature in *Ripley's Believe It or Not*. There are also people in the Philippines who regularly practice piercing themselves or hanging from hooks embedded in their skin as a kind of spiritual experience, while Native Americans practiced a similar ritual for their Sun Dances. Going back even further in history, the most prominent examples would have to be the Spanish Inquisition and their various pieces of equipment for deriving pain from their victims, as well as the writings of the Marquis de Sade.[2]

The look of the Cenobites was to be a kind of modern primitive, but perversely stylish, with clothes that intermingled with the wounds they had inflicted on themselves. Barker also had the initial sketches he'd come up with to help everyone visualize what he wanted, and, of course, descriptions in *The Hellbound Heart* like this one:

> Why then was he so distressed to set eyes upon them? Was it the scars that covered every inch of their bodies; the flesh cosmetically punctured and sliced and infibulated, then dusted down with ash? Was it the smell of vanilla they brought with them, the sweetness of which did little to disguise the stench beneath? Or was it that as the light grew, and he scanned them more closely, he saw nothing of joy, or even humanity, in their maimed faces: only desperation, and an appetite that made his bowels ache to be voided.[3]

So Barker's message to the costume designers was quite specific when it came to the Cenobites. Says Jane Wildgoose of a meeting she had with him:

> He gave me some very clear indications of what he'd like and then I did my research.... My notes say that he wanted:
> 1) Areas of revealed flesh where some kind of torture has or is occurring;
> 2) Something associated with butchery involved. And here we have a very Clive turn of phrase. I've written down "repulsive glamour." And other notes I've made about what he wanted is that they should be "magnificent super-butchers."[4]

The "repulsive glamour" comment is imperative, as it's something Barker has referred to a lot — the beauty of horrific images and even the attraction we as observers have to them. To quote him: "I certainly get a lot of letters from people who think that Pinhead in *Hellraiser*, for all his strange disfigurements, is sexy, endearing. There are more

Pinhead Cenobite concept sketch for *Hellraiser*.

things going on, in other words, in these kinds of strange disfigurements than simply saying this is disgusting, this is repulsive."[5] Pinhead is very much the embodiment of this mode of thinking, which is one of the reasons his character has endured and reached the heights of horror movie icon. But what are the others?

The horror genre is one that lends itself exceptionally well to iconography. The vampire with fangs and cloak, the hairy werewolf and shambling zombie with tattered clothes. Every so often a film comes along that delivers a momentous villain; and usually the actor playing the role will be forever linked with it. From the Universal stable, Bela Lugosi as Dracula, who became so interlinked with his character he was buried in the cape, and Boris Karloff as Frankenstein, with his flat head and stitches. Later, there was Christopher Lee playing the famous Count in Hammer productions, who must surely be a forerunner to Pinhead in every way. He is dignified but capable of unspeakable acts, tall and elegant but with an underlying barbaric quality. Bradley himself has commented, "That was very much an important element to me, that he had this love affair with the English language. Which as a demon from hell, committed to the sado-masochistic disposal of people, struck me as very exciting. When he spoke it was like an echo of Oscar Wilde or Noel Coward."[6]

In the '70s and '80s, slasher killers like Robert Englund's Freddy Krueger fulfilled the role of iconic horror monster in a very different way: with visual or verbal one-liners complementing their distinctive masks or ensemble. Then came Anthony Hopkins' portrayal of Hannibal Lecter to take us into the 1990s, which again has something in common with the Cenobite mentality. Fans of horror have always coveted their antiheroes and famous examples become such a part of popular culture they are recognized by all. This isn't something a director can plan in advance, although many have tried and failed. It is simply that certain characters immediately resonate with audiences.

The actor that brought Pinhead to life, Doug Bradley (courtesy Doug Bradley).

Doug Bradley's Pinhead is just such a character. To quote Barker again, "I think people came out of *Hellraiser* that first time they saw it, they probably said, 'Hey, check out the guy with the pins in his head'.... I would love to say that, oh yeah, God, it was all planned. It wasn't."[7]

This popularity trend is due chiefly to three factors. First, the performance Bradley gives is exceptional. He pitches the character exactly right, understated when necessary, authoritative when required, quite simply a powerful and terrifying screen presence. In this respect he was following advice from Barker to "Do less. Do less," ensuring even the slightest expression in make-up had a dramatic impact. What then comes across is a figure very much in control of the situation, and very confident in his own abilities. Pinhead is not a person to be crossed. The fact that

Bradley takes the role seriously makes us as viewers take him seriously. When questioned about the popularity of Pinhead, Bob Keen, who came up with the make-up, had this to say in two different interviews: "It's the combination of several elements. Perhaps the most important is that Doug gives an absolutely straight performance, and it was Clive Barker's genius in *Hellraiser* to present a character who was significantly different, strange and aloof from his surroundings, for the audience to be drawn to him."[8] "Ninety-five per cent of what Pinhead is, is what Doug Bradley brings to the role.... And Doug's voice was just fantastic. You hear him and he has these wonderful lines and the whole thing just grew and grew. So I think the look's important, but I think that if the wrong actor had been wearing this, Pinhead would never be the success that he is."[9]

It is a testament to Bradley, and more proof of his iconic status, that his lines in the film are the most quoted. Some were even used as taglines for the movie ("Angels to some, demons to others" and "We'll tear your soul apart.") His choice for the voicing of Pinhead should also rate a mention here. Obviously, he couldn't have pitched it like the asexual character from *The Hellbound Heart*. "The voice I gave to Pinhead is anything but 'light and breathy,' and certainly sounded like no 'excited girl' it's ever been my pleasure to know.... For the voice I simply went with how I was hearing the lines in my head, which was low, slow menace."[10] And the audio was enhanced even more in postproduction.

Secondly, as already suggested, the mystery surrounding the Cenobites at the start of the movie is vital. Who are they? Where did they originally come from? Why do they do the things they do? These questions are only vaguely answered in *Hellraiser*, and no background information is given at all. This mystique is part of what makes the Cenobites, and Pinhead especially, tantalizing. In conversations with Barker, Bradley was told that the character had once been human, but gave him no indication as to when this had been. Consequently there is also a melancholy behind the performance, a remembrance of something Pinhead had once been but can't go back to, a longing for his humanity. In successive films, this was expounded upon and he was given a back history: a British Army captain who sought the box after enduring the horrors of World War I. The other Cenobites, too, were depicted as once being human before their transformation in the labyrinths of Hell. It could be argued that the characters lost something that contributed to their success in the original film. Granted, the history gave the Cenobites much more emotional depth — allowing us to relate to them. But the unknown is often more frightening than the familiar. In *Hellraiser*, for the time being, that enigma, the puzzle of the Cenobites themselves, remains a secret.

We must also mention briefly the Cenobites as metaphors for our deepest instinctive fears — and we are always attracted to what we fear the most. Chatterer, with those wires pulling back his lips, revealing gums and teeth, crystallizes a very real anxiety about being eaten, possibly alive. On a more modern level, he brings with him connotations of dental work, too, the anxiety we all feel about this particular profession. Butterball represents fear about gluttony, of having overeaten until fit to burst, as he literally has. The stitches used on his flesh could be seen again as phobia about the medical profession and operations, which combines nicely with the terror of going blind when you realize his eyes are stitched shut under those sunglasses. The Female Cenobite's vaginal gash in her throat is clearly a representation of man's fear of female sexuality. The very fact that it is on display, not hidden, gives it the power to shock (and led to a raft of nicknames among the crew to diffuse the alarm, such as Deep Throat and Cunt Throat). As for Pinhead himself, he represents the greatest fear for both men and women, that of being penetrated against our will. He has been violated by the nails, not once, but dozens of times. And they remain there as a constant reminder of his defilement.

The third reason for the iconic status of Pinhead is that he was used to promote the film through posters and cinema trailers. His became the official face of *Hellraiser*. The marketing people at New World quickly recognized this potential, bringing Bradley back in for a photo shoot after filming had finished. When it came time to put the black contact lenses in, they discovered that one had melted, so the actual poster images show Pinhead with Doug's blue eyes. But it makes very little difference to the overall image, which was exploited in the first instance to draw audiences—up on billboard posters in the U.S., Australia, Japan. Then it was used to make money through merchandise.

Directors like George Lucas and Steven Spielberg had shown that films could be veritable gold mines when it came to spin-off merchandising, with *Star Wars* (1977) and *E.T.* (1982) both earning more from this than from actual box office returns. With slasher anti-heroes doing the same for the horror genre, it was perhaps no surprise that, soon after *Hellraiser*'s release, cups, T-shirts and jackets adorned with Pinhead appeared, backed up by promotional campaigns. Today, Pinhead models, toys, badges and just about anything else are available, further enforcing this icon's standing in popular culture. Can it be a coincidence that the video and DVD of the film has remained a constant seller, when it has Pinhead on the cover? As intelligent and as interesting as the film is, there should be no refuting the Cenobites' hand in its cult status.

4

SUCH SIGHTS TO SHOW YOU

As broached in the previous chapter, Barker is a champion of the horrific image as beauty, or what he has sometimes termed "The Revelation Response." This is, to quote him, "The sheer wonder of monsters and beasts and extraordinary things, which has always been one of the things that draws me to horror.... It's the appeal of the strange."[1] Without question, *Hellraiser* is a visually extreme film. There are fans who watch it simply to see if they can endure the intensity of the gore scenes. Yet, unlike splatter flicks such as *The Evil Dead* (Sam Raimi, 1981) and *Re-Animator* (Stuart Gordon, 1985), the bloodletting of *Hellraiser* is not the main impetus of the film. And it is shot in such a way as to inspire as much awe as it does repulsion.

The standout episode in this respect has to be Frank's resurrection. When New World saw the progress Barker was making on the movie, they gave him more money for special effects, and this was one of the scenes added afterwards. Originally the director was just going to cut from Larry's blood soaking into the floorboards to him reappearing on the night of the dinner party. In retrospect it is difficult to see how the film could work without this added Hitchcockian "ticking bomb under the table." But it is much more than just a narrative device to drum up unease.

The sequence itself is a carefully choreographed exercise in spectacular distaste, so riveting it is hard to look away. It begins with a heart beating under the floorboards, lifted almost directly from Poe's "The Telltale Heart," where the sound of a pumping heart forces a murderer to admit to his crime. As Frank pieces himself together little by little, accompanied by Christopher Young's score, we cannot help but marvel at the magnificence of the human body, even as we're reaching for the sick bags. Bob Keen, who was responsible for this scene, explains: "We'd already done it once. The first time we did it, it was a dried-up corpse that came out of the walls. None of us were happy with this. It was decided right at the end that we would go back and redo it, and it became this nightmare of visceral imagery."[2] With a combination of reverse shots and tricks—like using a rig for the floor shake and porridge pumped through holes— Keen came up with the most memorable scene in the entire film. The last shot, exquisitely back lit by Vidgeon, is quite literally breathtaking. Each stage of Frank's regeneration holds a fascination for viewers that elevates it above someone having an eye gouged out or their head cut off. Stimulated by the illustrations of Vesalius, Barker delivers lasting images which continue to disturb long after the final credits have rolled.

For the surrealism of *Hellraiser*, Barker also looked to the films of a favorite past director and artist, Jean Cocteau, for inspiration. One of his earliest memories is of seeing Cocteau on TV while he was at home sick in the autumn of 1960, and watching a clip from one of his movies: "It was called, though the title meant nothing to me at that time, *The Testament of Orpheus*, and in it this same old man appeared [Cocteau], dressed much as he'd been dressed in his interview. He was wandering in a rather fake-looking landscape of ruins, where he encountered a menacing woman dressed in a cloak and elaborate helmet, armed with a spear. Flanking her were men wearing horse masks...."[3]

Later he would get to see Cocteau's other movies at Film Societies in Liverpool, and another that holds a tremendous significance here must surely be *La Belle et la Bête, Beauty and the Beast* (1946). The poster for this alone should be enough to send chills of recognition through any *Hellraiser* fan, for its depiction of the two major players is an almost exact replica of Julia and Frank while he is still in his unfinished form. Says Barker of the film, "Garbo purportedly exclaimed, when the Beast, played by Jean Marais, who was Cocteau's best friend, turns into a Prince, 'Oh, give me back my beautiful beast!'"[4]

One cannot discount the effect of William Blake's (1757–1827) work on Barker in this respect, either. Blake proclaimed the supremacy of the imagination over the rationalism and materialism of the eighteenth century, juxtaposing the ordinary with the extraordinary, envisaging angels against the backdrop of Marylebone and Camden Town. This was a revelation for the young Barker, who immersed himself in volumes by the painter/poet, as well as in work by Bosch and Goya. This blurring of the normal with the

Skinned Frank concept sketch for *Hellraiser* (courtesy Clive Barker).

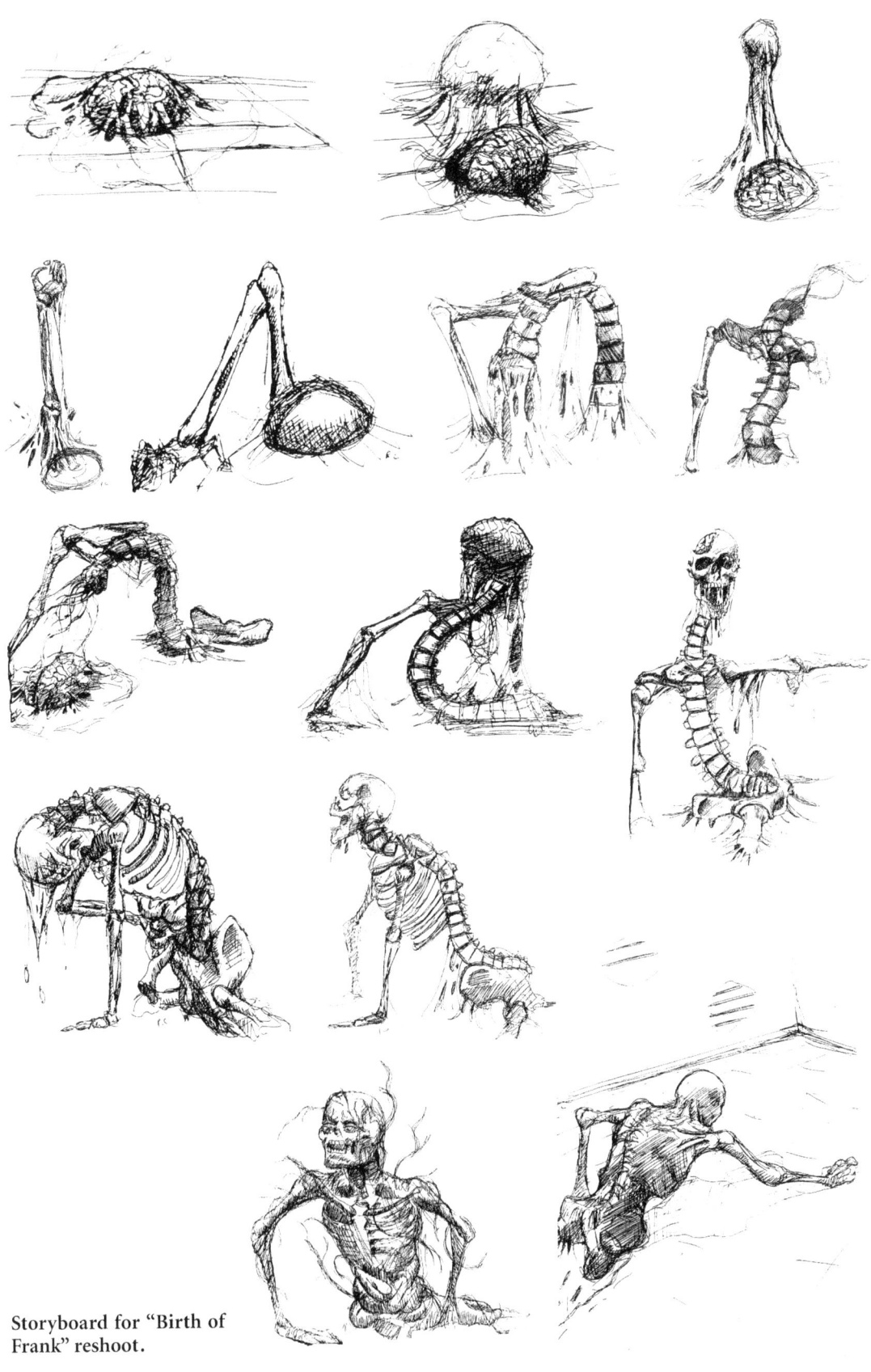

Storyboard for "Birth of Frank" reshoot.

abnormal, the palatable with the unpalatable, became the norm as far as Barker was concerned.

Understandably, the director was also eager to carry on the tradition of the Grand Guignol, just as he had done with his own theater productions. Founded in 1897 by Oscar Méténier, the secretary to a police commissioner whose duties included escorting condemned men to their death, the Parisian theater produced plays reliant on violent and bloody set-pieces. If meat was needed in a scene, then real meat was used and actors often "suffered" staged eye-gougings, strangulations and rapes night after night, all very effective and indistinguishable from the actual thing.

Barker has also quoted the playwright John Webster (c. 1578–1632) as being a strong influence on his work, especially regarding the depiction of violence and sensation. In plays such as *The White Devil* (c.1612) and *The Duchess of Malfi* (c.1614), we're presented with the familiar themes of revenge, but we also have the unusual, such as a suitor fooled into kissing the poisoned lips of a dressed up skull, or hints of witchcraft and lycanthropy. "My favorite playwright of violence is Webster," Barker has clarified. "He's the grand master of the violent set-piece, in which there's a broad configuration of events, circumstances, relationships, which are leading inevitably to some dire conclusion."[5]

Barker's love of Harryhausen and special effects in general has already been noted, and *Hellraiser* gave him the chance to simultaneously play with such devices and stay true to his own creed of gorgeous grotesquery. But like that other gore fest of the year before—David Cronenberg's remake of *The Fly* (1986)—the special effects do not overshadow the story. Indeed, Barker learned a very important lesson from Cronenberg and his penchant for staging shocking scenes quite early on in his films (the exploding head in *Scanners* (1981) for example). The introductory sequence in *Hellraiser* is radical, but it does grab the viewer and buy Barker exposition time. One of the reasons *Hellraiser* has stood the test of time is the fact that there is a solid, appealing and emotional story at its center. The effects only supplement this. To have it the other way around would be, as Barker says, "The tail wagging the dog."[6]

Hellraiser can be situated within the whole Body Horror subgenre, in which Cronenberg's films definitely belong, but again these are not mutations or disfigurements for the sake of them. As in the *Books of Blood*, the transformations of the flesh have a purpose beyond mere superficial spectacle: Frank's escape and taking on his brother's form, the Cenobites' intermingling of pain and pleasure. In a movie like *The Fly*, the slow deterioration of the body, the shock at what might be revealed next, starts to become the only impetus. Frank is the antithesis of Brundle, an attempt to make the ugly human and natural, instead of rendering the beautiful repulsive.

Similarly, jump-shocks do not age well in cinema. Films designed to be like Ghost Train rides, where one fright follows the next, date incredibly quickly. *Hellraiser* has two such shocks: when one of Frank's victims pleads with Kirsty for help; and the double whammy of Christ and the maggoty corpse dropping out while Kirsty is trying to hide from Frank. These scenes, added at the behest of New World, who thought that a horror movie should have some sudden scares in it, are the least satisfying in the whole film. They are obvious and seem unnecessary on repeated viewings.

But if *Hellraiser* by and large seemingly refuses to pander to these rules of horror cinema, it is still visually informed by other historical horror models. Indeed, it simultaneously pays homage to and transcends them. First, Barker acknowledges the mythology of the vampire subgenre—in his use of blood as a regenerative source. Frank may not have fangs and bite people on the neck, but he is still a vampire. As well as binding the family unit together, blood brings Frank back from the dead and he feeds off the victims Julia (his vampiric bride) lures to the house (their castle). So in this sense too, the blood and gore have value beyond the obvious.

Alternatively, the resurrected Frank could also be described as a zombie, one of the

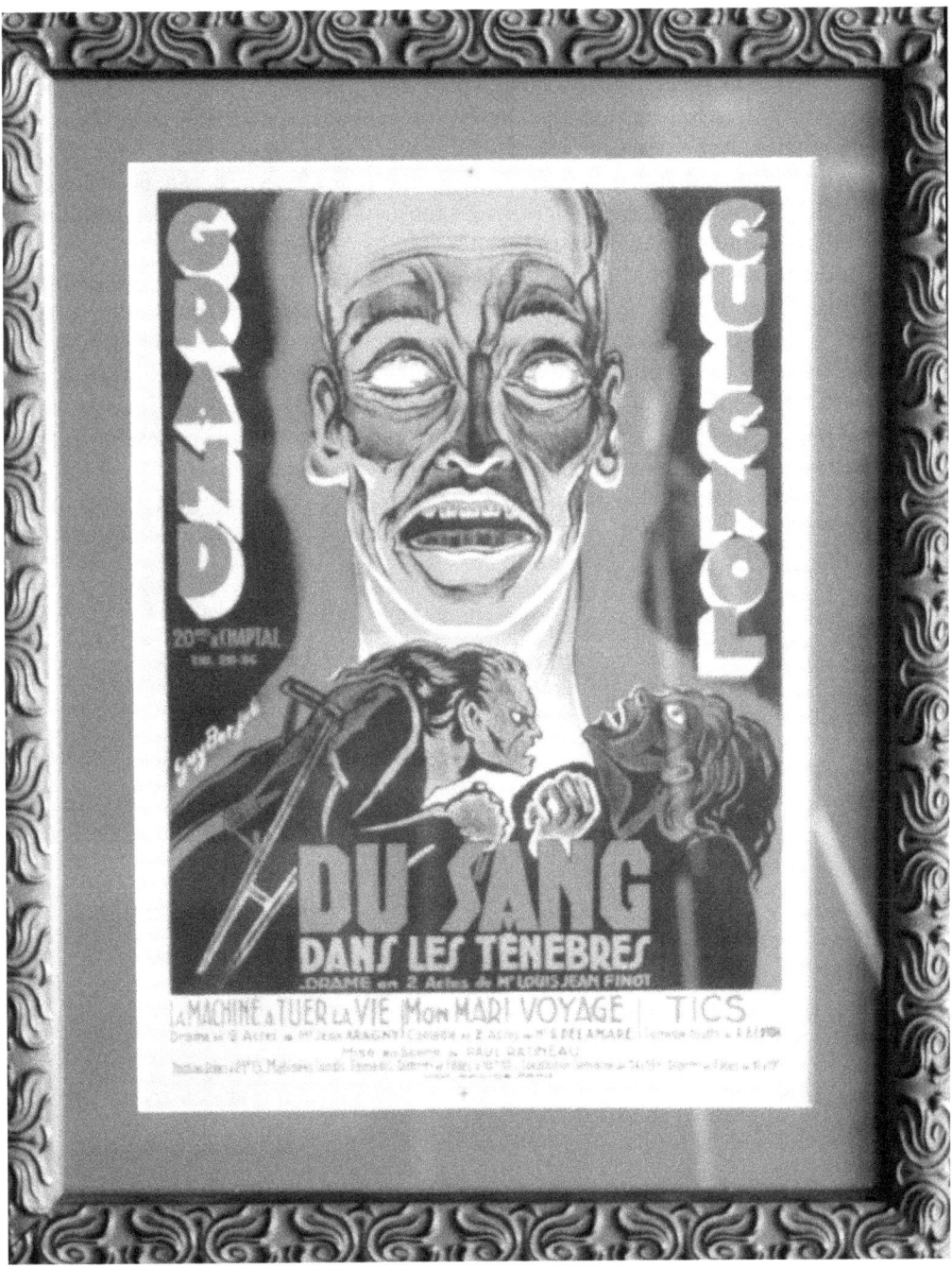

Grand Guignol poster (courtesy of Eric Horton).

walking dead, feasting on human flesh. True, he can think coherently, which is more than Romero's shambling corpses can do, but he is, to all intents and purposes, dead: we saw him ripped apart at the beginning. In a slightly different tone, there are some shots which are pure Gothic in nature, such as one high angle glimpse of Julia at the top of the stairs, her face half in shadow. And Barker pays homage to the haunted house and ghost film, in the most obvious way, with the location house itself, which looks suspiciously like a well-known property in Amityville, and with the ghost presence of Frank in the attic — the oldest form of shade.

Lastly, Barker includes a creature that would not look out of place in any monster or alien film. As we have commented, the Engineer does appear remarkably cheap compared with what might have been accomplished with more time and money. But thanks to Vidgeon's lighting again and Richard Marden's editing, it is nowhere near as deficient as Rawhead Rex. On the contrary, there is an inherent substance and charm to it that could never be replaced by computer generated trickery.

Both the British Board of Film Classification and the Motion Picture Association of America insisted on cuts to *Hellraiser*, to the tune of twenty seconds. But there was trimming only within scenes where both bodies thought the intensity was too much, and no scenes were lost in their entirety. For a final word on his motivations for creating such images, we'll turn to Barker once more: "I think it's a desire that the audience comprehend that these images are highly charged and mythic, and worthy of our close examination. And if we just go out and say, 'That was gross,' then we've missed most of the purpose of that image. It's difficult. You have to create very elegant images and very elegant metaphors. I hope there are places in *Hellraiser* where I have done that. It's a picture which should work on more than one level."[7]

5

No Limits

Critical reaction to Clive Barker's *Hellraiser* upon release was generally favorable on both sides of the Atlantic. London magazine *Time Out* had this to say: "Barker's dazzling debut creates such an atmosphere of dread that the astonishing set-pieces simply detonate in a chain reaction of cumulative intensity ... a serious, intelligent and disturbing horror film, *Hellraiser* will leave you, to coin one of Barker's own phrases, in a state between hysteria and ecstasy.'"

While *Melody Maker* proclaimed it was, "The best horror film ever to be made in Britain," which is saying very little at that time, *City Limits* encapsulated the attraction quite neatly with these words: "Barker exploits our deepest dreads about pain equals pleasure and the fears that our socially repressed primal desires will one day unloose and end in a sexual nightmare."

The Daily Telegraph commented that, in *Hellraiser*, "Barker has achieved a fine degree of menace." *The Daily Mail* called the film, "A pinnacle of the genre." And *The Scotsman* said, "It plays on the darkest fears and fantastical obsessions of the human psyche." The more academic magazines also took an interest, and horror writer and film historian Kim Newman hit the mark with his critique in *Monthly Film Bulletin*: "The most immediately striking aspect of the movie is its seriousness of tone in an era when horror films (the *Nightmare on Elm Street* or *Evil Dead* films in particular) tend to be broadly comic. ... the overall approach is straight, not to say relentlessly grim."[1]

And while *Q Magazine* echoed these sentiments, they also drew attention to the U.S. dubbing imposed by New World: "*Hellraiser* does have its share of problems: the re-dubbing of peripheral characters with a mid–Atlantic twang, the relocation of the film in a geographical limbo.... The film, however, cannot be faulted for the ambitiousness of its themes.... Sadly the moral and emotional complexity that is the film's greatest strength is likely to be deemed its greatest weakness by an audience weaned on the misplaced jocularity of *House* or *Fright Night*." *Screen International* also decided to concentrate on the scare tactics for their review, calling the film "The best slam-bang, no-holds-barred, scare-the-shit-out-of-you horror movie for quite a while."

Oddly, the most savage criticism came from the U.S., although industry magazine *Variety* did say in their Cannes review that *Hellraiser* was "a well-paced sci-fi cum horror fantasy which should appeal to a wide youth audience around the globe," and the *New York Times* called it "evocatively creepy." The first barrage came from famous film critic Roger Ebert of the *Chicago Sun Times*: "Stephen King ... may have seen the future of the horror genre, but he has almost certainly not seen *Hellraiser*, which is as dreary a piece of goods as has masqueraded as horror in many a long, cold night."

Richard Harrington was no less unpleasant in his *Washington Post* review of September 19, 1987: "Some things have to be endured.... That's what one of the characters says in Clive Barker's *Hellraiser*, and he might as well be talking about the first film written and directed by this new enfant terrible of the horror genre...." Thankfully, there were some who didn't share these views, Michael Wilmington from the *Los Angeles Times* for one. He said: "Clive Barker's *Hellraiser* is one of the more original and memorable horror movies of the year: a genuinely scary, but also nearly stomach-churning experience by a genre specialist who seemingly wallows in excess and loves pushing conventions to their ghastly limits.... *Hellraiser* is intelligent and brutally imaginative."

And the fact that *Hellraiser* won Le Grand Prix de la Section Peur at the sixteenth Fantasy Film Festival only added to its credibility. But from a financial perspective, which is something Hollywood takes more notice of than the written word, *Hellraiser* netted approximately $14,564,000 domestically and overall generated revenues of $30 million on its release.[2] It made Barker a major player and saw offers heading his way to direct the third film in the *Alien* saga, his response to which was, why would anyone want to make the third in any franchise? He wasn't even interested in helming the second in his own movie series. That would be the territory of two men, two men who would take us even further into Hell, and bring us back again.

6

TO HELL AND BACK

Even before the official release of *Hellraiser* there had been talk of a sequel. In fact, it was following early screenings of the movie at Cannes in 1987 that Barker and producer Chris Figg first pitched the notion of *Hellbound: Hellraiser II* to New World. Said Barker at the time, "We proved our point with *Hellraiser*.... We thought New World would only give novices enough money for one haunted house and no sets and it turned out to be true. There were clearly many questions left unanswered by the film which we couldn't do the first time around as we didn't have the budget. The sequel was conceived with this in mind.... In many ways I see *Hellbound* as an advance from the teaser trailer that was *Hellraiser*."[1]

Unfortunately, promotional commitments to the first film as well as for his next novel, *Weaveworld*, meant that Barker had time neither to write nor direct this. Instead he would settle for executive producer status, which would allow him to oversee the production but still maintain a reasonable distance from it. By this time, Barker and Figg had also founded Film Futures, seemingly tailor-made for this purpose. As Figg explained, "We set up Film Futures so Clive could executive produce, write plot synopses and supervise projects. Directors can get branded all too easily and neither of us wanted that to happen with Clive's film career."[2] Reading between the lines, one might speculate that, with the move into more fantasy-related fiction, Barker was attempting to escape the trap of being pigeon-holed as simply a horror writer and director, something a follow-up horror movie so soon would further compound. But at the same time the *Hellraiser* franchise was fundamentally his baby, so he was loathe to entrust it to just anybody.

The first person he turned to, therefore, was his old friend from the Dog Company, Peter Atkins. Atkins and Barker first met in 1974 when the former was only eighteen years old and had just finished his A-Levels—with an aim to go on to university the following autumn. Atkins was waiting in Allerton library, Liverpool, for his friend, Graham Bickley, who'd promised to introduce him to someone on Atkins' wavelength. "You're very alike," Bickley had told him, "you both read books."[3]

While he was waiting, Atkins actually bumped into this mystery person. His first impressions were not entirely favorable: "I saw an example of the type I'd learned to dismiss as the Would-Be Russian Poet—collarless shirt, tatty trousers, little wire-framed glasses, and a very embryonic beard. He needed only the long, black greatcoat and the volume of Pushkin to fit my arrogant preconception completely."[4] Atkins, himself dressed like a stereotypical musician, was gigging in bars with his school rock band. When Graham arrived, he introduced Atkins to the stranger, who turned out to be Clive Barker. Within an hour of meeting Barker, Atkins had already met the rest of his fledgling theater company and a week later he was preparing to work with them for the duration of the summer.

This time would be a revelation for Atkins, opening his eyes to the creative process:

> "You grow up in a working-class situation in a depressed industrial town like Liverpool and one always thought that the artistic life was something other people did. And Clive was very good—without lecturing or trying to make cod speeches about doing this stuff—he simply seemed to offer an example that, my God, actually you can do this. It's just up to you. If you want to try this there aren't any rules, you don't have to pass an exam, you can just start doing theater, you can start making movies, you can start writing, you can start drawing, painting, whatever."[5]

Abandoning his plans to become a teacher, Atkins pitched in with the group, acting in plays, and starring as the lead in *The Forbidden*: "In the same kind of arrogant assumption that we could make world-class theater on no money, we decided we could probably make world-class cinema on no money, too."[6] It was Atkins' first, but far from his last taste of making films.

Atkins was with the Dog Company for five years, then for about five years he followed his childhood dream of trying to make it with his band, The Chase. Although they never scored it big with a record contract, they were able to make a living playing regularly at pubs and clubs. "After the acting and music," explained Atkins once, "I turned thirty, and mid-life crisis hit. It was kind of financial and directional. In a way I had lived all my twenties for the pleasure principle."[7]

The music wasn't really satisfying him anymore and so Atkins returned to writing, something he had dabbled in before but never pursued aggressively. He produced some short stories and then a novella called *The Vampires of Summer*, which he showed to Barker. As a consequence, his old friend rang him in July 1987 and asked if he'd ever written a screenplay. Atkins replied that he hadn't but having been a cinephile all his life would like to try. Barker then encouraged Atkins to lie through his teeth at a dinner meeting in London with himself and Chris Figg, and suddenly he was being offered the job of scripting the next installment in the *Hellraiser* saga.

Following the meeting, Barker took Atkins back to his flat and, with the help of a bottle of bourbon, they came up with an outline for a story. Ideas were thrown back and forth, but what was paramount in Barker's mind was that this movie should show a lot more of the *Hellraiser* universe than they were able to before. "It would be great to get some sense of mythology," commented Barker later, "I'm very much into pulling the elements of myth together. I would be pleased if people could get a sense of the history of the Cenobites and this puzzle box."[8] The mythology would also include a reason for the Cenobites' existence, including the god that they serve. Barker was very keen on making Julia the central figure this time, though, someone who might even take the series into a third chapter.

Once the pair had a basic plotline, Atkins was sent to a hotel for the next two and a half weeks to write a first draft screenplay, armed with a copy of *Hellraiser* to help him lay it out correctly. During this time, both Barker and Figg showed a great deal of trust in the new writer; Barker avoided pressuring Atkins if he saw him out socially, and Figg would only ring to ask in passing what page Atkins was on. Remarkably, he delivered a 95 page screenplay on time, and one which showed he had a natural talent for it.

The story picks up just hours after the events in *Hellraiser*, with Kirsty in a psychiatric hospital. She tries to convince the authorities of what has happened, but the only person who will listen is the institute's director, Dr. Malahide. Unfortunately for her, Malahide is an occultist, desperate not only to open up the doorway to Hell again, but also to bring back a guide in the form of Julia by spilling blood on the mattress where she died. Add to this a young female patient called Tiffany who is obsessed with puzzles and Kirsty's compulsion to save her father from Hell, and you have the crux of what would eventually become *Hellbound*.

There was an agonizing three day wait for Atkins while both Barker and Figg read what he had done, but they were extremely pleased and had only made a few notes about changes. Typically—considering what he wanted to do with Julia and Frank's lovemaking scene—Barker wanted to take the sex between the doctor and skinless Julia even further, alluding to what he called "flayed fucking." Not even Frank and Julia had attempted this. Atkins did the rewrites back in Liverpool, which led to some embarrassing phone conversations dictating the skinless sex scenes to Figg's assistant, Louise Rosner, over a rather bad line.

In the meantime, the search for a director had been taking place, something that wouldn't prove as hard as Barker or Figg initially thought. Seven weeks into the shooting of *Hellraiser* New World had sent one of their employees to oversee the final stages of filming, and of postproduction. At first it was something Barker resented and he was prepared to fight this executive tooth and nail if he caused trouble. Thankfully, nothing could have been further from the truth. The person they sent was Tony Randel, who grew up watching late night horror films and whose favorite films included *Rosemary's Baby* and *Invaders from Mars*. He'd started out in the film industry toiling away in the mailroom at the old New World (when Roger Corman had been in charge) and worked his way up to special effects editing, soon moving on to trailer and feature editing. Randel eventually became postproduction chief for Corman's new Millennium company before rejoining New World and working on the rejigging of the Japanese perennial, *Godzilla*, for a Western audience.

When they met for the first time, he and Barker immediately hit it off and Randel was very supportive of the kind of film they were trying to make. He persuaded New World not to cut back on the usage of the Frank character (their reasoning being that the main villain shouldn't be seen as much as he is), brought Christopher Young on board, and helped out in the editing room. In addition, Randel suggested the shots of Kirsty down by the docks, to open up the film a little bit more, and even secured the £15,000 needed to shoot this scene. His help earned him not only a special thank you on the credits, but also the respect of Barker and Figg, all of which was leading, inevitably, inexorably, to Randel taking over the reins for the sequel: "Having done so much work on the original film I had become very familiar with the material, and had an affinity for it.... I had come to Chris and Clive and said I would like to do the sequel, because they'd actually hired or wanted another director to come onboard before but he had to drop out, and once he'd dropped out I said I think I'd like to come in and give it a whirl."[9]

As a consequence, the first draft of the script was passed on for New World's executives and the new director of *Hellbound* to read on August 8, 1987. The sense of urgency Atkins had experienced suddenly dissipated, as it took them until October 7 to get back to the team. Atkins was brought to London again to work on a second draft, but this time Randel was also flying in from Los Angeles to collaborate. Obviously, never having met Randel, Atkins was worried about how they might get on. "I had very little experience of the film world," said Atkins, "so my assumption when I heard that a former executive of New World Pictures is coming in to direct the movie and you're going to work together, was I pictured a guy at least ten years older than me in a three-piece suit. And Tony,

Director of *Hellbound: Hellraiser II*, Tony Randel (photograph credit: Colin Fletcher).

having read the script, apparently pictured a multi-pierced tattooed punk."[10] It must have been like déjà vu, being back in that library not knowing what to expect.

Randel did little to calm Atkins' fears when he rang him from his — more expensive — hotel to discuss the script: "Dr. Malahide. That's a great name.... I'm going to change it." Atkins' reaction was, "My God, all the stories are true. These directors, they fuck with you."[11] Upon meeting an hour later they discovered that none of their preconceptions were correct. The pair got on famously — and have in fact been firm friends ever since. Randel even introduced Atkins to the wonders of word processing on his own portable Compaq. (Atkins' first draft had been pounded out on a Smith Corona typewriter).

Naturally Randel brought some of his own ideas to the table, but the main concern was from New World, who wanted a whole new third act. The story points of the ending, such as Julia's revenge on Frank, the reversion of the Cenobites to their human forms and Kirsty and Tiffany's escape, would remain, but there was to be more made of the hospital sequences, including a chase sequence that resulted in one of the major myths about *Hellbound*. In this scene Pinhead and the Female Cenobite appear in full surgical regalia, and, as Atkins told *Dread* magazine some years later, "The girls got in an elevator, went downstairs, real creepy atmosphere. Two surgeons arrived and questioned them. As they were talking, the surgeons suddenly turned into Pinhead and the Female Cenobite.... It could have been a good scene. Then the Cenobites chased the girls."[12]

Sadly, due to technical difficulties when filming, the scene ended up looking quite bad. This didn't stop the marketing department placing pictures of Pinhead and the Female Cenobite in their gowns on video covers, causing much speculation about the deleted scenes.

Barker was out of the country when the second draft was written, but advised Atkins over the phone to simply make the changes New World wanted to keep them happy. So Randel and Atkins came up with a rough 150 page script incorporating New World's wishes and any more ideas they'd had themselves. Following another meeting with Barker, during which he offered his opinions, the screenplay was polished and reduced to a workable length. Storyboard artist Floyd Hughes was then brought into the equation and between him, Atkins and Randel — who was by now having meetings with members of the crew such as the director of photography, Robin Vidgeon, the production designer, Mike Buchanan, and Image Animation — they refined the second draft and had it ready for handing in to Chris Figg on November 2.

There are still quite a few differences between this script and the one that was finally filmed, though. At the beginning we have an extended version of the sequence that introduces us to Pinhead in his human guise, including a lengthy bartering scene at the bazaar which would have been in keeping with Frank's bargaining at the beginning of *Hellraiser*. Pinhead's first words also echo Frank, "Kirsty, come to Daddy," but somehow they didn't ring true. Much better is the line: "The suffering, the sweet suffering...." One of the police officers at Lodovico Street cuts himself on his own notepad and spills a few drops of blood on the mattress where Julia met her end.

The original speech that Malahide (soon to become Channard after Dr. Christian Barnard, the first surgeon to perform a heart transplant) makes during an operation is intact; it was later changed by Barker during postproduction to prefigure the link between the mind and Hell's labyrinths. There is a sequence near the beginning, where Tiffany has escaped and found her way to a deserted carnival and it is Malahide who brings her back, that emphasizes his control and domination over her. As mentioned, we have the more overt sex scene between the doctor and Julia, and Kirsty finds a room in Hell with photographs of her mother (a scene filmed and recently restored for the DVD release of *Hellbound*). Browning — the character who slashes himself with a knife on Julia's mattress — is shown in his own private "bug hell." And, of course, there is the scene with the Cenobites as surgeons. The major deviations, however, were not due to artistic determination at all. They were necessitated by two members of the returning cast.

When it became clear that a sequel was going to be made, several members of the ensemble from *Hellraiser* came onboard again. First there was Ashley Laurence reprising her role as Kirsty. Speaking about this, she said, "I was signed for a two-picture deal. I didn't know what that meant but I knew I was doing *Hellbound* when I was doing *Hellraiser*.... Oh, there's a lot of nastiness I have to go through this time. There's catwalks and abysses and labyrinths and all sorts of things."[13] Without her as its focal point the storyline would not have worked at all. Clare Higgins also agreed to return as Julia. "I had to come back," she told the media, "because playing the Queen of Hell was an opportunity I just couldn't miss."[14]

The actors who played Frank, in both his forms, with skin and without, were set to come back: Sean Chapman and Oliver Smith. Three of the original Cenobites, Nicholas Vince (Chatterer), Simon Bamford (Butterball) and Doug Bradley (as, who else, Pinhead) signed on again. And there was even a role reprisal for Oliver Parker as the removal man at the end. Most significantly, there was to be support again from the Hollywood actor and most famous member of the cast, Andrew Robinson, who would be playing Larry again.

Or so Atkins and Randel thought.

Larry had a vital function in the second draft of the screenplay. In his skinless form he appears to Kirsty at the hospital and entreats her to help him escape from Hell. This is the crucial motivational force for her to seek out the box and run the risk of confronting the Cenobites again. Once inside, she finds Frank and Larry fused together and they fight each other in Frank's "knife room." Larry then goes with both Kirsty and Tiffany to find a way out of Hell. It is a new Larry we see in the sequel, more determined and forceful, not willing to let anything or anybody hurt his daughter anymore. As the script says when Larry steps between the Malahide Cenobite and his two charges, "It is not fear, nor defiance. It is simpler than that. He is really, really pissed off."[15]

While understandable after everything he has been through — he's been lied to by his wife, killed and had his skin stolen — lines like, "Fuck you and the horse you rode in on" simply don't sound right coming from his lips. However, the scene where he is instrumental in helping the girls escape from Julia in the tunnel does blend in very well, and finally gives Larry his revenge. Sadly, very soon afterwards Larry has a heart attack and drops out of sight until the very end, where we just get a quick shot of him recovering in bed.

As it transpired, all the scenes involving Larry would have to be revised anyway when it was discovered that Robinson's casting hadn't been confirmed and he wasn't available for filming in early 1988. This news came after Atkins and Randel had flown to L.A. for meetings with New World and a final third draft of the script had been delivered in December. An emergency meeting was called at the offices of Pinewood, where the film was due to be made, and Barker, Randel and Atkins went through the script, factoring in this new development. Over the course of two days, a shooting script with these changes was produced which would pretty much resemble the film we now know as *Hellraiser II*.

I said there were two changes involving returning cast members, and the second revolves around the ending. As it was written and appeared in the second draft, the coda has Julia emerging from the mattress as the workman is left alone with it, a re-creation of the earlier scene with Browning:

SECOND WORKMAN: ... Gimme a hand with this.
Almost faster than the eye can register it, a hand shoots out from the mattress and grabs his wrist.
He has about half a second to issue a strangled shout and then, hideously quickly, a matter of two seconds or so, his body is drained of all life and the dried husk collapses to the floor.
The first WORKMAN appears hurriedly in the doorway and then freezes, an awestruck expression on his face.
JULIA is rising, headfirst and upright, from the centre of the mattress. The movement is smooth, magical, unsettling. It is graceful but not slow. JULIA is fully fleshed, fully skinned, and fully dressed. She is in a replica of the dress CHANNARD bought for her, but this one is jet black. She looks fabulous.
As the WORKMAN stands open-mouthed, her feet clear the mattress. But they don't stop there. She slows to a graceful halt about six inches above the mattress. She stretches and flexes her arms sensually. Then her head swivels and her excited, aroused eyes meet those of the WORKMAN.
JULIA: I'm Julia. Love me.
Suddenly, her head tips back and, accompanied by JULIA's delighted laughter, a wide beam of Hell's black light flies at the ceiling from her open mouth. Instantaneously, it spills across the ceiling and falls, like a fountain of blood, across the screen.
COMPLETE BLACKNESS
THE CREDITS ROLL.[16]

This was all calculated to carry Julia through into the next film, just as Barker wanted, making her the Queen of Hell and a recurring figure throughout the franchise.

There were just two problems. The first was that Clare Higgins, in spite of her enthusiasm for this sequel, had no wish to play the character in a further *Hellraiser* picture, nor did she have any aspirations to become a kind of female horror icon. The second thing was, as we have seen, the viewers and fans had already chosen Pinhead to be the recurring villain of the franchise. As Atkins clarifies, "Clive's original wish was that Julia from *Hellraiser* would be the Freddy Krueger of the *Hellraiser* series and Pinhead and the Cenobites would sort of be the background monsters.... What happened, of course, was the public got in the way. They fell in love with Pinhead."[17]

There were new members of the cast as well, though. Sixteen-year-old Imogen Boorman was chosen to play Tiffany because of the fresh-faced angelic look of innocence she displayed, so it was strange for other cast members to see her having a break to smoke between takes. Boorman's previous credits had included starring alongside Patsy Kensit, Daniel Day-Lewis and Elizabeth Spriggs in the 1982 TV adaptation of *Frost in May*, plus a stint on the popular Saturday tea-time science fiction show, *The Tripods*, based on the John Christopher novel. She also featured in the Dennis Potter scripted drama exploring the darker side of Lewis Carroll's Alice books, *Dreamchild* (Gavin Millar), in 1985. Speaking about the role, Boorman said, "She's basically the puzzle-solver. Without her no one would be able to get down to Hell. She's meant to be very intelligent.... The worst thing I have to do in this film is pull Julia's skin off.... But there are some nice bits in it that you don't find in most horror films."[18]

Canadian-born actor William Hope landed the part of the younger doctor Kyle, really a replacement for the character of Kirsty's boyfriend, Steve. Hope's first TV role was as Harry in the *Nancy Astor* miniseries of 1982, and from there he went on to star in the Dynasty-esque drama, *Lace* (1984), with Phoebe Cates, then *Tender is the Night* and *Behind Enemy Lines* (both 1985). His first film role was alongside a young Judge Reinhold in the 1983 film, *Lords of Discipline*, directed by Franc Roddam, which concentrated on racism at a military academy in the 1960s. The military theme would be carried on in the film that brought him fame: *Aliens* (James Cameron, 1986). For this he played an inexperienced young lieutenant in charge of the group of marines battling Xenomorphs on a distant planet. This portrayal of nervous Gorman showed off his acting abilities and proved he was worthy to share the screen with the likes of Sigourney Weaver and Lance Henriksen. Kyle would be just as much of a challenge, because he would have to react believably to scenes like the mattress attack in which Julia absorbs Browning.

Angus MacInnes was hired to play Detective Ronson, the first person Kirsty speaks to after she wakes in the Institution. Also born in Canada, this actor was the king of bit-parts, ranging from Gerry Anderson's *Space 1999*, *The Littlest Hobo* and *The New Statesman* on TV, to *Rollerball* (1975), Gold Leader in *Star Wars* (1977) and *Half Moon Street* (1986) in the movie world. While he again is not on screen for any length of time, his performance does have an impact — not least as the person who stands in for the audience when he says "Welcome back" to Kirsty. His cynical character is also a worthy counterpoint to that of the psychiatrists who believe her. The story goes that Atkins named Ronson after a razor company because he had just watched a film prior to writing where the main character's name was Gillette.

With Grace Kirby not returning as the Female Cenobite this time, Barbie Wilde stepped in as an excellent replacement. Her two credits up to that point were on TV as Mo in the

Puliski episode, "The Lone Granger," and as a punk in the Charles Bronson movie *Death Wish 3* (Michael Winner, 1985), which some might argue was perfect training for a Cenobite. Another new actress who had to endure the make-up process was Deborah Joel, who was actually a dancer by trade before *Hellbound*. She would become skinless Julia and, like Oliver Smith, had to be thin enough so that the suit looked right on her. Ironically, her first scenes in the film are shared with Smith, who was not only portraying Frank this time, but also the inmate Browning, who spills his own blood on the mattress so that Julia can come back. He was able to offer tips and advice about the process, ensuring that Joel's scenes are some of the standout ones in the whole film.

Another bit part player in the film was Tiffany's mother, Catherine Chevalier, whose role was actually reduced from an original complex backstory to the flashbacks Tiffany sees in Hell. Chevalier's first film role was as the French Girl in the U.K. made *Dutch Girls* (Giles Foster, 1985), where she featured along with Bill Paterson, Timothy Spall and Colin Firth, and she followed this up with parts as Rosita in *Riders of the Storm* (Maurice Phillips, 1986) and as Cosmo's secretary in Mike Figgis's *Stormy Monday*, released the same year as *Hellbound*. And while James Tillitt, who played Officer Cortez at the beginning of the movie, was a novice, his screen partner, Bradley Lavelle — Officer Kucich — had starred in everything from *Supergirl* (Jeannot Szwarc, 1984) to British TV fare like *Tales of the Unexpected* and *Robin of Sherwood*.

The wheelchair-bound patient who gets to deliver that immortal line, "one hundred and five years and he still doesn't know my name" (inspired by a wisecrack in a Jerry Lewis Telethon), was brought to life by *Who Framed Roger Rabbit* (1988) actor Edwin Craig. The removal man paired up with Oliver Parker was Ron Travis, who had been in *Scandalous* (Rob Cohen, 1984).

Possibly the most high profile and recognizable new member of the *Hellraiser* family, though — especially for English viewers — was thespian Kenneth Cranham as Dr. Channard. Born in Scotland, his career began in style as Noah Claypole in Carol Reed's Oscar-winning musical version of *Oliver!* (1968). Numerous TV and film appearances followed in the '70s and '80s, including *Up Pompeii* (Bob Kellett, 1971), *Vampira* (Clive Donner, 1974) and *Reilly, Ace of Spies* (Martin Campbell/Jim Goddard, 1983). He was perhaps best known at that time for his enduring title role in the much loved British TV comedy drama series, *Shine on Harvey Moon* (1982–85), set in post–World War II England. Here he played a likeable rogue struggling to keep his family together, so now Cranham would be playing completely against type.

Explaining his reasons for wanting the role, he said, "In my childhood I was very fascinated by such things and the chamber of horrors to me was the perfect place to go; and the first thing I ever built with my Meccano set was a gallows. My nephew, Ben Cranham, who's eight, thinks that this is the best career move I've ever made." He also made a good point about his approach to the material: "This sort of film, which is basically a special effects film, is like any other text. If you act it well, it works. If you don't, it doesn't."[19]

So with all the cast in place, excepting Robinson, and the rewrites done to accommodate this circumstance, filming could at last get underway. But if Atkins and Randel thought that would be the only problem they would encounter, they were to be disappointed. New World had increased the budget for this film, to enable them to top the first in terms of sets and effects, a general broadening out of the universe. It also allowed them to take the production from Cricklewood to Pinewood, where they could use real sound stages. Indeed, they were able to utilize some of the same stages that Powell and Pressburger shot their

A *Hellbound* reunion. From left to right: Pinhead, Bob Keen, Stephen Jones, Kenneth Cranham, Doug Bradley, Peter Atkins and Nicholas Vince at the Forbidden Planet signing for *The Hellraiser Chronicles*, London, June 13, 1992 (courtesy Forbidden Planet; photograph credit: Dick Jude).

films on, and many of the craftsmen there could remember working on *A Matter of Life and Death*, *Colonel Blimp* and *The Red Shoes*. Doug Bradley has recalled how delighted he was at the move: "Real sound stages! Dressing rooms (with your name on the door handwritten in the best copper-plate)! Proper make-up rooms! I was like the proverbial kid in the candy store wandering through all this."[20]

However, they couldn't get too excited. Just before filming was due to start, as the currency was being transferred over from dollars to pounds sterling, the Black Monday crash hit the stock markets of the world and suddenly there was a 20 percent cut in the budget. This meant that scenes such as the bazaar introduction and those between Kirsty and Kyle in his apartment — plus a much longer, more elaborate Cenobite fight sequence — had to be scrapped. But cost cutting could be made by using buildings that were to hand, such as the main administration building at Pinewood (as seen in *The Great Gatsby*) doubling up as the outside of the Channard Institute, and a house just across the road standing in for Channard's home. Nevertheless, it made sense for Atkins to remain on hand throughout the shoot in case anything else came up and more rewrites were needed, something Atkins thoroughly enjoyed because it was like a condensed film studies course.

Once again it was the technicians that turned what was still a relatively low budget film into something that looked much more expensive. Production Designer Mike Buchanan's sets were outstanding, from the creepy interior of the hospital and its underground basement cells — three years before *Silence of the Lambs* would give us Hannibal Lecter's prison — to the cool noirish look of Channard's living room, and, of course, his aptly named Obsession Room filled with occult items. And all of this was again lit beautifully by Robin Vidgeon. Cameraman David Whorley was able to pull off some masterstrokes, such as the dolly back and zoom out from Kirsty's eye at the start of the movie, and the superb 360° dolly where the camera swings around Channard and Julia as they kiss, necessitating many different changes in lighting. The matte paintings of Hell and the Carnival by Cliff Culley are breathtaking and seamless. Created over a decade before *Lord of the Rings*' C.G.I. castles and underground caverns, these painstaking paintings on glass, superimposed on the film, give the movie a grandiose feel and evoke a sense of scale that was barely hinted at in *Hellraiser*.

With Bob Keen directing in the States, his Image Animation partner, Geoff Portass, found himself acting as special make-up effects designer on *Hellbound*, but he proved more than up to the task. This would involve new make-up for the Cenobites, including giving the Chatterer eyes (largely at the request of Nick Vince, who couldn't see a thing during his time on the first film) and coming up with the look for the Channard Cenobite after he undergoes his transformation.

"The starting point for his design was your average household egg slicer," revealed Portass in an on-set interview. "We fitted him with a full headpiece on which wires were attached going through the ears. Then he's picked up by this bloody big tentacle. That's done by a composite of various shots—there's a mechanical tentacle, then a prosthetic headpiece that's actually stuck onto him with the tentacles shaped to look as though they're gripping then attached with a little coupling device to a tentacle when he's on a pole arm—or wires, which were used in one shot."[21] Cranham attempted the levitating scenes himself at first, but it hurt his neck and a stuntman called Bronco replaced him. Then there was the skinless Julia suit sculpted by Little John, the idea of which was "to make her look sexy," according to Portass. And Image Animation was also partly responsible for changing Hell's god, Leviathan, from an average monster to the diamond shape it now has.

Yet there were still problems in this department. After being given a pep pill—some sort of vitamin supplement—during one of the three a.m. early morning make-up sessions, Doug Bradley had a funny turn and ended up throwing Portass's filofax out of the window. He had to be strapped down to the make-up chair with gaffer tape. Bradley also found it hard coping with the waiting around on set, and took to wandering around, unable even to have a sleep because of the pins.

It was a sentiment shared by Simon Bamford: "I must admit I wasn't sure I wanted to do number two to put myself through that mental torture of having that costume on."[22] But being a Cenobite could also be quite a dangerous occupation, as Nick Vince soon discovered. During the scene in Hell with the Cenobites and Kirsty, there was a spinning pillar behind him, with a hook and chain attached. As he opened his mouth the big hook went inside and up into the roof of his mouth.

"The plan was," recounts Vince, "that I'd take a hit in the chest from Channard's flying tentacle in front of a spinning torture pillar. This meant holding the tentacle in my hand, thumping it into my chest and straightening up to give the impression I'd been knocked off my feet upwards, to be impaled on the torture pillar. The camera would pan up and we'd cut. Then I'd be put in a harness and attached to the pillar and spun for the next shot.... Chattering like mad I thumped the tentacle into my chest, I straightened up, I opened my mouth to scream.... Attached to the top of the spinning torture at a right angle was a piece of wood. Attached to that was a length of chain and at the end of that was a twelve inch metal hook.... It went between the false teeth and the point went a quarter of an inch into the roof of my mouth."²³ Luckily, apart from the pain and shock, Vince suffered no lasting injuries, but he can still feel the scar inside his mouth. It could have been so much worse.

To add to the misery, Randel split up with his transatlantic girlfriend during filming, although he claims that the pain allowed him to produce better work: the scene where Pinhead solves the Lament Configuration puzzle in his human guise, for instance, was put together right after he got off the phone with her. But as reporters like Alan Jones (for *Starburst*) and John Gullidge and John Martin (for *Samhain*) testified, the atmosphere on set was generally convivial. Jones stated that Randel was affectionately referred to on set as More Blood because of his penchant for "going full throttle," not just because of his penchant for gore.

Gullidge and Martin were also impressed by his enthusiasm and desire to open up the mythological elements of the series. Indeed, their only—possibly justified—criticism was about the Americanization of *Hellraiser*. After the dubbing of English actors in the first film, Barker and Randel fought hard to convince New World to film in Britain, but this still didn't stop U.S. references like "homicide" and cops with firearms creeping in. Writers John Skipp and Craig Spector also commented on the friendly working environment, but they put this down more to the presence of Barker than anything: "Clive is wonderful in that he knows how to diffuse tension and just bring people together around the project. We've witnessed less tension on this set, with the crew, than on any other shoot we've seen before."²⁴

But reporters weren't the only visitors. Brit director Ken Russell (*Women in Love*, 1969) also came to have a look around while they were filming the Channard/Julia scenes. Russell was no stranger to horror films himself, having made *Gothic* only two years previously, which revolved around events at the Villa Diodati in 1816 where Mary Shelley was inspired to write *Frankenstein* and Dr. Polidori would conceive of *The Vampyre*. (The director would go on to make another genre film, released not long after *Hellbound*. *Lair of the White Worm*, adapted from the Bram Stoker tale, starred Amanda Donohoe and Hugh Grant.)

Britain's answer to Siskel and Ebert, Barry Norman, also happened to be around filming his *Hollywood Greats* series for television, which he customarily introduced sitting in a director's chair, and he was given permission to use one from *Hellbound*. Norman had been very derogatory in his review of *Hellraiser*, so Barker and Figg saw their chance to have a word with him about it, allegedly asking him why he wasn't more supportive of their efforts. It seemed to work, because the review he presented of *Hellbound* for *Film '88* was altogether more positive.

Once the filming was completed, and Barker was relatively free from commitments, the editing process could begin. Richard Marden was again in the editor's seat, with both Randel and Barker offering their views. This helped with the pacing of the movie, and sequences such as the Cenobite battle and the climactic finale benefit from a buildup of quick cuts interspersed with the slower scenes. There would also be no question that Christopher Young would be handling the score a second time. His theme had become synonymous with the mythos and it was virtually impossible to imagine the sequel without it. Young was flown over to London from his native L.A. and spent a day at Pinewood with Randel and Atkins, then spent a couple more days with the director. According to the soundtrack notes, Randel "meant for *Hellbound* to be a 'celebration of horror,' rather than an obvious, conventional illustration of it. He also wanted the music to 'respond operatically to the film's mayhem.'" With this in mind, Young returned home to begin work on the piece, with Barker jetting over to spend time with him there, too.

The composer's *Hellbound* score managed to exceed all expectations. It is a rich, sweeping score that combines both orchestra (the Graunke Symphony Orchestra, utilizing eight French horns instead of the usual four) and choral arrangements to produce a truly Gothic complement to the visuals. Several of the themes from the first movie were woven in, most notably the signature title theme, and the chase music used when Kirsty first entered the corridors of Hell. But the rest of it was brand new and quite innovative. The "Devil's Horn," for example—played when Leviathan is first shown—actually spells out G-O-D in morse code, to counterbalance the evil.

The *Hellraiser* theme was also modified to fit the Carnival and Hall of Mirrors sequences, mixing the traditional band organ music with disjointed snare drums, voices and a blending of other themes in various tempos. But there are quieter moments, too. The

The score to *Hellbound* was once again written by Christopher Young (soundtrack cover courtesy Silva Screen).

music for "Second Sight Séance," for instance, utilizes the string section beautifully to deliver an unexpected purity. Once again Young elevates the film to a level beyond schlock horror, filling it with grace, dignity, excitement and multilayered textures.

While the composing was going on in early summer, Randel was also hard at work supervising the dub of the sound effects and dialogue, which is where the alternate Channard speech was added—an easy task because Cranham was wearing a surgeon's mask to operate on a brain. Randel was also overseeing the placement of optical effects, and wouldn't get to hear Young's final score until July, when he flew over to L.A. with Atkins to attend meetings with New World about a possible third film in the series. By the end of the summer, and after Barker had seen the latest cut of the movie, it was almost ready for release. It just had to go through the censors on both sides of the Atlantic, who were harsher this time, most of their attention being focused on the very uncomfortable mattress sequence. This shocked even Atkins when he first saw it: "It was one thing to write the stuff, it was 7:30 in the morning and watching that stuff made me feel sick."[25] It was not helped by Robin Vidgeon's suggestion that Browning draw the razor across his groin.

The M.P.P.A. came down especially hard on *Hellbound*, which was cut four times and still received an X, something that justifiably upset Barker: "I don't want that freedom to abuse it, I do want the freedom. I don't want to be thinking, shall we shoot that? will it get through? all the time. The thing is that special effects are expensive. And it's not worth shooting stuff that's not gonna get in."[26]

But all this was overshadowed by the financial returns of the film when it opened, which almost matched *Hellraiser* in its U.S. domestic gross ($11,090,000).[27] When asked what he wanted to achieve with the movie, Randel said, "I wanted to bring something new to the sequel.... I wanted to enlarge the scope of the picture. It eventually encompasses the entirety of Hell itself, which creates a kind of inverse claustrophobia: You're in this vast open space where anything can happen, which can be more oppressive than being in a closed, inescapable place."[28] This is, of course, the opposite of *Hellraiser*'s vision. What Randel—and Atkins—actually did accomplish was to polarize opinion, both fan-based and critical. People either loved *Hellbound* or hated it, there was no middle ground. But what of the merits of the film itself? What of the themes and influences? It is to those that we now turn our attention.

7

OPENING DOORS

Into the Underworld

As we have seen, Clive Barker's exposure to Jean Cocteau's films at an early age influenced his creative output later. It is an admiration that Barker shares with Peter Atkins, who has publicly stated that *Orphée*, or *Orpheus* (1949), is his favorite film of all time.[1] Small wonder, then, that in its central themes and story *Hellbound* should pay homage to the film, and the legend that inspired it.

The original Greek myth revolves around the greatest of all musicians, Orpheus, who sang songs about the creation of the universe and the battles of Zeus and the Olympian gods against the Titans. But his songs also had magical qualities that could calm nature and humans alike, and it is told that he soothed the sailors onboard the *Argo* when Jason was searching for the Golden Fleece. Upon his return he fell in love with a woman called Eurydice, but on their wedding day, while she was strolling through a meadow, she was bitten by a poisonous snake and died. Orpheus vowed to find her in Hades—the land of the dead—where his music allowed him passage across the River Styx and pacified the three-headed dog Cerberus guarding the Underworld. Orpheus sang his sad lament to the King and Queen of Hades, who granted his request: he would be allowed to take Eurydice with him as long as he didn't look back before reaching the living world. Unfortunately, on their way to the Overworld, Orpheus turned to look at his wife and she faded away. Returning to Thrace, he remained on a hillside singing sad songs for the rest of his days.

Cocteau's reimagining and updating of this myth is introduced by the director himself, and opens with the poet Orpheus in a Parisian café. Another bard called Jacques Cégeste appears, with the mysterious Princess. The drunken Cégeste is then run over and killed by a motorcyclist, but the Princess seemingly revives him and takes him through a mirror inside her villa. Unable to follow, Orpheus returns to his pregnant wife Eurydice, but is now preoccupied by what has happened—in particular the messages coming through from the Underworld on the Princess's limousine radio. Her driver, Heurtebise, reveals that both he and the Princess are ghosts. Complicating matters is the fact that Heurtebise is attracted to Eurydice and the Princess to Orpheus. But when Eurydice herself is killed in an accident, Orpheus is distraught and determines to find her in the Underworld. He is now told that the Princess represents Death, and mirrors are the doors by which death comes and goes.

Heurtebise gives him a pair of magical gloves so that he can travel through one of the mirrors. There he finds the Princess on trial for bringing Eurydice to her domain and desiring Orpheus. Orpheus is allowed to go free as long as he never speaks about what he has seen in the Underworld, and Eurydice can go with him if he promises never to look at her. But in their car he accidentally catches sight of her in the rearview mirror and she vanishes. In a variation on the original ending, Orpheus is shot but the Princess gives up her power so he can live again. Back in his world he finds Eurydice, who awakens, claiming she has had an awful nightmare. The pair go on to have their child, while both Heurtebise and the Princess are arrested by the guards of the Underworld.

Hellbound concerns itself with two other forays into the Underworld, each for completely different reasons. On the one hand Kirsty can be seen as Barker and Atkins' proxy for Orpheus and her visit is motivated not by a wish to bring back her partner, or husband, but her father. Yet, as we have discovered, the love Kirsty and Larry share is somewhat deeper than that of most daughters and fathers; indeed, they were initially ill-fated "lovers" in the original novella. The rationale for beginning the story almost immediately after the events in *Hellraiser* is to compound Kirsty's failure in the first movie. In spite of all she did, she couldn't save Larry from Frank, couldn't stop him from being taken to Hell by the Cenobites, although this is largely implied by subsequent events.

At no time do the Cenobites ever claim to have imprisoned her father; they just wanted Frank, and eventually Kirsty. Thus, when the skinless version of her father appears to Kirsty in her hospital room, slumped by the radiator, it is a potent reminder of that loss. If this in itself isn't reason enough to venture into the Underworld, he also writes in his own blood, "I am in Hell, help me," an entreaty she cannot possibly ignore. The bond between them is then highlighted by the camera circling around Kirsty, tracking her as she touches the blood on the wall and puts it to her lip, symbolically showing that they share the same life force, the same love. And where blood brought Frank back from Hell in the first film, it has exactly the opposite effect here — drawing Kirsty *to* Hell. She has no choice but to undergo the pilgrimage to free her tormented father.

To this end she seeks help herself, telling her story to Channard and Kyle, in effect singing her own lament to them. Kirsty recounts the events of *Hellraiser* in flashback and how her father met his end, bitten by the poisonous snake Frank. "Frank and Julia," she says, "they'd taken his skin and given it to Frank." What more could a reptile want than a fresh skin? At first it looks like they don't believe her, but secretly Channard knows she is telling the truth because he has made it his life's work to study this particular Underworld. Moreover, his intention is to journey there himself. As he tells Kirsty following her outpouring, "There is much we must investigate, much *I* have to do." To begin with, he must call forth his very own ghost princess, in the guise of Julia, whom he now knows died on the mattress at Lodovico Street. "You have to destroy that mattress," Kirsty warns. "See, Julia died on it and she can come back now like Frank."

Blood is the key again to communication with the other side, and Channard finds a willing volunteer in Browning, a patient so unstable he imagines insects are crawling over his body. Browning is asking for help of a very different nature, which Channard supplies by freeing him and presenting him with a straight razor. As Browning starts to cut himself on the mattress and Julia emerges, Channard, like Kirsty, comes into contact with the blood — except now it is involuntary, splattered over his face during the frenzied attack. Nevertheless, it is a signification that he will also be traveling to the Underworld soon. His motivation: not to find a long lost loved one, but rather to find *himself*. Earlier, Kirsty asked Kyle if Channard had got a ticket to Hell, the answer to which is yes. And now they both do.

Except the doorway on this occasion is not a river, a gate, or even a mirror, but the

Kirsty plays the Orpheus role but is hoping to bring her father back from the Underworld. *Hellbound: Hellraiser II* still (photograph credit: Murray Close).

Lament Configuration puzzle box. To this end, both Kirsty and Channard require someone to breach the gap, and they discover this in the newly introduced character of Tiffany, a mute girl who has an uncanny ability to solve puzzles. The connection is foreshadowed by the shots of steam from a radiator as skinless "Larry" appears to Kirsty being juxtaposed with Tiffany's solving of a wooden puzzle, not unlike the Lament Configuration. It is noteworthy that Kirsty herself is not allowed to open the box a second time. The obvious conclusion is that, just as Channard has Julia as his guide, Kirsty needs Tiffany for a companion. Kyle, although he comes to believe her story in the end, is little more than an echo of Steve—as ineffectual as he was. Kyle is merely a narrative device for delivering Kirsty to Channard's home, so that she can cross the threshold into Hell and meet up with her true guide: Tiffany.

Because Andrew Robinson was not available to play Larry, Kirsty—unlike Orpheus—was destined never to find her loved one again. But perhaps this was just as well, if his fate was to be comparable to Eurydice's. Instead, she discovers she has been tricked by Frank, summoned to his own private Hell to be his sex slave. But this doesn't mean she comes away from her quest empty-handed—far from it. Yes, she has failed again in her mission to save her father. But then again, there is no concrete evidence to suggest that he is even in the Underworld at all. When Kirsty says to Pinhead, "I've come for my father," the demon replies, "He is in his own hell and quite unreachable." It follows logically that if he is unreachable, then he might *not* be there. After all, Kirsty finds Frank easily enough. Perhaps Pinhead is merely referring to the hell of knowing Larry would never see his precious daughter again. Punishment enough for one who cares so deeply.

Frank, too, hints that her father isn't down here when he says, albeit rather tongue in cheek, "Oh come on, Kirsty, grow up. When you're dead, you're fucking dead!" But her story—comparable to the sad song Orpheus sings—stays the Cenobites' hands for at least a little while. The Guardians of this Underworld grant her the autonomy to look around before they take her. "Please, feel free to explore," Pinhead tells Kirsty, though, this being Pinhead, he caps the offer with another threat: "We have eternity to know your flesh."

Ironically, Pinhead and the other Cenobites are the ones Kirsty helps the most. After seeing a sepia-toned photograph of Pinhead before his transformation, she works out that they all must have been human at one point. Though they deny it when Kirsty first broaches the subject—"We have no more surprises," states Pinhead, and the Female Cenobite emphatically declares, "We have always been here"—when they meet up again, she convinces them. Kirsty hands Pinhead the photograph and he is forced to confront his past. "No, this one didn't escape—it's you. You haven't always been this way," Kirsty argues. "You were human, remember? Remember all your confusion, think.... You were *all* human." This revelation causes them to lose the ensuing fight with Channard, but also liberates them. The Cenobites revert back to their human selves, escaping from their own Hells. And in freeing Pinhead, doesn't Kirsty also free a sort of father figure, too? One who buys her time to escape from Channard.

Tiffany is the other soul Kirsty helps and frees in lieu of her father. She is the only person who manages to get through to the young girl. In return for her aid as a guide, Kirsty will help her to become more confident and even recover her power of speech. "Look, we're alone in all of this, and we have to help each other. Yeah?" Kirsty says. It is a bargain of sorts—well, this is *Hellbound*—but it is one of mutual consideration and benefit. This is the only offer of help that actually works, because there is support on either side. All the others fail because they are misguided or one-sided. Browning's plea for help leads to his spectacularly bloody death; Frank's supplication was—as always—grounded in deceit; and Tiffany's mother *definitely* asks the wrong doctor to help her daughter.

Channard's response to Julia's "Help me" request is to provide her with fresh bodies from his underground cells. Paralleling Frank's actions in the original, she uses Channard to make her whole again, finally providing her with skin. The pact they have made is for Julia to be his escort. But like Frank before him, Channard gets much more than he bargained for when Julia hands him over to her master, Leviathan, to be remade as a Cenobite. Though this might be interpreted as a betrayal, chiefly because the transformation process is so painful—both to endure and to watch—Julia is only giving him what he wanted. Furthermore, he has already indicated this himself. When Julia gives him a chance to back out and asks, "You're sure this is what you want?" he confirms, "It's what I've always wanted." His own evil, manipulative nature is given an outlet in Hell and he can be the creature he always wanted to be—powerful, sadistic, unstoppable. As he says himself when he comes out of the Cenobitization chamber, "And to think I hesitated." This is the only person Channard sought to free: the ultimate selfish act of a man who has devoted every waking minute to his own needs. For Frank, this was grounded in pleasure, but Channard's weakness is knowledge—of the labyrinths of the mind, of the occult, and ultimately of his true self. His eventual downfall is not Julia's doing, it is his own—attempting to kill Tiffany when his hand-tentacles get stuck in the ground, ripping his head in two.

Of the journeys Kirsty and Channard take into the Underworld, hers is the more successful. She may not have found her father or brought him back, but she did save the Cenobites from themselves and Tiffany from a life spent in solitude piecing together puzzles. Channard, even though he was given what his heart desired most, squandered the power and ended up annihilating himself in the process.

Mazes and Monsters

The Orpheus Legend isn't the only Greek myth *Hellbound* draws upon. In its depiction of Hell with the Channard Cenobite at its core, it also closely adheres to the tale of the Minotaur in the Maze. This begins with the story of Minos who, before he rose to power as King of Crete, prayed to the god Poseidon to send him a white bull as a sign of his favor. Minos had promised to sacrifice the bull, but instead kept it and sacrificed one of his own. As a result, Poseidon made Minos' wife Pasipha fall in love with the bull and the offspring of their union was a half-bull, half-man creature. Kept in a labyrinth built by the architect Daedalus and offered sacrifices, it was eventually defeated by the hero Theseus with the aid of Daedalus' daughter Ariadne, whom he had fallen in love with. She promised to provide the means to escape from the maze if he agreed to marry her, and, using thread, he was able to find his way out again.

For *Hellbound* we can easily substitute the Channard Cenobite for the Minotaur, the beast at the heart of this hell feeding on sacrifices of his patients. In this reading, Kirsty becomes Theseus, aided by Tiffany's Ariadne. (*Hellbound* has no real love interest, so friendship takes its place.) Together they are able to defeat the monster and find their way out of the maze — much to the chagrin of the monster's mother (Julia) and father (Leviathan).

You Wanted to See

Another important theme in *Hellbound* is that of voyeurism. Just as Frank was the supreme hedonistic thrill-seeker, Channard is easily his equal in terms of his desire not only to know, but to *see*. The very first time we encounter him, he is peering into a human brain, looking into the most private depths of the mind. The rewritten speech he gives goes:

> The mind is like a labyrinth, ladies and gentlemen, a puzzle. And while the paths of the brain are plainly visible, its ways deceptively apparent, its destinations are unknown. Its secrets still secrets. And if we are honest, it is the lure of the labyrinth that draws us to our chosen field, to unlock those secrets. Others have been there before us and have left signs. But we, as explorers of the mind, must devote our lives and energies to going further, to tread the unexplored corridors in the hope of finding, ultimately, the final solution. We have to see, we have to know.

It prefigures beautifully the unseen and unexplored corridors he will soon be venturing down in Hell.

Channard's underground cells, where he keeps the particularly gruesome cases, come with their own slots in the doors that he can peer through — and we, too, are given a sample of what's inside. Later, when he is walking with Julia along those corridors of Hell, we can see the similarities between his cells and the private purgatories prisoners are kept in. Channard once again has the opportunity to look through an opening and sees male and female figures writhing with a mixture of pleasure and pain. In a scene dropped from the second draft Channard was also to be granted a glimpse of Browning trapped in another cell at this point, the insects still crawling all over him.

Channard loves to witness the anguish of others, but always surreptitiously, without them knowing. It is his very own secret self. In contrast, Kyle — who is everything Channard isn't — kind, sympathetic and helpful — almost throws up when he is forced to watch Browning's demise from behind a curtain in Channard's house. A couple of glances are all he can take, and even these disturb him so much he has to escape as soon as possible. By the time he returns to the house, he has built up some nerve and compels himself to look inside the slaughter room, ignoring the warning from Julia that, "It's just terrible." And this curiosity will lead to his death when, after he sees the corpses, Julia kisses him in a parody of the kiss she and Frank once shared.

The "seeing" motif recurs with other characters as well. The first shot of Kirsty is a close-up of her eye, pulling out and slowly rotating as if to emphasize that she has already seen far too much, but there is more to come. Julia, also, when we first see her on the mattress, is identified by her eyes. Filmed in reverse, the stark whiteness against the red of her skinless body is both surreal and potent. Like Kirsty, she is no longer the person she once was; Julia, too, has seen things no one should ever have to see, the sights Pinhead spoke of in the first *Hellraiser*. Even when she is wrapped in bandages, it is her eyes that stand out, and she can't help raising Channard's finger to one orb, trailing it through the blood beneath.

Even the Chatterer Cenobite receives a pair of eyes in the time between our earliest meeting with him and our last. This was meant to be bridged by a scene showing him being altered, but as confusing as it is for viewers it does visually compound what the Cenobites go through when Kirsty tells them the truth, opening their eyes metaphorically to their past.

And it is not just the Cenobites who are shown a reflection of who they actually are. Mirrors may not be a means to travel to the Underworld, as they are in Cocteau's *Orphée*, but they do feature heavily in *Hellbound*. Julia smashes the oval mirror in Channard's lounge when she sees herself for the first time (itself a re-creation of the Princess smashing a looking glass when Cégeste dies in *Orphée*). Is it because she has lost her beauty or because the outside now more closely resembles the inside? Once dressed and mummified, she is able to cope better with her reflection, recognizing her potential as a sexual being again, a scene that was initially written with her standing and looking at herself in a full-length mirror in Channard's bedroom.

It is via a mirror in Hell that Kirsty realizes she has been duped into traveling there. On a dressing table she sees a repetition of the words her father supposedly wrote on the wall, "I am in Hell, Help me," but this time they are penned in lipstick. The association is clear: that it was the womanizer Frank who called to her using the mirror. Only now it shows her who he really is, if she didn't know already.

Tiffany is also the victim of voyeurism, and of mirrors. Kirsty is the first to watch her through a crack in the door and is startled when Kyle comes up behind her. Yet one can sense there is no malice there, more a sadness or the recognition of a kindred spirit, as we will see when we talk about their relationship in greater detail. More sinister—as is to be expected—is Channard's observation of Tiffany through a two-way mirror while she solves the Lament Configuration. Watching safely behind a wall, he and Julia expose the girl to the dangers of the Cenobites and Hell. There is even a close-up of Tiffany's eyes as she finally slots the pieces into place, indicating that she will soon see what both Kirsty and Julia have seen before her. Fortunately, the demons make the distinction that it is not Tiffany who has summoned them. "Wait," says Pinhead. "No. It is not hands that call us. It is desire." He might just as well have said "eyes," for Tiffany has no wish to see these sights. Unlike Channard.

Having already been subjected to voyeuristic attentions, Tiffany then finds herself in the carnival from Hell, complete with hall of mirrors. Here a sightless clown juggles with his own eyes, the balls plopping down into his bloody hands, the holes in his head weeping red tears. Not only is Tiffany unwilling to see the horrors of Hell, but there is also something that she doesn't want to see from her own past: a black-gloved hand over her mother's

Leviathan is Lord of the labyrinth — all seeing, all knowing (courtesy Eric Gross).

mouth and the last word Tiffany ever spoke, screaming for her mother. The mirrors throw back a reflection of a baby stitching up its own mouth, before the clown appears again and mirrors shatter. The mirrors can see who she really is, what has happened to her, and why she remains the way she is. It is something she must come to terms with before she'll be allowed to leave.

Channard, meanwhile, is shown his own reflection by Leviathan rather than by a mirror. The black light emanating from Julia's god has the power to delve deep into his very core, dragging out incidents he would rather keep hidden, such as the fact it was he who attacked Tiffany's mother. Leviathan is, therefore, an all-seeing, all-knowing deity, but it also coerces Channard to look within himself and face the reality of who, or what, he is. Leviathan strips away the pretense and gives him what he wants, the ability to see beneath the flesh. Only by bringing this monster to the surface can it turn him into a true Cenobite.

As Atkins clarified in an interview: "I think the implication is more that you get something that relates to what you wanted or something that relates to what you were or are, so it is the fact that Channard has *been* the great puppeteer, the brain surgeon, that is relevant here.... So each person's Cenobitization, let us assume, is personally relevant to whatever it was that drove them there in the first place."[2] This must surely explain why certain tentacles sprouting from the palms of his hands have eyes on the end, how he is able to find Kirsty and Tiffany wherever they go. The great voyeur has been furnished with the ability to truly *see* for the first time in his life.

Family Reunions

It could be argued that the family connections in *Hellbound* are nowhere near as critical as they are in *Hellraiser*. There are other plotlines to follow, there is more in terms of special effects and sheer spectacle. Director Randel himself has spoken out about this, stating that the scenes with the Cottons slow up the pace of the movie considerably.[3] To him they are requirements to get out of the way as quickly as possible so he can proceed with the next action set piece. But one cannot ignore the threads left hanging from the initial film which were begging to be tied up. It is why we are given not one but two recaps from *Hellraiser*; the first in a pre-credits montage and the second when Kirsty is relating the backstory to Channard and Kyle. It should be clear by now that there would be no storyline *at all* if Kirsty wasn't returning to Hell for her father. The fact that she doesn't find him is, for her, disappointing, but does allow her to settle things once and for all with Julia and Frank.

There is a scene that has only recently been restored to the film, where Kirsty finds a replica in Hell of her old home, comforting and bathed in warm yellows. There are photographs on the sideboard, including a black and white one of Kirsty as a young girl with her real mother. Blood then pours out from under the photographs, covering the sideboard and filling up the picture she's holding, which has turned into a photograph of Julia. Kirsty drops the picture, shattering the glass and frame, cockroaches spill from the drawers and the sideboard falls over in an outpouring of blood. Some might say it is an unnecessary scene, but it is a powerful one nevertheless, and Ashley Laurence's acting rams home the destruction and heartache Julia — and by extension Frank — has caused.

It also aptly parallels the scene a little later when Kirsty walks through a copy of the front door at Lodovico Street. This time she finds herself in Frank's Hell, filled with the obligatory candles which first guided him here when he solved the puzzle box. From arched openings, ghost women emerge on stone slabs beneath see-through material to tease and titillate, disappearing once the sheets are lifted. Frank appears, again wielding his phallic flick-knife, in an attempt to pick things up where they left off. He is still announcing himself as Uncle Frank, still desiring the forbidden. "That's why I sent for you, Kirsty."

This actually works better than in the second draft scene where Larry and Frank cohabit the same body. Here, instead of Larry taking his revenge by lifting his brother onto a wall of his own knives, thus giving him a taste of his own medicine and metaphorically raping him, Kirsty *must* take revenge for herself and for her father. It is vital that she do so, because only then will she have come of age. In both the wedding flashback and the photograph with her mother, Kirsty is shown as a little girl — vulnerable and ripe for Frank to abuse: "Don't be naughty, Kirsty, or I'll have to punish you first." But her journey into Hell and third confrontation with Frank enables her to shed the trappings of childhood completely. "Grow up," Frank barks at her, but she has already done that. The fact that she teases him herself, then turns the tables by setting the sheets and Frank on fire, shows that she now has the maturity to best him without having to rely on brute force.

This rites of passage theme is a momentous one and affects not just Kirsty, but Tiffany. Their relationship changes as the movie progresses. To begin with, Kirsty sees someone who is alone and subject to the evil forces at work: she basically sees herself. The pair could be sisters, and indeed they do mirror each other at times, especially when they both cry out for "Mommy" (Tiffany during the flashback sequence in the hall of mirrors, Kirsty while looking at the old photographs). In addition, they have both been the target of mistreatment, Kirsty by her uncle and Tiffany at the hands of Channard, another false patriarch with only manipulation in mind. However, the age difference between the girls makes a huge difference. Even though Tiffany is her guide in Hell, Kirsty is able to take on the mantle of big sister to keep Tiffany safe, at certain points even becoming the mother figure — not unlike Ripley and Newt in *Aliens* — particularly when Julia is around.

Paradoxically, Julia's relationship with Kirsty has been a volatile one. Julia never had the nurturing instinct, preferring instead to gratify her sexual needs with Frank. This is why any attempt she makes to adopt the mother persona always fails. When she takes Kyle into the slaughter room, she says, "Oh you poor boy, you look awful. Come here, come to mother." But it is meant more as a parody than a real inclination to comfort: signification that she has become a female version of Frank. This is borne out just minutes later when she betrays and kills Kyle with a kiss, as Frank did with her. When Kirsty confronts her in the ensuing scene, she describes her role as "the wicked stepmother." So when Kirsty, Tiffany and Julia are all together, the former feels obliged to take on a parental role to fill the void. Naturally Julia challenges this and attempts to undermine what she is doing: "You never could hold on to anything for very long, could you Kirsty?"

Julia does all she can to confuse Tiffany when the three of them are in the wind tunnel. But in the end the young girl realizes that Kirsty's warnings not to trust her were correct. It is how she is able to recognize Kirsty in Julia's skin at the denouement: Julia would never perform such a selfless act to save her. So Tiffany heeds the parental advice of Kirsty, rather than Julia. If more evidence were needed of this mother-daughter role-play, it comes when Kirsty breaks down and cries because she could not help her father. Tiffany hugs and consoles her, as a daughter might, which gives her new "mother" strength — "Tiffany, we're getting out of here!"

It isn't until Tiffany comes of age herself, learning to speak again and facing not only the Channard Cenobite — which she inadvertently defeats — but also Leviathan itself (consequently ridding herself of the obsession with puzzles) that the pair of them slip back into their sister roles once more. More than that, she has earned the right to become Kirsty's true equal, encapsulated by the look they give each other at the end before walking down the path — both dressed in black, both mourning their loved ones, and their loss of innocence.

The other parental role in the film is adopted by Leviathan. It remade Julia as a Queen of Hell, and transformed the Cenobites into their present form. Like they are naughty children it punishes them when they misbehave — pitting the newly-minted Channard Cenobite against the others when they start to remember who they are, and finally destroying its new son when he puts his own needs before his creator's. And how does it do this? By means of the umbilical cord still attached to Channard, the giant fleshy tentacle drilled into the top of his head immediately after he comes out of the Cenobitization chamber. Leviathan is the supreme parent, an all-seeing and all knowing father (or mother?) who is not scared to castigate its children if it sees fit.

Lastly, no reunion would be complete without mention of Frank and Julia's swan song. This comes just after Kirsty has seared the flesh from him, and it promises Julia her long awaited vengeance. With echoes of those mock wedding vows from *Hellraiser*, Frank says, "Julia, I knew you'd come. You're a girl who always keeps her promises." "Oh, I do.... I do...." she replies. Frank then seals his own fate by demanding that she kiss him, the means by which he betrayed her in the first film, and how she betrayed both Channard and Kyle. He is asking for trouble. The demand enabling her to get close, she uses this ruse to rip out his heart — taking back what she once gave to him — and then delivers her coup de grace: Frank's last words to her, "Nothing personal, babe." Thus concludes her metamorphosis into him. She has learned well from her teacher, seducing Channard and using him, knowing full well that he was never meant to be a part of this family. When she tells the doctor, "I'm cold," she means it in more ways than one. As Julia watches Frank's heart burn, there is blood on her lips; she scorns not only what she and Frank once had together, but also Kirsty's inability to find and rescue her father.

Fairy Tales

One final theme we must mention is that of Fairy Tales. Barker has commented in past interviews that the first imaginative stories he ever read were fairy tales: "I had several volumes as a kid, and found in their darkest corners images and ideas I never tired of examining. Back and back I'd go to keep company with cannibal witches and lunatic queens, dragons and phantoms and malignant spirits, passing over the simpery stuff ... to get to the business of the wild wood."[4] Obviously much of this can be detected in fantasy novels such as *Weaveworld*, *The Great and Secret Show*, *Cabal* and others. Anyone who has read the original stories of the Brothers Grimm can understand the horror potential therein, so it is hardly surprising that these should be an influence, and it was something Peter Atkins definitely picked up on when writing the sequel.

The first reference comes from the main protagonist herself. When Detective Ronson is questioning her at the very start he says, "Would you talk to me, and please, this time no demon fairy tales," to which Kirsty retorts, "Fairy tales, fairy tales. My father didn't believe in fairy tales either. Some of them come true, Mr. Ronson. Even the bad ones." Inevitably, Ronson tells her, "I'm sorry, I don't understand." Once again it points to Kirsty's childlike qualities at the beginning; the tantrum she throws with Ronson only emphasizes this, and the way she watches the rain trickling down the window like a bored kid on a wet Saturday afternoon. She believes in the fairy tales because she is still connected to her youth, whereas Ronson is an adult, and has closed off his imagination. This is why he cannot possibly help with this investigation, let alone solve it.

The next time fairy tales are mentioned is when Julia and Kirsty meet again at Channard's house. Julia, as we have seen, claims not just to be the wicked stepmother but also now the Wicked Queen—"So come on, take your best shot, Snow White!"—which is yet another reason Julia couldn't stand to look at herself in the mirror until she could claim to be "the fairest in the land" once more. Like Snow White, Kirsty has been the victim of a foul plot against her; but instead of being tricked into taking the poison apple, she has been tricked into entering Hell, none of which was Julia's doing, it has to be said.

But the allusion here does remind us of the jealousy aspect between these two women. Again, Kirsty has a good-looking man at her beck and call—another reason Julia had to kill him—and she probably fears that Channard might be interested as well. Just like Larry and Frank. "Kirsty, you have surprisingly good taste in men," Julia tells her. Not simply black humor with a double meaning (Julia has literally just *tasted* Kirsty's man), but also a sign of envy, as the Evil Queen envies Snow White.

One could also compare Kirsty to the character of Little Red Riding Hood. She enters the dangerous forest to help a relative—in this instance her father, not grandmother—then arrives at the house only to find the Wolf has disguised himself as that relative: Frank pretending to be Larry. And though it might be stretching the reading slightly, Tiffany is very much like Sleeping Beauty. She may not physically be asleep, but she still needs to wake in order to come to terms with what has happened to both her and her mother. It is not a Prince who comes to the castle to do this now, but Kirsty. And it is not with a kiss that she wakes her—for in the main these signify danger in the *Hellraiser* mythos—but with love and an embrace.

There is also referencing evident in the way the narrative and imagery draws on the Rule of Three. This is where patterns of three are apparent in the text, and fairy tales were riddled with them. As explained in Ansen Dibell's book, *Plot*, "One is an incident. Two is a pattern. Three breaks it. One tells us what the risk is. Two confirms what wrong behaviour is. At three, we know the rules, and so can appreciate what the smart third person is doing differently, to break the unsuccessful pattern and win."[5] It forms the basis of stories like *Cinderella*, *The Three Pigs*, *The Three Bears*....

In *Hellbound* there are two major patterns like this. The first involves Kirsty and Tiffany's encounters with the Channard Cenobite. The first time they meet is in the fake hospital on the wards. "The doctor is in," he bellows, before killing the patients in their beds with his tentacles. The second time, he appears behind Tiffany saying, "Tiffany, come. I'm your doctor, I'm here to help you." They are able to escape because of the other Cenobites' distraction, but we see the result if anyone tries to defy him: all the Cenobites die, slashed or stabbed by his tentacles. The third and final engagement occurs within sight of Leviathan, but Tiffany now knows how Channard kills — she has seen him do it twice now — and so avoids his tentacles when he attacks her, which leads to his own death. A perfect example of the rule of three.

The second key illustration of this is Tiffany's solving of the puzzles. The first time we see her she is putting together a wooden box, which allows Frank to send his message to Kirsty. The second time is when she solves the Lament Configuration, and it opens the door to Hell; the box is then reconstructed into a representation of Leviathan by Pinhead. The third time, she realizes that if she can turn the puzzle back into a box she can seal the rift and make the escape from Hell a permanent one.

In addition to these we can also identify the specific use of threes in the movie for dramatic and visual effect. There are three puzzle boxes in bell jars in Channard's home, for example. When Tiffany opens the gateway to Hell, three doors appear, two behind her in Channard's Obsession Room, and one behind Channard and Julia in their secret niche. When Kirsty and Tiffany pause after walking through the corridors of Hell, there is a pan from left to right which shows three different corridors they could choose. It is also at this point that Kirsty says, "We have to help each other. Yeah? Yeah? Yeah?" Repeating the question three times (although Atkins has joked that it is a homage to those other famous Liverpudlian exports, The Beatles).

The Channard Cenobite has three tentacles on the palm of each of his hands. There are three main villains in the shape of Julia, Channard and Frank, which balance quite nicely against the three main heroes: Kirsty, Kyle and Tiffany, except that the Cenobites upset this by appearing this time in long shot as a grouping of four, but we do encounter them three times during the entirety of the movie.

8

The Doctor Is In

As a character, Dr. Channard follows a long line of evil doctors in both literature and the cinema. Though perhaps misguided rather than wholly villainous, the first one that should concern us is the inspiration for *Hellraiser* in the first place: Dr. Faustus. However, Marlowe's tragic subject must be acknowledged as the direct ancestor of Channard if only because they both share a common goal — to uncover secret information. If anything, it is Channard rather than Frank who more closely embodies the ideas of this story, for he seeks knowledge instead of carnal desire. Any contact of this nature — such as his relationship with Julia — is purely a by-product of his search for answers.

The next most obvious forebears are Mary Shelley's Frankenstein and Robert Louis Stevenson's Dr. Jekyll, both characters from books that Barker read as a child. These literary inventions are perhaps the most celebrated examples of what the genre has termed mad scientists, people who tamper with nature for their own ends, creating chaos in their wake. For those not familiar with the tale, Dr. Victor Frankenstein was the eldest son of a high-class family from Switzerland, brought up with an orphan named Elizabeth. After the passing of his mother from scarlet fever, he started to take an interest in the human body and the subject of life itself, which preoccupied his studies at the university of Ingolstadt, Germany.

But his greatest obsession was to "bestow animation upon lifeless matter," which he finally accomplished by creating a monster out of body parts from graveyards and slaughterhouses, and passing electricity through it to bring it to life. This abomination of nature seeks refuge in a country hovel where a blind man and his two children reside. There he learns to read from the books on the shelves, one of them being Milton's *Paradise Lost*, which allows him identification with both the first man created, Adam, and the angel cast out of Heaven, Satan. When he reveals himself to the blind man's family, though, the monster is spurned and in a rage kills Frankenstein's brother. Frankenstein eventually finds him, and the monster demands that he build him a female companion. Frankenstein complies but when he destroys this work, the monster kills Frankenstein's new bride, Elizabeth, in revenge. The story ends with the doctor chasing his creation across the North Pole — actually the framing device for the book — but perishing himself.

In *Dr. Jekyll and Mr. Hyde*, the doctor becomes a monster himself, a deformed, stooping murderer, after drinking one of his own concoctions. The two beings, Jekyll and Hyde, are at complete odds with one another. The doctor has no control over the transformations, falling to sleep as himself and waking as Hyde, and he fears Jekyll will take over and remain indefinitely. At the end the potions he uses to turn himself back fail to work and he runs out of the salt needed for the mixture, so he is forced to commit suicide in order to free both Jekyll and Hyde from their torment. In these two stories the physicians are doing what they do with the best of intentions, for the good of humanity — in Frankenstein's case to try to prevent death, in Jekyll's case to separate the two halves of man, good and evil. But the results of playing God in this way are the same.

Channard is both Frankenstein and Dr. Jekyll at two different points in the film. His obsessive tendencies, like those of the two doctors mentioned, are evident by the set cast and crew would come to call The Obsession Room. In here we see various photographs of occult symbols, pencil drawings of faces in pain, organs in jars, extracts from Aleister Crowley on the walls,[1] more symbols on a blackboard, puzzles, anatomical drawings of a skinless man, Egyptian markings, drawings of the pyramids, skeletons, an altar, a replica skinned body in a glass case and the Lament Configuration boxes in bell jars. Kyle also finds a scrapbook filled with related articles belaboring the point, including "The Labyrinth of the Mind," "Children of the Vortex: Puberty and the Link with Psychic Phenomena" (giving us another reason for his interest in the young Tiffany), and "Is Death the Fourth Dimension?" There is also the sepia photograph of the human who used to be Pinhead, along with a diagram of a man's head cut into squared segments, which Kirsty finds later. We also see a book on the side called *The Internal Inferno* with a picture of Magritte's famous painting, *False Mirror Original* (1928), on the front cover (more eye imagery and references to mirrors). This has been Channard's line of inquiry for some time, or as Kyle whispers, "Jesus, he must have been into this shit for years."

That patience is about to be rewarded, as he is on the verge of reanimating his own carrion, just like Frankenstein; the only difference is there's no electricity involved this time: just blood. He "creates" Julia by letting Browning slash himself open on her mattress, but like Frankenstein he still constructs a monster, one which starts its new life by ravaging Browning. Julia is fully aware of her startling appearance, even before she sees herself in the mirror. She has only to cast her mind back to her own initial encounter with skinless Frank in the damp room at Lodovico Street. Julia is just as unpalatable to look at as Victor Frankenstein's creation, but, unlike him, she comprehends this early and takes steps to counteract it. "Don't be scared of me," she tells Channard almost immediately after her "birth," then with his help attempts to make herself more pleasing to the eye.

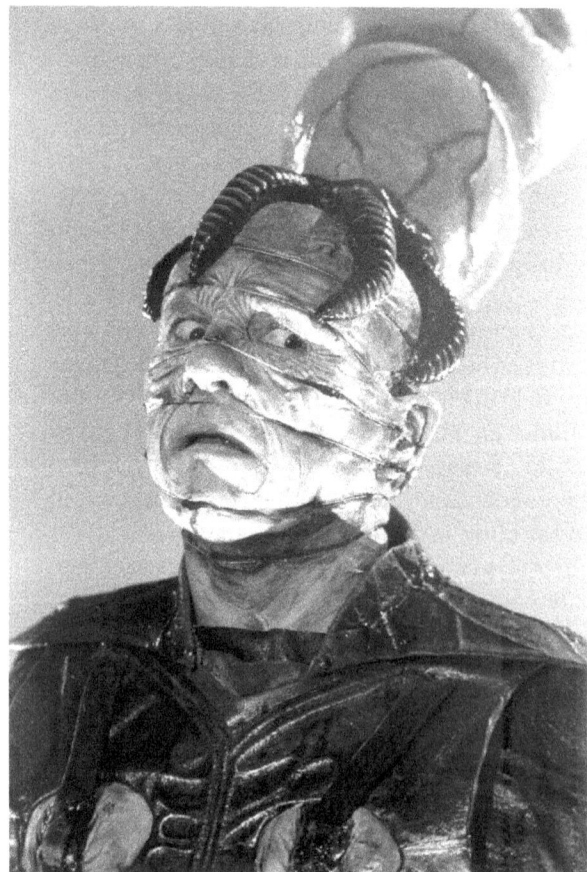

Channard follows in the tradition of Dr. Jekyll, who releases the beast within. *Hellbound: Hellraiser II* still (photograph credit: Murray Close).

First, she puts on one of Channard's white suits—which oddly makes for an alluring image. "Well?" she asks him. "Yes, yes. You look..." he answers. "Strange? Surreal? Nightmarish?" she finishes for him. The answer is all of the above, but at least she looks more human. The next stage is to wrap her in bandages to further disguise the monstrous (all you can see are her stunning blue eyes and lips), and to put on a light blue dress. Bit by bit, Julia is regaining the sexual power she once had, enough to attract Channard and encourage him to kiss her. When his hand rides up the back of her dress, the bandages there almost resemble stockings tops—the ultimate in sensual attire. "Now all we need is skin," she tells him. In one sense she means to be fully complete, with an epidermis, but skin is also a slang word for condom—a reward for when his work is over.

But for the monster to be whole again more victims must be brought to Julia. Unsurprisingly, the first casualty is a young naked woman, which hints at the beauty Julia will soon possess again. The scene then dissolves to show multiple corpses hanging, then Julia is revealed in all her glory when the bandages are removed. Channard has achieved something the original Frankenstein could not; he has redefined his creation, redesigned her into a more acceptable shape. In actuality, it is Julia who has done this to herself—Channard has merely provided the raw materials—so she has no reason to reap any kind of revenge on him. If anything, she only gives him what he wants: to see and to know. There is also the matter that she has been born again before Channard brought her back, changed in the depths of Hell by Leviathan. And the act of revival Channard has performed on Julia will soon be his fate, too. This is where the doctor becomes Mr. Hyde.

In the Cenobitization chamber, Channard metamorphoses into a monster. Rather than a potion, it is Leviathan that is the catalyst for his change. And instead of changing from good to evil, Channard simply becomes more evil, an extension of what he was on Earth. Though his process of rebirth is similar to Julia's, there is a crucial difference. While she goes to great pains to hide the monster behind a human façade, Channard's internal monster becomes visible. But just like Jekyll, he is unable to control it: the beast runs rampant, given free rein, for a time, at least. And because he had little or no conscience to begin with, after an initial struggle he embraces the mutation and, indeed, revels in it. His end comes not through suicide but because he let his newfound powers go to his head.

In terms of cinematic influences, there have been countless adaptations of both *Frankenstein* and *Dr. Jekyll* we can point to. Thomas Edison's *Frankenstein* (J. Searle Dawley, 1910), for instance, sees the doctor (Augustus Phillips) creating his monster (Charles Ogle) in a boiling pot which puts flesh on a skeleton's bones; then the monster dissolves into a mirror at the finale, which again links with *Orpheus*. Director James Whale's *Frankenstein* (1931) is the one most people remember, as it made a horror icon out of Boris Karloff, but it was based more on the play than the book and was set in modern times. Then, of course, there was Hammer's reworking of the story starring Peter Cushing as the doctor and Christopher Lee as the monster in *The Curse of Frankenstein* (Terence Fisher, 1957), which took the series back to a more period setting, and came to its conclusion—appropriately—with *Frankenstein and the Monster from Hell* (Fisher, 1973).

Film versions of *Dr. Jekyll and Mr. Hyde* have tended to emulate Thomas Russell Sullivan's play version of 1887, which centered more on Jekyll's suppressed sexual desires, turning Hyde more into a Jack the Ripper character. The basic premise, therefore, has been radically contorted in movies like the 1908 version of the same name, the 1931 adaptation starring Fredric March, Spencer Tracy's incarnation (Victor Fleming, 1941), right up to Christopher Lee's *I Monster* (Stephen Weeks, 1971) and Alexandr Feklistov in *Stannyar*

Isoryar Doktora Dzehila i Mistera Khaida (Aleksandr Orlov, 1985). The story has even been flexible enough to allow for gender reversals, such as Jekyll becoming a woman in *Dr. Jekyll and Sister Hyde* (Roy Ward Baker, 1971).

Adding to this, we must also mention those mad scientists of films like: *Island of Lost Souls* (Erle C. Kenton, 1933), an adaptation of H.G. Wells' *Island of Dr Moreau*; *The Invisible Man* (another Wells book — Whale, 1933) where once again bandages are used to mask the abnormality; *Dr. Cyclops* (Ernest B. Schoedsack, 1940); *The Man Who Could Cheat Death* (Fisher, 1959); *The Brain That Wouldn't Die* (Joseph Green, 1962); and *The Mutations* (Jack Cardiff, 1973). There are many others, of course, but one more deserves a special mention — Herbert West from Stuart Gordon's 1985 film, *The Re-animator*. Played to perfection by Jeffrey Combs, this character — which originated in an H.P. Lovecraft tale — is a distant relative of Frankenstein, and is also concerned with bringing dead tissue back to life, this time with a fluorescent green serum he has developed. There aren't too many parallels to be drawn from either the character itself or the performances of the "insane" doctors in *Re-animator* and *Hellbound*, but the obsession with what they are doing is what drives them both.

One more film that needs to be listed is a favorite of both Atkins and Randel.[2] Both have cited *The Bride of Frankenstein* (1935) as an influence and this is spectacularly obvious from *Hellbound*. *Bride* is the sequel to Universal's 1931 take on Shelley's novel, once again directed by Whale, but in actual fact utilizes elements from the book not used in the first film, such as the plotline where Frankenstein is to make his monster a mate. As the title suggests, the doctor (played once again by Colin Clive) creates a female this time, who would also become an enduring icon. As portrayed by Elsa Lanchester, the bride has a long flowing white gown, zigzag streaks in her dark hair, and bandages down her arms. In all but the hair, Julia's look matches hers. While there is a definite homage to another Universal movie, *The Mummy* (1932), as well as the Hammer films that came after it in the same vein (hence the Egyptian markings on Channard's walls), Julia is certainly more Bride of Frankenstein than she ever will be Mummy.

More clues can be found in the style of Channard's dress, the cut of his suit distinctly 1930s or '40s. Even his fondness for smoking reflects Hollywood movies of that era, with more than an indication of noir. The minimal use of color in the scenes with Channard and Julia — the exception being blood red — harks back to this era, and the lightning that strikes as Julia attacks her victims is pure Universal gothic, used in both *Frankenstein* and *The Bride of Frankenstein* during the creation sequences.

We've talked about the literary and filmic lineage that Channard has inherited, but there is more to his role as a doctor than facilitating *Hellbound*'s eligibility for this subgenre. Channard also embodies our fear of medicine, surgery and doctors generally, not just culturally. The first time we meet Channard he is performing one of the most horrendous operations one could possibly imagine. With his mask and gown on, he already appears something other than human — a prophetic indication of his later guise, and foundation for the aborted Pinhead-surgical scene — but what he is doing is enough to make even the strongest person cringe. Randel has spoken about the effect the *Ben Casey* TV series had on him as a boy. "This imagery comes from something that scared the crap out of me when I was young, with Vince Edwards doing surgery on somebody who was awake. I always thought, 'That's nasty.'"[3] And he's correct. (It was so nasty, in fact, that it was used again in *Hellraiser: Hellseeker* some years later.) The metallic implements on either side of the woman's head, gripping her face and nose, the cranium open with flaps of skin pulled tight,

Bride of Frankenstein French poster.

the scalpel hovering over the brain itself, and then the application of the drill, with the added touch of smoke rising as it connects with the gray matter, is extremely uncomfortable to watch. Even the nurses on hand and Kyle, observing his mentor, appear shocked. Channard, conversely, remains calm throughout. He doesn't really care about the patient, doesn't see her as a person: all that concerns him is what her brain can tell him. It is an apathy that — rightly or wrongly — many of us associate with the medical profession.

This is amplified only moments later when Channard walks down a corridor and discusses Kirsty with Kyle. "Now this case, Kyle, interesting but delicate." This is what she represents to him, another case to crack. "A speculative mind," he continues, "is an invaluable asset to the analytic man, but all diagnosis begins with..." "Examination," ventures Kyle. "Precisely. You must win from them their trust, draw from them their story, and take from them their pain." Channard has a plan all worked out before he even meets with Kirsty. It doesn't matter to him either way whether he cures her or not (the patients on his wards seem to have been there forever). What's important is quenching his professional thirst. The main factor in this equation, and the thing that terrifies us most, is that doctors are in a position of power. We are at our most vulnerable when sick, so the idea that someone could be using that to their own advantage is what scares us the most.

Later, of course, when Channard is placed in an even greater position of power, he becomes yet more frightening. As a Cenobite he no longer needs the medical equipment in that operating theater; it is all — quite literally — to hand. Scalpels spring from his tentacles, sharp enough to cut through chains, and perform an emergency tracheotomy on Pinhead. This makes his throwaway lines ("I recommend amputation") even more relevant and chilling.

But if Channard is the universal embodiment of our fears about medicine, his work with Julia more specifically focuses on one area: plastic surgery. In the 1980s, this kind of treatment was nowhere near as prevalent as it is today. Now, it is the norm to have face lifts, liposuction, breast enhancements, collagen injections; it has even become a fashion trend. There was much more anxiety attached to these procedures when *Hellbound* was made. The public was not as familiar with plastic surgery then, which meant it was a choice subject to tap into. What other explanation can there be for the resemblance of the bandaged Julia to Edith Scob in Georges Franju's seminal postwar European horror film, *Les Yeux Sans Visage* (*Eyes Without a Face*, 1959). This, too, trades on apprehension about bodily and facial disfigurement and plastic surgery, complete with uncompromising operating theater scenes which owe much to documentary shorts Franju made in the aftermath of the Second World War.

As she first appears to us, Julia is uncomfortable to look at: skinless, oozing slime. She may well tread that fine line between disgusting and hideously resplendent, but there can be no denying that she looked much better before her death. She has lost her natural beauty and is reliant on Channard to restore it, which he does by bringing her "food." The unwrapping of her bandages to reveal the face we all know is comparable to many a film or TV show (usually soap operas of the '80s like *Dynasty* when an actor was replaced) where surgery has been performed on the features. But somehow Julia's look *has* changed between films. She has grown even more beautiful, her hairstyle has changed, all of which supports the claim that villainy does indeed become this woman. A few final nips and tucks are needed, though, which Julia sees to herself. The tear at her back, where the new skin has been grafted on, is soon sealed by absorbing Kyle's life force when she kisses him.

On the face of it, Julia is better than ever before now: more stunning and attractive.

But this is only a temporary thing. In the wind tunnel when she is trying to deceive Tiffany, this new membrane is ripped off at the arm. Julia disappears, leaving a pile of skin on the stone floor. The "operations" she has been through may have given her transient beauty, but with one tug it is lost. In this way Julia personifies fears about whether plastic surgery will actually work, whether a facelift will somehow rip or tear, whether a nose will cave in after rhinoplasty. What brings this into even sharper relief is *Hellbound*'s accent on the fact that Kirsty doesn't need to undergo any of these procedures. She is shown in the shower, skin perfect, close-ups of her face emphasizing she has no wrinkles. Her youth is pitted against Julia's maturity. And in one final snub, Kirsty uses the skin Julia has left behind to fool Channard and liberate Tiffany. She dons this fake bodysuit, but she doesn't need it, which is why she peels it off with such glee once the rescue has been performed. Where Julia has been forced to put the skin on to retain her looks, Kirsty only has need of it to perform her heroics during the finale. After that, she can disregard it and all it represents. But as we have seen, Kirsty has matured herself during the film, developing fully into a woman. And when Kirsty is a little older herself, might Julia not have her supreme revenge?

9

THE DEVIL YOU KNOW?

Visions of Hell

In our discussion of *Hellraiser*, we touched briefly on the fact that the Hell it depicted—and its demons—were unlike any other seen before at that time. *Hellbound* took this basic premise, not to mention Barker's imagery, and extended it further. In the first film we get to see only one corridor in Hell. In the sequel, we are presented with Hell in all its awe-inspiring grandeur. But just how different is it to any renderings from the past? As we've already seen, in Greek mythology Hell is a cavernous Underworld, located in Hades and reached by crossing the river Styx. The Romans had their own equivalent, a kingdom ruled by their god Pluto. But possibly the most famous source about Hell is *The Bible*. Here the Infernal Region is described in a number of entries:

> The two of them were thrown alive into the fiery lake of burning sulfur.[1]
> And the devil, who deceived them, was thrown into the lake of burning sulfur, where the beast and the false prophet had been thrown. They will be tormented day and night for ever and ever.... Then death and Hades were thrown into the lake of fire.[2]
> But as for the cowardly, the faithless, the polluted, as for murderers, fornicators, sorcerers, idolaters, and all liars, their lot shall be in the lake that burns with fire and sulfur.[3]

There are also references to Hell being within the earth, somewhere that sinners descend into like an abyss. It expressly describes the earth opening up and the wicked being dragged down into Hell.[4] People have speculated that this might be a metaphor, however, to indicate a separation from God, the darkness of the abyss a direct contrast to the light of Heaven and all it represents. In addition, *The Bible* provides enlightenment about what life is like for the damned that dwell in the bowels of the abyss.

> If anyone worships the beast and his image and receives his mark on the forehead or on the hand, he, too, will drink of the wine of God's fury, which has been poured full strength into the cup of his wrath. He will be tormented with burning sulfur in the presence of the holy angels and of the Lamb. And the smoke of their torment rises for ever and ever. There is no rest day or night for those who worship the beast and his image, or for anyone who receives the mark of his name.[5]
> But the subjects of the kingdom will be thrown outside, into the darkness, where there will be weeping and gnashing of teeth.[6]

Not those of a certain Cenobite, but the teeth of sinners themselves. But what of the eternal torments they must endure?

It implies that all the pains and horrors of earth put together are nothing compared to what awaits the inhabitants of Hell. Yet the greatest torment of all is called the poena damni, or pain of loss: the soul's separation from God. A secondary torture is mentioned, too, the poena sensus (pain of sense). This could take on many forms, but the most familiar to us would be burning in the flames of Hell, which do not kill the victim, forcing them to endure the sensation of burning indefinitely. Their company in this place would be demons, liars, sorcerers, murderers, cheaters and fornicators, who would gloat over such sufferings. In effect, as the New Testament lays it out, Hell is a place of corruption, unquenchable fire and — of course — brimstone.

Muslims have a similar view of Hell, but the Islamic Hell, or Jahannum, is reserved only for all unbelievers in the Islamic faith, no matter how God-fearing they are in their own religions. Buddhists descend into one of many Hells because of evil karma (which means any action of doing). The eight hells or Jigoku are as follows: The first is for murderers, who kill for gratification: The Hell of Repetition. The next is the Black Rope Hell, for those who have killed as part of another crime; Tortures here include black birds plucking out eyes, demons ripping out entrails and tongues. The Crowded Hell relates also to killing or stealing and sexual indulgence. Desire is at the heart of the Fire-jar Hell, where you could have your eyes burnt out for dwelling on the vision of a desirable woman. The Screaming Hell is for those who abuse alcohol or other drugs, or encourage others to do so; while The Great Screaming Hell waits for those who have used their voices to spread evil. The Hell of Burning Heat is for those with dishonest viewpoints; and in the Diamond-beak Hornet Hell, the sinner is forced to drink his own blood and eat his own flesh. The Burning Hell of String-like Worms is concerned with sexual crimes of a religious nature; and, finally, the eighth, Hell Of No Interval, is the most serious, meant for those who have killed their own parents, or caused harm to the Buddhist community in some way.

Hindus have a comparable notion concerning multiple hells. Writers of law books, or Smritis, like Yogi Yajnavalkya and Vishnu, have given descriptions of the various Hells and the variety of pleasures in Heaven. For example Yajnavalkya mentions twenty-one Hells in his law book. In both these religions, Hindu and Buddhist, the sinner is given the opportunity to be freed once the bad karma has been worked through, and is then reincarnated. The punishment in Hell is not remembered by the soul when it is reborn; therefore, the chastisement in Hell is of a more reformatory or educative nature.

The idea of such levels of Hell was taken up by an Italian writer in the middle ages. Alighieri Dante (1265–1321) died shortly after producing his most famous piece, the *Divine Comedy*. It is a narrative poem in which Dante, with Roman poet Virgil as his guide, undertakes a religious pilgrimage to find God. His journey takes him through Hell, Purgatory and finally to Paradise. Dante's Hell, or Inferno as it's more popularly known, has nine circles. In each circle the pair witness sinners being punished for their misdoings on earth, guilty of three types of sin: Incontinence or loss of control; Brutishness; and Malice or Vice. The Inferno is intricately structured, covering the entire range of possible transgressions.

In Circle One we find pagans and unbaptized infants in limbo; in Circle Two the lustful; in Circle Three the gluttonous; in Circle Four the hoarders; in Five the angry and wrathful; in Six heretics; in Circle Seven (descending now to the lower regions of violence and fraud) the violent — split into sections that include murderers, suicides and those harmful against God; in Circle Eight we have sorcerers, fortune tellers, hypocrites, thieves, alchemists, impersonators and counterfeiters; and, finally, in Circle Nine there are the traitors to kin and country, and guests and traitors to lords and benefactors. It is also here that we find the Ultimate Destroyer Lucifer.

Pictorially, artists such as the Limbourg brothers (1380–1416), Franco-Flemish painters, have been hugely influential. One of their most original and beautiful miniatures, *The Fall of the Rebel Angels*, depicts the aforementioned Lucifer and the other fallen angels catching light as they touch the earth, the flames a golden color against shades of blue. Hieronymus Bosch (c.1445–1516) is another name synonymous with visions of Hell. His depiction in the right-hand panel of the triptych *The Garden of Earthly Delights* (*The Musical Hell*) shows all manner of strange and grotesque imagery. Here the sinners are being harassed by the likes of birds and swine with human attributes, as well as being surrounded by animal skulls and a pair of human ears with a gigantic knife-blade protruding from them. There may not be any fire, but there are plenty of demons representing the full spectrum of human fears.

Returning to William Blake, his illustrated *Marriage of Heaven and Hell* (1793) has images which imagine Hell as a dark place surrounded by flames. This is backed up by lines like "As I was walking among the fires of hell..." The sinners in his version of *The Last Judgment* are rising from the caves and flames, all naked and packed into tiny spaces, some praying for forgiveness. He was also responsible for illustrations such as "Dante and Virgil at the Gates of Hell," which shows the two men at the entranceway about to walk into a burning conflagration.

But perhaps the most significant of all was Gustave Doré's 1861 black and white illustrations that accompany Dante's *Divine Comedy*. These include winged creatures with pitchforks attacking Dante and Virgil, while cavernous regions and fire belch up from below.

Dante's Inferno: "The Thieves Tortured by Serpents" by Gustave Doré.

One of the most iconic images, though, has to be that of the doomed souls. These actively swayed how cinema would later portray Hell and those trapped inside.

For example, one of the earliest films to capture Hell on celluloid was *L'inferno*—a five-reel Italian epic that was directly inspired by Doré's pictures, and was brought to the U.S. by Warner Brothers in 1911. *The Devil's Assistant* (Harry A. Pollard, 1917) draws more on the classical myths—complete with Cerberus and Styx—but two more movies followed in 1924 and 1935 that also adapted Doré's visions for the cinema, both entitled *Dante's Inferno*. Although not given that much screen time—possibly because of the budget required—Hell has been glimpsed in films from that moment on, and usually as the underground, fire-ridden landscape that has seeped into our consciousness over the centuries—most recently in films like *Spawn* (Mark A.Z. Dippé, 1997) and *Constantine* (Francis Lawrence, 2005). It's also worth noting that "access" to Hell has cropped up in various locations, including a local fair in *Carnival of Souls* (Herk Harvey, 1962)—which *Hellbound* paid homage to in its own carnival sequence—a refrigerator in *Ghost Busters* (Ivan Reitman, 1984) and at the bottom of the garden in *The Gate* (Tibor Takács, 1987).

The depiction of Hell as seen in *Hellbound* is unique among those from the worlds of religion, literature, art and film. Certainly there are elements that bear a striking resemblance to those in this sequel. Yes, there are sinners here and, yes, they are being tortured: some in ways that the Bible and other holy books pre-empted. The Pain of Sense, for instance, could very easily be describing what the victims of the Cenobites are put through. And some of the ordeals from the Buddhists' Jigoku might prove adequate for the Cenobites to extract the maximum amount of suffering—especially when they combine the psychological with the physical. But there is one important distinction. When you die, you don't automatically go to this Hell. It is not a punishment for all the wrongs you have done in your life. You could have lived the purest existence ever and still fall victim to this particular Hell. All you have to do is open the box. And the pain the Cenobites inflict is intermingled with pleasure.

The look of the place—for which much of the credit goes to matte artist Cliff Culley—is labyrinthine in nature, as is only to be expected. Another puzzle like the box. But it also seems to have been inspired by three distinct artists. The first is Giovanni Battista Piranesi (1720–1778). His *Prison* etchings represent only a small fraction of his total output, and were not even of central importance to the artist, but they have become his most famous works and in them we can clearly see the later mechanics of Barker and Atkins' Hell. From stone archways to elaborate staircases and walkways, Piranesi's Prisons so closely match those of *Hellbound* that you fully expect to see Pinhead there.

The second is Maurits Escher (1898–1972). His wood engraving of Porta Maria dell'Ospidale, Ravello 1932, depicts another archway not unlike those Kirsty and Tiffany find themselves in, but it is his other work, like his 1938 lithograph *Cycle*, 1951's *House of Stairs* and *Relativity* (1953), which are characterized by their abnormal patterns or stairways appearing to double back on themselves with a warped perspective, that are most reminiscent of *Hellbound*'s delineation of Hell. If we now add the work of the more recent Swiss Surrealist artist H.R. Giger (the man responsible for the look of the monster in *Alien*) we are even closer to the depiction of Hell in our film. Giger's paintings mix the organic with their surroundings, and his biomechanical vistas in shades of grays and beige wouldn't be too out of place in *Hellbound*. What's more, Giger's work comes the closest in tone to what the mythos is really all about, that fine line between pleasure and pain. Between fear and enticement. Paintings such as *The Witches' Dance* (1977) and *Vlad Tepes* (1978) are definitely

Cenobitical in nature, and reveal more than a hint of that "repulsive glamour" Barker has talked about.

There are no caves in this Hell, only corridors, steps and dark storm clouds on the horizon. The captives aren't packed into small confines, but given the space of their own personal Hells. This Hades is not the epitome of chaos, but of order. And the flames are provided not by the environment, but by Kirsty when she sets fire to Frank's boudoir. They are not meant to be part of his punishment at all, just part of Kirsty's escape plan. Finally, this Hell shares the view that torment should be forever. Working through your bad deeds or repenting will not earn you a way out — karma has nothing to do with it. The only means of exit is to escape, as Frank does in the first film.

History of the Devil

Just as the idea of a fire and brimstone Hell is deeply rooted in Christianity, so, too, is the Devil as a personification of all-powerful evil. The word devil itself seems to be derived from the Sanskrit, *div*, although in biblical terms it came from translating the Hebrew "Satan" (originally a tester of men, or God's prosecution lawyer, only later turning into God's Adversary) into the Greek "Diablos." So two separate representations were merged into one. He was consequently used by early Church fathers to explain evil acts in human nature and to convert pagans to Christianity. This concept is far from peculiar to the Christian religion; indeed, it echoes Ahriman, the Zoroastrian epitome of destruction and lies, as well as other nature spirits and deities. However this religion is the one that made the figure their own, simultaneously incorporating and distorting it over the years.

The myth of Lucifer being a fallen angel also stems from The Bible. Lucifer — which in the Hebrew means "daystar" — is mentioned in the book of Isaiah: "How art thou fallen from heaven, O Lucifer, son of the morning." This was used to demonize Lucifer as an

A typical representation of the horned Devil (courtesy David A. Magitis).

outcast from Heaven, who was banished along with his followers for refusing to worship Adam. A subsequent connection was then made to the serpent that tempted Eve to persuade Adam to eat the apple in the Garden of Eden. The final piece of the puzzle comes in the Book of Revelation (12:9): "And the great dragon was cast out, that old serpent, called the Devil, and Satan, which deceiveth the whole world: he was cast out to earth, and his angels were cast out with him," thus to begin an ageless battle with God for human souls.[7]

This is the legend John Milton (1608–1674) utilized for his well-known poem, *Paradise Lost* (1667). Here Satan vows to corrupt God's new creation, man, and heads off to find Adam and Eve. To warn them, God sends the angel Raphael, who tells them the circumstances in which Satan fell. One of the principal angels in Heaven, Satan refused to bow before God's Son. He rallied angels to his cause and a three-day battle ensued, which ended in Satan retreating. God then made man to replace the void the fallen angels had left. Satan wrought his revenge on Adam and Eve accordingly, but when he returns to Hell he finds that he and his subjects are being transformed into hideous monsters, and that he himself is becoming a snake. Upon hearing Adam's appeal for forgiveness, God decides not to abandon the human race completely to Satan, his daughter, Sin, and his son, Death, but sends his own Son as a man to sacrifice himself and defeat the evil trinity.

The Devil has adopted other names over time: Abaddon, Behemoth, Belial, Asmodeus, Beelzebub. But the classical look is rooted in early patristic writings of the fourth century, giving the pagan god Pan—characterized by a goat's head and cloven hooves—a more human appearance. But the idea of a winged, horned creature again has more to do with illustrations like those of Doré's, where the tiny specks of Dante and Virgil come across Satan. This traditional form can be seen in many silent movies from *La Manoir du Diable* (Georges Méliès, 1896) to *Häxan* (Benjamin Christensen, 1922), then later in such films as *The Devil Rides Out* (Terence Fisher, 1968), *The Devil's Rain* (Robert Fuest, 1975) and *The Unholy* (Camilo Vila, 1988). The creature even made an appearance in Disney's 1940 cartoon, *Fantasia*. More often than not, though, the Devil in cinema has been portrayed in his human guise. Typical examples include *The Devil* (James Young, 1921), *Puritan Passions* (Frank Tuttle, 1923), *Heaven Can Wait* (Ernst Lubitsch, 1943), *Bedazzled* (Stanley Donen, 1967)—in which he was played magnificently by Peter Cook—and *The Witches of Eastwick* (George Miller, 1987), where Jack Nicholson made his mark as Old Nick.

In *Hellbound* we are introduced to an entirely different kind of Devil. The name Leviathan also originates from early Christianity and Judaism. The conjunction of Judaism and Zoroastrianism in the fifth century BC resulted in quite a complex demonology, which was incorporated into the former's religion. This was when Leviathan was given as a name to a demon of chaos. But if we consult the Bible once more—the Old Testament, to be exact—we discover that Leviathan represented a kind of malevolent creature, in the form of a serpent or crocodile, or even a huge sea beast. As with the Devil, it was customized over the centuries to become a more generic symbol of evil. More specifically, in the Ugaritic religion Leviathan is the actual name of a God of Evil, and it was ascribed to a demon of envy in medieval times. Interestingly, the English philosopher Thomas Hobbes (1588–1679) also named his most famous book *Leviathan*. In it he advocates absolute government as the only way of achieving order. He proposed a social contract under which the ruled agreed to obey the ruler if he in turn provided social peace.

Leviathan, we are told by Julia, is the "god of flesh, hunger and desire." Everything you'd expect from the Devil, apart from one thing. Surprisingly, Leviathan is also a god of stability and order. In its Hell, there is no mayhem—everything is methodically thought out and rules are followed or anarchy may destroy Hell completely. Like the society Hobbes is proposing, Leviathan provides the much-needed immovability of this region, in exchange for complete and utter obedience: from his Cenobites and in turn from their victims, even if force must be used — and actually it might prefer this. Julia tells us that Leviathan has sent her out to find souls, but it is not interested in waging any war against the good or even corrupting humanity. In the world of *Hellraiser*, humanity is already corrupt and all Leviathan is doing is taking advantage of the fact.

This logical fixation is reflected not only in the layout of its Hell but also in the mathematical and geometrical precision of its own shape. Gone are the serpent's features, the hooves and goat's head, even the red skin, horns and wings which connote chaos. Leviathan's perfect octahedral form is order personified. This is why the original interpretation of a Lovecraftian god would never have worked. H.P. Lovecraft's Old Ones, like Cthulhu, were notable for their alien visages and slimy tentacles.

Nor does Leviathan need to lie and cheat to get what it wants: the souls of the damned are there for the taking. If anything, it is the truth that this god deals in, penetrating the outer layers of human camouflage with its black light and seeing right into the very heart of a person, revealing who they truly are.

The Devil's Own

We've examined the demons that inhabit this Hell in chapter 3, but how do these differ from more traditional demonic interpretations? Greek Diamons were merely intermediary spirits that existed somewhere between humans and gods. But in Western religion and occult lore, demons have been classified into many elaborate systems connected with Hell. The most intricate of these was devised by Johann Weyer, who estimated there to be 7,405,926 demons at the command of seventy-two princes.[8] In the Christian religion, they have come to be associated with the angels that fell from Heaven with Lucifer. When the word is mentioned it immediately conjures up images of small, leathery creatures with pointed teeth and tails that populate Hell and torment humans on earth, exactly like The Yattering in Barker's short story from the *Books of Blood*.

The Cenobites are nothing like this. Sadomasochistic individuals with open wounds and butcher's implements hanging from their black garb, it is finally revealed in *Hellbound* that they were once human. In the first scene of the movie we are shown Pinhead's transformation process. The camera pans along a table of objects, a jacket, fly-brush, gun in a holster and safari hat — all of which pinpoint an occupation, as well as a rough date. It is clear from this that the person who was once Pinhead served in the army in India in the 1920s, when the English were in residence. (The additional bartering scene would have elucidated this.) We then see Doug Bradley sitting crossed-legged in long shot, solving the puzzle just as Frank did in the previous movie. His reward is a little different, for he is selected to become a Cenobite and we are witness to his bloody conversion, where the grooves are cut into his head and the nails are banged into it.

Later on in the film — after their deaths at the hands of Channard — we see who all the Cenobites were before their metamorphoses. The Female Cenobite was a beautiful woman with long, blonde hair. Butterball was an overweight man in his forties, and Chatterer was a young boy. Nicholas Vince later wrote a first person short story called "Look See" in which he redefined his character's back story as that of a more apposite stand-up comedian from New York in the 1930s: "Of course, now they've made movies of some of the Box's stories. They're quite good. They've got a lot of things right and most of them wrong. I mean, they've tried to say I was a kid when I opened the box — nice try, but no Kewpie Doll. But what can you expect from movie people?"[9]

To some extent, this revelation takes away from the menace that the Cenobites exuded in the original film. Their air of mystery had the dual purpose of keeping us intrigued and terrified. By providing an answer to our — admittedly inevitable — question about the origins of Pinhead and his colleagues, it decreased their ability to scare us. If we can relate to the Cenobites because they were once human, we can empathize with them; they are doing these things because they have been indoctrinated into Hell's legions by Leviathan. Granted, their worst character traits may have simply been given an outlet by the god, just like Channard; nevertheless it is hard not to feel some pity.

On the other hand, this does give the Cenobites another dimension. Bradley has said that in conversations with Barker before the filming of *Hellraiser* he not only told him to think of the character as, "some lowly clerk in a corporation,"[10] he also told him that Pinhead had once been a man. This knowledge hugely affected him when he initially put on the make-up and looked at himself in the mirror. "The first feeling I got was a deep sense of melancholia in the face, powerful and unsettling," said Bradley. "The layout of the nails being symmetrical helps. It was clearly something that was done to him. The melancholy showed me he was human, once. He was, in a way he could not express, mourning the loss of his humanity."[11] It allowed Bradley to foreshadow what would happen in *Hellbound* and also give his character that sense of sadness which set him apart from other villains and demons. Fundamentally, what was lost was a part of the monster, but what was gained was a deeper texture to the character itself. This was a dichotomy that would be more fully explored in the next film.

10

THE SWEET SUFFERING

There are no two ways about it, *Hellbound* divided critics and fans alike. Nowhere is this more apparent than in the first reviews from the Leeds International Film Festival (13–29 October 1988) where the movie received its UK Premiere, alongside Wes Craven's *The Serpent and the Rainbow* and Ken Johnson's *Short Circuit*. Peter Atkins was on hand to introduce the film and answer questions, but opinion was so divided that the magazine *Samhain* decided to print a "Case For" and "Case Against" feature.

In the more positive review, John Martin draws comparisons with *Aliens* because of the presence of Hope and the Kirsty/Tiffany storyline, but claims categorically that "*Hellbound* is far superior" not only to that film but to any other sequel in living memory[1]. He goes on to state that steps have been taken "to ensure that the poetry is not sacrificed on the altar of populism" but that it also "goes straight for the jugular," boasting an efficient screenplay by Atkins. Martin's only criticisms involve Randel's "attempts to convey the subjective nature of Hell via irritating optical effects," such as the scene where Pinhead confronts Kirsty again. "At one point ... he starts spinning around as though declaiming from inside a tumble dryer."[2] Martin ends with this meditation: "In an ideal world sequels wouldn't be made. It isn't, they are, they have to be judged on their merits and they don't come any better than *Hellbound*."[3]

Jeremy Clarke offered his views for the prosecution and didn't pull any punches. "*Hellbound: Hellraiser II* lacks all the elements that made its predecessor work so well whilst simultaneously incorporating and enlarging upon the one major flaw of the original."[4] He refers to the Americanization of the material, or, more accurately, the confusing mix of the British and American. "The sequel exacerbates this transatlanticity to an even more ludicrous degree. The first few minutes see a 'homicide detective' and a cop in an American uniform arrive on the scene of Frank's demise: later scenes show an insane asylum run by Channard, who has an unmistakably British accent."

Clarke's attack concentrates on the idea that if you don't start off the film knowing exactly where you are, or which country you're in, it makes it more difficult to suspend belief later. "No one in their right mind would buy the world of *Hellbound: Hellraiser II*. Not for one minute," he continues. "Any sense of reality, character or plot have been pared away from the original." In their defense, Atkins and Randel have always argued that the setting of *Hellbound* gives it a strange otherworldly quality that you can't pin down. "It takes place in the country of the imagination," claims Atkins[5] while at the same time admitting the more pragmatic reason was that a U.S. company was footing the bill and they wanted it to appeal to American audiences.

The movie was greeted with a similar mixed response from other magazines and newspapers. Martin Sutton's review in *Films and Filming* hinted that Barker took more of a backseat this time because he knew nobody could pull off a sequel to his movie, and centers on the two main female leads: "The sequel is particularly poorer for pushing aside the raunchy, forceful character of step-mother Julia, in favour of a far less charismatic actress.... Both her blandness and stateside turn of phrase ring quite false in the context."[6] Marc Shapiro's review from *Gorezone* was more of a cause for celebration for the cast and crew. "From the opening nightmarish flashbacks through to the slick/smart sequel-in-mind ending, *Hellbound: Hellraiser II* plays like the movie equivalent of a slaughterhouse tour."[7]

The Phantom of the Movies also sang its praises: "*Hellbound: Hellraiser II* represents one of those rare cases when a scare sequel actually surpasses the original.... *Hellbound* may be a mite strong for fainter-hearted viewers, but hard-core horror buffs won't want to miss what ranks as the best over-the-top terrorfest of 1988."[8] This was balanced out by Roger Ebert's predictably negative response: "It is simply a series of ugly and bloody episodes, strung together one after another like a demo tape by a perverted special effects man...."[9]

Variety, as well, was quick to judge it this way, "With marginal action and scattershot storytelling technique, helmer Tony Randel returns to the off-the-wall tale of a psychotic psychiatrist's long struggle to get the better of something called the Lament Configuration.... *Hellraiser II* is a maggoty carnival of mayhem, mutation and dismemberment, awash in blood and recommended only for those who thrive on such junk,"[10] while *Monthly Film Bulletin* drew comparisons with the original, complaining that before it can start its own story the sequel required two sets of flashbacks. But the *Film Bulletin* did have some good things to say: "Director Tony Randel and screenwriter Peter Atkins, working from a story by Clive Barker ... manage in the first half-hour to re-establish the boundaries of the story and the distinctive visual and aural style.... The best sequences appear early, as when the raw and skinless Julia flirts with the drawn and prissy Channard."[11]

Strangely enough, none of the reviews mention the quite blatant nods towards Hitchcock in the movie, which Randel — a massive fan — included. The first comes with the close-up on Kirsty's eye at the start, which is a tribute to Janet Leigh's death scene in *Psycho*. The scene where Julia rises from the mattress and wrestles with Browning was inspired by *Torn Curtain* (1966), where Paul Newman has to kill someone and it takes an agonizingly long time. The numbers on the cranes in the scene where Tiffany approaches the carnival exactly match those in a parallel scene in *Vertigo* (1958), and, of course, who could miss the reference to that same film when Tiffany falls off the edge of the walkway at the climax of *Hellbound*; the only difference is that Kirsty is able to pull her up, and Jimmy Stewart doesn't have the same luck with that fated policeman.

As for Barker's reactions, speaking in an interview for *Skeleton Crew* he said, "Tony has a very different take on this movie to me.... There are certain things that Tony has done with *II* that I as a director wouldn't have done. But they are his, and it's very important that people see Tony's vision through Pete's vision and my own. I'm very proud of *II*. I think it works."[12]

For Atkins, the main line of assault was the fight between the Cenobites. He actually received hate mail because Channard was so easily able to defeat Pinhead and the other Cenobites. Here was the new kid on the block suddenly picking on and beating up the established gang. The writer's rejoinder has always been that a more elaborate fight was written, but again because of money it couldn't be filmed. He also pointed out that because the Cenobites have just recalled who they really are, they are in a vulnerable position and, consequently, at the mercy of Channard, a person who embraced his Cenobite transformation. Atkins also maintains that, at his full powers, Pinhead would definitely trounce Channard in any brawl.

Speaking about the film in its entirety, Atkins has said, "A lot of hard-core fans of the first movie weren't too happy but I've met as many people at conventions, festivals and signings who prefer the second picture as I've met who dislike it. The critics, too, were split in their opinions.... But the real voters are the paying customers, and *Hellbound* did as well financially as the first movie, which is very unusual for sequels."[13] Which was a good thing, as a second sequel was already being discussed even as *Hellbound* was about to hit cinemas. Yet, in spite of the fact audiences had only had to wait a year to go to Hell, they would have to wait much longer before Hell would return to Earth.

11

Earthbound

Like its predecessor, preparations for the making of *Hellraiser III: Hell on Earth* were being made even before the current film had been released. In the summer of 1988, Tony Randel and Pete Atkins flew over to L.A. to have meetings with New World executives, while the finishing touches were still being put to *Hellbound*. The movie was again due to be a co-production between Film Futures (Barker and Chris Figg's company) and New World. Unfortunately, things didn't quite go to plan. A host of Film Futures projects were in the planning stages, while at the same time Barker was undertaking his first big budget director's job transferring his novel *Cabal* to film — with Morgan Creek financing it to the tune of $11 million. *Nightbreed* would reunite many members of the *Hellraiser* family, including Doug Bradley (now playing a prophet called Lylesberg), Nick Vince (as Kinski), Simon Bamford (as Ohnaka), Oliver Parker (as Peloquin), Catherine Chevalier (with a bigger part now as Rachel) and, of course, Bob Keen's effects crew. It would also headline Craig Sheffer as hero Boone, who would later return to star in *Hellraiser: Inferno*, Anne Bobby as his girlfriend Lori, and acclaimed horror movie director David Cronenberg as a deranged psychiatrist named Decker.

The story revolves around Boone who, believing he is responsible for several murders, seeks out the clandestine home of the monsters: Midian. There he unwittingly becomes their leader, and ultimately their savior. But the whole concept hinges on the fact that it is the human characters, such as the serial killer Decker and the brutal Sheriff Eigerman (Charles Haid), who are the *real* monsters, not Keen's impressive parade of creatures. Here the monsters were the good guys, working against the usual conventions of the genre. But it was a concept not everyone could so easily grasp.

Filming took place at Pinewood and on location in Canada, but owing to the sheer amount of make-up and other effects, plus the twenty-five sets that had to be built, the budget soon escalated (to a reported $20 million). Chris Figg resigned over disagreements with Morgan Creek, which entered into a distribution deal with Twentieth Century Fox. Fox was apparently expecting a *Hellraiser*-style film on a larger scale. What they got was something they'd never come across before and they didn't know quite what to do with it. At their insistence, new scenes were filmed and the running time—originally about two and a half hours—was heavily reduced.

But the worst part was Fox's marketing campaign, which promoted *Nightbreed* as a "slasher" flick, thereby completely misleading the potential audience. The result would be disastrous returns at the box office and a disillusioned Barker. "It was the worst creative time in my life," he later explained, "I felt there was so much I could have achieved and so many things that were getting between me doing that.... And I was painfully ignorant of

Clive Barker's early design for *Nightbreed* (courtesy Clive Barker).

the way that the politics of this business work."[1] Although *Nightbreed* would do well on video, its financial problems led to the collapse of Film Futures. This, coupled with New World going bankrupt, stranded *Hellraiser III* in its very own development Hell.

The main problem was this: because Barker had signed the *Hellraiser* rights away to get the first film made, they still belonged to New World, which now didn't exist. So who had the rights to make the next movie and would they even want to? The answer was erstwhile New World co-chairman Lawrence Kuppin who, together with Harry Evans Sloan and ex-Metromedia Broadcasting president Bob Bennett, formed Trans Atlantic Pictures. But there were reputedly some disagreements between Barker and Kuppin about this at the time, which inevitably led to Barker not being immediately involved in the project. Speaking in an interview with *Shivers* after the movie came out Barker said, "When I first heard about *Hellraiser III*, it was clear the production company ... didn't want me on board for financial reasons.... I was reasonably expensive and, frankly, I knew they wanted something cheap and nasty."[2]

Atkins was slightly more diplomatic in his explanation about Barker's lack of involvement: "I've got to be careful here, any explanation must be kept vague I'm afraid. Clive and the producers, unfortunately, couldn't come to terms about his participation in the project, meaning he has no hands-on or legal involvement with us. Of course, he's given us his spiritual support as guardian angels on a personal level."[3] Having acquired — or inherited — the theatrical and video assets of what was once New World, Trans Atlantic planned to bring out a number of sequels to their most successful movies; this would include *Angel IV*, *Wanted Dead or Alive II* and *Crimes of Passion II*. The third installment of the *Hellraiser* saga was scheduled to be the second in their line-up to go before the cameras, following on from *Children of the Corn II*. There was also some interest in *Hell on Earth* from Fangoria Films, who would have liked a co-production deal under the aegis of Trans Atlantic, but in the end this didn't come about.

Supposedly, one of the initial story ideas for *Hellraiser III* revolved around ancient Egypt. Back when it was still going to be a Film Futures-New World movie, Barker told Doug Bradley the idea was that the Great Pyramid was the very first Lament Configuration

Nightbreed poster artwork (courtesy Les Edwards).

to raise the Pharaoh. "It was one of those great conversations you only have with Clive," said Bradley, "and it was only after he left the dressing room I thought, well, that was great. Then I thought, no, hang on, that's not great because he's just told me that Pinhead will not be in *Hellraiser III*."[4] Luckily, with Peter Atkins scripting again and Barker refocusing this sun drenched preoccupation towards a possible Mummy remake, there was a shift towards tying up loose ends left in *Hellbound* regarding both Pinhead's origins and the torture pillar we last saw emerging from the bloodied mattress in Dr. Channard's home.

While *Nightbreed* was being made, a script was written which had Pinhead spending much of the movie floating around in a miasma made up of the various bits and pieces from the pillar, before being reincarnated and exploding out of a church altar. There was also an idea that the Lament Configuration could be a building this time and its corridors would make up the puzzle. All of these concepts made it into the finished movie, albeit in different incarnations: Pinhead does indeed explode out of the pillar, but the church scene comes much later on, and we are only given a quick glimpse of the Lament Configuration building right at the very end of the film — a story arc that would be completed in the ensuing film, *Hellraiser: Bloodline*.

However, just before the film's release, Atkins put paid to rumors that they had considered setting the movie in a bordello, turning Pinhead into a sort of Jason Vorhees clone. "Truthfully, that was just me shooting my mouth off because I was so worried the money men would turn him into a stalk and slash figure. A worry based on good reason, I might add, as one famous quote from a nameless New World executive shows. He said, 'Can't we get Pinhead on the streets beating up youths?'"[5] Tony Randel was also very much involved in the genesis of *Hell on Earth*'s plot, which is why he received a "story by" co-credit with Atkins, and was going to direct the movie himself until he, too, had a falling out with the producers, who thought he would make it too dark.

The first official draft of the screenplay was begun in March 1991 and completed in May. It contains much that should be familiar to fans of the finished movie, as the basic storyline remains intact. Rich, young, and successful nightclub owner J.P. Monroe spots the torture pillar in an antiques and curios store and buys it. Wannabe TV reporter Joanne "Joey" Summerskill then stumbles upon the story after witnessing a man from the club being torn apart by hooks and chains in a local hospital. The man was brought in by a punkish woman called Terri, who used to be Monroe's girlfriend. Joey's investigations lead her back to the club and she enlists Terri's help. Meanwhile she is having terrible dreams about her father's death in Vietnam, and it is through these that Pinhead's human half, Elliott Spencer is able to warn her that his demonic self is about to be unleashed upon the world. Pinhead, trapped inside the pillar, is awakened by a few drops of Monroe's blood. He then is able to make his escape by devouring one of Monroe's female conquests, Sandy, then Terri, and then finally Monroe himself, though not before talking the nightclub owner into doing his bidding. The script works towards a confrontation between Pinhead and Joey/Elliot, with J.P. and Terri brought back as Cenobites.

But there are also significant distinctions. When J.P. first arrives at the store there are "bums" in the street outside, used as a comparison to the one inside that "sells" him the pillar. The scene with the boy in the hospital is minus the head explosion, a homage to Frank's swansong on the original *Hellraiser*— although we do get a very apt description of the chain assault as "some vile variation on the Indian Rope Trick."[6] Monroe's nightclub is called Under the Underground, which was later changed to The Boiler Room. There's no sign of the barman or the DJ who work in the club, and who would be transformed into Cenobites themselves, but the workers J.P. employs are described as ethnic, which gives us a further insight into the man's exploitative character. There's much more character interaction between Joey and Terri, especially when she allows her to stay in her apartment. The scene on pages 28–32 includes a particularly relevant and poignant piece of dialogue by Joey, in which she tells her guest about a boy in a neighboring block who they can see through the window sitting staring at an empty pigeon coop:

JOEY: I don't know his name.... I saw the whole story. There was a wounded bird on his roof. I could hear its cries from here. He went straight to it. I couldn't have. I'd be frozen between pity and fear. But he wasn't. Its pain spoke directly to him. He picked it up. Caged it. Nursed it. Fed it. And it got better. Every day I'd watch him sit there. And every day he'd watch the pigeon. And every day the pigeon would watch him. I saw him learn. Learn that there was one more thing he had to do to make the rescue complete. And one day, just as afternoon became evening, he leaned over, opened the cage, and he walked away. Didn't look back. But he heard the sound of its wings...[7]

Terri is, of course, Joey's very own wounded pigeon whom she tries to help and, inevitably, has to let go.

Joey's car, a Mazda 323, makes more of an appearance — specifically during a ride to the store and during the climactic chase at the end. The store itself, like the nightclub, underwent a change of name. Here it is called Carducci's Antiques (soon to become the Pyramid Gallery, perhaps an in-joke referencing Barker's Egypt idea) and Mama Carducci herself is a minor character who lets Joey and Terri into the shop. Expositionally she isn't needed — having Terri break into the store further emphasizes her wayward nature and misspent childhood — but Mama Carducci does represent a missed opportunity to introduce another piquant character into the *Hellraiser* universe.

Sandy, the girl Monroe beds, is dragged to the pillar by a pair of hands rather than the chains that add a welcome special effect in the finished movie. And her life force is simply drained out of her, à la Julia and Frank's victims. In addition, we see more of the documentary footage of Kirsty in the Channard institute. The touch of irony where she says "And it might be metaphorical to you, Doctor, but you haven't had some blue-faced bastard come at you with hooks and chains"[8] cannot fail to raise a grin.

But the vast majority of the differences are towards the end of the screenplay, beginning with what happens at the nightclub. Whereas in the movie we are privy to some of the things Pinhead does to those poor unfortunates trapped in the club, here the scene ends with him contemplating what he is about to do: "A small smile forms on his face. He's just had an entertaining idea."[9] When we return to this location we find that, "The building that housed Under the Underground looks like a bomb hit it. Smoke and debris litter the streets. So do corpses."[10] Following this is a scene where Pinhead encounters two policemen on the streets who are beating up a runner for a drugs gang.

The exchange between Pinhead and the Elder Cop is comparatively out of character, though, and doesn't quite gel.

ELDER COP: I have the distinct impression I told you to fuck off. Unless I miss my guess, you've just disobeyed an officer of the law.
CLOSER ANGLE ON PINHEAD
— as he emerges into the (dim) light in the alley.
PINHEAD: I am the law.
ANGLE ON COPS
— as they halt in shock at this awesome presence, both of them instinctively drawing their guns. And both instinctively beginning to back up.
ELDER COP: You're one butt-ugly son of a bitch and you're about to be put down.
DIFFERENT ANGLE — ALL THREE
PINHEAD: I am the son of eternal night and you are about to discover pain has no ending.[11]

The first line of dialogue is so synonymous with the comic book character of Judge Dredd it would be hard to imagine Doug Bradley delivering it seriously (even if this was four years before the Sylvester Stallone movie). And the latter, though beautiful in its own right, jars against the utterances of the cop. The idea of turning the entire alleyway into a torture alley is a tantalizing one, though, and forcing the elder cop to pierce his own tongue with a handcuff bracelet counts as one of the most original torments in the entire *Hellraiser* canon.

The sequence where the Cenobites chase Joey down the street is gone, and while the controversial church scene is present it is the priest who faces Pinhead alone. All this is happening as Joey races home in her car, to find Pinhead waiting for her, "Like a spider or a lizard ... flat against the ceiling, his arms outstretched for balance."[12] This is a little too reminiscent of one of the best scenes in 1990's *Exorcist III* (William Peter Blatty), where one of the patients in the hospital looks down on George C. Scott's character from the ceiling.

Joey lures Pinhead through the window of her apartment, which she used to travel to Elliott's dream plane earlier. As in the film, it is in the Quonsett Hut where Elliott first opened the box that the final confrontation takes place. In this version both Pinhead and Elliott "erupt," then their essences merge together in the reflection of Elliott sitting cross-legged on the floor. The frozen scene comes to life and as Elliott works the box again in 1921 the box opens in 1992. In a replay of the first scene from *Hellbound*, the hooks and chains take hold of Elliott and Joey finds herself back in her apartment, alone.

Yet a number of extra twists await. Because the box is now open in her time, when Joey walks through to the kitchen she finds herself in Hell with Pinhead waiting for her. "Oh, no kiss of welcome after seventy years?" he says.[13] This is where we meet the Cenobitized versions of Monroe, Terri and Doc, Joey's cameraman. In one of the most dramatic and, I think, more satisfying changes, Joey must make her own Faustian deal with the Devil. The script has her dressed in Hell's bridal gown, "bound tight in a black leather bustier with decorative metal attachments.... The only flash of color amidst all this black are her blood red elbow-high gloves ... no ... as she gets closer we see it's real blood, as if she has dipped her arms elbow deep in a pool of blood. The skin exposed between blood and bustier is a rich Cenobitic blue."[14] Joey walks up the aisle of her own accord, taking Pinhead's hand — and then the camera pulls out through the circle of the puzzle box, just as it did at the end of *Hellraiser*. We discover the box is in "Ms. Summerskill's Office," on a plinth inside a bell jar. Seated behind the desk is a more confident and successful variant of Joey. All her dreams have come true, she is now a TV celebrity with her own show. Brad, her boss at the station, is now beneath her. A final bit of dialogue ends the movie perfectly:

> SUMMERSKILL: You have to ask yourself, Brad — What do I really want ... and what am I prepared to pay? You have to ask yourself ... The Question.
> BRAD (off): The Question?
> SUMMERSKILL leans her elbows on her desk, interlocking her fingers and leaning her chin on the bridge they make.
> She stares straight ahead — at BRAD and us. A mysterious smile plays about her lips.
> SUMMERSKILL: What's your pleasure, sir?[15]

A backwards nod to the previous films, the lines also make more of the romantic possibilities between Elliott and Joey. This was also an undercurrent in the Pinhead/Kirsty relationship and because, to all intents and purposes, Joey takes Kirsty's place in *Hell on Earth*, one option was to make her the bride.

But as with *Hellbound*, there would be more drafts and the screenplay eventually fell in line with what we saw on the screen. It wasn't an easy process, something Atkins confirmed when the task was completed: "Every time someone made a stupid suggestion,

I would ... give 'em an earful. And, thank God, they listened — even if it did take four different versions of the script and more drafts than I care to remember to get it where it is now."[16] This would filter out some of the components mentioned, completely revamp the climax, add two more "Pseudo Cenobites"— C.D. and Barbie — an on-foot pursuit through the streets, the construction site scene, a deception involving Joey's father, and her triumph over Pinhead. The box also became more of a driving force for Pinhead, because if it is in his possession he cannot be sent back to Hell, and it would be the catalyst for turning the office block not yet built into a veritable shrine to the Lament Configuration.

There is just one more point to mention with regard to the script: the wavering between English and American settings completely disappeared. *Hellraiser III* is told against a backdrop of an American City — unnamed in the first drafts of the screenplay, but most definitely New York when it came to filming. Those holding the purse strings were insistent this time. Besides which, it would be virtually impossible for the film to cling to its English origins now that almost all the cast were American and the movie was slated to be shot in North Carolina. But, ironically enough, the director chosen to replace Tony Randel at the very last minute, though he lived in the U.S., was in fact British himself.

Born in 1964 in London, Anthony Hickox came from a family of successful cinema people. His father was Douglas Hickox, who directed *Entertaining Mr. Sloane* (1970) and *Zulu Dawn* (1979). He was also the man responsible for *Theatre of Blood* (1973) starring Vincent Price, which he helmed at the behest of his horror- and Hammer-loving son. His mother, Anne V. Coates, edited such well-known classics as *Lawrence of Arabia* (David Lean, 1962) and *The Elephant Man* (David Lynch, 1980). Both Anthony's brother, James, and his sister, Emma, followed her into this line of work: James was assistant editor on two of Anthony's movies (*Waxwork II* and *Hellraiser III: Hell on Earth*), and Emma also edits for a living. As if that wasn't enough, Hickox's great-grandfather was none other than Lord J. Arthur Rank, founder of the famous Rank Film Company. Hickox's contributions to cinema were slightly more modest; indeed, he began his career in front of the cameras rather than behind them.

After some commercials, television and film work as a child, Hickox thought about pursuing acting when he grew up, and this explains why he always makes cameo appearances in his own films (in *Hell on Earth* he's a dying Vietnam soldier in Joey's dreams). But his father had other ideas, "When I was young I vividly remember my dad throwing down the *Spotlight* book (an actor directory used by casting agents), saying, 'Most of these people are starving! Is that the sort of career you want?'"[17] He bought Hickox an 8mm camera to experiment with and took him to work, in order to steer him towards making movies. Hickox decided to go to film school, but with no A or O levels, it wasn't going to be that easy. Thankfully, the London College of Printing gave him five days to make an 8mm short as part of the entrance exam. Hickox used Ralph McTell's famous song, "The Streets of London," as inspiration and his father helped him to acquire a photographic model for the film. The College liked what he'd done and he was accepted onto their Foundation Course, which lasted four years.

After all that hard work, Hickox dropped out two months in and changed direction completely. The club scene was taking off in the early eighties and he tried his hand at this. While this experience would make him eminently qualified to get inside the head of J.P. Monroe's character later on, he almost wound up running nightclubs for the rest of his life. It was his girlfriend at the time who provided the impetus for change. Daughter of actor Simon Ward, Sophie Ward convinced Hickox to direct again. He wrote and filmed the

16mm short *Rock-A-Bye Baby*, which he financed with his own money and which Sophie starred in. Helping out again, his father also facilitated Vincent Price's role as narrator.

It eventually came to the attention of stage and film producer Michael White, best known for *The Rocky Horror Picture Show* (Jim Sharman, 1975), who asked Hickox to come in for a meeting. White wanted to know if he had anymore projects lined up, and Hickox told him about a cheap sci-fi flick he was trying to get off the ground called *Death Star* (which coincidentally Bob Keen was set to work on). Hemdale had agreed in principle to finance the picture for $800,000, so White paid for Hickox to travel to Los Angeles to close the deal. The director flew to New York instead and took the Greyhound bus on to L.A., due to his notorious aversion to flying, but he heard nothing after the meeting. Fortunately, White backed him to the hilt, telling him that he'd sort out anything he needed over there.

Finally Hickox got his lucky break when he met Stefan Ahrenberg of Vestron Pictures, who showed interest in yet another project he was developing. This one was called *Waxwork*, about students who visit a waxworks chamber of horrors in an old dark house, only for the exhibits to come to life. On the same day Vestron agreed to make the movie, Lorimar made an offer, but his loyalty was with the former company, which put $1 million into the venture. The 1988 movie starred Zach Galligan—famous for his role in Joe Dante's smash hit *Gremlins* (1984)—as Mark, and cult starlet Deborah Foreman as his companion Sarah. It also featured ex-Avenger Patrick Macnee, while Bob Keen was called upon again to re-create the gallery of famous monsters from filmland.

Waxwork definitely set the tone for Hickox's early work: derivative, but well-paced, visually stimulating, with interesting camerawork, and tongue firmly placed in its horror-comedy cheek. It was something the director justified by stating, "When we made *Waxwork*, horror comedies weren't the big thing aside from *Monster Squad*, so I felt it was quite original to spoof the genre."[18] He also saw it as a clever way of getting around the ratings system. The movie was due to be released in 1,200 cinemas, but then Vestron's title *The Unholy* did badly at the box office and Vestron got cold feet. Nevertheless, the movie found its niche on video, doing extremely well financially. This had two consequences: first, Vestron were impressed enough to payroll Hickox's next venture, a spoof vampire-western; and second, Electric Pictures bought the rights to *Waxwork* and offered Hickox $2 million to direct a sequel. The first of these, *Sundown: The Vampire in Retreat* (1991), was a self-confessed homage to Polanski's *The Fearless Vampire Killers* (1967) that revolved around a peaceful vampire town called Purgatory. Enter the great-grandson of Van Helsing (a bespectacled Bruce Campbell) who has tracked down the oldest of them all, The Count (David Carradine). Throw in a splinter group threatening to destroy the community, and you have the essence of the movie. Interesting ideas, such as six-shooters that pack wooden bullets, sit well alongside jokey one-liners (when she becomes a bloodsucker, one woman moans, "What am I going to tell my mother?"). But there are some distinctly soap opera moments—exacerbated by the presence of *The Colbys*' Maxwell Caulfield—and the action appears overblown and staged. If it did nothing else, the director claims it taught him the "real nuts and bolts of film making,"[19] although the more relaxed method of filming would prove time-consuming and led to his next film being made at breakneck speed.

Waxwork II: Lost in Time (1992) was another parody. Gallagher returned to reprise his role from the original, but with model Monika Schnarre replacing Foreman. The protagonists are not confronted by waxworks of the monsters on this occasion, but are transported via a time bubble to meet them personally. Martin Kemp's Dr. Frankenstein rubs

From left to right: writer Pete Atkins, director Anthony Hickox, producer Lawrence Mortoff and effects man Bob Keen. *Hellraiser III: Hell on Earth* publicity still (photograph credit: Keith Payne).

shoulders with Dr. Jekyll and Mr. Hyde, Godzilla, and a shopping mall full of zombies. Hardly the credentials, you might think, for a *Hellraiser* director — a concern broached by Barker himself. "I was nervous about this choice. I wasn't a fan of his previous efforts.... He's a slick cameraman with movements to match and he makes great-looking pictures. But I didn't have a great deal of faith in his story abilities. I made this quite clear when he came round my Hollywood home to discuss the film. I told him in no uncertain terms that I hoped, (a) it wasn't going to be funny, and, (b) he told the story properly. These were the two main obstacles in my view."[20]

His supporters, on the other hand, felt that it would make a huge difference that he wasn't directing one of his own screenplays. In any event, the opportunity itself arose immediately after the filming of *Waxwork II* because of a good turn Hickox had done. After giving movie insurance broker Buckley Norris a small role in the film as the judge, Norris repaid the favor by mentioning Hickox during dinner with Larry Kuppin. Hickox received the phone call in the middle of the night asking if he would like to do *Hellraiser III*, "And I was like, yes, I wanna do *Hellraiser III* please. And that was basically it."[21] But the director did admit to being concerned not only about the rigors of having to start another film so soon after one had wrapped but also about his change in style: "This represents a major U-turn in my directorial approach. I'd be lying if I said I wasn't worried about pulling it off."[22] What did help was Hickox's admiration for the first two films, something that would give him a pointer as to how to pitch number three.

The next step after securing both the writer and a new director was casting. With only two actors from the previous films returning—Bradley as Pinhead, and Ashley Laurence as Kirsty (her scenes were filmed on a barren dubbing set with a video camera long before the movie began shooting)—the task of filling the vacant roles remained. It was something Hickox found both exciting and frightening: "It was scary, but there was an amazingly good response because people want to be in *Hellraiser* movies. We basically auditioned people. Terry Farrell came in first and she was great."[23] So great that the director started dating her after they worked together on the movie, Hickox having something of a reputation at the time for romancing his leading ladies. The beautiful twenty-eight-year-old Iowa-born actress had already starred in a number of TV shows and films. She first appeared as an Elite Model in Robert Goralnick's *Portfolio* (1983), reflecting what she did for a living before acting. Next came a part as Laurie Caswell in the TV series *Paper Dolls* in 1984, then as Nicki Phillips in *The Cosby Show* in 1985. She featured in *The Twilight Zone* and *Family Ties*, both 1986, and *Beverly Hills Madam* with Faye Dunaway.

She gave up her promising career to live with actor Mickey Rourke for a few years, but was ready to start again by the early nineties. Hickox had wanted Farrell to star in *Waxwork II* but it clashed with a commercial assignment, so he promised if the lead in anything else came up he'd contact her, little realizing that would be a *Hellraiser* movie. For the young actress it would mark something of a comeback, and would almost immediately springboard Farrell to her most prominent role as Dax in *Star Trek: Deep Space Nine*. Speaking about her character, she said she saw Joey as "A driven career woman who has not come to terms with her father's death. It is because of his death in Vietnam that she has a connection with Elliott. He is able to come into her world in her dreams."[24] To prepare for her role she studied tapes of TV reporters and read a book by famous journalist and television producer Linda Ellerbee.

The substantial part of J.P. Monroe went to thirty-year-old Kevin Bernhardt, who had something of a soap opera background. Bernhardt had starred in *General Hospital* as a temporary replacement in 1984, then as Dr. Kevin O'Connor (1985–1986) and in *Dynasty* as Father Tanner McBride during 1989. The intervening years saw him feature in the European films *Le Feu sous la peau* (Gérard Kikoïne, 1985) and *Escuadrón* (José Antonio de la Loma, 1987), as well as Charles Norton's actioner *Kick or Die* (1987). Genre fans would also remember him for a stint on the appalling *Superboy* television series in 1989. Bernhardt had the same dark good looks as Sean Chapman, which was quite appropriate as the characters of Monroe and Frank have much in common.

For Monroe's girlfriend and pivotal character, Terri, they plumped for relative newcomer Paula Marshall, who in spite of playing a woman younger than Joey was in fact the same age as Farrell. Coincidentally, Marshall had also been in *Superboy*, though much later than Berhardt, but it wasn't her first brush with a comic book hero. Her inaugural role was as John Wesley Shipp's girlfriend in the pilot of DC's *The Flash* (1990). Subsequent TV work took in the crime series *True Blue* and *Mancuso, FBI* (both 1990), and she would later go on to star in *Grapevine*, *Life Goes On*, and coming of age show *The Wonder Years* (all 1992). Marshall's look combined just the right amount of vulnerability and attitude. It was an important casting decision, because along with Bradley and Farrell she would make up the third member of the nucleus of characters at the very heart of *Hell on Earth*. As Hickox explained: "This one was really driven by Doug and Terry and Paula. If they didn't work, that movie would be a disaster."[25] The director was so impressed that he used her again, not once, but twice, in *Warlock: Armageddon* and *Full Eclipse* (both 1993).

For Joey's cameraman and friend, Daniel "Doc" Fisher, Lawrence Kuppin had the perfect actor in mind. A friend of his, Ken Carpenter, had just the look they were after: a rough and ready jobbing technician, one of the unsung heroes of the media that holds the reports together. Carpenter's first taste of film work, and of genre work, was on Brian De Palma's *Phantom of Paradise* (1974), a rock reworking of the famous *Phantom of the Opera* story, with, aptly, elements of Faust included. In this he played another behind the scenes hired hand, almost prophetic considering Doc's calling. On TV he was A.L. Alexander in *The Lindbergh Kidnapping Case* (1976), but there was a considerable gap before 1989's children's adventure *Spirit of the Eagle* (Boon Collins). Apparently Hickox thought that the tall, bearded man was too cleaned up for the film — a process which involved a hair trim — but he still managed to retain that earthy, hard-working appearance. The movie would also mark his first time playing a monster, when Doc is transformed into the Camerahead Cenobite, of which Carpenter enthused, "It's incredible. I'm fascinated with what I have to play with in this movie. I sat there in awe as they were applying my make-up ... and I thought, I've become another person. I don't know who I am...."[26]

Veteran actor Clayton Hill was chosen to play the priest who opposes Pinhead in the church scene. Hill had started in show biz at a very early age, singing in beer gardens with a three-piece combo when he was just six years of age. When he was a teenager he sang on the radio station WTAE-Pittsburgh, then after the army and drama school he took the role of lead zombie in George A. Romero's *Dawn of the Dead* (1978), for which he also served as weapons coordinator. He worked again with Romero for *Nightriders* in 1981, as second assistant director. Adding further strings to his bow, Hill also did some stunt work and location scouting for films.

Peter G. Boynton secured the part of Joey's father, who still haunts her dreams. His first role was in *Big Apple Birthday* (Nick De Noia, 1978) as the Frog Prince. Boynton appeared in *The Catlins* TV series as Beau Catlin (1983–1984), before taking a role in Luis Aira's *Miloha* a.k.a. *The Pool* (1987). Aimée Leigh — sometimes created as Aimee Lee — joined the cast as Sandy, the blonde whom Monroe has sex with before discarding her. Her portfolio consisted of an uncredited part in Russell Mulcahy's cop thriller, *Ricochet* (1991), alongside Denzel Washington and Ice T. According to Hickox and Bradley,[27] she apparently hadn't read the script, and wasn't at all happy about the bedroom scenes with Bernhardt. She was eventually talked around, but only if the actor covered her breasts with his hands — which, if anything, adds an even more perverted twist.

As for other minor parts, this wasn't "Blond Nurse" Sharon Hill's first medical role, as she had starred as the unfeasibly-named Nurse Flovilla Thatch in Russ Meyer's *Beneath the Valley of the Ultra-Vixens* (1979); "Female Cop" Shanna Teare had been a stuntwoman on Hickox's two *Waxwork* films and *Sundown*; "Male Cop" Bob Bragg had been stunt coordinator on those films as well as many others; "Second Male Cop" Bob Stephens had also worked in the stunt industry — most recently on *Cape Fear* (Martin Scorsese, 1991), while Brent Bolthouse from *Waxwork II* filled in as the DJ, a dual part shared by an uncredited Eric Willhelm as the C.D. Cenobite. Young Bobby Knoop and Hickox's brother, James, played yuppies, and the go-go dancers were ably brought to life by Tonya Saunders, Angela Thomas, Kim Ball, Cassandra Perry, Anna Marie Isaacs and Flame.

"Of course," admitted Hickox afterwards, "there were lots of people that were friends of friends and anybody who would actually arrive who could act in Greensboro would be grabbed and put into a part."[28] There were even producers onscreen. Larry Kuppin is a derelict, and Lawrence Mortoff the tramp who sells J.P. Monroe the statue, not to mention Pete Atkins returning to acting as both the barman and the fire-breathing "Barbie" Cenobite.

On the production side, the crew was made up of virtually all new people. But after working on *Nightbreed* and *Waxwork II* production designer Steve Hardie was more than qualified for the assignment of making places like Joey's flat and the nightclub a reality. Taking over from Robin Vidgeon was cinematographer Gerry Lively, who had worked with Hickox on *Waxwork II*. Editing chores would fall again to another Hickox regular, Christopher Cibelli, from both *Waxwork*s and *Sundown*, and James Hickox. Costume designer Leonard Pollack had also worked on the first *Waxwork* and *Sundown*. Completing the team was art director Tim Eckel.

It was left to Bob Keen and Image Animation to bridge the gap from the first two movies, but at the same time they came to the project having worked on Hickox's movies as well. Keen and his crew were the ones primarily responsible for the look of the new Pseudo Cenobites. On board in the make-up department was Paul Jones as make-up effects

Gary J. Tunnicliffe's first *Hellraiser*, pictured here with helper Fiona Leech (courtesy Gary J. Tunnicliffe).

coordinator, Martin L. Mercer as make-up artist and Gary J. Tunnicliffe as part of the make-up crew. The latter, who had worked on the short-lived forerunner to *Buffy the Vampire Slayer*: *She Wolf of London* (1990), would also be responsible for the Lament Configuration boxes and would play a huge part in the *Hellraiser* story from this movie onwards.

Possibly the most worrying news, though, was that Christopher Young would not be scoring the film. Four years after Barker wanted to use Coil for the soundtrack of *Hellraiser*, *Hell on Earth* was all set to have a full-blown rock soundtrack. The makers gathered together some of the most original heavy metal musicians around to lay down their songs. Obviously, some would be used for scenes within J.P. Monroe's nightclub, Armored Saint, for example, singing "Hanging Judge." But others would be there just for the sheer hell of it, including a genuine "Hellraiser" song performed by Motorhead, with lyrics by Lemmy Kilmister and that famous Prince of Darkness, Ozzy Osbourne. Other artists and songs on the soundtrack included "Divine Thing" by the Soup Dragons; "What Girls Want" by Material Issue; "Go with Me" by Ten Inch Men; "I Feel Like Steve" by the Electric Love Hogs; "Waltzing with a Jaguar" by the Chainsaw Kittens; "Baby Universal" by David Bowie and Tin Machine; "Down, Down, Down" by House of Lords; and "Troublemaker" by Triumph. Unfortunately, upon test screenings it was decided to cut back on their usage in the main body of the film, with a cinematic soundtrack taking its place.

That job went to Randy Miller, whose first score had been for the 1988 movie *Witchcraft* (Rob Spera). Miller was given just over three weeks to compose an hour's worth of music, which — due to budgetary constrictions — would be performed by Russia's Mosfilm State Choir and Orchestra. Miller became the first American to score a Hollywood film in the newly privatized Russia, spending ten days there recording the material. However, he himself had concerns about their ability to play the score he'd written and their recording techniques: "You can throw the most difficult music in front of an American studio orchestra, and they'll be able to play it in a minute," he said, "but Mosfilm wasn't used to that quick pace, and it took a lot of rehearsals to get the score right. I insisted on a certain level of excellence, and while the Russians may have gotten a bit annoyed with me during rehearsals, they were glad that I pushed them."[29] Much of this annoyance is translated into the music, making it the angriest *Hellraiser* score yet. The subtler, more suspenseful moments with violins—for example in the track "Back to Hell"— are suddenly interrupted by violent booms and a repetition of the composer's main *Hell on Earth* theme. A more pacy, action oriented melody, this is at times disjointed and has none of Young's majesty. Thankfully, Young's themes do appear sporadically, as in "Cenobites Death Danse," used in its entirety for the opening credits sequence, but here they only serve to remind us that the days of the first two movies are long gone. Miller did, though, come up with a memorable new theme for "The Pillar," which he uses again in "Elliott's Story." None of this is to say that Miller's score is bad; it simply reflects how different *Hellraiser III* is to its forebears.

Shooting began in late 1991, with Bradley and Atkins being flown over to the U.S. and meeting Hickox for the first time. Said Bradley, "I didn't meet Tony until I got to North Carolina, which was my first experience of working in the States. And I just got on with him straight away. Maybe the English sense of humor thing worked as well? It was a curious kind of crossover point. It was the point at which the A-Team, so to speak, who had been responsible for *Hellraiser* and *Hellbound*, were starting to move out of the equation. But Pete was still there, Bob Keen and the Image Animation Team was still there, and I was still there."[30] Atkins, who was needed on hand in case there were anymore changes to be made to the script, summed it all up more succinctly: "I guess we're not in Cricklewood anymore, Toto," he commented to Bradley as they were driving to film a location scene, "and it sure ain't Pinewood."[31] The movie itself was shot in Greensboro and High Point, a tiny town which is the furniture capital of America. It would double as the New York setting, and a furniture factory would be transformed into the Boiler Room. In complete contrast to the conditions on the first movie, the studios were right at the back of the hotel, with one huge soundstage and four sets which were within walking distance of each other — good in one sense, but quite difficult if the second unit films a scene at the same time as the first in close proximity, especially when working at such a fast pace.

Undoubtedly this was one of the major criticisms of the shoot. Zach Galligan had remarked during the filming of *Waxwork II* about the speed Hickox worked at: "The first two or three days were difficult, getting used to the pace at which Tony operates. He does 50 or 60 set-ups a day, which is almost unheard of. It's three times more than I usually do, and there are no stand-ins, so we're constantly on the set, constantly working."[32] The fact that there was only an eight week break between that movie and *Hell on Earth* seemed to do nothing to slow the director down. It was something that Bradley saw as a downside as well. "Clearly Tony enjoys working fast and doesn't mind the long hours. Yesterday, I clocked up my longest day ever, seventeen hours in total. It has to be fast to achieve everything in the six weeks Trans Atlantic Entertainment allotted the production. But you can't linger to get things right and that's frustrating."[33] Hickox also preferred to edit in camera, which again speeded things up but occasionally made it very difficult for the actors. In effect they were working in close-up with just the storyboards to give them some idea of how the finished thing would look.

Bradley also experienced a number of other problems on the set. The first was his scenes inside the giant Pillar of Souls. The actor had to hold on to two bars inside and put his head through the gap; not the most comfortable of positions. And deprived of any movement other than facial, Bradley had to make his words count even more. It is a testament to his dedication, and to Atkins' writing that these Pillar scenes work so well. The next concern was make-up related. With Paul Jones taking over from Geoff Portass, when it came to applying the make-up there were noticeable changes. The application was much faster, with the look totally redesigned. There were fewer pieces of latex and the nails were now plastic instead of metal, which helped them sit better on Bradley's face. But they had a tendency to bunch up, making it not quite as clean as the first two make-up jobs. This might be the reason Bradley has said it is his least favorite make-up of all the films.[34] Pinhead's flesh color is also different, more beige than blue-white, not helped by some of the lighting effects and a completely misjudged dream sequence where he is filmed outside in a field. Meant to be seen on a set or at night, the make-up simply doesn't look right in daylight. One good thing, though, was that Bradley was able to find an optician in Greensboro who could make him prescription black lenses. Whereas before he had only been able to wear the contacts for twenty minutes at a time, now he could comfortably shoot scene after scene.

A final concern revolved around the shooting of the climax when Elliott and Pinhead are seen at the same time. As he related in his diary for *Fangoria*:

> Saturday, October 19 — It's a positively schizophrenic night for me as we shoot the climactic confrontation between Pinhead and Elliott, starting out in human form and switching to Cenobite at about 2 a.m.... I'm completely tripped out by the sight of Pinhead standing there, waiting for me. Kevin, my stand-in, has won the nomination to double Pinhead. I point out that he's the only other person ever to have worn the full Pinhead make-up and costume.... I suddenly realize just how jealously protective of the character I've become. It is deeply unsettling for me.[35]

A *Fangoria* cover showing that schizophrenic moment when Elliott and Pinhead merge (courtesy Starlog Group).

But in spite of these niggles, Bradley was more than happy during his time in the U.S. His part had more depth, he got to perform as both a human and a monster, and he had nothing but praise for both the production team and the film's director. In several different interviews he's claimed that *Hell on Earth* was one of the happiest working experiences he's had.

The smoothness of the shoot and professionalism of the crew were also noted by both Alan Jones on a set visit for *Shivers* and *The Dark Side*, and Philip Nutman for *Fangoria*. Nutman's visit coincided with the filming of the scene fourteen days into principal photography where the Pseudo Cenobites are harassing Joey on an abandoned work site. "The director talks his young thespians through the next shot. It's taken from Joey's point of view, as J.P. and the female Cenobite (Marshall) circle her, while Barbie, Camerahead and C.D. advance from the background."[36] After four takes, everyone was satisfied and they set up the scene again to film it from Pinhead's point of view. The only major reproach was about the skimpiness of Marshall's costume—fishnet stockings and a leather bodice in the freezing cold of a winter's evening.

By the same token, Jones's interviews with Atkins, Bradley and Hickox reveal a general air of conviviality about the shoot, with the possible exception of some unrest when it came time to film the black mass scene. Hickox had already been refused permission to film in an actual church — hardly surprising, given the content of the scene: Pinhead's very own reworking of a Christian sacrament — so a matte background would have to be painted around the Church's aisle and altar. But, due to Carolina being in the heart of Bible Belt country, many members of the crew were startled by the display itself, murmuring "sacrilegious" under their breath, according to Jones. Hickox's reply to that was, "Is it really so controversial? I don't see it as that, well, no more than Christopher Lee storming around a church setting light to curtains in umpteen *Dracula* movies. The crux of the sequence is that Pinhead fights back against the power that abandoned him. So the Church fights back, too, by crumbling around him and turning into Hell, the one place he doesn't want to be."[37]

Aside from a little healthy rivalry in the acting stakes between Marshall and Farrell, which Hickox actually welcomed because it meant they upped the ante in their scenes together, there weren't that many more obstacles during the filming itself. These, it would seem, were being reserved for post-production. The first problem came in the shape of the infamous EDIFLEX editing technology that Larry Kuppin suggested Hickox use, because he owned the company. But the process itself proved incredibly onerous, involving banks of videos in the editing bay. It was so time-consuming that in the end they had to revert to film. By this stage, the independent distribution company Miramax had picked up *Hell on Earth* for an American release and a rough cut was shown to them.

This is where the story splits into two versions, depending on who is telling it. Hickox maintains that Miramax's co-owner, Bob Weinstein, who wanted to pick up a horror franchise and start Dimension films, saw a rough cut and loved it. But he asked the director, if he had a week more to shoot and some more money for effects, what would he do? Hickox told him that he'd like to add some more substance to the nightclub scene where Pinhead attacks the revelers, and redo the ending. So he was given the time and budget to do just that. This is how *Hellraiser III* became a groundbreaking film in terms of special effects technology.

Computer Generated Images, or CGI, was still only in its infancy in Hollywood. A few artists had dabbled with this new toy, one of the earliest examples being the Knight from

Young Sherlock Holmes (Barry Levinson, 1985). But it wasn't really until James Cameron's spectacular *Terminator 2: Judgment Day* (1991), with its impressive liquid metal T-1000, that people in industry circles started to take notice. *Hell on Earth* was the first horror movie to utilize CGI, expressly for the scene where a glass of liquid solidifies and spears one woman in the face, Sandy's skinning — and morphing effects when Joey's father turns into Pinhead, as well as when Elliott and Pinhead merge. Remember, this was still a year before Steven Spielberg popularized CGI with his blockbuster *Jurassic Park*.

Conversely, Clive Barker has a different recollection of events. In his version, Larry Kuppin showed him a rough cut of the movie, which Barker was less than impressed with. "I told him that although it contained some great moments, there was a lot of stuff missing; the ending wasn't right, there was no climax, I didn't understand some sequences, and in parts the story was incomprehensible. But, true to his [Hickox's] skills, it was beautifully composed and photographed, the actors were nicely framed and the images did look slick."[38] According to Barker, the low budget was also to blame when it came to the less than impressive effects.[39] Barker says he turned down an offer to put his name to it, wished Kuppin good luck, then returned to his own duties serving as executive producer on *Candyman*, an adaptation of Barker's own story "The Forbidden." This would be around the time that the Miramax deal was struck.

A few weeks later, Barker reports that Bob Weinstein called and asked for his honest opinion of the film, which he gave him. As he'd done with Kuppin, Barker told him what he thought were the weaknesses, so Weinstein asked if he could come in and fix these. Once more, Barker declined because he felt that the changes would be too extensive. Barker also felt that more special effects filming needed to be carried out. But Weinstein was extremely

Pinhead with rock band Motorhead (courtesy Shelly Berggren, Singerman Entertainment).

NOSTRADAMUS PICTURES
OFFICE (919) 889-4403
FAX (919) 889-4495

CALL SHEET

HELLRAISER III

7:00 A.M.

DAY _MONDAY SEPT 23 1991_
_1_ DAY OUT OF _34_
CREW CALL _7:00 A_
SHOOTING CALL _8:00 A_
LOCATION _620 Francis St_
HIGH POINT N.C.

PRODUCER: _MORTORFF_
DIRECTOR: _HICKOX_
SUNRISE _7:18 A_
SUNSET _7:15 P_
WEATHER _Lo 60 HI 70_

SET	SCENE	CAST	D/N	PAGES	LOCATION
INT- HOSPITAL EMERGENCY ROOM — NOTHING TO REPORT AT HOSPITAL	3	3, 6	N-1	2 1/8	STAGE
INT- HOSPITAL CORRIDOR — BOY WHEELED IN	4	3, 4, 12, 13	N-1	3	↓
INT- HOSPITAL EMERGENCY ROOM — BOY DIES	5	3, 12, 13	N-1	1 2/8	↓

CAST & DAY PLAYERS	PART	LEAVE	MAKE UP	SET	REMARKS
1.					
2.					
3. Terry Farrell	Joey		7:00A	8:00A	REPORT TO STAGE
4. Paula Marshall	Terri		9:00A	10:00A	
6. KEN CARPENTER	DOC		7:00A	8:00A	
12. ROB TREVEILER	PARAMEDIC #1		W/N	W/N	
13. CHRIS FREDERICK	PARAMEDIC #2		↓	↓	↓

ATMOSPHERE AND STANDINS
1 - NURSE (NIKKI STAND IN) 7:00 A
1 - TEENAGE BOY 8:00 A
1 - DOC / 1 - NURSE (SHADOW IN) 10:00 A

SPECIAL INSTRUCTIONS
VIDEO PLAYBACK: JOEY (IN CAMERA) Need working Camera with monitor

KFX: DANGLING CHAINS ON BOY,

BFX: CHAINS DROP TO FLOOR, EKG MONITOR SPARK & SPUTTER

OPFX: Electric Energy runs along chains, Fibrillator Pads arc

SET DRESS: HOSPITAL
PROPS: T.V. CAMERA CREW STUFF, CELL-PHONE,

ADVANCE SHOOTING

DATE	SCENE NO.	SET	CAST	LOCATION
SEPT 24	5PT	INT-N- HOSPITAL To complete Boy dies	3,12,13	STAGE
SEPT 25	48, 41PT, 50, 18, 20	INT-N- DOCS BEDROOM Doc wakes up goes to club INT-N- J.P BEDROOM JP and Sandy get it on and then Pinhead	5, 6, 8	↓

UPM Phil Smoot   1ST A.D. Paul Martin

Second unit schedule for *Hellraiser III: Hell on Earth* (showing scenes were shot back-to-back for *Children of the Corn II: The Final Sacrifice*) (© Trans Atlantic Entertainment).

keen to get him involved. Said Barker: "So I did a deal with Miramax ... to remake and remodel the picture."[40] This included, according to Barker, the addition of Farrell's bondage scene at the end, many of the insert deaths for the nightclub and the extra CGI for the girl's skinning (while Hickox says that this was inspired by a commercial he saw where the "skin" was pulled off a car). Barker's standpoint was that Hickox was very good on the set, making decisions and handling actors extremely well, but it is during the postproduction period that the film is truly made. This painstaking task took time to get right long after the shoot was over. "There's no trace of accusation in my comments," Barker added. "We all have our own ways of working and that's obviously the way Tony works best."[41]

Whichever way one looks at it, *Hellraiser III* needed quite a bit of work before it was released. But Barker's involvement in postproduction meant that now not only would the film receive a Clive Barker Presents and executive producer credit at the beginning, the makers would also be able to call on him to publicize the movie while he was doing the same for *Candyman*. Although he saw *Hell on Earth* as being representative of one type of horror film — the in-your-face variety — and *Candyman* as being more suspenseful and subtle, he declared he was proud of both of them. He even agreed to direct the *Hellraiser* video for Motorhead's rock song, a one-day shoot of seventeen hours. In this, Motorhead are performing in a large Hellish space to "The Damned," creatures characterized by their prosthetic claws and beaks, while props from *Hellraiser III* decorate the background. As Pinhead enters, the demons thrash about to the music, then he takes a seat and drinks blood from a boiling cup. In a further scene we see Pinhead playing cards with Lemmy, lead singer of Motorhead — all intercut with clips from the movie.

"While I hadn't been invited to the party at first," Barker said afterwards, "I turned out to be the surprise guest only too happy to join in the festivities late in the day!"[42] And what festivities they happened to be. Upon screening, *Hellraiser III: Hell on Earth* endeared itself to the fans, with horror audiences generally warming to the cranked up action. But while the movie notched up another gear with regard to energy and pace, it didn't sacrifice the story to do so. At its very core, the third film in the series contains some very piquant themes and propositions.

12

COMPLETING THE PATTERN, SOLVING THE PUZZLE, TURNING THE KEY

War is Hell

There is really only one overriding theme in *Hellraiser III*, that of warfare. This permeates the movie to such a degree that it can be felt — if not always seen — in almost every frame. On the most obvious of levels, we have the blatant homages to films like Francis Ford Coppola's masterpiece, *Apocalypse Now* (1979), and the thought-provoking motion pictures of Oliver Stone — chiefly *Platoon* (1986) and *Born on the Fourth of July* (1989). The Vietnam flashbacks that Joey experiences when she is dreaming about her father could have been lifted directly from any of these. The iconography is exactly the same, the death sequences comparably harrowing, the tone unmistakably grim. When Joey, walking through this terrifying landscape in a white, billowing nightdress, claps her hands to her ears and closes her eyes to shut it all out, we can sympathize. We do not want to be confronted with the reality of war any more than she does. But for her there is an added sadness, the pain of loss associated with the death of her father in that conflict. He represents all those who never made it back alive from the jungles of Vietnam, and she, in her own way, represents those who were forever changed by what they had seen there.

Through this imagery, the film deals with not only the visual trauma of battle but also its devastating aftermath: the effect it has on those waiting at home for their loved ones to return. Her father's demise has had such a profound impact on Joey that it still has the power to reduce her to the helpless child she was when she heard the news. In her dreams she reverts to this state, calling out to the soldiers who leave her father behind: "Where are you going? My Daddy's still alive. Come back and save my Daddy!" It is this weakness that Pinhead exploits when he pretends to be Joey's father. "Daddy," she shouts again as she runs to him, falling into his embrace. It is the safety she yearns for, which was denied to her because of the war, but which will be denied again by another battle entirely.

Yet it is not just the after effects of the Vietnam war that the movie dwells on, but of every war throughout history. To quote Elliott Spencer, "A dream of one war is a dream of all wars." We see Terri alone in Joey's flat, reading a book about battles of the twentieth century, but the way *Hellraiser* actually underscores this point is by exposing us to the horrors of the First World War in graphic detail, using the character of Elliott as our escort. Basically, it was the rigors of World War I that drove Elliott to become Pinhead. As he explains to Joey while he strolls through the streets of India in 1921, "The war pulled poetry out of some of us. Others it affected differently.... I was like many survivors, a lost soul with nothing left in which to believe but gratification. We'd seen God fail us ... so many dead. For us, he too fell at Flanders. The war destroyed my generation. Those that didn't die drank themselves to death. I went further. I was an explorer of forbidden pleasures; opening the box was my final act of exploration. Of discovery." This is backed up by Doug Bradley on the audio commentary to *Hell on Earth*:

> Just before we came out to film it, there was a documentary on the BBC about survivors of the Somme and one of the guys said this extraordinary thing I just grabbed hold of, talking about all his comrades who had died on the first day of the Battle of the Somme — something like 60,000 British troops were killed or injured in the first twenty-four hours. He felt as though he had cheated, that he was in the wrong place, that he shouldn't have lived, that he should be dead and he should have been buried along with his comrades in France. And I thought that's exactly Elliott's thing. That's exactly what leads him from there to this."[1]

Two different characters, two different generations, both affected in different — but no less devastating — ways by the wars that impinged on their lives. It drove Elliott and Joey to search for something, perhaps a meaning for what had happened? And it shaped who they were later to become. In the case of Elliott, his search was for the Lament Configuration, for answers to the great questions about what we are and what's beyond this reality. He assumes, quite wrongly, that nothing can be worse than the horrors he has already seen. His own search will draw out the monster inside him, the dark side of his nature that, possibly — although we are not shown this — somehow enjoyed being in charge of those men on the battlefield. Like Channard, who was transformed into a warped version of his former self, Elliott is Cenobitized and turned into another commander of sorts: working for Leviathan in charge of the other demons. "Monster that I was," he tells Joey, "I was still bound by laws. Hell has its commandments, too, you know." As Elliott Spencer he followed the orders of his superiors, for King and Country — and for God as well. As Pinhead, those same orders now came from another god entirely.

For Joey, it is the constant search for reasons: the reason why her father was left behind, what really happened to him, where he is now, and maybe even the reason for war itself. In her dreams she has been searching for those answers since she was little, but never finding them. Her own personal Hell. But it is this investigative temperament that has caused her to become a journalist. These are traits which will help her to unravel the puzzle of where the young man in the hospital emergency room came from, and what the box he was clutching really is. Two searches, at different times, initiated by completely separate wars, will nevertheless draw Elliott and Joey together. And it is worth observing that both their quests can only be completed within the limbo world between Heaven and Hell, rather than in either of their own realities.

In an effort to enforce this war theme, the film parallels scenes, linking past and present, unreality and reality. Joey's first experience of Elliott's "dream" is in the trenches of World War I. She walks through the muddied channel, dead bodies littered on either side of her, close-ups of cold, staring eyes and body parts. Joey tries not to look, but again she can't shut any of this out. Stepping up into No-Man's-Land, she walks over to meet Elliott for the first time, the churned up ground and barbed wire recalling scenes from Lewis Milestone's superb *All Quiet on the Western Front* (1930). Later, when she tracks Pinhead down to the nightclub, she finds the victims of his rampage, and once more has to walk through the death and devastation — nightmares even more grotesque than the First World War could offer. Young men and women hung up by their tongues, with pool balls stuffed into their mouths, electric lights wrapped around their heads and dice inserted into their eyes. The scene also echoes those illustrations by Gustave Doré from Dante's *Divine Comedy*, a credit to the talents of production designer Steve Hardie, DP Gerry Lively and the effects team. But the true horror is brought home to her when she walks into the room filled with candles and discovers her cameraman, Doc, sitting with his severed head in his lap. As if to compound her grief, Pinhead offers, "Oh, it's unbearable isn't it? The suffering of strangers, the agony of friends. There is a secret song at the center of the world, Joey, and its sound is like *razors through flesh*." Two battlefields separated by 80 years (as well as the veil between waking and dreaming), the remains of the dead scattered over them both. Each, in equal respects, a Hell on Earth.

Similarly, the Vietnam scene, with its gunfire and helicopters, mirrors the sequence when the Pseudo Cenobites chase Joey down the street at nighttime. *Final Destination*-style explosions abound, electricity cables crackle, the current conducted by the water running down the road — the result of fire hydrants bursting — and the police shoot at the creatures to no avail. Instead of returning fire with bullets, the Cenobites have in their own arsenal: fire, spat out blow-torch-fashion by the Barbie Cenobite, sharp and lethal Compact Discs— thrown by the C.D. Cenobite — and a deadly extendible camera lens with which Doc (a.k.a. Camerahead) punches holes into his victims' craniums, harking back to the method the Alien used to dispatch Harry Dean Stanton's character Brent back in 1979. "Ready for your close-up," he grunts before the kill, and "That's a wrap!" just afterwards. This street has suddenly become a war zone.

When the Terri and J.P. Cenobites corner Joey at the building site — a barren stretch of land which closely resembles the setting for Stanley Kubrick's own Vietnam epic, *Full Metal Jacket* (1987) — we see that the one directing this conflict is Pinhead. Standing above them and watching, he has orchestrated their movements like a general moving toy soldiers around a board. It was a connection director Hickox was eager to make: "There is a strong analogy between warfare and how Pinhead learns to kills people. Because Pinhead was a human being in war, I am really saying that he has learned most of his methods of killing from human beings, not from any Devil."[2] And Pinhead admits he is acting out this role himself: "They're handmade, a shadow of my former troops. Over eager, but let them play. Our game will come later." Terri, J.P., Barbie, Doc and C.D. are all unwilling conscripts in his army (Monroe even emptied a whole round of bullets into him, which Pinhead spat out one by one) but they are necessary, as he does not want to dirty his own hands. It is interesting that in earlier drafts of the script Pinhead was seen to do things physically, such as putting the handcuff through one policeman's tongue; there was even talk of him using the sharpened C.D.s to kill instead of the DJ. However, now even the killings at the club are done at a distance — by Pinhead psychically manipulating not his troops this time, but whatever comes to hand. And, of course, the obligatory hooks and chains. Even though he is "unbound," he is still Pinhead and it would go against his modus operandi to have him connect in any other way to his victims.

The Key to Dreams

Dreams are an essential element in *Hellraiser III*. As we have seen, they hold the key to bringing Elliott and Joey together, but dreams hold a much greater significance for the characters than simply as doorways. Joey's nightmare is a manifestation of the failure in her own working life, her inability to break through the glass ceiling in the television industry. Her true dream is to be a reporter, or have her own TV show. At the start we see her in the hospital waiting for a story to come up, but her first gig which is not reporting about "kindergarten kids"—once again linking her to childhood and children—seems to have coincided with the only day when nothing newsworthy is occurring. Pictured through the blue viewfinder, a color which prefigures her later dealings with the Cenobites, she bemoans: "It's as if death took a holiday. It's a mystery to me. A mystery to me how those assholes at assignment knew it." As Doc points out, there's no way they could have bought off every accident victim in the city—it is just a case of her bad luck again. To add insult to injury, Doc is called away just before the man with the chains arrives, so there is no video evidence of what happens in the emergency room. This further compounds Joey's failure, but it does pique her curiosity enough to follow up the lead.

"The story of your life," Doc says before he leaves, "could be just around the corner." The story of Joey's life up to now has been the story of many women's lives in the late '80s and early '90s, a battle in itself for recognition in their chosen fields. We're given a sense of this when she's back at the studio, and co-worker Brad is commenting on her technique after a recent TV appearance. This seems to involve Joey showing more thigh so she'll get noticed. In an early script this sexism is even more explicit:

Brad: What, you think I'm kidding? I guarantee it. An inch more flank. Boys upstairs get hot. Bingo, you're an anchorwoman.

> JOEY: (to herself) Jesus Christ ...
> DOC: Ah, give her a break.
> DOC leans over and stops the tape.
> BRAD (to DOC): What's with you?
> He swivels his chair round to face JOEY.
> BRAD: C'mon, Joey. I'm just trying to help you climb that ladder.
> JOEY: Yeah? The one to my bedroom window?[3]

The wonderful line, "I want to do it the right way. Tight stories, not tight skirts," survived intact, though. But the irony is Joey spouts this while wearing the shortest and tightest of skirts herself. It could be read that Joey already knows this is one way to make her dream a reality, and in spite of her protestations is just playing the game. Or were the makers of the movie just as guilty of this as Brad?—while they had Terry Farrell on hand they would exploit how she looked to please the horror audience? Certainly the S&M shots of her towards the end, strapped up in leather, are more for titillation value than anything else.

That said, Joey definitely follows in the tradition of feisty female reporters from the past, the most famous of which has to be Superman's love interest, Lois Lane—brilliantly rendered by Margot Kidder in the Richard Donner movie version from 1978. But the closest pure cinematic comparison must be Jane Fonda's character of Kimberley Wells from *The China Syndrome* (James Bridges, 1979). Wells, too, is a TV reporter hoping to advance from cutesy features to hard news, and she even has her own Doc in the shape of Michael Douglas's Richard Adams, whom she hires for a feature on nuclear energy. Like Joey, they just happen to be in the right place at the right time (depending on your perspective) when a crisis arises. It must say something about how the world has changed that this is exactly the predicament a man finds himself in as part of the premise for the recent *Bruce Almighty* (Tom Shadyac, 2003). Here Jim Carrey is the lowly TV reporter so desperate to distance himself from giant cookie stories that he uses the powers God (Morgan Freeman) has given him in order to *create* news, such as a meteor crashing just over his shoulder.

The all important "Pillar of Souls" under construction (courtesy Gary J. Tunnicliffe).

As the first ending stood, Joey's dreams—in the real world and in other dimensions—actually do come true. But the price she has to pay is allegiance to Leviathan. In the version that was made, Joey finds the "story of her life" but it gets away from her again. She thwarts the Pseudo Cenobites by solving the Lament Configuration, and sends Pinhead back to Hell. But there is no evidence, no footage to back up her story. She ends the film in exactly the same position, no further along the road to becoming that serious television reporter. So while victorious in one way, in another way Joey still remains a failure.

Elliott's dreams are, like Joey's, that of a war-torn landscape and a past he'd rather forget. Yet, although this is never stated outright, it is obvious he also yearns to return to his human state — much of this a tribute to Bradley's acting. Elliott's most immediate concern is to take back control of the Pinhead husk and prevent its rampage. But below the surface is a pining for love, for understanding — and companionship. The close-up when he shakes Joey's hand signifies a meeting of kindred spirits—literally. "Brave girl," he says admiringly, "probably never shaken hands with a ghost before, am I right?" But Joey is a ghost herself, like the Pseudo Cenobites a shadow of the woman she was and still could be. In her long, white nightdress, she unquestionably looks the part, and her haunting of the Vietnam scene denotes that she has much in common with Pinhead's alter ego. Elliott's haunts are the trenches, and the particular moment he solves the puzzle box in India. Frozen in time, a crossed-legged soldier sits holding the Lament Configuration, leaving his more mobile counterpart to wander through the dream limbo.

We are not shown J.P. Monroe's dreams as such, but one suspects they would revolve around power, sex, death and art. His bizarre and very dark taste in ornaments and paintings is what draws him to the pillar of souls— his club a haven for all manner of weird sculptures, like a baby covered in barbed wire and a hand protruding from a wall holding a heart (which it later crushes). The picture in his bedroom that Sandy admires just after their tryst depicts a blinded man screaming with his scalp opened up. "It's really ... really dark," she comments. (In the original script Atkins describes another painting here, called "Biker Crucifixion," a Hell's Angel stripped to the waist and tied to a tree with barbed wire.) Moments later she is skinned and sucked into the pillar by Pinhead who, in his speech to Monroe, paints a much more vivid portrait. "You enjoyed the girl," states Pinhead matter of factly. "Yes," Monroe replies. "Good. So did I. And that's all."

To Monroe she is one in a long line of women he has used for sex, trading on his station as owner of the club. For Pinhead she was nourishment. There is little to choose between each. "If you have a quality, let it define you, whatever it is," Pinhead continues, repeating the lines Monroe used to seduce Sandy. He refers to Monroe's art collection as "tawdry representations." What Pinhead is offering is the ability and imagination to use "the body as canvas, the body as clay. Your will, and mine as the brush and the knife." He knows that J.P. murdered his own parents with the gun he possesses, to gain their wealth and power. Just as the club owner seduced Sandy, Pinhead does much the same to Monroe with his promises of even greater supremacy and the answer to his wildest dreams: "There is a place at my right hand for you, Monroe. For a man of your tastes. Tastes I can help you to indulge. Flesh. Power. Dominion." As for any qualms he might have, Pinhead assures him: "There is no good, there is no evil, Monroe. There is only the flesh, and the patterns to which we submit it." And the first target of their attentions is another one of Monroe's conquests: Terri.

Terri is the odd one out in *Hell on Earth* in that she doesn't dream at all, not in the common sense of the word anyway. When Joey explains about her nightmares, Terri discloses, "I don't dream; never have.... Maybe it'd help if I slept sometime.... Just kidding." It's a source of concern and also of envy. "No, so it's always neat for me to hear about dreams. I'm jealous. It's like everyone has another world except for me, you know? Be nice to see something else. Have a nighttime world." As he does with Monroe, Pinhead uses this to control Terri. When Monroe's attempts to sacrifice Terri to the pillar go awry, Pinhead must talk her into drawing closer. She is poised at the door to Monroe's apartment, struggling with the locks, as he utters his first persuasions: "Do you know where you are? You are at the door to dreams, Terri." It is what she has always wanted and his enticement causes her to forget all ideas of escape.

"Now, there are two keys in this room," Pinhead continues, "One is in the pocket of this fool. You could take it out without me reaching you — probably. You could use it to let yourself back into the world you know. The world you've always known; banal, dreamless, hopeless...." "And ... the other?" asks Terri. "The other is the key to dreams, to black miracles, dark wonders. Another life of unknown pleasures. It's yours. Complete the pattern. Solve the puzzle. Turn the key." For someone who has never known such a life, it is an offer hard to refuse. In a reversal of what might have happened, Terri gives Monroe to Pinhead and consequently frees him from the Pillar of Souls. He holds out his hand, ready to give Terri her reward: to give her that nighttime life she spoke of—as a Cenobite who smokes through her throat and whose skin is pulled back so far up her arms it looks like she is wearing bloody gloves. "I can dream now," she tells Joey at the building site. "Oh, you wouldn't believe what I can dream of now...."

But these are not Terri's only dreams. Though firmly rooted in reality, her own dreams are about belonging, and someone who will love her. At first she believed she had this with Monroe. We can imagine him going through the same pantomime with Terri that he did with Sandy, offering her a rose, smooth talking her into bed. And just when she thought she'd found what she was looking for, he abandoned her just like everyone seemingly has done in the past. As she elucidates to Joey, "All I know is—this is it for me. Just me, my bag, and a series of shithead boyfriends." Her background is kept deliberately vague, but from the clues we are given we can easily piece it together. Terri is comfortable on the streets; she is able to break into the back of The Pyramid Gallery ("Five minutes, we're browsing"). She looks the part of a punk — or even a Goth — but underneath there is a loneliness reflected in her expression and eyes.

She's never been in a home like Joey's before, as her excited reaction shows: "This is great. And it's yours? You, like, own it? ... I've never owned anything. I haven't even had a room of my own since I was fifteen years old." Terri is over the moon when Joey lets her stay, so much so that she attempts to cook her breakfast. This goes horribly wrong, naturally, and the kitchen ends up looking like a war zone of its own. "Can I ask? Is it always this ... exploratory?" Joey ventures. "Ha! I don't know yet. First time. I'm a kitchen virgin." She can't cook, can barely look after herself, let alone anyone else. Atkins' scene about the wounded bird would only have driven home the message that Terri would give anything to stay with Joey, to be her friend. It is a dream that Pinhead shatters to lure her back to the club, leaving a false message at Joey's about a nonexistent job in Monterey. Terri assumes she has just been using her, like everyone else, and flees the apartment. A scene only recently reinstated shows her sitting in a café with a cup of coffee, staring at the couples having intimate conversations. It is then that she sees a reflection of Monroe's face in her coffee and we know her fate is sealed.

The final important dream is, of course, Pinhead's. It is to be free from the Pillar, free from Elliott — his "conscience"—from Leviathan and all his duties. Free to do whatever he wants on Earth. Given the opportunity he will shape the planet in his own image, creating a Pseudo Hell. "My evil was too strong," Elliott tells Joey. "It hid, waited.... The shell of the beast has been fleshed. What I was is out there in your world, unbound. Unstoppable." Only Joey stands in his way.

Devil's Radio

It is wholly appropriate that a film which used such innovative special effects should also have a technological theme running through it. The most prominent examples of this all have a link to communication devices; the first featured in *Hellbound* as well, right at the very start. Instead of drawing us through the circle on the side of the Lament Configuration box — as Barker did in *Hellraiser*— we enter the movie via an old-fashioned radio dial with a needle pointing to various cities of the world, London, Paris, Nice, Moscow, Oslo— a hint that the story is about to open up globally.[4] The voice of a BBC World Service announcer filters through as we pan along a table with Elliott's belongings on top: the jacket of an English army officer in India, a gun in a holster, a fly brush and helmet. This radio was used once again in *Hellraiser III* in the scene where Joey wakes and hears a transmission coming from downstairs. She takes it out of her wardrobe and turns the knob, tuning in to Elliott's signal, which instructs her to go to the huge window of her apartment. But as an audience, we see that the radio is not even plugged in. Like the Limousine and Ham radios in *Orphée*, it is a means by which to convey information across dimensions or even between the living and the dead. And like the radio in the unmade sequence with the Evangelist and Kirsty in *Hellraiser* it can be used to issue warnings.

A more modern spin is put on this in *Hell on Earth*, when Elliott uses television to talk to Joey — fitting, as she works in the TV industry. He does this through the set in her bedroom and the monitor where she works. The latter comes just after Joey has watched the tape of Kirsty that Channard made. This in itself is communication through time — and a passing of the baton from one heroine to another. "I don't know what else to call them," Kirsty informs Joey through the blue-gray tinted screen, "Demons ... demons live in the box; it's a gateway to Hell." Her hand movements show Joey how to work the Lament Configuration, information that will prove vital later: "It kind of opens itself. Your fingers move and you learn. It wants to open, that's the thing." Then Elliott appears in a haze of static to reinforce her words. "She's telling the truth, Joey," he cautions. Like the ghosts of *Poltergeist* (Tobe Hooper, 1982), Elliott is forced to choose an up-to-date piece of technology to commune. In a similar way to Carol Anne (Heather O'Rourke) in that movie, Joey will have to pass through a barrier in order to meet the ghosts on the other side. But like the TVs in David Cronenberg's surreal cult classic, *Videodrome* (1983), the recorded images have much more sinister overtones.

Joey's unplugged TV shows her reports of mayhem from the Boiler Room club, which spur her to go. But she calls Doc first to meet her there. He flips through the channels but cannot find the report she means (only a quick glance of Anthony Hickox being interviewed and a clip of *Waxwork*). This is why she feels so guilty about his death, because *she* sent him to the club, all of which makes the next scene so much more compelling. When Joey stops to rest in the street during the climactic chase sequence her likeness appears on the multiple TV screens behind her in a shop window. Just as she was at the start of the movie, Joey is framed by Doc's viewfinder, trapping her in the square. Now the camera is housed in Doc's head, replacing his right eye, a cable running from it into his chest. The Pseudo Cenobite uses his zoom to kill an innocent man passing by—and he is somehow also able to fire projectiles at the police cars out of the lens. Yet he is not the only one to employ technology for killing.

Pinhead utilizes moving piston parts from Monroe's beloved motorbike to slay him initially, implanting them into the side of his head. Joey then sees the club owner hanging from the ceiling on his bike, dead. At the end he is brought back as another Pseudo Cenobite, the pistons pumping in and out, imitating the Japanese film *Testsuo*'s fusions of man and machine (Shinya Tsukamoto, 1988). "Relax, baby. This is better than sex," he promises Joey, flicking his tongue in and out of his mouth. The DJ who works in Monroe's club suffers a similar fate. One of the victims of Pinhead's massacre, his own spinning C.D.s hover above his head, then imbed themselves firmly into his skull and mouth. Pinhead subsequently brings him back as the C.D. Cenobite (a particular fan favorite) with the compact discs still protruding, a uniform distance apart. These are the weapons he uses to murder people, with a robotic whirring sound.

C.D. Cenobite is the epitome of technology used for evil in *Hellraiser III*. Replica figure by NECA (courtesy NECA; photograph credit: Nicolle M. Puzzo).

Hellraiser: The Next Generation

Though there are no actual family ties between the characters in *Hell on Earth*—if anything one of the few things they have in common is their very lack of family connections—they can very easily be read as the antecedents of the characters in the first two movies. Joey is able to take on Kirsty's role in the series as the female protagonist, almost "becoming" Kirsty for the purposes of this story. And there are overwhelming parallels between the two women. Both have been left fatherless, though Joey's loss happened much earlier in life. Both are independently minded, with a knack for thinking on the spot and getting themselves out of trouble. Both have been drawn into the mythos by accident. But, perhaps most importantly, both have been given young charges to look after. In Kirsty's case it was Tiffany, her "sister" and guide in Hell. Joey's lost soul is Terri, who will guide her to the club, and eventually to Hell on Earth.

They, too, could be described as sisters. Terri looks up to Joey and even unconsciously emulates her. Terri's behavior after she meets Joey definitely changes; we would not have seen her reading books before, and the investigation into the Pillar of Souls gives the young girl a taste of what Joey does for a living. She tells Monroe on the phone with hope in her heart, "Joey's going to get me a job at the TV station, and I'm meeting a lot of new people." Even so, there are moments when Joey adopts a more maternal position. It's obvious she disapproves of Terri's smoking, saying, "I'm trying to quit," when she's offered a cigarette. She takes over in the kitchen after Terri makes a mess, and the expression on her face when Terri is about to break into the Pyramid gallery is one of concern — even though it will get her the answers she wants. This is why we get a sense that Terri is actually leaving home when she departs from Joey's. Disappointed by her surrogate mother's behavior, she retreats into the arms of the bad boy lover, a scenario familiar to many parents with teenage daughters or sons.

For his part, J.P. Monroe's resemblance to Frank is uncanny. He could almost be one of the bastard children Frank Cotton must have fathered in his travels around the world. Monroe sports the same dark hair and good looks, the same hedonist tendencies, and the same attitudes towards women. Like Frank, Monroe has bedded countless women over the years and none of them have meant a thing to him. He has used them for his own gratification, then told them to get out, just like he does with Sandy. "Who do you think you are?" she says. "I'm J.P. Monroe, right? You stupid little bitch. Gimme back my shirt and get the fuck out of my life." But, like his predecessor, he has to turn on the charm when he wants something from a particular woman. In this film, Terri stands in place of Julia, and Monroe is able to talk her into returning to his apartment. The difference is, he doesn't ask her to kill for him so he can be whole again. He needs to kill *her*.

If we are even the slightest bit unsure about his origins we need only listen to his supplication when trying to persuade her to join him by the statue. "Come to Daddy," he sneers. And his phallic weapon? Not the flick-knife that Frank preferred, but a large silver pistol. Terri once again becomes the Julia figure when she takes her revenge on Monroe, rolling him closer to the pillar so that Pinhead can feed on him. "Hell hath no fury," Pinhead utters, "except for a woman scorned." Like Julia in *Hellbound*, Terri delivers her reprisal for all she has endured at the hands of her very own Frank. She may not take as much delight in it, crying as she struggles to kick the prone body, but one cannot help making the comparison.

In another reading altogether, Pinhead himself becomes the Frank figure. Imprisoned in the Pillar of Souls, just as Frank was trapped in Hell, he waits for someone to set him free. This occurs when Monroe, alone in the club and hearing a noise inside the statue, reaches inside one of its crevices (a scene, Hickox says, which was modeled on the tree beast test from *Flash Gordon* [Mike Hodges, 1980] where novice Peter Duncan has to play a form of Russian Roulette with Timothy Dalton's Baron). He is bitten by a rat for his trouble, the creature's own revenge for what happened to its cousin in the first movie, when Frank sliced it open with his knife. Here it is Monroe's blood that wakes Pinhead, so in this sense J.P.

is an imitation of poor Larry. But when Pinhead is talking him into supplying more flesh and blood, Monroe becomes Julia, sweet-talked into doing what the more charismatic figure demands.

It could be said that Elliott is the true father figure in the film — at least to Joey. There is an ambiguous admiration between them, love possibly, which also perfectly mirrors what was happening with Kirsty and Larry. Hickox has stated outright that there's more than a hint of this in their relationship:

> Elliott manages to bring her to his domain by entering her psychic level. Because she is concentrating on her career, Joey does not have any love interests. So Elliott offering her the task of fighting Pinhead is probably the closest thing to a love interest. He comes along and offers her responsibility, something which people have not been doing because she is a woman. In the end, he makes Joey feel useful.[5]

But it's much more than this. It is appropriate that Hickox should say that Elliott "enters" Joey's psychic level. He connects with her on a level no one has ever done: in her mind, in her dreams, the kind of intimacy only lovers share. He respects her; he respects her abilities. This is why in the earlier draft of the script, when Pinhead and Elliott merge, Joey is taken as their bride. It is a desire that spills over into Pinhead's consciousness as well.

If we are to read Joey as a replacement for Kirsty, then that longing is now transferred to Joey. Pinhead recognizes the similarities himself when they first meet face to face at the club. "I'm here to stop you and send you back to Hell," she says, which straightaway sounds very familiar. "Oh, spirited? Oh, good, oh, *very* good," he finally says to cap off their exchange. Just like old times, the pleonastic banter, the sexual tension. Pinhead and Kirsty played an identical cat and mouse game in the first two movies, but he gets closer than ever before with Joey, even to the point of wrapping her up in leather bonds and suspending her from the ceiling. One imagines that Pinhead would be anything but a gentle lover.

Finally, the Pseudo Cenobites, though the offspring of Pinhead in *Hell on Earth*, are more correctly the progeny of the three main Cenobites from *Hellraiser* and *Hellbound*. Immature and, as Pinhead points out, over eager, they might be a shadow of his former underlings, but they do correlate to them quite closely. Just as Chatterer preferred the hands on approach — grabbing Kirsty and silencing her in the first film — so too do C.D. and Doc. And Barbie, comparable to Butterball in size and shape, crashes through walls just like his forefather smashed through the debris of that collapsing house on Lodovico Street. Terri, who also looks suspiciously like the Female Cenobite, is just as eager to get Joey to play as her "mother" was to entice Kirsty. While the former ran her hook along the wall and made it bleed, the Terri Cenobite runs her hands over Joey's body and burns her with lit cigarettes. Their demise is also akin to that of Barker's Cenobites. When the puzzle box is solved at the building site, it blasts them with a beam of light — blue this time instead of yellow — which causes them to vanish.

Alter Egos

The last theme to consider is that of the alter-ego. Every main character, and some of the peripheral ones, in *Hellraiser III* has a dual identity. The Pinhead and Elliott scenario exemplifies this in the most extreme way possible, by splitting one personality into two. Elliott and Pinhead are two sides of the same coin and can't — or shouldn't — exist in isolation. Without Elliott, Pinhead is even more terrifying than he was before and less in control of his anger. His performance at the Boiler Room proves that he cannot restrain himself (indeed, he doesn't want to), and his lack of patience when dealing with Joey is telling. Elliott is therefore Jekyll to Pinhead's Hyde, a necessary part of him that needs to be returned.

Terri, Monroe, the Bartender, D.J. and Doc are all transformed into Pseudo Cenobites, monsters that reflect what they once were. Like Channard before them, their Cenobitization contains some element of their human selves. For example, we see the barman mixing drinks behind the bar at the Boiler Room, while a sudden gush of flame erupts behind him. This translates into him spitting fire from his mouth and throwing cocktail bombs. The others we have already discussed, all changed but with something linking them to their former selves, whether it be CDs, a camera, motorbike parts or cigarettes.

Joey's alter ego is her dream-self. The Joey that struggles to make it through the day in the real world becomes a vision in white gliding through this other reality. Her personality changes when she makes this transition, regressing mentally to a young child (yet another trait she shares with Kirsty). But what of the means she uses to travel to Elliott's plane of existence? Like the Lament Configuration being disguised as a puzzle box, this particular doorway is the window in her apartment. Obviously based on the mirror doorways from Cocteau's *Orphée*, and continuing the trend of putting hands through mirrors set in *Waxwork*, some credit must also be given to Lewis Carroll's famous tale, *Through the Looking Glass*, from 1871.[6] The thematic likeness between Joey and Alice is plain. As Camille Paglia observes in her introduction to a reprinted 1990s illustrated version: "On her travels over meadows and through the woods, Alice never turns into Huck Finn, a smudged vagabond scamp. She remains the well-bred young lady, her crisp apron and pinafore undisheveled even when she falls into a pool of tears or rockets up and down, bizarrely changing size."[7]

Joey's real-world persona might swear, get dirty and generally play dirty, but her dream self is exactly the same as Alice during her adventures. Simply compare Joey's "walk into madness" that she makes through the window to this description in Carroll's novel:

"Oh Kitty! how nice it would be if we could only get through into the Looking-glass House! I'm sure it's got, oh! such beautiful things in it! Let's pretend there's a way of getting through into it somehow, Kitty. Let's pretend the glass has got all soft like gauze, so that we can get through. Why, it's turning into a sort of mist, now, I declare! It'll be easy enough to get through." She was up on the chimney-piece while she said this, though she hardly knew how she had got there. And certainly the glass *was* beginning to melt away, just like a bright silvery mist. In another moment Alice was through the glass....[8]

Joey's apartment has, it would seem, its very own alter ego on a par with her own. And one which lets her gain access—either in bed while asleep, or through the window—to this dream-self she has created.

13

Pinhead Unbound

The Cult of Pinhead

A lot had happened between the making of *Hellbound* and *Hellraiser III*. Not only had rights changed hands, directors been swapped, and the storyline altered dramatically, but the character of Pinhead had taken on a life of its own. If his popularity had increased between the release of *Hellraiser* and *Hellbound*, then by the time the cameras rolled on *Hell on Earth*, it was at an all-time high. Doug Bradley had been Guest of Honor at *Fangoria*'s Weekend of Horrors in Los Angeles in 1989 — it wasn't the last invitation he would receive — and recounts a humorous incident in his book, *Behind the Mask of the Horror Actor*, whereby he had to get past immigration guards in the States:

> "You're an actor? You work in horror movies? What've you been in, maybe I seen you?"
> "Well, do you know the *Hellraiser* movies?"
> "*Hellraiser*? Oh man, that's my favorite! But I don't remember you in that."
> "Don't you? You know the guy with the pins in his..."
> "No kiddin', man! You're Pinhead." Handshake, handshake. "Would you mind signing your autograph?"[1]

A somewhat typical reaction. Bradley was being recognized on the street more and more. He found he couldn't just walk around the dealers' room at the convention without being encircled by Pinhead fans. But all this was something he could definitely relate to. "I've gotten used to being a cult figure now," he said during an interview to publicize *Hell on Earth*. "All the attention came as a big surprise initially.... But I was a huge fan of horror movies before I wanted to be an actor. So I can put myself very easily into the minds of the people who've taken the character to their hearts."[2]

In light of this level of attention, it made sense for the filmmakers to focus on his character. Fans were demanding more of Pinhead on-screen, and additional information about his past — alluded to only briefly at the beginning of *Hellbound*. It was Hickox's belief that Pinhead had been largely unexplored and underused in the first two films[3] but both Atkins and Bradley were determined not to do anything that would go against the grain of the established character.

Atkins may have joked about Pinhead turning into a slasher-style villain, but some of this did actually manage to creep in. The slaughter scene at the Boiler Room comes as close to a Freddy Krueger nightmare sequence as *Hellraiser* ever will, in which as many original ways of killing people as possible are dreamt up. In the *Nightmare* series up to that point Krueger had murdered the residents of Springwood by strangling them with their own bedsheets, trapping them inside a school bus, drowning them, and even through television. Granted, the murderous activities of Pinhead are more sadistic, but the ploys with the drink morphing into a representation of his face, the razor-sharp CDs, and hooks that no longer just rake the skin but slice off fingers do smack of slasher film lore. Pinhead may not crack jokes per se, but his answer to Monroe's, "Jesus Christ!" is a wry, "Not quite." He is even called Pinhead for the first time — by Joey — implying that if he is going to become a serial killer icon he will need a nickname on-screen as well as off.

By the same token, it may not be Pinhead himself who is stalking Joey through the streets outside the club, but his creations do a very good imitation of slasher movie antiheroes, each with their own special powers, impervious to bullets, and unable to be stopped by the authorities. The fact that the location where the shooting took place was called Elm Street only adds to the irony. This is *Hellraiser* as an action-thriller, as a monster film, and as a gore film with set pieces to match — in keeping with its move to the U.S., where everything is done on a grander scale. It is exactly the opposite of the original film's intent, which made it stand out from the crowd back in 1987. We talked a little about the impact of the Cenobites in chapter 3, and the fact that their limited screen presence was a prime cause of our fascination with them. That particular enchantment resulted in saturation here. Our knowledge that the Cenobites were originally human meant we were suddenly able to relate to them on a brand-new level, sympathizing with their predicament, empathizing with their pain. When applied to the Pseudo Cenobites, whom we have seen as human beings throughout the film, this effect becomes even more perceptible. They cannot scare us with subtleties, so they must rely on theatrics.

There is also a link to be made between Pinhead and Hammer's Dracula. As I mentioned before, Christopher Lee's portrayal of the Count has much in common with Bradley's. They exude fear without having to do anything at all, and when physicality does come into the equation it is sometimes to the detriment of the character. When their animalistic qualities are caged, there is more cause for alarm. Dracula, also one of horror's most popular characters, was resurrected in film after film: from his debut in *Dracula* (Terence Fisher, 1958), to *Dracula — Prince of Darkness* (Fisher, 1966), *Dracula Has Risen From the Grave* (Freddie Francis, 1968), *Taste the Blood of Dracula* (Peter Sasdy, 1970), finally bringing the mythos up to date in *Dracula A.D. 72* (Alan Gibson, 1972) and *The Satanic Rites of Dracula* (Alan Gibson, 1974). By the third movie in the *Hellraiser* saga it began to look like Pinhead would be repeating the trend.

He was supposedly killed in *Hellbound* by Channard, yet he was back again in the sequel — revitalized, it has to be said, by blood. He also featured more heavily, something that the later films in the Dracula cycle did, too, banking on Lee's charisma and screen presence. Joey even stakes Pinhead in the heart at the end of the film. This was a resemblance Bradley noticed as well, but he was quick to highlight the differences: "It wasn't just going to be a typical Dracula sequel; O.K. so he died at the end of the last one, so let's get him back to life in a quick pre-credits sequence and get on with it. The whole *Hellraiser III* plot is driven by Pinhead's reincarnation and, in particular, resolving the conflict established at *Hellbound*'s climax where he'd split into two.... It's Elliott Spencer's story too."[4]

Herein lies the crucial distinction. By allowing Bradley to play dual parts, the movie not only catered to the fans who wanted to know more about the character, it also balanced out the time Pinhead spent on screen. It added a greater depth than one would ever get with a slasher villain, articulating and commenting on the monster within the film's narrative itself. We were not simply presented with a beast running amok, but with the yin to

Christopher Lee as Dracula (© Hammer Studios).

its yang. The predicament Elliott finds himself in also gives the filmmakers an excuse to let Pinhead off the leash; he is no longer tempered by his human side. Gone are his qualities of control and mercy, if such a word can be used about a Cenobite. This incarnation of Pinhead would not have let Kirsty go quite so easily, would probably not have bargained with her in the first place over Frank. His tendency is to act first, and think about the consequences later.

Another reason why we can never write Pinhead off as merely a slasher villain is the Shakespearian-like speeches he gives when imprisoned inside the Pillar of Souls. At this stage in the proceedings he has neither the freedom nor the strength to rebel, so is forced to use the "softly, softly" approach of his former self. As Elliott warns Joey, "He can be very persuasive ... and very inventive." These virtual monologues written by Atkins are what elevate the movie beyond the fright flick it could so easily have been. Unbound as he is, Pinhead is still Pinhead and cannot be distorted that much. Thomas Harris did this with the famous characters of Hannibal Lecter and Clarice Starling in *Hannibal* (1999), ending the novel with them living happily ever after together, a climax that was changed considerably when Ridley Scott made the film version in 2001. Even with these indulgences, the main crux of what made Pinhead so appealing is definitely still present in *Hell on Earth*.

The Church of Pinhead

We cannot end this analysis without looking at the religious implications of *Hellraiser III*, and what some might call blasphemous scenes involving Pinhead. The first time he appears, Monroe uses Christ's name to indicate his surprise and panic, which Pinhead seizes upon. No, he is not Jesus—but later in the film he mocks the Christian belief system by holding a black mass in a church. Joey seeks refuge in here during the chase sequence, and tells the priest that demons are after her. "Demons? Demons aren't real. They're parables, metaphors...." Right on cue, Pinhead steps through the doors and Joey points and says, "Then what the fuck is that?" He proceeds to shatter all the stained glass windows and melt a cross that the priest is holding. "Thou shalt not bow down before any graven image," states Pinhead, ridiculing one of the Ten Commandments. Going even further, he takes two nails out of his head and pushes them through the palms of his hands. Spreading his arms out wide, he tells them, "I am the way." (This was nicely prefigured by the sign on

Joey's bus at the start which reads: "Prepare for the second coming.") The flames on the altar candles rise higher and the window behind him shatters. Pinhead then forces the priest to eat some of his flesh in a warped take on Holy Communion.

At first sight this is controversial in the extreme. But what the casual viewer must understand is that in the context of *Hellraiser*'s mythos accepted religions hold very little sway. The Hell Pinhead belongs to is not the Christian one; as far as he is concerned that doesn't exist. Logically then, he doesn't believe in their God, either. Furthermore, this is Pinhead "unbound." He is no longer even listening to his own dark god, Leviathan, so why should he respect the one Christians worship? In addition, Elliott has already told us that, for him, God fell at Flanders, too. The War made him question his faith in religion, and this drove him into the waiting arms of Hell. So in this respect, the scene in the church can be construed as Pinhead's very own act of vengeance against God. This goes some way to explaining its relevance and importance to the movie.

"You'll burn in Hell for this," screams the priest when he sees the spoliation of his church. "Burn?" is Pinhead's reply. "Oh, such a limited imagination." We have already seen that the Hell of *Hellraiser* bears very little resemblance to that of the Christian belief system. And yet fire marks the characters of *Hell on Earth* as damned. The first shot of J.P. Monroe pans upwards from his feet to show him lighting a cigarette. Later, Terri does the same in Joey's apartment, the matches she has left behind indicating where she has come from. The barman at the club serves drinks as fire spurts up behind him: indeed, everyone under its roof is in danger because the very name of the place is The Boiler Room. In a newly restored scene, the barman also asks the DJ on their way out, "Wanna cigarette?" Only Joey is saved because she is trying to quit smoking. She momentarily gives in when Terri offers her one, but only keeps it lit for a few seconds. Joey doesn't light up *herself* until she is watching the tape of Kirsty. In the original script Kirsty was the one smoking, but here we cut between the cigarette clamped between Joey's fingers and Kirsty's hand movements as she mimes opening the puzzle box—a signal of the peril to come for Joey.

14

What Started in Hell

All things considered, reaction to *Hellraiser III: Hell on Earth* was much better than that of *Hellbound*, which might have had something to do with the commercial considerations of the film. As Phil and Sarah Stokes from the Barker site, Revelations, comment in the booklet accompanying a recent *Hellraiser* boxed set, "More accessible than the first two films, this was Pinhead Unbound, *Hellraiser* for the MTV generation, and beautiful American youths were finally slaughtered in great numbers. What the film lost in the glorious perversity of the original, it gained in scope, scale, pacing and sheer spectacle."[1] But there was none of the *Life of Brian* style furor the makers had expected due to the religious aspects of the movie — if there had been such a response it might have made even more money.

The movie had its World Premiere in Milan at the famous Dylan Dog Horror Fest in May 1992 — where they realized a full-on rock soundtrack didn't work. Its British premiere was at the London Film Festival later in the year, screening alongside Barker's *Candyman* and Sam Raimi's manic horror comedy, *Army of Darkness: The Medieval Dead*. Genre magazine *The Dark Side* sent along Nigel Floyd, who wrote that it erased "all memory of Tony Randel's disastrous *Hellbound: Hellraiser II* with its bravura camerawork, gruesome effects, nerve jangling sounds and adrenalised excitement." Actually, the camerawork was what a lot of people picked up on, especially Hickox's trademark deep-focus technique, where a character remains in the background while a close-up of another character fills half the screen (especially prevalent in the Pinhead/Elliott/Joey finale). While Hickox's apparent footwear fetish seems to have been ignored by all (close-ups of Monroe's boots at the start, Joey's high-heels in the hospital corridor and her bedroom slippers...), Floyd went on to call the movie "a worthy successor to Clive Barker's visceral, flesh-ripping original,"[2] with Atkins' skilful script receiving just as much praise.

Reviewing the film for *Monstroid*, Richard Griffiths gave it four skulls, commenting that it was "much better than it deserves to be ... a cracking example of what sequels are all about." Picking up on the fact that it was a showcase for Pinhead — "but who cares" — Griffiths also credited Atkins for taking "the useful bits of the original *Hellraiser* mythology and then adding a whole lot more as the main story twists around clever subplots, all the time building to the exciting climax."[3]

Variety also seemed impressed this time, crowning the movie a "well produced effort" that is "an effective combination of imaginative special effects with the strangeness of author Clive Barker's original conception." Its review singled out Farrell and Bradley's performances: "Farrell is a strong heroine binding the film together, and British thesp Doug Bradley is a commanding presence as Pinhead, while also doubling sans make-up as the good guy captain." Sheila Johnston of *The Independent* was more offhand in her praise, saying, "It is competent and accomplishes the small feat of being better than its predecessor." But the tabloids were more forthcoming, the *News of the World* drawing attention to the "gut wrenchingly imaginative special effects ... truly shocking," and *Today* stating that *Hell on Earth* was "great entertainment for those who love being frightened out of their skin." *The Daily Mirror* went one step beyond and proclaimed it "better than the first two horror movies in the *Hellraiser* series."

Backing this up were the box office returns, ensuring that the third movie did just as well as the last two (total U.S. gross $12,525,537,[4] and encouraging interest in yet another sequel. The tagline might have read: "What started in Hell will end on Earth," but there looked to be no signs of the *Hellraiser* series finishing. Barker was apparently going to be much more involved in the fourth film, and Atkins was again to script. But what would this one be about? A prophetic comment by a cast member at the wrap party for *Hell on Earth* pointed the way. According to Bradley, who'd had a little bit to drink by that time, the cast member said, "You know what they ought to do with Pinhead in the next one? Send him into space!"[5] One can imagine there might have been laughter at this "joke." Who could have predicted that in *Hellraiser: Bloodline* we would indeed see Pinhead spacebound?

15

PRODUCTION HELL

The seeds of *Hellraiser IV*'s storyline were planted by the addition to later versions of *Hell on Earth*'s script of a coda sequence: much like the one in *Hellbound* where the Pillar of Souls emerges from the mattress. In this one, however, we are shown a building based on the Lament Configuration, caused — presumably — when Joey buries the box in the concrete at the building site. Anthony Hickox had actually found the location of this site purely by accident; the huge golden statue outside with the world wrapped around a box drew his eye on a drive around Charleston (South Carolina) one Sunday morning. It is a monument that would anticipate the global magnitude of the fourth film's tale.

The idea for the structure of the movie would again, though, come from Clive Barker. He would be serving as executive producer from the start of the project — already in its planning stages by early 1994. "My only concern was to do something fresh and new — for God's sake this is number four!" said Barker. "So it was important to find something that hadn't been done before."[1] He came up with the notion of a three-part film tracing the fortunes of one particular family through different time periods, suggesting that it start in Victorian London. And although Pete Atkins had envisaged the third film being the end to a trilogy, this piqued his interest. He extrapolated the concept, adding the twist that this new family should be the Lemarchands: the clan that created the puzzle box. This decision would dictate that the story started in France, with the most obvious historical choice being during the Revolution, the period of atrocities and bloodshed providing a fitting backdrop. Barker had also established the occupation of Lemarchand himself in *The Hellbound Heart*, stating he was a "maker of singing birds"[2] In other words, a toymaker.

An outline wasn't required because both Atkins and Barker were familiar with the executives at Miramax from *Hellraiser III*, and the studio was keen to make another film. So the initial meeting took the form of a pitch presentation where they both fired off ideas and Miramax gave the green light. In retrospect this freedom would prove both a blessing and a curse, and would lead indirectly to many problems later. But with their go-ahead Atkins went away and started writing the most ambitious of all the Hellraiser scripts: *Bloodline*. As usual, the screenplay would go through several drafts, but the sixth version gives us an idea of just how much changed between page and screen.

Atkins' script begins with a series of extreme close-ups of human hands delicately working on tiny cogs and machinery, a huge eye grotesquely "expanded through a magnifying glass."[3] It is Phillip Lemarchand described as 30, handsome and obsessed with his craft. These images call to mind the beginning of the original *Nightmare on Elm Street* where Freddy is making his famous razor-glove. We are then told via a caption that the year is 1784. Phillip's wife, Genevieve, does not share her husband's enthusiasm for the new piece he is making. "It doesn't actually do anything, then." she says. "I meant no offence, Phillip. I'm sure it's terribly intricate. It's just ... *dull*. I prefer your acrobats and lovers."[4] She alludes to the toys he usually makes, including monkey musicians and Harlequins, all of which fill his workshop. Undeterred, Phillip sets out to deliver the puzzle box to the Chateau Du Reve, where he is greeted by Jacques, "a 19-year-old servant-cum-apprentice to the chateau's owner."[5] This is the powdered and periwigged Duc de L'Isle, whose face is covered with layers of white powder but whose red and rheumy eyes and spidery limbs place his age in the late 50s.

Lemarchand is taken through a room filled with gamblers and introduced to the person behind the commission of the box: the Princess Angelique, "dark, mysterious, exquisite."[6] Atkins emphasizes that Lemarchand is beguiled by her beauty even at this early stage. Lemarchand is dismissed, but continues to watch through a window. Eager to test the box, Angelique gives it to the gamblers. Corbusier is a natural leader, good looking with a sardonic smile. At the other extreme, Delvaux is fat, ruddy and libidinous. L'Escargot is amoral, and De Conduite is a dandy. Finally, L'Hiver, Printemps, L'Automne and L'Été (named after the seasons) are young army officers present to learn the ways of the world. L'Isle issues them with a challenge: "Gentlemen, a new game..."[7] Corbusier is the one who takes the box and begins to manipulate it, encouraged by a striptease that Angelique performs. Like a twisted version of pass the parcel, it is handed around and with each new turn of the box, the Princess removes another layer of clothing until, finally, it returns to Corbusier and the inevitable occurs. But as the box opens, so too does Angelique show her true demonic form, her flesh rippling and eyes turning completely black.

Atkins writes: "The entire room TREMBLES as if caught in a quake. Unearthly WINDS explode up from the floor sending the candle flames shooting upwards in powerful RED FIRE, casting NIGHTMARE SHADOWS on the walls."[8] As Lemarchand flees from the chateau, he encounters a derelict at the gates selling spices and wonders from beyond the sea. He shakes himself free, shouting back, "No more wonders! An end to wonders!"[9] The toymaker seeks help from his friend, Auguste, a young professor of science and philosophy at the Sorbonne. At first he doesn't believe a word of Phillip's story, then tells him to design a machine that can destroy the demons.

Lemarchand is in the middle of doing just that when he is visited at home by Angelique, who asks him to produce more of the boxes. Again, the attraction is apparent and she offers him rewards beyond his wildest dreams. De L'Isle was merely an initial contact, but she can offer him so much more than money: "When I say 'power,' I mean real power. And when I say 'reward,' I mean real rewards."[10] Genevieve interrupts them just before they kiss, and Auguste only just manages to stop him from ripping up his new designs. Auguste's *reward* is to be killed by Angelique's troupe of clowns (Harlequin, Columbine, Pierrot, Pulcinella and the Surgeon) and acrobats, based on Lemarchand's toys. A black bird watches as the professor is hurled into a giant maw of Hell, which Atkins describes as "a dark infinity, like an impossible tunnel opened between dimensions. Circular, ribbed, and pulsing, it resembles a GIANT ESOPHAGUS."[11]

Phillip leaves his bed that night to go to the chateau, but wakes his wife in the process. It is here that he finds out she is with child. In his eyes, this is even more reason to go—to give his offspring a better life. When he arrives, Phillip finds that there is a *Masque of Red Death* style celebration taking place, the ballroom filled with people in grotesque masks; Angelique is dressed as a black bird. This time Lemarchand cannot resist her and they kiss, but three guests intrude, one of them Corbusier. De L'Isle then reveals a pentagram beneath

One of the Gamblers from an original version of the script (courtesy Gary J. Tunnicliffe).

a circular rug. "That's what your box is designed to replace. That and a few words of Old Latin," the magician explains.[12] It is how he summoned Angelique in the first place, and how he is able to exert some degree of control over her; a summoned demon is the summoner's to command. But now they want more of the boxes so anyone who stands in Hell's way is forfeit. There is a fight and Angelique throws De L'Isle across the room. This snaps Phillip out of his daze and he lets slip his plans to make an anti–Lament Configuration (or Elysium Configuration as it comes to be known). The gamblers pull off their masks to reveal the hideous scars of the dead, and attack him.

Meanwhile Genevieve has followed her husband to the chateau. She finds him close to death, and he tells her to save herself and the child. Angelique overhears and cannot allow any of his bloodline to survive. But before she can kill Genevieve, De L'Isle intervenes, dragging the demon through the pentagram. With her gone, the gamblers dissolve into human towers of worms, then finally to dust. Genevieve flees the chateau, giving the puzzle box to the derelict outside. We then witness Jacques calling Angelique back so he can control her: "He who summons the magic, commands the magic."[13] The next scene shows Genevieve onboard the clipper *Liberté*; Genevieve is heavily pregnant and bound for New York with the designs Phillip set to paper.

The script then jumps forward to present-day New York, where Phillip's descendant, John Merchant, is having terrible nightmares involving his grandmother. He also dreams about a beautiful dark-haired woman and wakes up screaming, frightening his wife, Bobbi, and son Jack. Much of the following section runs exactly as it does in the finished film, with Angelique tracking him down via the building he has designed (from the end of *Hellraiser III*) and summoning Pinhead in the basement. The main differences concern the fact that there's more rivalry between the two demons. Angelique represents Hell's past and Pinhead represents Hell's "more ordered" present. Atkins even comments during their first meeting, "It's already clear that these two aren't going to like each other."[14] This lends more credence to Pinhead's impatience when Angelique tries to seduce John, forcing him to take matters into his own hands. Hence, we are privy to some excellent exchanges between them:

> ANGELIQUE: Your Hell has forgotten not only chaos and laughter but the slow delight of temptation.
> PINHEAD: I've harvested more souls than you could dream of and their suffering is with me always. *That* is a slow delight.[15]

We get a magnificent showdown at the end of this section where Pinhead asserts his authority over her when she double crosses him and uses the Elysium Configuration. Her motivation:

she no longer wishes to be a slave, neither to Pinhead nor his new Hell. During the battle, Pinhead spits out a chain from his mouth which anchors itself in the ceiling and he flies it, "like a spider sucking itself back up a web strand."[16] Then he virtually cocoons Angelique in chains, which wrap themselves around her—the ultimate retort to fans who were aggrieved about the Channard-Pinhead fray.

This is the second of two special effects set-pieces. The first involves a security guard called Valerie Dyson (who would be replaced by twins in the finished film). The 40-year-old single mom comes across Pinhead and Angelique "in conference." For her trouble she is chased by the Chatter Beast, which Atkins describes as "like something the scientists at Cenobite central made as a joke from what was left of a man and what was left of a dog after a particularly nasty car crash." It also has chattering teeth, "showing a distinct family resemblance to Pinhead's old ally, the Chatterer."[17] She escapes this creature by hiding in a lift, which proceeds to descend at a rapid pace: in effect she finds herself on an express elevator to Hell.

But these effects-laden scenes are as nothing when the script finally takes us into the future—the year 2204 AD—and into space. A speech Bobbi gives to Jack, after his father's death, about keeping the box in the family ends in a camera track towards the boy's eye until the blackness of his pupil fills the screen. We cut to a passenger shuttle in deep space. Government Ship *Endeavor VII*, then shift to the Minos, a crater-covered asteroid (named after the king from the Greek Minotaur myth), with towers and buildings laser-cut from the rock. (In a production note, Atkins stipulates that corridors shouldn't be the stereotypical metal sci-fi fare, but rather partially rock.) A TV broadcast—originally an in-flight briefing onboard the *Endeavor*—presents us with the necessary exposition. The trillion-dollar facility has dropped out of radio communication and is also out of its geo-stationary orbit. We're then introduced to Paul Merchant, another descendent of Phillip. His room is a shrine to his family's history.

In the screenplay, Paul has been helped by Minos's administrator, Corrine Cotton, a woman in her mid–20s and, one can only assume, a descendant of Kirsty. In a previous draft there was also a character called Gary Gerani—possibly a mirror character of Auguste? Paul leaves the task of aligning the station to Corrine while he operates the robot that opens the Lament Configuration box. We also see that the computer is using a holographic image of Paul, which prefigures his subterfuge at the end. The shuttle arrives, bringing with it four military figures and two civilians, themselves almost reflections of the gamblers from the first part. Edwards is a government official sent to take over from Corrine, and Chamberlain is a young scientist, while the soldiers include two males, Commander Carducci (presumably Mama Carducci's descendent) and Parker, and two females, Roscoe and Rimmer (originally a male prior to draft number six).

Paul is arrested by Roscoe and placed in jail, then spends much of the remainder of the script trying to persuade Edwards and Carducci that there are now demons on Minos. When Parker and Rimmer let the Cenobites out of the holding pen—tricked by a monitor showing frightened and hungry children—they are immediately dispatched. Angelique's Cenobitization has more of an impact here because we know she has been made a slave once more. Moreover, Pinhead's line "No time for games" is a complete contrast to her philosophy in France. Chamberlain is killed by Cenobite twins and Roscoe by the Chatter Beast; Carducci is dispatched by Angelique using a mirror—dragging him so far through and slicing him in half.

Corrine is forced to strike Edwards in order to free Paul, who tells them both to flee.

Corrine makes it only after blasting the Chatter Beast with the exhaust of her escape vehicle, but Edwards isn't so fortunate and encounters both Angelique and the Twins. The scene is then set for Paul to face off against Pinhead, and there is another dramatic release of chains before Pinhead grasps he's been fooled by the hologram. It also allows for a final scene between Angelique and Lemarchand's descendant. In the end, the hologram only buys time for Corrine to activate the Elysium Configuration, not for Paul to escape, and he shares the Cenobites' fate as Minos breaks apart. The camera then tracks in on a piece of the debris—the puzzle box—and suddenly we pull out to show the box resting in the hand of Phillip Lemarchand in his workshop in France, bringing the script completely full circle.

In a post–*Bloodline* interview Doug Bradley described a couple of very interesting variations on this ending that were considered: "The ending originally involved the space station folding up into the puzzle box. Then a hand came through space, picked up the box and dropped it onto a merchant's table. Back to the first film, we had completed a time loop. When that was dropped, the final shot was going to be the shuttle returning to Earth with a trail of pins following it. Then they dropped the pins, so all you have now is the shuttle flying away."[18]

This screenplay is definitely one of the best of the *Hellraiser* sequels. It is intelligent, thorough, self-reflective — with superb parallels between the time zones— and hugely ambitious. Therein lay the first stumbling block. To make a film of this script would have required a considerable financial investment from Miramax. What was on offer was closer to that of the original film, an estimated $4 million. Without even taking into account inflation it was an impossible feat. Immediately, certain scenes involving special effects were scrutinized then dropped, and the space effects and Cenobite fights needed to be scaled down. The next step would be finding a director used to making less seem like more, someone able to make the impossible possible.

The search was not an easy one. Barker was an obvious choice, but quite apart from the fact he'd publicly stated he didn't want to direct *any* sequels, he was also about to film *Lord of Illusions* for United Artists, an adaptation of his own short "The Last Illusion," starring Scott Bakula as Harry D'Amour. Factor in executive producer duties on *Candyman 2: Farewell to the Flesh* (directed by Bill Condon), and Barker was well and truly crossed off the list. The other main contenders were Guillermo del Torro, whose 1993 vampire film, *Cronos*, had seriously impressed everyone in the genre, and Stuart Gordon, a director who thrived on low-budget horror fare, known largely for H.P. Lovecraft adaptations like *From Beyond* (1986). Gordon was all but signed up for the project when an artistic disagreement forced him to back out. It was now that special effects maestro Kevin Yagher was approached via his agents. Yagher had been in the film business several years, providing make-up for horror movies such as *Friday the 13th: The Final Chapter* (Joseph Zito, 1984), *Trick or Treat* (Charles Martin Smith, 1986) and a couple of *Nightmare on Elm Street* films. Yagher was also well known as the creator of the withering corpse-like Crypt keeper —from the anthology TV series, *Tales from the Crypt*, and designer of Chucky from *Child's Play* (Tom Holland, 1988).

In fact it was these two projects that afforded him the opportunity to direct. Famous producer Joel Silver, who had an office across from Yagher's effects shop, was instrumental in securing him the *Crypt* effects work. When the technician promised he could shave the costs off a season of the series in exchange for directing an episode, the result was "Lower Birth," which explained the origins of the Cryptkeeper. This in turn led to Yagher directing yet another episode in 1989, "Strung Along," and finally to the second unit director's job on *Child's Play 2* (John Lafia, 1990). By turning his hand to directing, Yagher was following in the footsteps of other effects men, now filmmakers, such as Brian Yuzna (*Society*, 1989) and Tom Savini (*Night of the Living Dead*, 1990).

"When I got the call," Yagher said in an on-set interview, "I told my agents that I didn't want to do *Hellraiser IV*. I mean, what could I possibly do that was different and hadn't been done before in one, two and three? I thought the original film was great! Then I got Pete Atkins' script and I fell in love with it."[19] Yagher was especially taken with the eighteenth century scenes and going back to the *Hellraiser* origins, or "visual circularity," as Barker described it to him.[20] So with a director secured, the cast came next. Doug Bradley would be reprising his role as Pinhead, a given after his reaction to seeing some else in the make-up during *Hellraiser III*. However, he agreed that Pinhead should be slightly less prominent than in *III*. For the other characters, just as they had done in previous entries, the makers would hone in on relative unknowns.

Twenty-seven-year-old Canadian-born actor Bruce Ramsey was cast in the three important main roles: that of Phillip Lemarchand and his descendants John and Paul Merchant. After small TV roles and a part as a teenager in Sandor Stern's creepy horror film *Pin* in 1988, Ramsey went on to star in films such as the cannibal survival movie *Alive* (Frank Marshall, 1993) and *Killing Zoe* (Roger Avary, 1994). Speaking about the part, the actor said, "Phillip is a young man with great ambition and he wants to be recognized, so he is seduced by Angelique's power.... Lemarchand is not an evil man, but he is attracted to the dark side."[21] About John and Paul, he mused: "In the second story, his descendant, who is a husband and a father, is more mature and

Pinhead with director Kevin Yagher (courtesy Gary J. Tunnicliffe).

understands himself better. The third character is an old and weathered man who has spent his whole life trying to secure the ultimate trap for the horror which has plagued his entire family for several hundred years."[22]

Cast as principal female villain Angelique was Chilean Valentina Vargas. With her dark, sultry looks she was perfect. Her acting CV began with European TV work, playing Laure in an episode of *Le Petit Docteur* (1986), then a role as La masseuse in Pierre Jolivet's *Strictement personnel* (1985). But it was in Jean-Jacques Annaud's *The Name of the Rose* (1986) that she made a real impact starring alongside Sean Connery and Christian Slater in this fourteenth century murder mystery. Parts followed in Luc Besson's *Le Grand Bleu* (The Big Blue, 1988) and *Street of No Return* (Samuel Fuller, 1989). The uneven *Twin Sitters* (John Paragon, 1994) marked something of a low spot, but did at least prophesy what her character would be doing in *Bloodline*. Though she almost didn't take the role because she was having nightmares about Pinhead coming to kill her,[23] she soon warmed to the idea and even embraced tapping into this side of her character. "For the first time in my career, I'm playing a villainess in a horror movie, and I'm really loving it," she said. "In the first two tales, she's like a serpent because she'll trick, seduce and manipulate people. They'll think they're in Heaven until she turns around and backstabs them."[24]

For the role of John Merchant's wife, Bobbi, Kim Meyers was selected. Meyers had worked with Yagher once before on *A Nightmare on Elm Street Part 2: Freddy's Revenge* (1985), where she played Lisa Webber, but her other credits included parts on TV's *L.A. Law*, *Tales from Hollywood Hills* and the Chuck Norris vehicle, *Walker, Texas Ranger*, as well as the films *White Palace* (Luis Mandoki, 1990) and *At Risk* (Elana K. Pyle, 1994). Playing a similar part was Charlotte Chatton as Genevieve. Chatton also had TV experience, most notably in popular British detective series *Inspector Morse* (1992). That same year she starred as Jen Cross in *Dakota Road* (Nick Ward) opposite Alexis Denisof before going on to feature as Emma in the show starring Jane Seymour *Dr. Quinn, Medicine Woman* (1995–6).

Bit-part actor Mickey Cottrell was chosen for the role of the evil Duc de L'Isle, having established himself in a number of parts in addition to serving as a unit publicist for movies like *Bagdad Cafe* (Percy Adlon, 1987). His first big film role was alongside Keanu Reeves and River Phoenix in Gus Van Sant's *My Own Private Idaho* (1991) where he played Daddy Carroll.

Up for the role of De L'Isle's apprentice, Jacques, was 21-year-old Californian Adam Scott, who was also building his career on TV appearances. The first of these was as Dan in the pilot episode of *Dead at 21* (1994), followed by a couple of turns in *Boy Meets World*. Post–*Hellraiser*, the actor could be seen in such high profile shows as *E.R.* and *Murder One*, as well as Martin Scorsese's *The Aviator* (2004).

Louis Turenne — another Canadian by birth — stepped into the role of Phillip's friend, Auguste, bringing with him over twenty years of acting experience starting with *Happy Birthday, Wanda June* (Mark Robson, 1971) right through to *Mystic Pizza* (Donald Petrie, 1988) with Julia Roberts. Louis Mustillo would play Sharpe, a victim of Angelique who opens the puzzle box and calls forth Pinhead. But audiences may have recognized him from brief appearances on *Quantum Leap*, *Married with Children* and *L.A. Law*. A child actor with the requisite experience was required for the scenes with Jack and Pinhead and they found this in Courtland Mead. At only seven, the young actor had nonetheless amassed a serious number of parts, from *For Parents Only* (Bill Shepherd, 1991) to *Little Rascals* (Penelope Spheeris, 1994).

Due to a reshuffle and cull of characters, there was no need to find anyone to play Roscoe or Corrine Cotton. Rimmer was now to take on a more central role and would be played by Christine Harnos. Though she had appeared in films like *Cold Dog Soup* (Alan Metter, 1990) and *Dazed and Confused* (Richard Linklater, 1993), most viewers would recognize her as Mark Greene's wife, Jennifer, in *E.R.*—from 1994 onwards. Making up the rest of the SWAT team were Wren T. Brown as Parker (from *The Hidden*—Jack Sholder, 1987), Tom Dugan as Chamberlain (*The Puppet Masters*—Stuart Orme, 1994), Pat Skipper as Carducci (*Predator 2*—Stephen Hopkins, 1990), and Paul Perri as Edwards (from *Manhunter*—Michael Mann, 1986), now their commander.

Replacing security guard Valerie Dyson were twins Jimmy and David Schuelke, who had only appeared together before *Hellraiser IV* in Ruben Preuss's horror film, *Almost Dead* (1994). Story-wise this would make more sense, as they are supposedly transformed into the Twin Cenobites we see on Minos, but under the latex were two other twins, first time performers Michael and Mark Polish.

This was an assignment handed to the new head of Image Animation's U.S. branch, Gary Tunnicliffe. "Basically what happened was that myself and Bob Keen were jointly running the company in England," explained Gary. "We were taking on more and more projects and a lot of work was coming from America. We therefore decided to set up a U.S. shop and I ended up coming out here to run it."[25] Tunnicliffe had already been involved in the effects for *Hellraiser III*, in particular the re-shoots suggested by Barker, so he was no stranger to this universe. But upon hearing that effects-man Yagher would be directing, he was worried that Image Animation might be surplus to requirements, fears that were to prove unfounded: "Kevin rang us up and basically said, 'Hey, I want you to be involved, you're the only people who've been around doing all of the films, can we meet?'"[26] This secured IA's position on the movie and led to Tunnicliffe handling the make-up on the Twins, actually based on Greek comedy and tragedy masks (sculpted by Steve Norrington). Tunnicliffe was also responsible for the design of Angelique's stunning Cenobite, some of which he got from watching the film *Sister Act* (Emile Ardolino, 1992): "It's true, honestly! I was watching these singing nuns and seeing the way their cowls fall down and I thought it would be interesting to do something with flesh rather than material."[27] Thankfully, there was also a touch of slinky Morticia Addams thrown in, the skin-tight outfit actually securing Vargas a place on the cover of *Femme Fatale* and *Fangoria* magazines.

Fortunately, Tunnicliffe was also keen to return to the original Pinhead look, having been a great admirer of the work done in the first two movies. The make-up in the third film had been designed for speed and it was reduced to a two-piece appliance; Tunnicliffe always felt that the pins were a little too long and cumbersome: "Personally, I thought Pinhead was fine the way he was, so we went back to the original design and pattern."[28] This would involve one-inch gold pins and a grid closely copying Geoff Portass's original. The return to this old look would also help Bradley to get back into character. After loosening up his performance when Pinhead was set free in *Hell on Earth* he would now have to rein that in again and re-establish the boundaries of Pinhead's persona.

Though Yagher left Tunnicliffe to handle these make-ups, he couldn't resist designing the Chatter Beast himself and letting his own shop bring it to life. But it would take the talents of Jody St. Michael, who had been one of Rick Baker's apes in *Gorillas in the Mist* (Michael Apted, 1988), to truly animate the monster. "There's a center that an animal has that a human doesn't," St. Michael clarified. "Humans do human things, have human intentions and human emotions. Animals all have this one center, and it takes some practice to

A design for Valentina Vargas's costume, which was inspired by *Sister Act*. Gary Tunnicliffe's idea is rendered here by Myles Teves (courtesy Gary J. Tunnicliffe).

capture it."[29] Other notable crew positions were filled by Ivo Christante as production designer, costume designs by Dayna Cussler and Eileen Kennedy, Rick Kerrigan as visual effects supervisor, and David Douglas designing the spacecraft.

Filming began in August 1994 in order to meet Miramax's proposed release date of January 1995. The location for the first few weeks of principle photography was L.A., specifically floor three of Hollywood's old I Magnin building, transformed into expansive corporate offices for the purposes of the shoot. Before setting up here, rumors abounded that, like the house in Dollis Hill from *Hellraiser*, this place was haunted. The ghost of the woman who was married to I Magnin was said to roam the building and didn't want a group of filmmakers invading her territory. By the time they were finished, even Yagher had cause to believe this might be true.

Cast and crew had bad luck right from the start. There were concerns about the cinematography—rightly so—leading to the dismissal of a DP and drafting in of Gerry (*Hellraiser III*) Lively. Indeed, according to Bradley the entire art department and camera crew were sacked after just one week.[30] A strike shut down production for a whole day, resulting in loss of footage. A fire broke out at the building that set off the sprinklers and caused a flood. An emergency called the assistant director away from work for a couple of weeks, and Courtland Mead developed a bad case of chicken pox. To his credit, Yagher remained composed, patient and professional, something he said he inherited from his dad: "My father was a very patient man, and I inherited a little of that. I've been concerned here and there, but I've stayed pretty calm...."[31]

Shooting the eighteenth century France scenes were much more satisfying, it seemed. Likening the shoot to making three separate films, Yagher said on the set, "It's a great experience to start on something this difficult and hopefully, *if* I work again, the projects will not be as tough. Right now, I'm tired, but I'm happy tired."[32] He also sang the praises of Barker—who would drop by when he had any free time and offer his advice—Atkins, who was on hand to do any rewrites, and the Weinstein brothers at Miramax. Publicity photographs from that time also reveal Tunnicliffe's work on the transformed gamblers, one of them with his eyes healed over and another with his lips pulled back even further than the Chatterer.

The production then moved to an abandoned A-1 Spaghetti factory, only a few blocks from where Barker was filming *Lord of Illusions*. This would be transformed into a makeshift soundstage, and technicians recreated the Minos corridors—reverting to sci-fi type by making them completely metallic. The Minos was now a free-floating space station rather than part of an asteroid and the year had changed to 2127. Here the crew encountered yet more difficulties, including Vargas suffering from a reaction to the glue and prosthetics used in her Cenobite make-up. The whole experience had been too much for some, so much so that, looking back, Bradley said that, "*Bloodline* was the shoot from hell; it was the most miserable professional experience of my career."[33] One of the few highlights for the actor was his sixty-fifth appearance in the Pinhead make-up over the course of eight years, for which Tunnicliffe presented him with a specially made bus pass from Leviathan City Limits Public Transportation.

Regardless of all the horror and heartache, Yagher managed to deliver the movie on time and within budget. Running at about 110 minutes, it was screened for executives at Miramax in early 1995. Their reaction was less than favorable. Their main concern was that the most important character in any *Hellraiser* movie, Pinhead, didn't appear until well over half an hour into the film. "I'd written six versions of this script: six drafts," Pete Atkins told an interviewer in late 1995, "and [Miramax] always knew that the eighteenth century came first and Pinhead didn't appear until the twentieth century story. So it's not that anyone could blame Kevin for delaying Pinhead's entrance.... But, I think that when they saw the movie they suddenly felt, 'Hey, wait a minute, where's our monster? We made a terrible mistake!'"[34]

Consequently, they requested changes to the film, the first of which would be rearrangement of the story sequence. The space section would have to be brought in sooner, to give audiences at least a glimpse of Pinhead and let them know he would be featured later on: the historical parts would now be introduced by Paul Merchant as if he was telling his family's tale. There were other alterations that would be necessitated, too, such as the expulsion of the gambling scene in favor of Angelique's "birth." She became a young street urchin that the Duc and Jacques murder so that she can play host to the demon they summon. A happy ending would be required as well, whereby Paul gets away with Rimmer in a shuttle. All of this would require more footage.

After spending so much time and effort on such a traumatic shoot, Yagher was naturally hesitant to commit himself. "I could understand the changes that they wanted me to make but, for someone who has slept with it, which they didn't do, it's tough to give up what you've kind of created. I had given everything to the one script. So, the bottom line was that I had to decide either basically to dedicate another year to the film or go on with my life and continue other projects. In the end, it wasn't so much the direction that they wanted to take, as it was that I just didn't have the time and energy."[35] To watch it change day by day would have been like, in his words, "pulling butt hairs out."[36] Instead, he threw himself into work on Universal's *Sleepy Hollow* project, to be directed by Tim Burton.

Enter director Joe Chappelle. He had previously directed a movie called *Thieves Quartet* in 1994, a surprisingly good low-budget film in the *Reservoir Dogs* mold. His other credential was *Halloween: The Curse of Michael Myers*, the sixth film in the series. This movie had also gone through many difficulties, beginning with eleven drafts of the script. Chappelle reportedly wanted to excise many of Donald Pleasance's scenes as Dr. Loomis; then a combination of the actor's death, creative differences between Chappelle and the producer, and an allegedly bad test screening forced re-shoots and post production re-editing. The result: most of the cast and crew vowed they would never make another *Halloween* movie again. If nothing else, this experience should have prepared him for work on the troubled *Hellraiser IV*.

Atkins penned three of the new scenes but wasn't available for further rewrites, so at the suggestion of Barker the extra rewrites were handled by Rand Ravich, co-author of *Candyman: Farewell to the Flesh*. His was the rewrite that enabled them to slot material into a framework the studio would be satisfied with, and Chappelle directed the new footage in April and May 1995. Said Bradley of these: "I mean, I did two weeks of re-shoots, which weren't really re-shoots at all, they were [shooting] whole new material, and there were at least two other sessions which didn't involve me."[37]

When the new version of the movie was shown to Yagher, he felt it didn't represent his artistic vision. The film had changed so much he decided to remove his name from the project. Yagher exercised his right to anonymity by using the Alan Smithee pseudonym. Alan (or sometimes Allen) Smithee is the name designated by the Director's Guild of America as screen credit for a filmmaker who wishes to remove his or her own name from a movie.[38] It was hardly surprising. The film suffers greatly from its lack of overall supervision and views like a movie made by *several* directors, not just two—reflecting the number of different people who worked on it at different times, including three editors: Randy Bricker, Rod Dean and Jim Prior.

Of the major changes, the dynamics between the main characters are most conspicuous. Angelique and Phillip are not given sufficient time to develop their relationship in eighteenth century France, so when they meet again in New York the rekindling of it feels rushed. "We were good together, John," she says to him, and yet they only encountered each other briefly, when Angelique killed him at Jacques' behest. Their encounter on the space station, which would have been a final tying up of their business, is totally absent.

Similarly, Angelique and Pinhead's attitudes towards each other are now ill-defined. The way the film has been spliced together, it plays as if Pinhead actually misses the chaos that the Princess once brought to the underworld. "Hell is much more ordered since your time," he tells her, "and much less amusing." In the original script this was a chastisement—a sly remark about her use of the clowns as tools of death—but here it is more like a lament. To add to the perplexity, he says, "You've been away too long, Princess." Not an admonition, but a confession that he has missed her, which is strange in itself as Pinhead didn't exist before the twentieth century. The one-upmanship has no grounding at all, and it appears that Pinhead may be jealous of her relationship with John.

An extremely sexual scene replaces the argument they have about which methods work best to secure souls. "Your human admirer may not sense it, but I can smell the exquisite stench of what you really are!" he says, then rakes a finger hook between her breasts, much to Angelique's delight. This, in turn, throws the conflict at the end of the New York scene into confusion. It is not made clear why Angelique wishes John to open the Elysium Configuration, nor why Pinhead suddenly punishes her and they all disappear into the puzzle box.

When Angelique appears at Pinhead's side again, it seems to the audience that she has simply reverted to a more Hellish demeanor. Gone is the undercurrent about her being a slave to Pinhead and Hell, about her own desires being quashed in favor of the order he spoke of. She is Pinhead's companion now, taking the place of the female Cenobite from the first two movies. How much of this has to do with Barker's intention to finally see Pinhead paired up one can only speculate. "We're actually taking the mythology places it hasn't gone," he told Imagi-Movies back before the film was even made. "We're going to see Pinhead in some situations we haven't even remotely seen him in. We've got female Cenobites, and we're determined that somewhere down the line the Black Pope of Hell himself is going to get laid!"[39] The attraction between Lemarchand/Merchant is definitely muted, possibly so that Pinhead might get that bride from the unfilmed ending of *Hellraiser III*, after all.

What does impress is the soundtrack by Daniel Licht. The composer began his career with music for Tony Randel's *Children of the Night* in 1991, then went on to work almost exclusively in the horror genre. While Licht does touch on Christopher Young's themes for *Hellraiser* and *Hellbound*, most apparent when Pinhead makes his first real entrance — he doesn't leech from them constantly. The new, haunting theme he came up with to accompany the credits is a tremendous Gothic tune and a worthy successor to Young's, as is the chase sequence music that accompanies Bobbi, and later Rimmer's, flight from the Chatter Beast (recalling Kirsty's encounter with the Engineer). The whole score is powerful, blending unconventional instrumentation occasionally augmented by a chorus.

The film — in a lean eighty-five minute version — was finally released in American cinemas during March 1996, well over a year after Miramax's projected date. And while it didn't do a roaring trade, it did manage to take $9,321,492 at the box office domestically.[40] It would eventually surface as a straight-to-video offering in the UK a couple of years later. While it was not what anyone — Yagher and Atkins especially — would have hoped for, as Bradley so succinctly summed up: "It was something of a minor miracle that we had a movie at all."[41] He even went so far as to state, "The results are uneven, but the first 20 minutes — the bit I'm not in — are as strong as anything in any of the previous movies. I'm happy with it, overall."[42]

Yagher's defense just after its opening was: "My whole idea was that I didn't want to do a *Hellraiser IV* where Pinhead slaughters a bunch of people. It's been done before, and *III* was a good example of that, turning people into C.D. Heads and Cameraheads. I wanted to do something a little different."[43]

For better or worse, it can truly be said that he got his wish.

16

OPEN THE GATES, LAY LOW THE RAMPARTS

Time to Play

It should be self evident from an examination of both the script and the resultant film that the predominant theme of *Bloodline* is time. The three sections of the linear story are all set in distinct time zones, which further prevents the movie from retaining a single identity. These were to be roughly two hundred years apart, until the final setting was changed to 2127, possibly to keep it more in line with what near future technology might be like. But as the restructured non-linear movie plays it casts Paul Merchant not only in the role of narrator but also that of a time traveler.

He takes both Rimmer and the audience through time via a series of flashbacks, first to an unspecified date "centuries ago," which we know to be 1784 from the script, then to the modern day New York of 1996. Like the main character in H.G. Wells' *The Time Machine* (1895), Paul is also determined to alter the course of that history, or at the very least alter the course of the present. In Wells' book, The Time Traveler returns from a future where the Morlocks have bred the weaker Eloi for food, while in the recent 2002 film adaptation, directed by Wells' great-grandson Simon, inventor Alexander Hartdegen (Guy Pearce) is motivated to travel back and save the love of his life when she is murdered. Both Phillip and John have been killed because of their dealings with the forces of Hell and it is Paul who will take his revenge using the Elysium Configuration, sent *forwards* through time by his ancestors. This is also another perfect example of the Rule of Three. Where the first two incarnations failed in their task, Paul will succeed because he is aware of the pitfalls.

Time haunts the characters in all three periods. During the opening introduction, Paul Merchant impresses upon Rimmer that "Time is of the essence," and tells her, "I don't have time to help you understand." But because it is the only way, he has to relate his story. When we move into the France section, we see that Phillip's workshop is littered with clocks, the sound of ticking all around; indeed, this is part of his profession. In his eagerness to deliver the finished box, he walks past a huge clock face lying on the floor — shown in a low-level point of view shot — as wife Genevieve asks: "It's midnight, where are you going?" On his way out, she again reminds him, "It's late," and the chiming of a bell is heard from far away ringing out the hour. When Phillip arrives at the Chateau du Reve, the Duc de L'Isle congratulates him on his timing: "As precise as your pieces, as *timely* as your toys...." Then as

Genevieve sets out to track down her husband after he visits the Chateau for a second time, the clocks in his workshop all chime mockingly, as if to emphasize that his time has run out.

In the New York section, Bobbi is woken early by Angelique's phone call and enquires, "What time is it?" John's reply covers up the indiscretion: "Japanese client, has no sense of *time*." Pinhead himself grows impatient with Angelique's progress, so much so that he takes matters into his own hands and kidnaps John's son. "The time for trickery is past," he informs her. When Bobbi finds that Jack is in the clutches of Pinhead, she puts her hand to her mouth and her watch is very clearly in the shot, linking her terror directly to time. And John and Pinhead's eventual meeting compels the demon to impart: "No longer will we have to seep into your world like pests through cracks in the baseboards; once and for all we will open the gates, lay low the ramparts.... It is *time* to open the pathway, forever."

Returning to the future section, after Pinhead and his cohorts are summoned, one of his first lines to Paul is: "We'd almost given up waiting for you to play." Paul counters: "Long wait, demon, for such a short game." But, as always, Pinhead is ready with a rejoinder of his own: "Tell the truth, Merchant, you're pleased to see me. Your impatience has matched my own." The waiting is once again linked to agony, as well as curiosity.

During the climactic finale, a red digital clock counts off the time to a solar alignment that will allow completion of the Elysium Configuration, accompanied out loud by a computerized female voice. "Twenty-three minutes to complete mission," she tells Merchant as he is trying to convince Rimmer about the Cenobites. Edwards, too, sets a time limit, ordering his officer to "Escort the prisoner to his cell and be prepared to leave at 0430 hours." Sadly, he will not make his own deadline. Later we see a close-up of the clock as the computer states: "Twelve minutes to complete mission," and we're granted a tight close-up of the seconds speeding away. When Pinhead catches up with Merchant in the control room, the doctor's eyes flash up to the clock once more, which shows him there are only six minutes left. Immediately afterwards he tells Rimmer she's got five minutes to get to the shuttle. Lastly, Pinhead's final speech shows he is still preoccupied with time. Upon hearing the computer counting down, he offers these words of wisdom: "Two minutes; two centuries, it all ticks by so quickly." Yet when told he is about to die, he claims, "I am forever!"

The clock device in this section, as well as drawing our attention to the theme, serves the purpose of increasing viewer tension, utilizing the teachings of that Master of Suspense, Alfred Hitchcock. To quote him: "The element of suspense is giving the audience information. Now, you and I are sitting here. Suddenly a bomb goes off, up we go: blown to smithereens. What does the audience have watching this scene? Five or ten seconds of shock. Now, we do the scene over again, but we tell the audience there's a bomb underneath this table and it's going to go off in five minutes.... Then their anxieties will be as long as that clock ticks away."[1]

In *Bloodline*, the ticking bomb is the countdown for the Elysium Device activation. The audience has been given information about this, they have seen Phillip drawing up his plans, seen John's attempt — and failure — to successfully operate it in the basement of the building he designed. We know, because Paul is trying to learn from past mistakes, that he will probably succeed this time. At first it is the SWAT team that are oblivious to what is happening, which leads to their deaths at the hands of the Cenobites. Then it is Pinhead himself who is unaware that he is walking into a trap.

Toys and Games

Considering that the central human character in the film is a toymaker — the name by which he is referred to in all three time periods — it should come as no great revelation that there are numerous references to both toys and games throughout the film. This theme has actually been a recurrent one throughout the whole series. All the important characters have played games at one point or another. Frank plays with Julia's emotions, and in turn she plays a dangerous game with her prey in the bars. Frank also plays a game with Kirsty at the end, pretending to be her father, until this is revealed, giving rise to one of the most memorable lines in *Hellraiser* history: "So much for the cat and mouse shit."

Kirsty plays a bargaining game with the Cenobites, as we saw in chapter 2, and the demons themselves enter into games with their human subjects, "Time to play," being one of Pinhead's preferred sayings. In *Hellbound*, Tiffany's obsession was bound to her playing with puzzles (coincidentally, the wooden box she slots together at the Institute bears more than a passing resemblance to Phillip's rudimentary Lament Configuration), while in *Hell on Earth*, Pinhead encourages Joey to let the Pseudo Cenobites play: "Ah, more friends come to play with you." Even when he slips inside her mind, he is toying with her memories of her dead father. "Couldn't resist playing games, could you?" snaps Elliott when he comes face-to-face with his alter ego.

In *Bloodline* these correlations are much more blatant. In France, the peasant girl Angelique assumes the Duc is playing a game when Jacques binds her hands to the table; this is further compounded by his producing a handkerchief from behind her ear. In the original script, the gamblers are playing card games at the chateau when Phillip arrives, but the delivery of the box initiates a new, more deadly game. "Will you play, sir?" the demon Angelique asks Corbusier, offering him the Lament Configuration. In the film, though, it is Jacques who plays sexual games with Angelique once she is demonized, and she is condemned to do his bidding. This doesn't prevent her from wishing that things were different, especially when Phillip arrives. "Toymaker! You have such pliant fingers," she says seductively. "I want them to play with me." In the previous version of the story, she does play a mating game with Phillip, but now is ordered to dispatch him quickly, then to join Jacques back in the bedroom.

In the present day there are even more games to be played. Angelique is at the forefront this time, and the first involves revenge on Jacques. "Close your eyes," she tells him. "Don't move." "Why?" he asks, and in a replay of what was said during her original demise she replies, "So you won't bruise." Jacques' reaction to that: "Is this a new game?" "Oh yes," she tells him. "It might hurt ... just a little." And when the game is over, Jacques will be dead.

In New York, Angelique recruits another volunteer to help her. Bumping into overweight, balding businessman Sharpe at the unveiling of John Merchant's new building, she entices him to the basement — just as Julia did before her, except they are descending instead of going up into an attic. Their conversation harks back to the most famous villainess of the series. "Do we really need to know each other's names?" she says when he asks hers. "Oh, a mystery woman, huh?" Sharpe concludes and follows her eagerly down the stairs. When they reach the basement, she asks directly, "Do you like games?" and gets him to close his eyes while she searches for the box — punching a hole in one concrete support to free it. This signifies that it is "Time to play another game." Sharpe is the one who plays with the box now and his reward is to be dragged into Hell by a hook and devoured by the

Chatter Beast, his departure signaling the grand entrance of Leviathan's favorite son, Pinhead.

More subtle is the game Angelique plays with John, the art of seduction which we will discuss more fully later. In reference to this, Pinhead says to the architect, "Isn't that the game you've been playing?" "This isn't a game," protests John. "Oh yes," Pinhead assures him, "this *is* a game." The very fact that Pinhead then affects Jack's voice and calls out "Daddy!" should be enough to prove that this is child's play. It also foreshadows the use of this trick on the space station — the Cenobites calling out in distressed childlike voices so Parker will free them. John's recreation of the Elysium design on his monitor, which he shows to Angelique in his office, is tantamount to a computer game, one where only logic and skill can sustain the Configuration, working with mirrors and lasers. "Trapped light, feeding off its own reflections," John explains. It will work only for a few moments before losing its definition, and when he puts this into practice in the basement — at the behest of Angelique — his gaming skills again prove lacking. This failure will cost him his life as Pinhead shouts, "No more games!" before slicing off his head. It is left to Bobbi, who has herself been playing a real-life version of a scrolling computer game with the Chatter Beast, to send Pinhead back to Hell with another apt phrase: "You go and play with your dog, you bastard!"

The scenes onboard Minos are even more reminiscent of a "shoot 'em up," with winding corridors and laser guns. We've already heard that Pinhead had almost given up waiting for Merchant to play, and, as Paul has told Rimmer, "I'm playing an endgame here!" He warns her, "You don't know what you're playing with...." Only *he* is qualified to participate in this final game, which he does using a hologram. Angelique lures another man, Carducci, to his death by pulling him so far into a mirror; and Pinhead plays a game of hide-and-seek with Chamberlain, who thinks he has escaped only to find the jaws of the Chatter Beast lurking in the darkness. Rimmer takes Bobbi's place as the dog's prey, but destroys it completely by trapping it in a decompression chamber. "Play dead," is her own contribution to the game.

The most obvious toys are the three pivotal constructions of the Lemarchand/Merchant clan, which grow bigger in each time zone. And all have dual purposes. The first is the Lament Configuration that Phillip creates, a toy puzzle that is actually a gateway to Hell — replacing the cruder Pentagon that de L'Isle relies upon. The second is the office building John has designed, which earns him a place on the front cover of *AE* magazine but which also has the potential to become a much bigger pathway. It

The Chatter Beast that terrorized Bobbi. Replica figure by NECA (courtesy NECA; photograph credit: Nicolle M. Puzzo).

is, as Pinhead comments, "a holocaust waiting to wake itself." During this section the movie also shows us little Jack building a Ferris wheel out of a Meccano-like toy set, showing that the need to build is in the Merchant family's blood. When Jack survives and passes his genes on, as well as trace memories, the result is Paul's masterpiece: the Minos Station, which hides the workings of the Elysium Configuration — and the ability to transform into a giant puzzle box in space.

On a much smaller scale we have the toy figures that Phillip makes. These are seen only briefly in the movie, as part of the box-making montage. But in the script there was much more detail. Genevieve mentions the acrobats and lover figures, and examples of the Harlequin dolls are present in Phillip's workshop. These are what Angelique bases her killer troupe on, and the lovers are almost certainly meant to represent herself and Phillip. Later, Paul uses a much larger doll he's built — a robot, which he manipulates using sensor gloves — to work the puzzle box. In just the same way, the toy dolls serve also to highlight the manipulation of mankind by Hell — and by the Cenobites. First, through de L'Isle, they orchestrate the conception of the Lament Configuration. Then, through Angelique (in both the script and the film) they demand more boxes be made. The Cenobites use human beings for their own entertainment and pleasure. They are latter day Greek or Roman gods, moving human beings around as if on a gigantic chessboard, an analogy the series would return to in *Hellraiser: Inferno*. Human beings are their own dolls to do with as they like. Pinhead's speech when he sees Earth on the monitor enforces this argument: "Ah! Glorious, is it not? The creatures that walk on its surface, always looking to the light, never seeing the untold oceans of darkness beyond. There are more humans alive at this moment than in all its pitiful history. The garden of Eden ... a garden of flesh!"

Sex, Death and ... Adultery

We have touched on the complex relationships between Phillip, his descendants and Angelique, as well as Pinhead and the Princess. But this warrants further exploration, as it ties in with yet another one of *Bloodline*'s fundamental themes. In the script the attraction between Lemarchand and Angelique is much more pronounced. When he first visits the Chateau and sees her, Philip is spellbound; how much of this is magic and how much pure, animal lust, Atkins leaves to the reader's imagination. However, he does state that Lemarchand is "Visibly struck by her beauty...." and is "the subject of her penetrating stare and ravishing smile."[2] Seeing her true demonic features during the game with the gamblers sends Phillip fleeing from the house, but not even this can bring him to his senses when she calls at his workshop. Again, the puissant attraction draws them together during a heated scene. Phillip wouldn't be the first or last man to be seduced by power. Their meeting ends in them almost kissing, were it not for Genevieve's interruption. With this knowledge, the New York section of the film now makes much more sense. When Anqelique says to John Merchant, "We were good together," it's a statement of fact, not a panging for what might have been had she not murdered him within seconds of setting eyes on him. In the movie version, Phillip's reaction to Angelique is one of disgust; when she demands that he play with her, he fears only for his soul; there is no lust or love in his eyes.

Had we not known about their relationship in the script, it would seem very strange that Angelique's seduction of John would be so quick. He has been dreaming about her, but in those dreams her mouth is smeared with blood and she is holding a heart, hardly an image that would make him desire her. Additionally, it would make more sense for him to become flustered when he sees her during his speech, if this had happened before to his ancestor Phillip. "You think you don't remember, but your blood knows. Let it remind you," Angelique says when they eventually meet in person. "You know me from dreams, John Merchant. John Lemarchand." But the film in its current form would suggest that those memories and dreams are merely bad ones. In any event, John is soon fixated with her and his dreams are filled with much more erotic fare: Angelique straddling him naked in bed, promising that whatever he wants can be his. So, when the double cross comes again, it is following the same pattern as the scripted France section: seduction and betrayal, ending ultimately in death.

Hence, in the screenplay's futuristic setting, Paul is able to twist this around. Allowance is made for a final confrontation between the two, where Angelique wishes they could return to the past, perhaps to change what happened. Thankfully, it is Paul who betrays *her* this time, leaving her in the clutches of Pinhead before destroying them all by triggering the Elysium Configuration. The movie version denies the audience this final satisfying meeting between the two, thereby withholding any kind of resolution to this subplot, or any form of closure to the affair, which brings us to another aspect of this scenario.

In the script, Phillip and Angelique raise Genevieve's suspicions because they exhibit all the signs of a couple having an extramarital relationship. Phillip leaves his house twice at night to venture to the chateau, once even leaving his bed. Then Genevieve catches them virtually kissing when Angelique comes to see Lemarchand. This is why, in order to win him around, she reveals that she is pregnant, divulging the information just as he's about to leave her. But even this fails to stop him. Genevieve plays the spurned wife in this scenario, who cannot compete with Phillip's stunning new admirer. Of course, in the film we have none of this tension. Phillip is happily married and knows about the child Genevieve is carrying right from the start, even before he knows of Angelique's existence. "Stay with me. Stay with us," says Genevieve in the very first historical scene, placing his hand on her stomach. So, when he departs to take the box to the chateau at midnight, this makes his motivation more about providing for his family than seeing his other woman.

In the New York setting this infidelity is present in both the script and the finished movie. John's strange behavior alerts Bobbi to a possible liaison between her husband and another woman. John is distracted, is having trouble sleeping and unashamedly lies to her. The close-up of Bobbi's face as she rolls over in bed tells the audience she doesn't believe a word he says. This section recalls the first *Hellraiser* and Larry's growing suspicions about Julia. But Bobbi is much more astute than Larry: if Jack hadn't been kidnapped one suspects she would have uncovered John's secret anyway. And, once more, the punishment for this deception — for his guilty pleasure — is to almost lose his wife and son, and to be killed at the hands of Pinhead. Could this be why there is a hint of sarcasm in his voice when Pinhead says, "Stand your ground, *family man*"? Through his behavior, John has damaged his family unit beyond repair. Bobbi no longer has a husband and Jack will now grow up without a father. The imagined future that Pinhead speaks of to John, where he watches his son grow up and loves him, is snatched away not — as John originally thought — by the death of Jack, but by the untimely demise of himself. The ultimate price of any extramarital affair is the break-up of the family unit, the estrangement of husbands and wives, fathers and children.

Maybe this is the reason why Paul Merchant has not taken a wife. He is very different to his predecessors, not simply focused and dedicated to his work as they were, but obsessive to the exclusion of all else. In the script the love interest is represented by Kirsty's descendant, Corinne. There is potential for a relationship to develop, but because his bloodline is cursed it is necessary for Paul to sacrifice himself and obliterate the demons. In the film, Rimmer replaces Corinne, and she has studied the doctor in depth, which we deduce from Edwards' line: "I wasn't asking you, Carducci, I was asking the expert. Well, Rimmer? Great man didn't live up to your expectations, did he?" It is apparent from her interview that there is a certain amount of hero worship on her part, and possibly attraction as well. Before they can embark on a relationship, though, Paul must rid himself of the guilt from his past by erasing all trace of Pinhead and Angelique. This done, he is allowed to fly off in the escape ship with Rimmer to start a better, and, it's to be hoped, happier existence. Paul doesn't succumb to temptation; he resists and reaps the benefits that were beyond the grasp of Phillip and John. It is his act of recompense on their behalf.

But Phillip, John and Paul are not the only characters Angelique finds herself involved with. Once summoned, she is forced to enter into a sexual relationship with Jacques. Phillip sees him through the open bedroom door, a naked Angelique attending to his needs. The epitome of the jealous boyfriend, Jacques' answer to Angelique's attraction for Phillip is to hit him over the head then damn him for all eternity: "Demons will walk the earth and you're responsible." His order for Angelique to kill Phillip is the ultimate masculine triumph over both her and him. She has no choice but to obey, even though she wants Phillip for herself. But when the bloodline continues, Jacques is doomed. Angelique sees John on *AE*'s cover and determines to go to America. "I'm restless and you're bored," she says in an effort to talk him into going. Jacques tries to stand in her way — and in Hell's way; therefore his punishment is *Hellraiser*'s infamous "kiss of death," this time ripping a bloody hole in his cheek.

Angelique's relationship with Sharpe is brief and founded upon a misunderstanding on his behalf. He believes that she wants him for sexual favors, when she is only using him to call forth the next man in her life: Pinhead. As already discussed, there is a discrepancy between the technicalities of their relationship on page and on-screen. In Atkins' script they do not care for each other at all. In the movie there is a definite undercurrent of physical, and possibly emotional, magnetism. His entrance impresses her, and she circles him, looking him up and down. In the film this is also the first time she is called Princess. This could mean she was high up in Hell's echelons. Or is it a term of endearment? As Pinhead is sometimes known as the Dark Prince of Hell, it would seem that the two are well suited. The rest of the section reads visually like a mating ritual between them, with each vying for superiority. Like Jacques, Pinhead manifests a certain degree of jealousy about her fascination with Merchant men; then he asserts himself at the end by encasing her in chains, a scene that recalls Joey's bondage at the climax of *Hell on Earth*. When we see her again, she is dressed in the attire of a Cenobite, insinuating that she has relinquished herself fully to Pinhead.

As for Carducci, his fling with Angelique is even shorter than Sharpe's. Unable to ignore Angelique's cries in the mirror on the Minos, he reaches out, only to be killed when it solidifies around him. In any and all cases, just as they are in all the other *Hellraiser* films, sex, love, pain and punishment are intertwined: one is never present without the others.

He Who Commands

Connected very closely with this is the theme of slavery—or even bondage—contained within the movie. Like most slaves, Angelique comes from a poor background: "All alone in this dark, dark world," as the Duc de L'Isle puts it, which suits his purposes exactly. Skinned in the traditional *Hellraiser* fashion, she is used as a vessel for a Princess of Hell—and yet, still she finds herself in servitude. "He who summons the magic, commands the magic!" de L'Isle teaches Jacques. In the original script, it is he who commands Angelique, but in the film the young apprentice steals that power. For two centuries she remains his slave, and it is implied that his treatment of her has not been lenient. When we catch up with them in 1996, the scene between them speaks for itself. Grabbing her by the back of the neck, Jacques elucidates: "Angelique, let's make this clear, what you want is irrelevant. It's about what *I* want. After two hundred years, you should know what those things are." But her chance to escape comes when Jacques ignores the rule about standing in Hell's way. "You like it rough, don't you?" she says, grabbing him by the throat and slashing his face.

Unfortunately, her moment of freedom is short-lived, if it ever truly existed at all. Although personally her reasons for going to New York are to see John Merchant, this overlaps with Hell's bidding; and Hell, as we know, speaks through Pinhead. In the script these contrary forces—the chaos of the Old Hell and stability of the New—are defined by their sparring and her eventual surrender to Pinhead's wishes. In the movie this is much more subtle, expressing itself first in the way Pinhead grows impatient with her progress, then in his line: "A lesson, Princess. Work with me, or *for* me." When it becomes apparent she wants to send him back and regain her freedom, she is forced to return to Hell for Cenobitization. In the last section of the film, we see a more subdued Angelique, once again a slave, this time to discipline. When Pinhead gives her the order to kill the soldiers on the station, there is no argument, no spirited retort as there was back in Merchant's buildings when she told him he was "no different than the beast that sucks the bones you throw to it." Now, she simply obeys; Angelique is bound to Hell's new rules.

Though he is more in control than Angelique, Pinhead, too, is a slave to Hell. We know from the previous movies that there is a human side to him, trapped in the "shell of the beast." His orders come from Leviathan and his efforts to open the larger Lament Configuration in New York are all in the name of his dark god. At the same time, Phillip, John and Paul are slaves to what they have created. Phillip's device has allowed the door to be opened between Earth and Hell, and will cost the lives of many. John has inadvertently done the same thing only on a grander scale. Paul has been a slave to this history and sees it as his responsibility to end the curse, to seek both redemption and retribution. He is tied to this destiny just as surely as the slave-like manacles bind him to his chair when Rimmer is interrogating him. Paul, in turn, has also used the robot in the holding cell as a slave, getting it to perform the task he would rather not, which results in its total obliteration. Lastly, the first two Lemarchand/Merchant incarnations are, to some extent, slaves of Angelique, intoxicated by her, Phillip more so in the script than in the film.

Mirror Images

Mirrors have played a very important part in the mythology of the *Hellraiser* series. They've hidden voyeuristic tendencies, allowed passage into dream landscapes and reflected the inner qualities of the person. In *Bloodline* this trend continues. De L'Isle offers the demon Angelique a mirror so she can look at her new face immediately after he has summoned her. "You are Angelique," he informs her. She studies the guise carefully and smiles before rubbing blood across her lips—as Kirsty does when she sees Larry's skinned figure in *Hellbound*—indicating that de L'Isle is her "father." But there is an aspect that is not revealed until she kills Jacques, her monstrous clawed hand and black eyes hinting at the creature she keeps hidden. This is referred to when Pinhead catches her looking in not one, but two mirrors, symbolically and physically reflecting her two personas. "You look like death, Princess," he says admiringly, as the camera closes in on the pair of them framed in the mirror. It is unclear whether the tear on her cheek is because she hates the form that she now takes, or because she has another one beneath that John Merchant is liable to discover. Quite possibly she is crying for the person she would like to be, one expunged of the evil that dwells inside.

There is one final scene with Angelique and a mirror, during the Minos sequence. Here she is actually on the other side in her human appearance, asking Carducci to, "Help me, please help me!" It is a ruse and when he is pulled through he sees her as the Cenobite she has become. There is something very sad about this, that Angelique's human self has now become merely a shadow used to confuse her victims, like Elliott Spencer, the ghost of what Pinhead once was.

Paul Merchant is also plagued by mirror images. He is cursed with looking exactly like his predecessors, which creates even more pressure for him to conform to their mistakes. "You are so very like your ancestor," Pinhead says to him, "did you know that?" Facially this may be so, but there is a difference. In his current incarnation, with his shaved head (which Ramsey willingly volunteered for just to get this point across), Paul more closely resembles his adversary than he does either Phillip or John. In order to beat the demon he has taken on some of its traits—the obsession, the allegiance to order, the ability to play games. But only Paul and Angelique actually take on *three* different personas at various times: in the latter instance, her human, demonic and Cenobitic likenesses; in the former, his three different generational incarnations

A more tangible representation of the mirror image is presented in the shape of the twins. A staple of horror cinema, these have been used time and again in films like *Dead Men Walk* (Sam Newfield,

A mirror image, the Twin Cenobites of *Hellraiser: Bloodline*. Replica figure by NECA (courtesy NECA; photograph credit Nicolle M. Puzzo).

1943), *The Dark Mirror* (Robert Siodmak, 1946), *Twins of Evil* (John Hough, 1971), right through to the more recent *Dead Ringers* (David Cronenberg, 1988), the brothers chillingly portrayed by Jeremy Irons. In *Bloodline* we first encounter the twins as inept security guards. "What's this?" says the first when they come across a section of John Merchant's building they aren't familiar with. "It's a door," replies the second. "I know it's a door, but it isn't on the chart," his brother replies. The solution is to put it down to "Genius college boys" and investigate. This ends in a confrontation with Pinhead, and their ultimate Cenobitization: "I know your pain, I hear it. Please don't separate me from my brother. I give you my word, that will never happen." The pair are merged forever, a drill winding their faces tightly together. Moments beforehand, their conversation actually alluded to a repressed Cenobitic nature:

> "So she starts asking me all kinds of weird questions," says the first brother, "Like would I do it with a woman who used to be a man."
> "With a guy who had it cut off?" asks twin number two. "So what did you say?"
> His answer is: "I mean, I guess so, if she was cut and all...."

A transformation brought about through pain, exactly like their own. When we see them a second time on the Minos, they have been radically altered: their faces are contorted, one smiling, one frowning. And they have the ability to absorb other people, just as they do with Edwards—disconnecting and coming back together with their victim in the middle. In addition to their mirror image twin faces, they now have another personality as Cenobites taking direction from Pinhead and Angelique.

Darkness and Light

At its most simplistic level, the darkness and light motif represents good versus evil. Pinhead tells John in the corridor that "Darkness is where you'll find me." In contrast, it is "the light" that allows Paul to defeat Hell, solar energy powering the Elysium Configuration. "The light, demon," Paul explains as he makes his escape, "the light." But, as we're aware, nothing is that simple in *Hellraiser*.

Leviathan churns out a black light, itself a paradox, and the demons can be seen as angels to some. The main female demon in this film even takes part of her name from this concept: Angel-ique. The monster she hides beneath her human guise and the Hell she originates from is more in keeping with those described in chapter 9. She is a demon of the Old Hell—and thus could only find a home in an unchristened host. Therefore, her radical metamorphosis into a Cenobite could be seen as a rebirth, a baptism to wash away the elements of chaos she once defended.

Pinhead, as we've noted, turned his back on the Christian God after his experiences in the First World War. His opinions haven't altered and this gives rise to one of his finest lines: "Do I look like someone who cares what God thinks?" He is asked to question who he is in this movie at least twice, by Angelique and by Paul. In this last scene Pinhead tells Paul that he has the "same faithless hope in the light" as his ancestors. "And what do you have faith in?" Paul asks. "Nothing," is the reply, "I am so exquisitely empty." Except we know this isn't completely true. Somewhere deep inside, Elliott Spencer is begging to be released—a release that comes when the Elysium Configuration is activated. As he dies, Pinhead—or Elliott—whispers: "Amen." Could this one word mean that he is again embracing the light? That at the end he has sought forgiveness from a God he once turned his back on? The very name of the Elysium Configuration is taken from the Greek Elysium Fields, a heaven where souls go to rest upon their death.

But if the lines between the light and dark are blurred again, we can be sure of one thing: the black magic that de L'Isle practices is the very embodiment of evil. Most surely influenced by the Marquis de Sade, who was alive around that time, though probably more by the Satanist Gilles de Rais (a French nobleman from the 1400s who kidnapped, tortured and murdered hundreds of peasant children in his black magic experiments) with a pinch of Frankenstein, de L'Isle's ritual to summon a demon uses iconography that will be familiar to most horror fans—the pentangle, the Latin incantations, the blood sacrifice. These are shorthand to identify the true forces of darkness in this movie.

17

A Distinct Sense of Déjà Vu

More than any other picture in the series so far, *Bloodline* relies upon previous filmic references to tell its story. As Doug Bradley said in the U.S. press kit: "In a way, we made three films in one: a Gothic horror film, a contemporary horror film and almost a genre-crossover, a science fiction horror film."[1] In some respects the movie couldn't help referring to those that had gone before it. Simply in terms of the iconography and setting, the eighteenth century section closely resembles films like *The Scarlet Pimpernel* (Harold Young, 1934). But both the storyline and décor match when examining Stephen Frears' 1988 film, *Dangerous Liaisons*. This film is set in baroque France, circa 1760–1770, and tells the story of a bet made by a widow, the Marquise de Merteuil (Glenn Close), and her ex-lover Vicomte Sébastien de Valmont (John Malkovich) to corrupt a married woman, Madame de Tourvel (Michelle Pfeiffer). Full of intrigue and sexually charged, it could easily be taking place not far from the Chateau du Reve in *Bloodline*.

Furthermore, this section, as Bradley suggests, does owe much to the Gothic tradition of horror films, typified by the Universal movies of the 1930s and Hammer films of the '50s and '60s. But its closest cousin must be a production that only just beat *Bloodline*'s release: *Mary Shelley's Frankenstein* (Kenneth Branagh, 1994). An extremely faithful adaptation of the original novel, in look and theme it is another good mate. A comparison of the birth scene in both — Angelique's and Robert de Niro's monster — should be enough to convince, the organic nature of both so close in conception. Similarly, Branagh's Frankenstein shares many of the same qualities of Phillip's inventor: dedication to his work; realization of their one true masterpiece, no matter what the cost; dabbling in areas they definitely should not be.

Yet, it is in the future section that cinematic comparisons are abundant. One might even speculate this was done on purpose because of the success of those it emulated. The first is the shot of the Minos's interior, accompanied by a very good imitation of Jerry Goldmith's and James Horner's respective scores for the opening of *Alien* and *Aliens*. The corridors also recall the dirty, industrial look of these seminal films, in direct opposition to the look Atkins wanted:

> (*NB: PRODUCTION NOTE*: This area and all the areas (mainly corridors) that are not function-specific have a half-finished laser-blasted look to them. There are grooves in the walls of the rock where corridors and walkways were blasted through. Unless specifically described otherwise, *everywhere* on the Minos is *rock*, not steel or wood or plaster.)[2]

Rather like the caverns of the Christian Hell. He knew that this would have given it a more original look, more in tune with lesser known sci-fi movies such as *Saturn 3* (Stanley Donen,

1980) and *Outland* (Peter Hyams, 1981). The combination of lack of money and the insistence on using such cinematic shorthand combines to give this sense of déjà vu. Though the outside of the Minos station is original in design — clearly an unfolded box, which gives the dramatic ending less impact — the shuttle that arrives is an almost exact replica of the drop-ships used by the space marines in Cameron's sequel to *Alien*.

When they infiltrate the station, their movements resemble those of Cameron's marines, too, as they hunted for Xenomorphs on the remote Terra-forming colony. However, in dress, they look more like the futuristic Detroit police officers of another classic sci-fi franchise, *Robocop* (Paul Verhoeven, 1987). In their dark blue riot gear and face shields, as they make their way through the corridors to Paul Merchant's quarters, they are merely extrapolations of the police teams of the day — just like Robocop's contemporaries — with Rimmer an adequate replacement for Nancy Allen's Lewis. More robotic resemblances abound when Paul uses a droid to open the Lament Configuration. Sat crossed-legged, the same position Frank and Elliott had occupied in previous *Hellraiser* entries, the robot is an exact duplicate of the T-1000 endoskeleton from *The Terminator* (James Cameron, 1984) and *Terminator 2: Judgment Day*, even down to the red, glowing eyes. The only difference is that this one is more docile and cannot fight back when the Cenobites tear it to pieces.

We are granted more *Alien* references as the section continues. The female voice of the computer is comparable to "Mother," who counts down the time Sigourney Weaver's Ripley has to escape from the Nostromo (and, to a lesser extent, the countdown to evacuation in *Aliens* when Ripley sets out to rescue Newt from the Alien Queen), while Rimmer does a passable impression of the same heroine when trying to outwit the Chatter Beast in the corridors, substituting a shuttle's rockets for a decompression chamber.

The use of a holographic character is informed not only by *Star Trek: The Next Generation*'s holosuite — which could conjure up people from thin air — but also *Red Dwarf*'s holographic officer played by Chris Barrie, coincidentally enough called Rimmer. Lastly, the final condition of the Minos station, a metallic representation of the puzzle box, looks suspiciously like a Borg ship, also from *The Next Generation*. The Borg race, ironically enough, were themselves possibly modeled on Cenobites; or are, at any rate, futuristic versions of them due to their ethos.

18

A BLOODLINE CURSED TO THE END OF TIME

The critical response to *Hellraiser: Bloodline* was almost universal. Reviewers lined up to criticize and condemn the movie, with *Variety* being one of the first: "Except for the most undiscriminating gorehound, the pic is a pointless mess." Richard Harrington at the *Washington Post* in his review of March 6, 1996, shared some of these sentiments, applauding Yagher's decision to take his name off the film: "Yagher's move was a good one, for this fourth installment in the Clive Barker-inspired 'Hellraiser' chronicles is the least imaginative…. The three episodes do not hang together all that well and the Configuration mythology is never really illuminated. Even poor Pinhead seems bored; other visually distressing creatures don't show up until the last reel, far too late to rescue the film." He does, though, concede that it has the widest scope of any of the movies so far.

John A. Lavin of *Movie Magazine International* was slightly more balanced in his evisceration of *Bloodline*: "So, is this great science fiction? No. Is it great horror, sending endless chills down one's spine? Not really. What this movie is, though, is a decent distraction. It's certainly not a bad little time at the movies."

Scan O'Neill at *Box Office Magazine* was not quite so restrained: "'Whither Pinhead?' might have been the question that the … fans out there in movieland were clamoring to have answered in a third sequel to Clive Barker's 1986 horror masterwork, *Hellraiser*. 'Wither, Pinhead!' might be what each of them says after paying good money to see this…." He continues: "Whenever Alan Smithee is credited as the director, informed audiences know they're in trouble."

The *Deseret News* reviewer, Chris Hicks, commented, "Though the *Hellraiser* movies have traditionally taken place in dark, dank abodes with 'haunted house' written all over them (along with those long, spooky hallways that inevitably shoot chains and hooks into the flesh of innocents who pass through), this one begins like an episode of TV's 'Space: Above and Beyond,' as a 22nd-century space station is boarded by armed troops."

The most considered, and perhaps the longest, review came from Anthony Tomlinson at *Shivers* magazine, who really took the time to go through the history of the project, making the viewer aware of all the bad luck that had befallen the venture before passing judgment: "Even by Smithee's demanding standards the production of *Hellraiser — Bloodline* was … difficult."[1] But the overall response was still the same: "Fundamentally, *Hellraiser — Bloodline* fails to achieve the key aim of any film: to tell a story, and on this occasion it's hard to know where to point the finger of blame."[2]

Perhaps it was a testament to the dedication of *Hellraiser* fans that the film did so respectably at the box office — so much so that speculation was rife about a further sequel. When asked if this was the series end, in an interview for *Lost Souls*, Peter Atkins said, "You never can tell. Miramax is very interested, but you have to look at these questions from a creative viewpoint and a financial one. As far as I was concerned, part three was the end creatively. It seemed to round things off.... But Miramax wanted to do a fourth part and Clive had the nice idea of a three part story, which excited my interest.... But I think from this point on it would be just telling more stories about the box and the demons. So I am not particularly interested in pursuing it. Miramax certainly want to preserve the franchise. One reason why they are spending the extra money in having this extra shoot is to keep the franchise alive for parts five and six." And when the subject cropped up of Pinhead versus Jason, he said jokingly: "You'd better believe it! Actually, they don't own Jason, but they do own Michael Myers. So Pinhead versus Michael Myers might be a distinct possibility somewhere down the road."[3]

Doug Bradley's reply when asked if he would be vowing never to play Pinhead again was, "Not at all, I'd certainly consider another *Hellraiser* movie. I hear rumors about a fifth film, although I know nothing about it."[4] And Clive Barker's reaction? "*Hellraiser 4* has been released in the States. It's not very good. I think they are making another one. Oh, God!"[5]

19
Dante's Footsteps

In part because of the reaction to *Bloodline*, there would be another gap before the next *Hellraiser* film arrived—regardless of the fact that Miramax were keen to start on a follow-up as soon as possible. They did not want to let this franchise die, especially when they were still planning sequels to films like *Children of the Corn*. The *Hellraiser* fanbase remained a strong one and there was room to tell more stories in that universe, as the *Hellraiser* comic series had shown. (See chapter 33.) Dimension listened to potential pitches and developed scripts for some time, many of which picked up plotlines from the previous entries, set in modern day America.

However, one sought to bring the *Hellraiser* story back home to London for the millennium. This was a treatment by the unit publicist on the first three films and a well-respected editor of books like *The Hellraiser Chronicles* and *The Mammoth Book of Best New Horror*, Stephen Jones, working with his friend, bestselling author of *Only Forward* and *Spares*, Michael Marshall Smith (nowadays also known for his *Straw Men* thrillers written as Michael Marshall). Their idea, entitled *Hellraiser: Hellfire*, revolves around Jack Credence, a businessman with his finger in every pie and the head of a cult called The Nine. Members of The Nine think Credence draws his power from ritual magic, whereas actually it comes from a pact he made in the '80s with a figure very familiar to *Hellraiser* fans: Pinhead. Pitted against the forces of Hell this time was a shy but tough American, Christine Freely, who works in a bookstore Credence happens upon, and who has access to antiquated tomes that might just help in her battle.

Smith and Jones brought back familiar characters, such as the original Cenobites (including a deadlier CGI incarnation of The Engineer) and Kirsty—now an insane derelict after her earlier encounters with the demons—and even returned to the house at Dollis Hill, where Christine thinks she spots a figure in the attic window. But they added to these traditional elements a determination to use the city itself as a character, weaving a multi-layered story from its history, including the positioning of abandoned tube stations and Hawksmoor churches. The climax involved a giant Lament Configuration pattern encompassing the whole of London, and a race against time to stop a gateway to Hell opening as Leviathan breaks through into the real world and panic grips the streets. In essence, it would be a lost *Hellraiser* classic that tied up a lot of loose ends, adding much depth and humanity to the mythology in the process. Though it was written in response to a commission from Miramax's London office, encountered a warm welcome at a pitch in Los Angeles, and received strong support from both Doug Bradley and Peter Atkins, *Hellraiser: Hellfire* ran aground on the mechanics of the film industry.

Or perhaps still bides its time in the shadows …

Concurrently there were moves to put the original *Hellraiser* onstage in the West End. Barker gave his blessing to the theatrical production, which was due to open around May 1999, and Doug Bradley was approached to play Pinhead again. A veteran theatre actor, the only thing that bothered him would be the make-ups every night, but as he told Nick Joy, "The bottom line is I don't want some other bugger doing it. I can't face the thought of someone else opening the show in the West End or taking it all over to Broadway."[1]

Banking on a fresh start for the celluloid series, Miramax producers eventually settled upon the creative team of Scott Derrickson and Paul Harris Boardman. The pair met at USC's film school where Boardman wrote and directed *The Roof*, a short film that won a CINE Eagle Award and several festival prizes. Derrickson edited the project and became quite a fan of his friend's writing, so much so that he asked Boardman to co-write his own thesis film: a short called *Love in the Ruins* (1995). This enabled them to attract an agent, and they co-wrote a full-length screenplay together called *Darkness Falling* which Derrickson was slated to direct with Bryan Singer serving as executive producer. Even though the movie went into turnaround, the duo found this put them in a good position regarding a potential *Hellraiser* film.

After passing on all the other ideas they'd been presented with, Dimension asked if they had anything original they could bring to the table. They returned to the company with an idea Derrickson called "outrageous."[2] He went on to explain, "It was a detective story and a bizarre concept, but they loved it and commissioned us to write it. I was not attached to direct at that point. They were thrilled with the script and we got a three-picture writing deal."[3] When Derrickson told Bob Weinstein that he would like to direct the picture as well, he gave the young director $10,000 and sent him out to film a test scene from the movie in 16mm. Weinstein liked what he saw and agreed to let Derrickson direct. It was around the time that they were negotiating this deal for *Hellraiser* that Boardman and Derrickson also became involved in a possible *Urban Legend* (Jamie Blanks, 1998) sequel. The producers of that one liked their *Darkness Falling* script and they were also commissioned to write *Final Cut* (John Ottman, 2000). They wrote both the scripts back-to-back and handed *Inferno* in first.

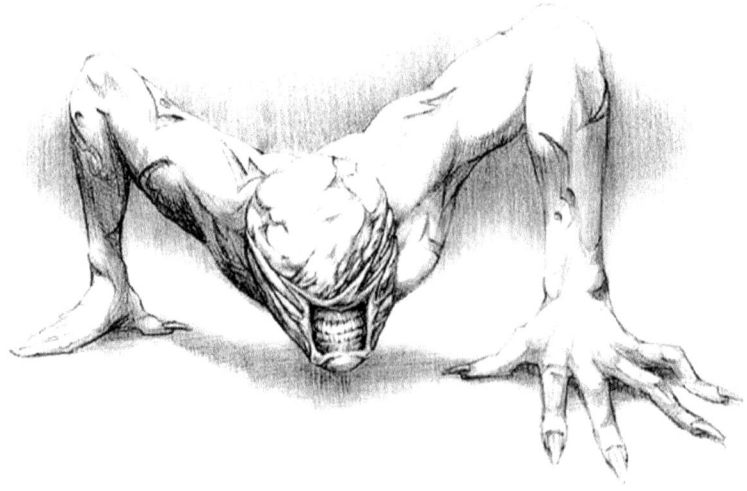

Chatterer Torso sketch by Steven Lawrence (courtesy Gary J. Tunnicliffe).

The script revolves around Detective Joseph Thorne of the Denver P.D. and his investigation into the death of Jay Cho, a man he hasn't seen since high school. When he discovers a child's finger inside a wax candle at the crime scene, he soon finds himself chasing a serial killer who has a proclivity for young victims. On his journey he experiences weird hallucinations and begins to question his own sanity, which results in a visit to see psychiatrist Dr. Paul Gregory. His enquiries also lead him into conflict with a mythical crime boss called The Engineer, whom we don't get to meet until the very end. It isn't long before Thorne realizes that not only is he racing against time to save the child whose fingers are being severed, but also to save himself. There are obvious heritages to the screenplay, the first being—coincidentally—from Singer's *The Usual Suspects* (1995), as well as David Lynch's surrealistic *Blue Velvet* (1986), *Twin Peaks: Fire Walk with Me* (1992) and *Lost Highway* (1997), plus popular serial killer movies *The Silence of the Lambs* (Jonathan Demme, 1991) and *Se7en* (David Fincher, 1995). There is also a huge film noir influence which we shall explore in the next chapter.

Doug Bradley has always said that the script was a pre-existing one about a troubled cop, which was then turned into a *Hellraiser* movie,[4] and there are definite grounds for this case. The mythos elements seemed forced or disjointed; for example, Jay Cho's murder is quite obviously related to the Lament Configuration found in his home, yet the box itself appears to be part of the candlestick holding the candle with the child's finger inside it. This begs the question of how he opened it. The Cenobites also usually take their victims away with them to Hell and clean up the evidence left behind, so as not to arouse suspicion or necessitate a police enquiry, as happens here. Jay Cho's murder could have occurred in any way for the purposes of the tale; it just so happens that chains and hooks were the methods used.

Thorne's descent into madness, too, albeit a creditable personal Hell Dante would have been proud of, could simply be explained away as guilt about the kind of person he is and the actions he has taken—without any involvement of the Cenobites at all. Undeniably, it is the moralistic tone of the piece, almost as if he is punishing himself rather than letting the demons do it for him, that negates the previous ground rules of the *Hellraiser* series. This in particular was of great concern to Bradley: "I had also felt uneasy about the distinctly avuncular, moralistic tone that Pinhead had been given, particularly in his 'summing up' speech towards the end of the film. Whatever else he may be, I have never exactly seen him as a moral guardian."[5]

Something else that troubled Bradley was the scarcity of Pinhead scenes, and Cenobites in general. Disturbing though they are, the new creations are relegated to the position of hallucinatory glimpses that may or may not be part of Thorne's imagination, much like the monsters in *Jacob's Ladder* (Adrian Lyne, 1990). While it was probably true that the franchise needed to regain some of the mystery of the first films by cutting back on Cenobite appearances, they still needed to be present for it to be classed as a *Hellraiser* film. As Bradley clarified, "I was surprised I was in it so little. The irony is, and I said this to them [Dimension] ... that I think we need to hold back a little bit. I think you can overexpose, and the law of diminishing returns kicks in, but I think they went to another extreme."[6] Nevertheless, the actor agreed to be involved because he didn't want to be left out of the loop completely; besides that, the stage *Hellraiser* project had fallen through.

In response, Derrickson argued: "The thematic concerns and philosophy are closer to the original. What's so fascinating about the original is that you go through the entire movie and eventually you realize that the Cenobites are not the monsters. The monsters are Frank and Claire. That's what Paul and I gravitated towards with this one, and we tried to figure out how to do that again."[7] And to counter the worries about Pinhead's brief appearances, "His importance to the story is probably as great as it has ever been in any of the movies."[8]

In spite of all this, principal photography was set to commence towards the end of 1999 on a hectic thirty day schedule, with a predicted budget of $2 million. Derrickson had a lot of freedom from start to finish, first working with Dimension executive David Jordan, who let the first draft of the script pass through (this became the shooting script) and then afterwards when Jordan resigned during preproduction for his own reasons. As a result Derrickson and Boardman were left much to their own devices, and with bigger Dimension movies in production at the same time — like the third installment in the hugely successful *Scream* trilogy — *Inferno* was, according to Derrickson, "barely on people's radar."[9] Some might say that this level of independence was not necessarily a good thing. Certainly Barker's input might have straightened out some of the more obvious kinks, but as he told the Sci-Fi Channel's Web site at the time, "I'm not invited to their [Dimension's] meetings."[10]

But casting went ahead, with the main role of Thorne going to Barker alumnus Craig Sheffer, whom Bradley had worked with ten years previously. Since his turn as the savior Cabal in *Nightbreed*, the 39-year-old actor had been quite prolific, starring in films such as *Blue Desert* (Bradley Battersby, 1991) as Randall Atkins; Robert Redford's *A River Runs Through It* (1992) alongside Brad Pitt; true life alien abduction story *Fire in the Sky* (Robert Lieberman, 1993); *Wings of Courage* (Jean-Jacques Annaud, 1995); the comedy *Head Above Water* (Jim Wilson, 1996) with Harvey Keitel and Cameron Diaz; *Shadow of Doubt* (Randal Kleiser, 1998) opposite Melanie Griffith and Tom Berenger; and *Merlin: The Return* (Paul Matthews, 1999), where he took on the part of Mordred, with Rik Mayall as Merlin, Patrick Bergin as King Arthur and former *Highlander* actor Adrian Paul as Lancelot.

Sheffer had the difficult task of making the unappealing character of this detective — who cheats on his wife, frames his friends and beats up his snitches — watchable, something he does very well. Whether the previous Barker credit works for or against him is subjective, but one thing is indisputable: Boone is the complete antithesis of Thorne. Where the former tries hard to control the monster within him, the latter lets it out and doesn't care who sees it. Finally, something that might have indicated he was destined to be in a *Hellraiser* movie is Sheffer's real-life hobby of solving jigsaw puzzles.

Playing his partner, Tony Nenonen, would be Nicholas Turturro, brother of John and cousin of Aida. Known for his early associations with Spike Lee on the movies *Mo' Better Blues* (1990) — in which Denzel Washington steals the show as the trumpet-playing Bleek Gilliam — *Jungle Fever* (1991) and *Malcolm X* (1992), Turturro was also familiar to viewers as Detective James Martinez on the long-running TV series *NYPD Blue*, a role he played for seven years. This didn't stop him from taking movie assignments, as his performance as Grasso in *Shadow Conspiracy* (George P. Cosmatos, 1997) alongside Charlie Sheen, Donald Sutherland and Linda Hamilton confirms. Turturro would bring just the right amount of humor (the wordplay banter between them is particularly effective) and realism to the part, evidenced in scenes where he displays his disappointment at Thorne's behavior and rising suspicions that he could actually be the killer.

Character actor James Remar, distinguished by his intense stare, was hired as psychiatrist Dr. Paul Gregory. Remar trained at New York's Neighborhood Playhouse and made an impact playing Richard Gere's lover in the Broadway production of *Bent* in 1979. His role as a punk in the movie from that same year, *The Warriors* (Walter Hill), gained him something of a cult status, which he built on with William Friedkin's *Cruising* (1980), *48 Hours* (Hill, 1982), where he played a homicidal prison escapee alongside Eddie Murphy and Nick Nolte, *The Cotton Club* (Francis Ford Coppola, 1984), and *Drugstore Cowboy* (Gus

Van Sant, 1989). He was cast as the original Hicks in *Aliens* but had to be replaced very early in the film by Michael Biehn (who even used his outfit). His other genre credits include *Tales from the Darkside: The Movie* (John Harrison, 1990), *Judge Dredd* (Danny Cannon, 1995), *The Phantom* (Simon Wincer, 1996), *Mortal Combat: Annihilation* (John R. Leonetti, 1997), and Gus Van Sant's ill-advised remake of *Psycho* (1998). The actor is probably best known, though, for the recurring television role of philandering Richard, high society boyfriend of Amanda (Kim Cattrall) in *Sex and the City*. Oddly enough, he also starred as Dr. Coleman West in a 1998 telemovie called *Inferno*.

Nicholas Sadler was drafted in as Bernie, Thorne's repugnant informant and drug supplier, who drives around in an ice cream van to attract the young children. His career began with the telefilm *A Town's Revenge* (Helen Whitney, 1989), playing Billy Dryer. He graduated to *The Cosby Show* in 1990 before starring in the TV version of Stephen King's *Sometimes They Come Back*

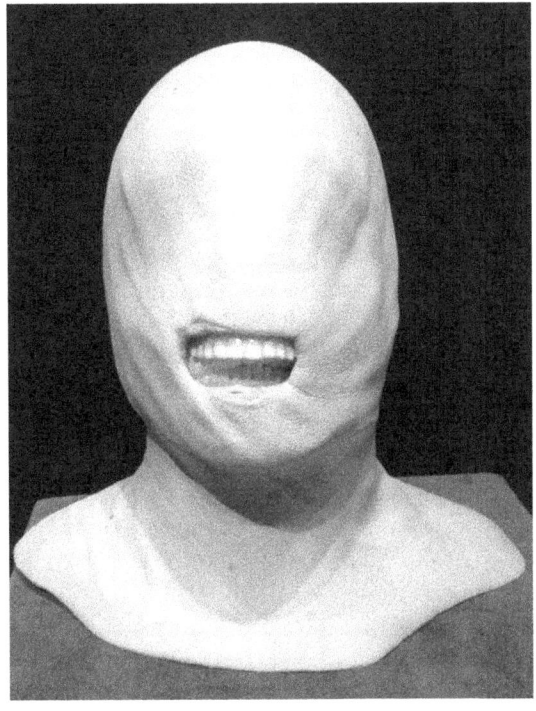

The Faceless Killer mask. Original item like many props sold at the Prop Store of London (courtesy Stephen Lane).

(Tom McLoughlin, 1991). Later standouts included *Twister* (1996), Jan de Bont's phenomenal special effects extravaganza, and the low budget horror movie *Idle Hands* (Rodman Flender, 1999) with *Buffy*'s Seth Green.

Boasting fewer credits were Noelle Evans, who portrayed Thorne's wife Melanie, and Lindsay Taylor, Thorne's daughter Chloe. Noelle had previously starred in *Dangerous Proposition* (Brad Sanders, 1998) a character-driven low-budget thriller, and an episode of *Ally McBeal* in 1999. Young Lindsay's only film role up to that point was as the Little Girl in a 1999 episode of *Buffy the Vampire Slayer* entitled "Gingerbread." Next came Matt George, who puts in a memorable performance as the tattoo artist and body-piercing expert, Leon, at a parlor Thorne visits. George had featured in an episode of *Red Shoe Diaries* (1995) and *Charmed* (1999) as well as the Zalman King movie *In God's Hands* (1998).

Michael Shamus Wiles' screen roles were many and varied, beginning with *Divided We Fall* in 1982 (Jeff Burr and Kevin Meyer). His films included *Leatherface: Texas Chainsaw Massacre III* (Jeff Burr, 1990); *Up Close & Personal* (Jon Avnet, 1996) with Robert Redford and Michelle Pfeiffer; *Dune* (Joseph D. Kucan, 1998); *Fallen* (Gregory Hoblit, 1998); *Fight Club* (David Fincher, 1999); and *Magnolia* (Paul Thomas Anderson, 1999) with Tom Cruise. Interestingly, he also had a part in David Lynch's *Lost Highway* as a guard, which further emphasizes the bond between the two pictures, although his character in *Inferno*, the gun-toting cowboy Mr. Parmagi, is definitely more peculiar.

Eighteen-year-old Sasha Barrese was cast as Daphne, the prostitute Thorne sleeps with just before he opens the puzzle box, and who turns up dead in the shower not long afterwards. The former model, born in Hawaii, got her first acting job at the age of just eight in *Homer and Eddie* (Andrei Konchalovsky, 1989) with her mother Katherine Barrese. In 1990 she starred as Young Jezebel in *Jezebel's Kiss* (Harvey Keith), then appeared as the Random Cute Girl in *American Pie* (Paul Weitz, 1999). Since starring in *Hellraiser V* she has landed parts in Hollywood blockbusters like *The Ring* (Gore Verbinski, 2002).

Kathryn Joosten, bit-part actress from TV shows like *Picket Fences, Grace Under Fire, Roseanne, ER, Seinfeld, NYPD Blue* and *Dharma and Greg*, took the role of Thorne's older mother in both the hospital scenes and the flashbacks at the finale, while Jessica Elliot from *Cityscrapes: Los Angeles* (Michael Becker, 1994) played the younger version. Likewise, Thomas Crouch would be Thorne's father in the present day for the coma scenes and the gunfight at the climax, while Timothy "T.J." James Driscoll played the younger incarnation.

Sadly, veteran actor Carmen Argenziano was to be shamefully wasted as the captain at the police precinct, featuring in just the one scene where Thorne plays back the tape of Bernie's murder. Argenziano came complete with a lengthy credits list, beginning in 1970 with *Cover Me Babe* (Noel Black), and would take in *The Godfather Part II* (Francis Ford Coppola, 1974), *Sudden Impact* (Clint Eastwood, 1983), *The First Power* (Robert Resnikoff, 1990), *Broken Arrow* (John Woo, 1996), and *Blue Streak* (Les Mayfield, 1999), in addition to countless TV roles in shows like *Quincy, Hill Street Blues, L.A. Law,* and *JAG*. His most famous role, and the one for which he would be recognized in genre circles, was as Samantha Carter's (Amanda Tapping) father in the hugely successful spin-off series from the movie *Stargate* (Roland Emmerich, 1994), renamed *Stargate: SG-1* (1997).

Other actors signed up were Christopher (*Enemy Action* (Brian Katkin, 1999)) Neiman as the pathologist; Christopher (*The Landlady* (Robert Malenfant, 1998)) Kriesa as the older detective; Brian Sostek in a quirky turn as the Crime Lab Technician; J.B. Gaynor from *The Contract* (Steven R. Monroe, 1999) as young Joseph Thorne; Winifred (*The Naked Gun* [David Zucker, 1988]) Freedman as Front Desk Nurse; Michael Denney, who played a demon in Derrickson and Boardman's *Love in the Ruins*, switching to a Security Guard; Ray Miceli as The Faceless Killer; Kazuhiro Yokoyama and stuntman Akihiro Noguchi as the karate-kicking cowboys; Lynn Speier and Trisha Kara as the Wire Twin Cenobites; and Michael Regan as the uncredited Chatterer Torso (Regan would go on to executive produce Gary Tunnicliffe's short *Hellraiser* film, *No More Souls*).

In terms of Crew, Gary Tunnicliffe returned thanks to his superb make-ups for *Bloodline*. On this occasion he'd work in conjunction with the visual effects supervisor, Jamison Goei, on certain shots, such as the Torso Chatterer, which had to have its lower body removed digitally. Goei would also be responsible for the excellent cracking and shattering of Thorne's frozen wife and child, chained to a pillar near the end of the movie, although again this was in tandem with live effects such as Thorne snapping off his daughter's arm (calling to mind the superb work with the T-1000 in *Terminator 2: Judgment Day*). One of the few things Tunnicliffe wasn't overly happy about was the Wire Twins' make-up. "They were compromised by money.... I would love to go back and re-work the jaw that holds up the wire pulls, as during the day it got stretched and their jaws got kinda long and wacky," he said in an interview afterwards.[11] Nonetheless, these two women, who perform a highly sexual and graphic "under the skin" massage on Thorne that is possibly the highlight of the movie, have become definite fan favorites. Their serpent tongues, also provided by Goei, might well have contributed to their appeal.

Cinematographer on the shoot would be Nathan Hope, who had worked only on *Suckers* (Roger Nygard, 1999) and *Nice Guys Sleep Alone* (Stu Pollard, 1999). He would ensure at least the slick look of the picture, with cool, icy blues and stark lighting for the snow scenes, and sepia tones blended with tinges of green for the Thorne childhood flashbacks. In charge of production design would be Deborah Raymond, whose credits included *Scanner Cop* (Pierre David, 1994); *Leprechaun 4: In Space* (Brian Trenchard-Smith, 1996); *Wishmaster* (Robert Kurtzman, 1997, written by Peter Atkins); and *Ringmaster* (Neil Abramson, 1998). She would be responsible for some great sets on what — it has to be said — was a shoestring budget. Possibly her most important contribution would be young Joseph's room that he keeps returning to throughout the movie.

Editing would be handled by relative newcomer Kirk M. Morri, whose only experience was on TV with *Jeopardy!* and *Assault on Dome 4* (Gilbert Po, 1996). He would need to add essential suspense and pace to what is largely a thriller film. For sound design, Derrickson hired Creative Café and sound designers Peter Brown and Byron Miller to come up with the movie's vital auditory scares. Said the director: "Those guys gave 150 percent — honing and working it to build the best sound design they could. That was one way to make this movie feel bigger than it actually is."[12]

Last, Walter Werzowa was chosen to provide the music — after working on *Tales from the Crypt*, supplying additional music for the final fight scene in *Mortal Kombat* (Paul W.S. Anderson, 1995) and the main title music for the Arnold Schwarzenegger vehicle *Eraser* (Chuck Russell, 1996). His new *Hellraiser* theme would be a world away from those used in the past, but still incredibly powerful with its use of strings and drum base, not to mention a choir, harking back to *The Omen*. His cool jazz riffs recall those composed by Angelo Badalamenti for Lynch's *Twin Peaks* TV series, with cymbals, violins and trumpet used to excellent effect. The movie would also feature the song "From Eden," performed by MOD: I.

As is to be expected when any director is left to his own devices, the shoot went quite smoothly; compared with all the trouble on *Bloodline* this was a new direction for the series in more ways than one. Bradley's scenes took just three days to shoot, for which he flew over to L.A., and when he got there he was able to talk to Derrickson about Pinhead's phrasing. The director told him that writing for the character had been the hardest thing they had faced, so with his permission Bradley was allowed to change aspects of it to more accurately reflect the

The popular Wire Twins from *Inferno*. Replica figures by NECA (courtesy NECA; photograph credit: Nicolle M. Puzzo).

Pinhead audiences had grown to expect. "He's a Shakespearean actor at heart," said Derrickson, "and he added quite a few lines to that final speech that made it a lot better."[13]

But despite its brevity this was a shoot Bradley was unlikely to forget, thanks to a very special celebration on-set. On his third and final day at work, Gary Tunnicliffe presented him with a mock telegram from Her Majesty the Queen. The effects artist had calculated that it was Bradley's 100th day in the Pinhead make-up, so the crew was celebrating accordingly. At lunchtime there was champagne and a cake in the shape of Pinhead's face with candles in place of the nails. Some old friends dropped by as well, including Peter Atkins and production designer Steve Hardie from the early *Hellraisers*. "Steve brought me the most fabulous present," said Bradley. "He gave me a framed piece of Pinhead's face with a huge, two-foot long nail and a big gout of blood dripping off the end of it. It's quite impressive."[14] Additionally, the cast and crew were given Access All Areas Pinhead badges, and Bradley got a certificate for all his hard work over the years. "I wasn't expecting any of it," he admitted.[15]

The film wrapped on schedule, but Derrickson still didn't know whether it was going to be given a theatrical release like the previous *Hellraisers*. *Inferno* was shot with both media in mind and was actually transferred in widescreen. As Boardman commented not long after completion: "My impression is that Dimension didn't necessarily know, either, because some of the movies they've done before have gone theatrical and some have not."[16] This turned out to be the case. *Hellraiser: Inferno* was the first in the series to debut on TV screens at home — in November 2000. Although the "direct to video" label no longer has the stigma attached to it that it once had, due in no small part to the boom of the DVD industry, it was nevertheless a disappointment for followers of the series not to see the new release playing at their local cinema.

But this would be the start of a trend that saw the next three films premiere in exactly the same way.

20

A World Full of Riddles

Crime and Punishment

Hellraiser: Inferno is at its heart a crime film. The central character is a policeman who is attempting to fathom out who has killed Jay Cho. He is also trying to track down the serial killer responsible for kidnapping a child and cutting off his fingers one by one, with each digit representing a kill. Yet it is not a straightforward crime drama by any means. Its roots lie firmly in the film noir genre, a term used by French film critics of the 1940s to describe American thrillers derived from the kind of hard-boiled fiction written by Raymond Chandler, James M. Cain and Cornell Woolrich. *Inferno* adheres to this mode of filmmaking in several ways, not least in its overriding sense of pessimism and social malaise.

Firstly, noir pictures are usually cheaply made, and the ones these critics were originally referring to were B movies. Secondly, *Inferno* mimics the visual style favored by so many noir films of that age, contrastive lighting being a specific example of this, used to objectify a protagonist's psychological states of mind. In *Inferno* the lighting switches from soft and warm when Thorne is with his family, to hard and cold — and even shadowy — when he is on the streets. The noir setting is usually an urban one, highlighting the grimy underbelly of the city, in this instance the world of prostitution and drug dealing.

Minor characters are expected to be stereotypes: the weaselly snitch (Bernie); the loving and long-suffering wife (Melanie); the by the book partner (Tony); the whore (Daphne). The only female character who counteracts this is the *femme fatale*, an intelligent, active woman who manipulates the protagonist. Granted, one is not present as such in *Inferno*, but Dr. Gregory/Pinhead certainly manipulates Thorne by the use of these women.

Thirdly, the main protagonist himself is morally ambiguous. Thorne might be a cop, but he has more in common with Humphrey Bogart's Sam Spade from *The Maltese Falcon* (John Huston, 1941) than he does with the clean cut heroes of other police dramas. For most of the movie he operates alone, keeping things from Tony. (He even comments, after Thorne has withheld information about the case, "Thanks for keeping me informed, *partner!*") Only when he requires Tony's help, or backup, does he ask him along — such as when they cover up evidence at the scene of Daphne's murder or when they visit Parmagi. The rest of the time he is a loner, a drug addict with a cruel streak and a hidden agenda.

Thorne is a thoroughly dislikable character, but like all noir heroes he has one or two

"Whipping Boy" Bernie, with make-up by Gary J. Tunnicliffe's crew (courtesy Gary J. Tunnicliffe).

redeeming qualities. His love of children and their innocence is what compels him to catch the killer. "That child was still alive," he says to himself as he looks through the missing children on his computer screen, "and if I could just keep it that way I knew it would be the best thing I could do in my lifetime." This extends to devotion for his own daughter, signaled quite early on by a close-up of him pressing his face against hers while she sleeps, though the tilted angle warns that something is wrong with this picture. Thorne would be the perfect family man were it not for his warped views on marriage. "I believe in loyalty, fidelity," he tells us as he picks up Daphne. "I understand the concept. My parents have been married for forty years. But I live in a different world. Most marriages fail, most men just leave; I know that would kill her. But if she doesn't know, if doing this keeps me coming back, then who's to say what's right and what's wrong?"

This constant use of the voice-over is our fourth film noir prerequisite. Most of the early noir films relied upon this device to convey the protagonist's internal thoughts to the viewer and it is still used in many modern noir movies, from *Blade Runner* (Ridley Scott, 1982) to *Memento* (Christopher Nolan, 2000). We are privy to Thorne's thoughts right from the beginning when he gets changed in the locker room: "Even as a little kid I was wanting to examine things closely. The world was full of riddles and mysteries and puzzles. I learned early on I had a gift for solving them."

Closely linked to this is the use of flashbacks to tell the story, often facilitating the solving of the central mystery. As Thorne has commented, he is the ultimate solver of riddles, but the one he must solve now will explain what's happening to him and where exactly he is—and only through the flashbacks to his boyhood can he do this. Not only that, time itself is looping, as it does in *Groundhog Day* (Harold Ramis, 1993). Thorne is reliving the same events over and over, waking up in the bathroom with the box, waking on the bed at home after visiting his parents. Such is the way *Inferno* has been constructed, the flashbacks are intermingled with real time, and vice versa.

Interlaced with this are the serial killer aspects, where Throne tracks down the killer using police procedural techniques, as Agent Starling (Jodie Foster) does in *The Silence of the Lambs*. But the film is closer in tone to *Se7en*, in that it offers a gimmick for the murders. In Fincher's masterpiece it was, of course, the Seven Deadly Sins, whereas in *Inferno* it is the loss of innocence represented by the severed fingers. "Doesn't this guy usually give us the finger," deadpans Tony at the scene of Bernie's demise. The calling card of this killer is to leave a child's digit with each victim, thereby doubling the jeopardy — not only must Thorne stop the killings, but he must also rescue the little boy. As is common in so many slasher movies, the murderer wears a mask. Here it is a little different because the mask appears to be his own skin: like the Wire Twins, he has no eyes to speak of, just healed over holes where they should be. This is what a Cenobite would look like if he were to take up serial killing: the triumphant lick of Bernie's cigar with a black elongated tongue is his proof of allegiance. Yet we're also furnished with the reveal at the end, where the rubber of the mask is peeled back to show Thorne's bloody face beneath, a trick worthy of a Scooby Doo mystery.

This peppering of surrealism is what draws the comparison to Lynchian crime narratives. The discovery of the ear in *Blue Velvet*, for example, is what leads Jeffrey (Kyle MacLachlan) inexorably into the seedy and disturbing world of gang lord Frank Booth (a chilling performance by Dennis Hopper). The death of Laura Palmer (Sheryl Lee) in *Twin Peaks* opens up the door to another dimension inhabited by the backwards dancing dwarf, one-armed Mike and the evil spirit of Bob.

After finding the puzzle box at Jay Cho's house, Thorne enters his own world of insanity, where characters and events are just slightly off kilter. When he visits Leon's parlor, he sees the tattoo on the man's back come alive. At first it is the Wire Twins, then a hand with a nail driven through it, an essential clue as to who is behind all this. But the one blatant homage has to be the encounter he has with Mr. Parmagi, a character straight out of Lynchian mythology. A gambler with six-shooters on his hips—"I have a license for these"—he is flanked by two karate-kicking cowboys, too weird even for fans of Derrickson's work. "Even my friends who love the film give me shit about that," he told *The Hellbound Web*. "It was the one thing about the movie that Bob Weinstein didn't like. Oh, well. Live and learn."[1]

But *Inferno* also lifts an idea from another recent crime film. The notion of an almost mystical underworld boss comes directly from Bryan Singer's *The Usual Suspects*. In that movie we are told a camp fire tale about Keyser Soze, who apparently vanishes into thin air after committing his crimes. Instead, we have Bernie's story about The Engineer (itself a reference to the monster from Barker's original, and a new moniker for Pinhead). In it he describes how The Engineer leaves a severed head — Godfather style — in the bed of one of his enemies. The moral of this: "Hunt for the Engineer and the Engineer will hunt you."

Ultimately, the punishment meted out for the crime is what Thorne is doing to himself. It is implied that he killed all the murdered people in real life (utilized again in *Hellraiser: Hellseeker*) and will have to live with this knowledge in his own personal Hell.

Loss of Innocence

The theme of childhood and innocence is one of two carried over from *Bloodline*, *Inferno*'s immediate predecessor. When Pinhead snatches John Merchant's son, Jack, he says as he strokes his hair: "Young, unformed. Oh, what appetites I could teach him." Later, when John comes to his rescue, the lead Cenobite once again alludes to this theme: "Oh, I understand. You love this boy, you have plans for him. Hopes and dreams, a whole imagined future where you love him and watch him grow." In *Hellraiser V* Jack is substituted for Chloe, Thorne's daughter. She is his hope for the future and, as such, represents a way for the Cenobites to hurt him most.

When he returns home at the end to find her and his wife strapped up to a torture pillar, dying of exposure, Thorne realizes that his dreams for the future are dying also. The twist is that by living the life he has, Thorne has himself destroyed these: the vision he is seeing only reflects what he has done to them both mentally. When his daughter asks him, "Daddy, are you home yet?" he replies, "No, sweetheart, I'm here for a little while then I've got to go." Which initiates the plea: "When are you coming home?" The next time we see her, she's crying that she wants her Daddy, but in his rush to get to the hospital and check on his mother, he completely ignores her. "Daddy's gone," Chloe's mother says. This neglect will come back to haunt him at the end. Thorne might state that "Children are the only sacred thing left in this world," although in his quest to save the child that's missing he is forced to sacrifice his very own daughter.

When Thorne goes to see Dr. Gregory he enquires about the picture in the frame, a little girl who turns out to be the psychiatrist's daughter, Melissa. "She's the best thing in my life," says Gregory. "I envy children. I envy their innocence" (forming a tangible association to *Bloodline* as we later discover Gregory *is* Pinhead). It is a sentiment Thorne readily agrees with. But he also seems willing to turn a blind eye to the loss of innocence of the children who frequent Bernie's ice cream truck. (The use of this symbol itself is twisted.) Because Bernie is supplying him with narcotics—his "birthday present"—the detective lets him go about his business even though it is obvious he is a child molester. When he enquires about Daphne, Thorne adds that she's a little too old for this man despite being barely out of her teens—and bear in mind this is a hooker Thorne has actually had sex with. The beating he gives his "whipping boy" cannot balance out such transgressions. These are contradictions that do not sit well together and give the character a schizophrenic edge. If children are sacred and it is Thorne's job to protect them, can he really be so cold as to let a known pedophile roam the streets selling ice cream? The reminders of children throughout, playing in the park, crossing the road in the rain, serve only to enforce where his priorities should lie.

But the problems stem from his formative years. "What are you gonna do?" Tony asks as he's off to see Gregory. "I'm gonna go lie down and talk about my childhood," is the answer. Except Thorne does nothing of the kind. Not until he is forced to return "home" at the climax does he discover what his flashbacks are about—walking through his first bedroom (filled with icons of his innocence: toy planes hanging from the ceiling, a stuffed animal on his bed), seeing himself completing a jigsaw on the floor, and then ripping apart the idealistic memories he has of his mother and father. The child's voice he keeps hearing calling out, "Help me," is actually his own. The fingerprint from the last digit found matches his, and Thorne is at last confronted with the truth. He has been torturing *himself*. For each bad deed he his done, he has lost a part of that happy childhood. "This is the life you chose, Joseph," says Pinhead, the judgmental words ringing somewhat hollow. "All the people you hurt, all the appetites you indulged. You have destroyed your own innocence, allowed your flesh to consume your spirit." In *Inferno* the most significant loss of innocence is Thorne's own.

Winning and Losing

The second theme to feed in from *Bloodline* is that of playing games. This is certainly true of the scacchic opening, with Thorne and his opponent—the Professor (the Vietnam name Jake Singer went by in *Jacob's Ladder*)—sitting in the typical *Hellraiser* bargaining position: on opposite sides of the frame with the table in the middle. The quick cuts as they make their chess moves and hit the clock not only underscore the competitive nature of Thorne, but also indicate that games will figure largely in the plot. If one needed any more convincing, the setting itself is a basketball court with players still in the background. As if to emphasize his need to win, a call comes through on Thorne's cell from Tony and he tells him, "We won by seven, but it should have been twenty." It is not enough that he win, he must win outright—as he proves by trouncing the Professor: "You played right into my game...." It's also one of the first things he tells his wife when he returns home. On asking how the game went, Thorne tells her, "We won."

In the word games he plays with Tony, Thorne also likes to be the victor. Tony's futile attempt to get the better of him ("What's an eight letter word for slaughterhouse ... ?"—"Abattoir") is met immediately by a much more complicated test. Thorne throws back, "What's a ten letter word for your name?" and delights in watching him struggle. The next day Tony begs him, "What's the answer?" and Thorne replies, "You've given up quicker than usual, Tony," thus implying it is a regular ritual humiliation. Tony's surname is in fact a palindrome—Nenonen—because it reads the same backwards as it does forwards. "Oh I get it," says Tony, "it's like the name Bob. That's one, too, right?" But Thorne has no idea how pertinent his puzzle is, for he is the victim himself of a much larger palindrome. "It ends the same way as it begins," he informs Tony—just like his own private Hell. Thorne will be destined to live out the same events over and over on a loop, forwards and backwards.

Thorne has no idea that he is playing yet another game, one he cannot possibly win. And his opponent this time is Pinhead. The chess game should have been a clue, as it is a distant cousin to Lemarchand's dolls. This is investigated more fully in Pinhead's speech at the climax: "It's all a puzzle, isn't it Joseph? Like a game of chess. The pieces move, apparently aimlessly, but always towards a single objective: to kill the king." Thorne's reality is Pinhead's own giant chessboard and the people on it no more than expendable pawns.

The allusions to the sport of fishing serve to illustrate this, too, when they enter Jay Cho's crime scene—"Ever go fishing, Tony?"—and when Thorne informs his wife, "Actually I *caught* a case." Thorne is used to being the one with the rod, but suddenly things have turned around. The hooks and chains are directed at him during the finale. And now that the viewer realizes Tony is merely a construct of Hell, it is safe for him to admit to Thorne that he's been fishing as well.

Once again, this desire to win probably stems from Thorne's lonely upbringing. We see him in flashback playing alone in his room; the adult Thorne looking out of the window to show us we are on a farm miles from anywhere. Thorne had only his parents for company, and subsequently abandoned them in later life. "Why don't you visit us, Joe?" asks his mother sitting by his father's bedside. This isolation accounts for the reason why he uses his magic tricks to entertain himself rather than his daughter. The sleight of hand as he palms the coke at the first crime scene, then brings it out again when he's with Daphne, is just for his own amusement, as are the worry balls he plays with constantly during the film. "That's a Chinese thing, isn't it?" says Gregory with tongue firmly in cheek, an obvious reference to the puzzle box. Thorne has spent so long challenging himself he thinks nothing of trampling over his rivals.

But in *Inferno* the competition is the greatest game player of them all.

Pins and Needles

Still, the most interesting aspect of *Inferno* is the fact that *Hellraiser*'s influence — like Thorne's word puzzle — has come full circle. When the original came out, body piercing was more of an underground scene, and certainly not as prevalent as it is today. The series must take some credit for popularizing the art of adorning one's flesh with metal. In the documentary *Hellraiser Resurrection*, Barker enforces this: "Now there's a whole movement of people who've made an art form of their bodies, piercing, scarification, brandings of various kinds. Back then [when *Hellraiser* was made] it was much, much harder to see that; there was much less of that around."[2] The performance artists Puncture, who also feature, confirm: "*Hellraiser* is like a breeding ground for our imaginations, for our next performance."[3]

In *Hellraiser V* we are taken to Leon's Stigmata body piercing parlor, introduced by shots of the pictures on his wall. Black and white images of needles through the eyebrow and nose, stitched lips, latticed backs, hooked nostrils, give way to a live procedure of someone having their tongue pierced with a large spike. Into this world comes Thorne, to ask Leon about the Lament Configuration. Leon himself is bald, covered in tattoos, and has a hook through his nose. On his walls hang studded collars and a lethal multistranded whip with hooks on each of its ends — the same one used in Bernie's death later. This is the influence of *Hellraiser* in the real world, but it is an effect Thorne cannot possibly understand. The only metal he has on him is his badge and his gun, which is why it takes him so long to figure out the enigma and why the Cenobites appear so alien to him. Here *Inferno* is art imitating life, which in turn has been already been influenced by art.

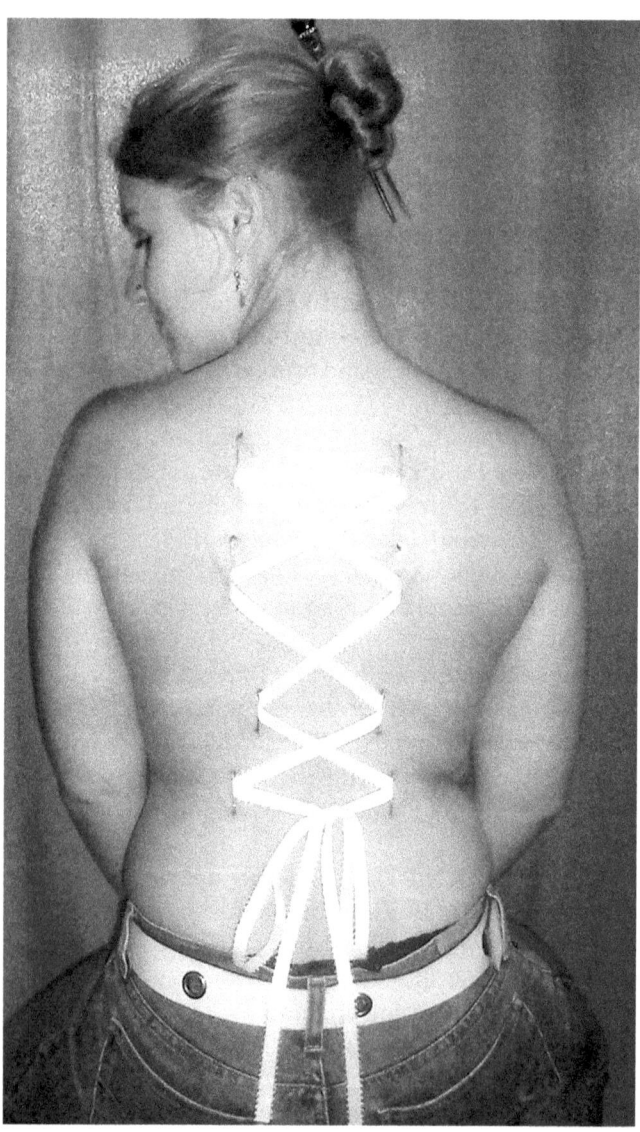

Life imitating art imitating life. An example of body piercing, the back corset. Piercer: Shorty, West Palm Beach, FL. Model: Kacey (www.theshorty.com. Photograph courtesy Marc Calma).

21
WELCOME TO HELL

It was anticipated to a certain extent, but no one could have predicted the sheer disappointment of *Hellraiser* fans who bemoaned the virtual absence of their favorite Cenobite in the new film. "The series had become the Pinhead show," stated Derrickson in retrospect. "Personally, I'm very happy about the lack of Pinhead in *Inferno*, but if I had to do it over again, I'd put a bit more of him in there for the sake of the fans."[1] To have held back with Pinhead was one thing, but it was the use of his image for promotional purposes that seemed to upset people, as Bradley suggested: "What irritates me, and I know it upsets the fans as well, was that they then smothered the video cover with pictures of Pinhead, and that tells everybody it's his film again — he's the featured character. Well, no, he isn't, so don't sell it on that."[2]

Barker, too, was displeased by the film, as evidenced in a question and answer session at a *Hellraiser* screening in Los Angeles in August 2000: "I really don't like to say this about another's work but I really hate this movie and it seems to have violated a lot of the things that I like about *Hellraiser*."[3] They were thoughts he reiterated in the *Lost Souls* newsletter: "[*Hellraiser: Inferno*] is terrible. It pains me to say things like that because nobody sets out in the morning to make a bad movie...."[4]

Derrickson's chess move was to send an e-mail to *Esplatter* arguing his case, "[Clive's] reaction, I must admit, was not entirely unexpected.... I never expected that he would appreciate seeing the treasured iconography of his brainchild tossed out of the window and replaced by a whole new set of rules. But it seems to me that I made a movie that is too good, or at least too provocative, for him to just simply dismiss.... This is, in fact, a very good film. It is philosophically ambitious (unlike *Hellraiser* II, III, or IV), and it represents a moral framework outside that of the previous *Hellraiser* films and (apparently) outside that of Clive Barker's personal taste. Quite simply, I subverted Clive Barker's franchise with a point of view that he does not share, and I think that really pisses him off."[5]

The reviews, on the whole, came down on the side of Barker and Bradley. *Fangoria*'s Allan Dart compared the film to that of *Halloween III* and *Friday The 13th Part V*, which also abandoned their original concepts in favor of a new start but were lambasted by the fans: "And while *Hellraiser: Inferno* doesn't completely disregard its Pinhead origins, it is guilty of demoting everybody's favorite Cenobite to a bench player on a losing team...." He goes on to compare the lead character of Thorne to the director, saying, "The person who is really in over his head is co-scripter/director Scott Derrickson. His demon-haunted detective tale, while not bad on its own, doesn't belong in the *Hellraiser* storyline. It's an odd and uncomfortable fit that makes Derrickson, like Joseph, damned from the beginning."

David Trier at Movie Vault reported that *Hellraiser* was a series close to his heart and so approached this new installment with the lowest of expectations. But he was impressed that this was a self-contained movie with coherent beginning, middle and end (unlike, in his opinion, *Bloodline*) and liked the sense of style it displayed. His reservations, though, revolve around those same questions again: "There are two main things that keep this from being a 'good' movie. First and foremost, it is not a *Hellraiser* movie. The presence of the box and the minute or two of Pinhead's screen time are the only things that tie it to the series.... Pinhead's provoking commentary has always been one of the greatest assets to the series and I could tell Doug Bradley just wanted to cry. It's really just a supernatural detective story...."

Efilmcritic.com reviewer Scott Weinberg, like Bradley, was concerned for the fans: "Here's what I don't get: A studio goes to all the trouble of producing a new horror sequel, but time and again they simply refuse to acknowledge that these movies have fans and followers, people who love the series and will pretty much rent any movie with a number in the title."

The consensus of opinion tended to be that as a stand alone film this might have worked better, but as a *Hellraiser* movie there weren't enough elements from the mythos to warrant the title. Incredible as it may seem, Derrickson was asked if he wanted to direct the next film in the sequence as well, but he declined as he and Boardman were already working on other projects, one a thriller for Dimension. So it would be time for yet another person to take charge of the franchise. Would that person stay faithful to the mythos or carry it on in the direction *Inferno* had taken it? Only time would tell.

22

Hide and Seek

The person chosen by Dimension to immediately follow up *Inferno* was cinematographer Rick Bota, who had begun his career — like Kevin Yagher before him — working on episodes of *Tales from the Crypt*. Not the best omen *Hellraiser* supporters could have wished for. But he also had ten years of experience on films such as *Final Embrace* (Oley Sassone, 1992), Pamela Anderson's flashy — in more ways than one — comic book flick *Barb Wire* (David Hogan, 1996), the interesting though inferior remake of *House on Haunted Hill* (William Malone, 1999) and serial killer jaunt *Valentine* (Jamie Blanks, 2001) starring *Angel* heartthrob David Boreanaz. In addition to this, Bota had been a second unit director on Guillermo del Toro's impressive monster movie *Mimic* (1997) starring Mira Sorvino, and *Kiss the Girls* (Gary Fleder, 1997), with Morgan Freeman taking up the role of Dr. Alex Cross from James Patterson's successful novels.

Providing the script this time would be two writers. Carl V. Dupré had been a writer on TV's *Bone Chillers* (1996), had penned *Detroit Rock City* (Adam Rifkin, 1999), *Prophecy 3: The Ascent* (Patrick Lussier, 2000) and *Broke Even* (David Feldman, 2000), but had cut his teeth in the industry working in a variety of positions since 1992, from assistant editor to production assistant. This was also true of Tim Day, who had started out as electrician on *9½ Ninjas!* (Aaron Barsky, 1991) and Anthony Hickox's *Waxwork II* (1992), before working as best boy and key grip on a number of productions. Day was actually an old friend of Bota's from his *Tales from the Crypt* days. The now titled *Hellraiser: Hellseeker* would be his first writing assignment, but between the pair of them they had a wealth of filmic experience which they could draw on when fleshing out the story. They were also, quite obviously, fans of the *Hellraiser* canon, which is why the script is peppered with homages to previous films in the series (even down to calling places of work Cubic Route and Kircher Imports after the character who provides Frank with the box in *The Hellbound Heart* novella).

But it is fair to say that without *Inferno*'s influence *Hellseeker* probably wouldn't have been the screenplay it was, hinging, as it does, around the gradual descent into madness of a man who loses his wife in a car accident, then has to piece together the mystery of what's happened. A further resemblance arises when we discover that someone has been killing the other people in his life, such as his boss, his neighbor and his best friend at work. Time is also nonlinear, as it was in *Inferno*, and the lead character of Trevor experiences flashbacks and jumps in time, which may or may not have been caused by a head injury after the accident. And he gets his just desserts at the end, exactly like Thorne, when he discovers he is dead, too. What was particularly exciting about the script, though, was the missing wife's name: Kirsty.

Dupré and Day had originally intended to bring back the character of Kirsty from the first three *Hellraiser* films, a fascinating and attractive idea for long-term devotees of the mythos, but Bota and the team had trouble contacting Ashley Laurence. The character then had to be altered to make her a new one, the name remaining in deference to both the character and the early films (and the couple's friendly pit bull took on the name of Cotton). This was the version of the script sent to Doug Bradley, who was initially intrigued to read that Kirsty was in it, then disappointed to discover that it wasn't Kirsty Cotton. Because negotiations for the role of Pinhead were left until quite late into preproduction, Bradley didn't get the chance to discuss this with Bota. He got on with the director immediately, impressed by his enthusiasm and distinct vision: Bota had been very influenced by avantgarde art and was extremely interested in colors because of his director of photography background.

When the story became clear, Bradley offered to get in touch with Laurence himself, as they had kept in contact. In the intervening years the actress had starred in movies such as *Lurking Fear* (C. Courtney Joyner, 1994) based loosely on the H.P. Lovecraft tale *Felony* (David A. Prior, 1996) and *Cupid* (Doug Campbell, 1997), as well as appearing on TV in *Legend*, *Hercules: The Legendary Journeys* and *Suddenly Susan*, before taking some time out from show business to concentrate on her family. She'd just started back, featuring in *Warlock III: The End of Innocence* (Eric Freiser, 1999) and *Beyond Belief: Fact or Fiction* on television — still firmly established in the genre — when the *Hellseeker* offer came. Laurence accepted it, delighted to be able to play alongside Bradley once more. "[It] was really nice for me [after] so many years, to come back and be in an environment as an adult that I had started as a child," she said in an interview on *Hellseeker*'s release, "to come back and look at things through those eyes."[1]

But this didn't leave long to rewrite the script again — she was actually added back in just days before filming started — and so information about where the character had been and what had happened to her since we last saw her was included in a title sequence with Trevor in the car. This was subsequently dropped in favor of Jamison Goei's spinning digital puzzle box over which the credits play, something he came up with in his spare time. The script also alluded to money Frank and Larry had left her when they disappeared "under some rather unusual circumstances" and which might have been a motivation for Trevor to kill her. The most enticing addition, though, was actually embroidered upon by Bradley — a lengthy conversation between Pinhead and Kirsty when she re-opens the puzzle box. "I gave it to Doug Bradley," said Bota, "and asked him to put it into the words of Pinhead but also expand on the story if he wanted to.... And he did a great job and added a lot of pages of great dialogue and great backstory which we already had in there, but he filled in between the lines. It's great stuff."[2] Sadly, most of this was also excised, although it survives as an extra on the finished release. The very fact that Bota was open to this and wanted the *Hellraiser* mythos to gel pleased Bradley enormously.

The rest of the cast and crew were now in place as well, ready for the February 2001 shoot in Vancouver, Canada. When casting for Trevor, the director looked at a number of different actors before executive producer Jesse Berdinka sent him a tape of Dean Winters playing Ryan O'Reily in the HBO series *Oz*. Winters' brother Scott had originally persuaded him to attend acting school, and he made subsequent appearances in *Homicide: Life on the Street*, *NYPD Blue*, *Millennium* and *Sex and the City*, as well as in the films *Conspiracy Theory* (Richard Donner, 1997), *Undercover Angel* (Bryan Michael Stoller, 1999), *Snipes* (Rich

Murray, 2001) and *Bullet in the Brain* (David Von Ancken, 2001). The script for *Hellseeker* was sent to him and three weeks later he was shooting the film.

Because of what had happened with Thorne on *Inferno*, the makers developed Trevor into a more likeable character the audience could care about before revealing too much of his true persona. In earlier drafts of the script he had less of the endearing qualities that Winters brought to life on-screen, such as his own interpretation on how much he loved his wife. "I think he did a great job with Trevor," said Bota. "It was a really difficult part to play because he goes through a range of emotions and I think that's what essentially was appealing to Dean."[3]

Because the script had so many morally bankrupt characters in it, one nice person was introduced: Dr. Allison Dormere (the name itself being an in-joke as it is French for "sleeping"). Described by the director as "a sort of guardian angel," in the script it goes on to say, "Something about her just radiates a calming presence"[4] It was Canadian actress Rachel Hayward's mission to sell this to the audience. Hayward's first film role was as Angie in *Breaking All the Rules* (James Orr, 1985), before graduating to, aptly enough, "woman in morgue" for the adaptation of Dean Koontz's *Whispers* (Douglas Jackson, 1989). Further movies included *Time Runner* (Michael Mazo, 1993), *Voyage of Terror* (Brian Trenchard-Smith, 1998), and *Cabin Pressure* (Alan Simmonds, 2001), while her TV series CV featured parts in shows such as *Sliders*, *Highlander*, *Stargate SG-1*, *First Wave*, *Xena: Warrior Princess* and *Cold Squad*.

Trevor's vampish boss, Gwen, was to be played by Sarah-Jane Redmond, who initially came in to read for the Kirsty part. She had such a presence that Bota wanted to use her somewhere, and she proved to be perfect casting for this dominating and sexually aware woman. Born in Cyprus, Greece, Redmond's first movie was *From Pig to Oblivion* (Simon Barry, 1993) and she filled in the time between her next one—*Disturbing Behavior* (David Nutter, 1998)—with roles in *The X-Files*, *Millenium* (as The Devil, for which she was voted the Internet's number one villain), *Sleepwalkers* and *Poltergeist: The Legacy*. She had recently enjoyed a lengthy stretch on the new reworking of the Superman legend, *Smallville*, as well as James Cameron's televisual brainchild, *Dark Angel*. As research she viewed dominatrix sessions at a local dungeon and said, "When I auditioned for the part, I used a photograph out of Stanton's illustrated book, *For the Man Who Knows His Place*, as my headshot. It's a photo of a man on his hands and knees slaving to his female master in his office."[5]

The part of his equally rampant neighbor, Tawny, was taken by twenty-four year-old actress Jody Thompson from *Death Game* (Randy Cheveldave, 1996) and *Fear of Flying* (David Mackay, 2000). Completing Trevor's harem of women was Kaaren de Zilva as the acupuncturist Sage. De Zilva's acting experience involved work on *Final Round* (George Erschbamer, 1993), John McTiernan's *The 13th Warrior* (1999), based on the Michael Crichton book and *This Is the Disk-O-Boyz* (Morris G. Sim, 1999). Bota wanted Sage to have an accent because it would add to her exotic charms, but because de Zilva looked quite exotic anyway, the decision was taken to have her speak with a British lilt, for which she copied her English mother's accent.

Bota came across Canadian actor Trevor White in a play. "When I first got to Vancouver and we were doing the casting I was taking in some local theatre on the weekends," the director explained.[6] Bota tracked the thespian down and asked him to read for the part of Bret, Trevor's best friend. The actor, who has a look of Clive Barker about him, had previously starred in films like *Groomed* (Trent Carlson, 1996), *The Rememberer* (Coreen Mayrs, 1999), *The Vigil* (Justin MacGregor, 1999) and *Epicenter* (Richard Pepin, 2000).

For the role of Detective Lange the filmmakers needed someone who could play an almost father figure to Trevor. They found this in the shape of kindly William S. Taylor, whose first film character was anything but amicable — a gang member in John Carpenter's classic *Assault on Precinct 13* (1976). His lengthy back catalogue included such movies as *Certain Fury* (Stephen Gyllenhaal, 1985), *The Fly II* (Chris Walas, 1989) *Omen IV: The Awakening* (Jorge Montesi and Dominique Othenin-Girard, 1991), *The Silencer* (Robert Lee, 1999) — where he played another detective — and *Romeo Must Die* (Andrzej Bartkowiak, 2000). The yin to his yang, Detective Givens, was a role that would go to Michael Rogers, who had impressed Bota in the latest installment of *Children of the Corn: Revelation* (Guy Magar, 2001), also through Dimension. His career began with the Rex Hamilton musical, *Staircase* (Stanley Donen, 1969), where he was part of the opening song. Other films included *The Mosquito Coast* (Peter Weir, 1986) and *Mission: Impossible* (Brian De Palma, 1996). Rogers had also made a bit of a name for himself as a producer on the Lloyd A. Simandl films *Escape Velocity* (1998), *Lethal Target* (1999) and *Fatal Conflict* (2000).

Other actors playing smaller parts were *Breaking Point*'s (Bob Clark, 1976) Ken Camroux as the doctor/coroner Ambrose (who has one of the best lines in the whole film, when Allison is talking to the dead body of Trevor: "You're creeping me out, and I'm the coroner!"); Dale Wilson, veteran of cartoons like *Spider-Man Unlimited*, as the chief surgeon who operates on Trevor's brain at the start; Gus (*Black Point* (David Mackay, 2001)) Lynch as Tawny's overprotective boyfriend; Kyle Cassie, also from *Children of the Corn: Revelation*, as the ambulance driver who has significantly fewer lines in the final cut than he did in the script; another voice artist — for cartoons like *Transformer Beast Wars Metals* (1999) — Alec Willows, in the only comedy role of the film, that of the janitor whom Trevor catches smoking ("Okay, you caught me. At least let me finish, will ya, I got one puff left."); Brenda (*Mr. Magoo* (Stanley Tong, 1997)) McDonald as the older nurse who assists in the brain operation at the start then repeats the ongoing line, "We're all here for you, Trevor."; Basia Antos from *First Wave* as the naked woman Trevor spies on through his window; yet another *Corn* actor, John B. Destry as a minor detective; with the Cenobites being played this time by Sarah Hayward (Stitch Cenobite), Michael Regan (Surgeon Cenobite) and Nancy J. Lilley (Bound Cenobite).

Following up his special effects work on *Inferno* was Gary Tunnicliffe, who did a marvelous job working for very little money — "Stitch and Bound were sculpted to be worn by feminine petite women and Rick Bota wanted and cast very large, heavy women ... that stretched the masks.... [The director wanted to veer away from the "sexy Cenobites" of recent entries in favor of the original exaggerated concept.] The Surgeon, I was pretty happy with him. It was kind of a big idea that worked out well."[7] Also returning was Jamison Goei, whose favorite effect was the eel sequence that must surely have been influenced by the worm creature in *Poltergeist II: The Other Side* (Brian Gibson, 1986): "We had an actual eel made out of silicone, used in the shots of the eel flopping around on the ground after Trevor pukes it out. Then I shot photos of the silicone eel for textures that are mapped onto the [digital] eel models. A model of the human head was then modified to roughly match Dean's head and then match-moved to Dean's movements on the plate with him acting as if the eel was working its way out of his throat...."[8] In addition, Goei handled the realistic needle through the neck scene and the blackbirds emerging from behind the merchant, some of which were recycled from the *Prophecy* clip in which Lucifer explodes into birds.

Cinematographer on the show was John Drake from *Christina's House* (Gavin Wilding, 1999). Because he is a director of photography by trade, Bota had a difficult time deciding whether or not to hire someone at all, but it freed him up more to concentrate on other aspects of the movie. "Sometimes we butted heads," admitted Bota, "but I think it was to the advantage [of the film]."[9] Meanwhile, production design fell under the remit of Troy Hansen, who had just finished working on *Children of the Corn: Revelation* and was able to re-use some of the same sets: Trevor's flat, for instance, and the police station. The morgue, too, came from another film — *Valentine*, for which Bota had served as DP — but an actual office was taken over for the day to double as Trevor's place of work, perfect for what the script describes as a "honeycomb of cubicles,"[10] and an old mental institution in Vancouver was a stand-in for the hospital and the underground tunnels at the police station.

Anthony Adler of *Tales from the Crypt* and *House on Haunted Hill* was to be the editor, along with first-timer Lisa Mozden, although she had been a second and first assistant editor on *Bound* (The Wachowski Brothers, 1996) and *Halloween H20: 20 Years Later* (Steve Miner, 1998). In charge of music was old hand Stephen Edwards, whose varied credits spanned *She's Been Away* (Peter Hall, 1989) and the song "Work Me to the Bone" from *What Women Want* (Nancy Meyers, 2000). His take on the score was totally different from anything that had gone before, bringing in electric guitars and pianos that would have been unheard of during Christopher Young's time. His new title theme put a powerful spin on the old *Hellraiser* material and his haunting "Kirsty's Theme" has to be one of the highlights of the entire production.

Apart from the time factor involved, akin to that of *Inferno*, there were other pressures on cast and crew, most notably the stunt with the car and the underwater scenes. Because of the low budget ($3 million) other ideas were discussed that could trigger Trevor's hallucinations and headaches, such as a fall down the stairs or a bicycle crash, but Bota was adamant there be a jaw-dropping incident right at the very beginning that Trevor could keep flashing back to. "The car accident keeps interest.... It had to be a mechanism for Kirsty to apparently die and suddenly disappear, and Trevor to survive...."[11] It would not prove easy.

In the script, the cause of the smash is a goat in the middle of the road — described as "the most exotic one available in Vancouver ... for scale [with] weird twisted antlers...."[12]; this would not only have linked in to the old woman on the bus, who we would later see knitting from the goat, but also the theme of Hell and the Devil. In reality it was simpler just to have Trevor nearly missing another vehicle then crashing over the bridge. Bota had one take to achieve this, but the car spun over and landed upside down, which would not have matched the underwater scenes with Kirsty and Trevor. Ingeniously, the director filmed the climax of the movie where the car is being lifted out of the water, then dropped the car in the water upright.

Much of the underwater filming was done in a tank, but Ashley Laurence — famously like Winona Ryder in her aquatic scenes for *Alien Resurrection* (Jean-Pierre Jeunet, 1997) — wasn't very comfortable in the water. Bota had to film her scenes just under the surface, which meant that an effect where we see Kirsty's drowning face in a vending machine had to be dropped. The rest of the footage was shot in water six feet deep, with the car cut in half and a bubble machine working overtime. "I think studios, producers and everyone else, as soon as they read 'underwater,' they start to panic," said Gary Tunnicliffe. "Logistically, it's a nightmare. Filmmaking is hard enough, but as soon as you're in an environment that's more dense than the air we breathe, it gets very, very complicated."[13]

Bota also ran into trouble because he was promised that the giant fans that could be heard in the basement of the mental institution would be switched off during the scenes between Lange and Trevor on their way to the morgue. When he came to shoot he found that they couldn't be shut down, resulting in the actors having to do it as a scratch track then dub in their words afterwards. An asbestos pipe also broke in the abandoned hospital location, causing the production to be shut down for three days.

After Bota had handed in his tentative director's cut, he asked Clive Barker if he would watch the movie with him and offer advice. "He was gracious enough to take a look at it," said Bota, "and he actually liked the film."[14] The director noticed Barker smiling wryly when references to his original came up (like the money/box exchange with the merchant). Barker made notes during the screening and Bota addressed as much of this as he could in post production, the main suggestion being to add some more graphic imagery. On Barker's instruction, a cutaway was added during the morgue scene, for example, with some raw meat and mealworms. In general though, the creator of the franchise seemed pleased with the product this time — as did its star, Bradley, who thought it fitted in with the mythos' ideology: "*Hellraiser* is very much an 'ideas' series. I've always been impressed over the years that that's what the fan base has reacted to. The ideas in the *Hellraiser* films bubble under the surface. They rise to the top here and there, but they remain largely subtext."[15]

But the real test would be when the film was released, straight to video and DVD, to an eager viewing public in 2002.

23

ALL PROBLEMS SOLVED

The Surface of the Real

Like *Inferno* before it, *Hellseeker* is reliant on a surfeit of surrealistic elements to tell its story. Much more than its direct predecessor, it models itself on the narrative of films like *Jacob's Ladder* and *Videodrome*. In both of these, something sets off a chain of bizarre events—in the former, Jake Singer (Tim Robbins) is wounded in Vietnam and in the latter, Max Renn (James Woods) watches a pirate videotape—and the main protagonist experiences waking hallucinations and time shifts. Singer starts to see faceless demons, on trains, driving cars, and Renn slips further into the body horror nightmares that Cronenberg is famous for, pushing his face into a flexible TV screen, pulling a tape out of a slot in his stomach....

In Trevor's case, it is the car crash that triggers his hallucinations, which are superficially explained as morphine-related or connected to a head injury. The audience is even led to believe that he might be undergoing emergency brain surgery ("Over the course of this ... procedure," says the surgeon, "I will be triggering memories, disrupting the unconscious, so our patient may experience some ... distress."). Nevertheless, like Singer and Renn, he is anchored to that one central image of being in the car with his wife and crashing through the bridge into the lake. It is this that he keeps flashing back to time and again, enforced by all the water imagery in the movie (dripping water, Trevor washing in the sink, the puddles at the warehouse).

He first notices something strange is happening when he sees bowls of blood on the hospital ward. When he comes out of the brain operation hallucination, Trevor comments that, "It felt like a dream but it just seemed so..." "Real?" Allison finishes for him. Then Lange tells him that over a month has passed already since the accident, even though Trevor appears to have just woken up. As the film progresses there are more and more of these: Trevor sees the wet hand inside the vending machine, coughs up an eel, witnesses people being tortured at the police station and Lange splitting in two. He has a conversation with Allison in a corridor, but she suddenly disappears, and he is stabbed with a *Basic Instinct*-style ice pick by Sage only to wake up in an ambulance on his way to the hospital. "Remember what happened back there?" asks the paramedic. "Some woman," replies Trevor, "on top of me, naked, trying to kill me..." "Ar ... yeah, not quite that good," the ambulance man tells him. "You were riding on a bus and then you just collapsed on the floor."

Not only that, wherever he goes a masked man—who Trevor believes might be the killer—seems to be stalking him, and he has a *Videodrome*-style encounter with a camera. Here he is watching himself and Gwen make love on-screen but there is nothing in front of the lens (in a neat trick shot, Trevor waves his hand in front of the camera and it appears on-screen), just before Gwen is suffocated with a plastic bag by unknown assailants. Later, neighbor Tawny is killed—Trevor finds her bloodied body tied to a chair—but the next day she answers her door alive and well.

A further misdirection is offered in the form of the images that crop up on Trevor's computer at work, throwing back a QuickTime movie of his steamy romp with Gwen in the recreation room and a news clip with the headline: "Accident Leaves One Hospitalized, Another Missing." This, coupled with Laser Pacific's manipulation of the film color to give it those blue and green hues, might lead one to believe that Trevor is actually inside an artificial reality like the Matrix. Indeed, the office he works in is almost identical to that of Neo (Keanu Reeves) in the first film. (Neo goes on to have his own hallucinations of a living bug inside his stomach, his mouth being sealed over and his hand puncturing a liquid mirror.)

But there are clues as to what is really happening imbued in the narrative. Allison's comment, "We're still going to have to run a few more tests, to see if we can '*pin*point' what's causing your headaches," right at the start, followed swiftly by Lange telling Trevor, "You look like Hell warmed over" should have rung warning bells enough. If not, then perhaps the Lament Configuration-style clock on the wall in Trevor's apartment, plus the detective who practices origami and makes a puzzle box, might offer some insight ... or even the torture that's going on at the police station or in the morgue.

The main giveaways, however, are the flashbacks Trevor has when he sees the calling card "pinned" to his board at work with the legend "All Problems Solved" printed on it. This transports him into several disjointed recollections about a warehouse where the employees sit at sewing machines, stitching human flesh, and a merchant stands behind a counter telling him, "I can see into your soul." It is where the transaction took place and Trevor bargained for the puzzle box, which he fully intended to give Kirsty. It changes shape from round to square as it rolls across the counter and the old man reveals, "It is a means to break the surface of the real.... Once you have chosen to cross the threshold, there is no returning."

So, Trevor is the architect of his own hallucinations, and we shouldn't be surprised when Pinhead appears at the acupuncturist's to thrust a lengthy needle through his throat, then again in a mirror and in a puddle reflection (walking *under* the water in direct opposition to that other religious figure). It is Pinhead who resolves the enigma at the end, in his recounting of the deal he struck with Kirsty: how she killed Trevor's lovers and his best friend as an offering to Pinhead, and finally her husband, too—shooting him in the head and causing the initial accident. If anything, it is Trevor's recollections of Kirsty, presented as soft focus flashbacks, that are the fantasy. Their life as he remembers it was a sham, something Pinhead confirms: "Welcome to the worst nightmare of all, reality."

But there is one last surreal moment before the end, when the characters who have populated his Hell appear in slightly different guises, just as they do in *The Wizard of Oz* (Victor Fleming, 1939). Allison and Ambrose aren't doctors at all, but coroners here to examine Trevor's corpse, fishing the eel out of his airway. (In the script the ambulance man was the one who drove Trevor away, but this scene was cut.) Only Detective Lange appears to be the same, although there is no sign of his "partner," Givens. One might extrapolate from this that others featured in Trevor's nightmare had dual, or even triple roles, the nurse, for instance, a Cenobite, as is the surgeon. Pinhead might well have been the one performing the brain operation, and even the merchant selling Trevor the Lament

Configuration (actually portrayed by Bradley). Nothing in *Hellseeker* is as it first appears, and that is the beauty of this complex story.

See Anything you Like?

Hellseeker taps into the voyeurism aspect of *Hellbound* and simultaneously expands on this, adding another dimension. Whereas Channard's observation of his patients was limited solely to looking through doorways or two-way mirrors, *Hellraiser VI* takes this concept into the twenty-first century. There are obvious references to people watching using surveillance devices. At work, after he has walked down the corridor and drawn stares from his fellow employees, Trevor is warned by Bret, "Hills have eyes, remember?" and he points to the closed circuit TV camera in the corner of the room. Gwen makes a similar statement after their fumble in the recreation area: "Now get some fucking work done," she says nodding up at another camera, "we're watching you." We're then shown an electronic image of Trevor from

One of the new Cenobites for *Hellseeker* was Bound. Model painted by Dan Cope and sculpted by Chris Elizardo for CD Publications (courtesy Dan Cope).

the camera's point of view This is the means by which his indiscretion has been recorded and broadcast to his computer console, an even more twisted version of Orwell's *1984* (1949). As we see more of the movie, it becomes clear that the people doing the watching are, obviously, the Cenobites. When characters repeat the phrase, "We're all here for you, Trev," what they really mean is they're here to make him remember as the Cenobites observe him like some animal in a zoo. As Pinhead tells him, "You were an interesting study."

Moreover, if one's own Hell relates to personal preferences, then this voyeurism is a reflection of Trevor's obsession with videoing everything. When he wants to recall Kirsty he has to bring down the box full of tapes from the closet and watch them. One in particular shows him looking at himself in a mirror, holding the camera, as if to show him who he really is. It's their anniversary and Kirsty is urging him to put down the camera and come to bed. "God forbid you should let one event go unfilmed," she says. Which will ultimately be his ruination.

When Gwen visits him at home and takes her clothes off, she asks, "Where is it...? You usually have it up and running by now." We cut to the camera watching as she straddles him, the same tapes Kirsty found to incriminate him. In a longer version of the scene where Kirsty confronts him in the car, she states, "I know about Gwen ... and the others. You think I don't know what's going on. I've seen the fucking tapes, Trevor. All those women in our home, in my bed!" It is the only way he can "see"; Trevor needs the aid of this device to fulfill his sexual fantasies. It is not enough to scrutinize the naked woman in the window of an apartment across the road, as she can see him, too, and closes the curtain.

"You have seen many things that you will wish you had not," Pinhead informs Trevor as he writhes around, hooks and chains holding him fast. Trevor was hoisted by his own petard, his love of watching finally turned around and aimed at him.

Good and Bad

Another theme in *Hellseeker* is the one crystallized by Lange and Givens. Lange was meant to be a caring figure, like Allison, who guides Trevor through the search for his wife. "How's that head of yours feeling?" he asks as Trevor comes down to the station for a talk. When he inquires whether something might have happened, just before the accident, that Trevor is withholding, Lange says in his softly spoken voice, "Don't take it the wrong way, I'm just a guy trying to do a job here, okay?" Later, after they catch Trevor at the scene of Sage's murder with a bloody ice pick in his hand, Lange appears genuinely disappointed in the man.

His partner, Givens, is a completely different character. Mean, cynical and bad tempered, the grilling he gives Trevor about Kirsty and her inheritance oozes malice: "How many zeroes was your wife worth? ... Don't play fucking stupid with me, all right? ... If Kirsty's dead, like you seem so *fucking* certain, well, then I guess it all goes to you, Trev." He continues, "My partner, Detective Lange, he's softer around the heart than I am. Me, I'm hard as they come and when I get a feeling about something I'm usually right. And I get a bad feeling about you, Trev."

Toward the finale, when Lange takes Trevor down to the morgue, we discover that they are, in fact, one and the same person, augured by Givens' sudden appearance after Lange walks down a corridor, and when Trevor hears the two of them talking in an office, but only Lange emerges. "I believe each of us is the sum of two entirely different people...." says Lange. "Good and bad, honest and dishonest, righteous and evil. That's how we're all made. It's just a question of how much of each." In the original script, we see Givens' face on the back of Lange's head. In the finished movie, thanks to Goei's visual imaging, Givens separates his head from Lange's and it hovers on his shoulder — a little like Johnny Knoxville's character in *Men in Black II* (Barry Sonnenfeld, 2002). "I believe you and me have a lot in common," Lange tells Trevor, which is true.

Lange/Givens are Trevor's twin characters, used to highlight the fact that Trevor *also* has a light and a dark side. But instead of being the ultimate good cop/bad cop like them, Trevor is torn between the love he felt for Kirsty (his imagined past with her) and his sordid vices — women and money. This is only fully revealed when Pinhead forces him to remember what really happened that anniversary night when he handed over the Lament Configuration. "I trusted you," says Kirsty, "Goddamn it, how could you do this to us? You told me you loved me..." Trevor answers coldly, "Just open the fucking box," which she does, much to his eventual regret.

No Mercy

The title here comes from deleted lines that Pinhead utters in the script: "Jealousy arouses a spouse's fury. And no mercy will be shown when that revenge is given."[1] It is an appropriate one as it underlines the final major theme in *Hellseeker*, that of revenge. Without a doubt, it is Kirsty's vengeance that is the driving force for the entire narrative. She takes her revenge against the women who have slept with Trevor by killing them one by one, and then murders the man with whom he conspired to kill her. Her final act is to shoot Trevor and then ensure he takes the blame for the murders. And why is her retribution so brutal? Not only had he betrayed her sexually — possibly the worst thing a man can do to his wife — but he had also brought the box to her again, confronting her with a past she thought she'd left behind. Trevor offered up Kirsty. "I can't believe this is happening. I have a deal," he says in the car. "No, you *had* a deal," Kirsty takes great delight in informing him, "but I made a better offer, and guess what? He took it!" She sacrifices Trevor just as he was willing to do to her.

But hers is not the only revenge on display. The women whom Trevor used — and who are now with Pinhead — also get to take their revenge on him. Gwen shocks him when she is suffocated by the plastic bag; Tawny's bloody corpse appears in his apartment, and then she rejects him when he knocks on her door; and Sage leaves him to Pinhead's devices in the acupuncture room, stabs him with the ice pick, and coerces him into pulling that same pick out of her head, thereby incriminating himself. Bret, too, compels him to watch as he blows his own brains out, after accusing him of reneging on their deal: "You had to go solo with your little car accident bit, then you fucked it all up. What were you thinking?"

Finally, Pinhead is granted a revenge of sorts when he catches up with Kirsty. She escaped him twice in the past, and, indeed, the last time they met he was killed at the hands of Channard. Now, at last, is his opportunity to play with her; to watch her squirm at his hands (although there is an altogether different reading of this that can be made as we shall see in the following chapter). He is the one who gives her the opportunity for revenge, but at the same time he is also the one who turns her into a killer.

It is a revenge any Cenobite would be proud of.

Homage to Hell

In addition to the return of Kirsty, *Hellseeker* contains references to every single *Hellraiser* movie thus far. The guardian of the box, or merchant, if you prefer, is back striking deals with the damned. In the screenplay the warehouse Trevor finds contains a tribute to the Pyramid Gallery from *Hell on Earth* with "erotic, sometimes grotesque sculptures, paintings, and other collectibles from all over the world depicting lust, ecstasy and torture."[2]

The brain operation scene at the start is a direct lift from *Hellbound* when Channard gives his "labyrinths of the mind" speech. The all-important mirrors from *Hellraisers II*,

III and IV are referenced when Trevor is lying on the acupuncture bed ("What's the mirror for?" asks Trevor and Sage replies, "To help see into your soul"), and the chart through which Pinhead appears bears a close resemblance to those seen in Channard's obsession room.

Infidelity as a theme reappears from parts *I*, *II*, *IV* and *V*, while the entire plot strand of tracking down a killer and solving a mystery is pure *Inferno*. But far from making the material clichéd, all this simply shows is that there is an acknowledgement on the writers' and director's behalf of the *Hellraiser* history, and that some attempt has been made to incorporate this into *Hellseeker*.

24

Hellbound Hearts

Much has been made, particularly in fan circles, of the relationship between Pinhead and Kirsty. Since they met in *Hellraiser* there has been a fascination between the two. She has been the only person Pinhead has bargained with instead of taking straight to Hell. This indicates some form of connection, possibly sexual, but definitely one based on admiration on Pinhead's part. It could be argued that on one level theirs is the only union that has ever worked in the entirety of the series' history. Though on the surface they are supposed to be enemies, as the Female Cenobite stated in *Hellbound*, they "do keep finding each other."

Kirsty is drawn to Pinhead and the box, just as much as he is to her, and *Hellseeker* plays with these issues, while Pinhead and Kirsty play with each other. The look, the smile that passed between them when he was in his human form the last time they met, insinuated that without his dark side there might have been a chance for a friendship — and possibly more. On Kirsty's behalf this could be read as a surrogate father figure attraction after the loss of Larry, while Elliott may have viewed her as someone he could put his faith in after both God and Leviathan had failed him. In *Hell on Earth*, Joey is Kirsty's substitute, and a romantic undercurrent could certainly be detected.

But Kirsty is the one Pinhead has always truly longed for, "a far more interesting creature," as he refers to her. The much longer encounter between them, found in the extras section of the DVD (bizarrely taken out of the movie because Bota didn't want to exclude viewers who hadn't seen the other *Hellraiser*s) confirms what many have suspected about these two for so long. In it Pinhead spells out his intentions quite clearly: "You opened a door a long time ago and it will not be closed until I get what I came for," he says. "My soul," Kirsty acknowledges. As if to verify this, he goes further: "I will not rest until I get what I want, and what I want is you!"

Adding more weight to the claim, he also draws attention to how she has been hurt and left alone in the past. "It was your *loving* husband who did the hard work. He made it easy for me. It seems your family always does." Kirsty retorts, "That was Frank. I gave him back to you. I did what I promised." "Don't think I'm not grateful," he says. "I am. Eternally grateful ... But there was another bargain, wasn't there. You will not have forgotten that I gave myself to let you run. Did you think that gift was nobly and freely given? Did you?" In essence, Trevor betrayed her, Frank betrayed her, but Pinhead allowed her to escape from Channard. He is attempting to make her see that out of all the men she has known — apart from her father — he was the only one willing to sacrifice himself for her. Kirsty owes him, and he won't let her forget it. But perhaps she doesn't want to. Pinhead's first line is extremely telling: "Still playing the innocent, Kirsty? You disappoint me. After all these years surely you've realized it's *you* that wants *me* here." It's interesting that she doesn't contradict him.

An unfilmed version of this exchange from the script presents yet more evidence:

> KIRSTY: How did you find me?
> PINHEAD: I never lost you. I've waited. Watched and waited. Seen how the bud blossomed and ripened into firm fruit. But what to do? Pluck it and consume it? Or watch it fall from the bough, rot and wither into dirt?[1]

Hardly subtle, which is possibly why it was cut. But one last piece of dialogue remains:

> PINHEAD: Ah, a little understanding at last. It [her soul] is mine Kirsty. I possess it utterly. More completely than your pathetic Trevor ever could in his haphazard couplings. I touch the deep, dark, secret center of your self. And you know it. You welcome it.[2]

More metaphors that need no explanation. Yet the question remains: why let her go again?

There are two possible explanations. First, he is impressed once more with her bargaining skills and that she is willing to kill this time ("You'll get your five!"), something she gives him the credit for ("I had a great teacher," says Kirsty in the extended scene). In the script it has Pinhead smiling like a "proud parent" at this point, but reading between the lines it could be more than simple emulation. Second, if Kirsty is released, not only will she be granted her revenge as we've seen, but also the game can carry on, as will the sexual tension. "The box will never let you go," Pinhead tells her, and he is talking about himself as well. As long as the *Hellraiser* saga continues the question of whether Kirsty and Pinhead will ever meet again — and what will happen next time — remains.

Theirs are the real Hellbound Hearts of the series.

25

SOUGHT AFTER?

Hellseeker was released in October 2002 and met with another mixed response from critics. Garth Franklin at *Dark Horizons* on the Internet questioned the logic of making a movie so similar to the last one: "Again this is a character drama about a man who may be suffering delusions, though there's a more ... unsettling horror tone than the previous paranoid venture." He also laments the shortage of Kirsty: "Where this film truly bites, though, is that the great Ashley Laurence is back but totally underused and appearing in only a few minutes of footage at best."

Meanwhile, Jason Myers at *Revolution Science Fiction* sang the film's praises, declaring, "Imagine my surprise, then, to find that *Hellraiser: Hellseeker* was not only better than most direct-to-video horror movies, but also better than a good portion of the horror movies that get a theatrical release." Although he admits to having only seen the first two films in the series before this one, he says: "Questions about the movie's innate '*Hellraiserness*' aside, *Hellraiser: Hellseeker* is actually a decent horror flick."

Horror Express's Scott W. Davis saw the positives as well: "[The puzzle] appears briefly, but in fact it's all around us. That's the trick of the latest *Hellraiser* film. The entire film is a puzzle. Every time the film shifts, it reveals one part of the picture while concealing another. During the entire running time, we're wondering which end is up? Actually, people who are familiar with this type of story may guess where it's all leading, but there's enough of a surprise in the final revelations to make it all satisfying. Yes, I said satisfying. *Hellraiser: Hellseeker* has defied all expectations and is actually a good little horror film, the best this series has seen in some fourteen years. Clive Barker is allegedly happy with the film, too, since it seems to treat the mythology, surroundings and, most importantly, the characters with respect." On the other hand: "Writers Carl Dupré and Tim Day's script likes to walk the fine line between fantasy and reality, but rarely does it cross the mediocrity line from TV movie to feature film," claimed Travis Eddings of *Film Threat*. "Even the sets stay, the majority of the film, grounded on Earth, unlike previous prequels, which ventured into nether worlds."

The Surgeon 1:1 scale head. Replica sculpted by Ian Frost (courtesy Ian Frost).

Kage Alan of Modamag.com felt cheated by the cuts made to the movie: "While it's fantastic to see Kirsty again, the director didn't want to alienate viewers who weren't familiar with the *Hellraiser* series by giving too much exposition about events in previous installments, so he cut much of those sequences out. Personally, I find this extremely insulting. The people who are watching this 5th sequel are the ones who have stuck with it all along, even through the unforgivable *Inferno*, so why alienate us?"

Still, the reaction seemed to be in favor of *Hellseeker*, certainly over *Inferno*, in spite of any similarities. Of course, by this time Bota was already hard at work not just on the ensuing film, but on the next two *Hellraiser* films.

26

DEADER CERTAINTY

Aping *Inferno*'s genesis somewhat, *Hellraiser 7* began life as a pre-existing script, this time written by Neal Marshall Stevens. Stevens' first writing credit was on the TV show *Monsters* in 1988. From here he went on to direct *Stitches* (2000), about an evil sorceress who sews together the body parts of her victims, and then to write Dimension's *Thir13een Ghosts* (Steve Beck, 2001). Stevens' *Deader* script was sold to Dimension as a stand-alone, an intriguing horror story about the boundaries between life and death. In it, we're introduced on page one to a feisty reporter called Amy Klein, who works for *The Underground*, a weekly newspaper in the *Village Voice* mode. The poster outside their offices promotes her most recent story "How to Be a Crack Whore." She's dressed all in black, with black sunglasses, except for a white complexion "so translucently pale that it bespeaks only the most rare and grudging familiarity with daylight,"[1] so much so that she is described sarcastically by her editor, Bud, as an "Angel of Light."[2] He plays her a low resolution tape he's received set in a dingy apartment where people drift in and out of frame and the narration is provided by a girl of Chinese descent called Marla Chen, Official Deader Archivist.[3] Amy watches as Sheila — a new recruit — mouthing the mantra that she "isn't real," lies on a mattress, puts a gun against her head and pulls the trigger. Their leader, Winter, kisses a Deader called Carl, who then straddles her and apparently brings her back to life in a non-penetrative sexual orgasm of heavy breathing.

Colleague Larry believes the tape is a hoax, but Amy takes the story, the return address on the video envelope leading her to Marla's apartment. There's a rancid smell coming from inside, so she gets the super to break down the door because he doesn't have a key. The super's unwilling to come in, so Amy steps inside — to find Marla's dead body. She's hanged herself on the toilet with her own bootlaces. Next to the sink is another manila envelope that looks like it, too, has a tape inside. Amy tells the super to go and phone for the police, while she enters the bathroom and grabs the video. Searching the flat, Amy finds a stiletto knife and photos of another Deader party Marla attended. Hearing noises from the bathroom, Amy sees Marla's fingers twitch and her head turn, which causes her to scream and flee the building. Later, Amy watches the video at home, which was made just after Marla's own initiation. When Marla removes her sunglasses we see a pair of dead eyes looking out of the screen. It is at this moment that Larry calls Amy, startling her. When Amy calls Marla's number to see what has happened, she ends up speaking to the dead woman herself.

Amy subsequently enlists the help of Joey, who let her inside the drug scene to do the crack whore story. She finds him in the subway, having a private party in one of the coaches:

> The interior of the car has been transformed into some oddball cross between a very small nightclub and an opium den. Anyway, there are PERFORMERS at the far side who start playing as the train pulls out....
> In the uncertain light Amy can see the various CELEBRANTS hanging out — some on the seats, some on the floor, some dressed, some partially undressed, some engaging in desultory drug use, others in desultory sex acts.[4]

Joey tells her all he knows about the Deaders, that they're more than simply the Frankensteins or zombies Amy thinks. "It's all about minds, and believing and what's real and what's not."[5] They are playing with the concepts of the real and unreal, and it was all started by a man named Winter. Joey gives Amy the address where the group hang out — Avenue B and Third Street — but warns her away from the place.

Upon leaving the carriage, Amy sees a dead figure in a green plastic raincoat. Then she spots Winter dressed in black. He falls backwards in front of a train, but when she reports this to the police they can find no sign of his body on the tracks. When she sees Winter again she chases him, only to be arrested by the police. Bud bails her out and in a conversation between them it's revealed that Amy has an appetite for information, but he's the one who is curious about what's on the other side — and what the Deaders might have discovered. Amy herself is not tied by any religious guilt, which makes her the perfect person to find out.

After tracking down the Deader hideout, as she moves through a darkened corridor with only her lighter to guide the way, Amy feels the walls closing in on her. Finally, she arrives at the room where the first video was made and finds it full of people staring at her. Amy is sent in to see Winter and tells him she wants to join the Deaders. It is here that Winter elaborates about the real and unreal. Taking her hand he explains that it is not the flesh that defines this, but the spaces around it and in-between. "In all essential qualities, it is less than nothing. ... you are less than nothing. Not solid, not here, not real."[6] The reason Marla is decaying is that she's still clinging on to the real world instead of letting go. There follows an impressive special effects sequence in which he forces Amy to place her hand on the table and close her eyes. The surface feels wet, something is sucking at her fingers, and when she opens her eyes she sees a baby's face embedded in it; then the table turns into Sheila, who bites her.

Amy escapes and returns to her flat, ringing Larry to tell Bud that she is off the story. But while she is in bed that night, trying to sleep, she is shocked to find blood on the pillow — and a knife sticking in her back. She manages to remove the knife and stem the bleeding. Realizing the blade belongs to Marla, she returns to the woman's apartment by traveling on the subway, encountering a strange old man on the train. When Amy arrives, Marla says, "I'm sorry.... It's the way it's supposed to work. The one who initiates you is the one who has to be your guide,"[7] a guide who makes it easier to believe in coming back. She tells Amy that the apartment is too solid and that she's been drifting in and out of its reality all night. A crack appears in the window, but it's more than just a hole in the glass: the shafts of light illuminate figures from the real world, like the policeman from the subway. "In their world, in the daylight, a knife in the heart is fatal. If you stay ... then you'll have to live by their rules. The rules that make you dead."[8] So the choice is clear: the light is reality, the dark is unreality, and the women slip into the Night side.

In the Nightworld anything is possible, as we see in a series of hallucinatory scenes, the first involving a restaurant with dead cats hanging from the ceiling and a cluster of grotesque chefs. Following these incidents, Amy wakes to find herself in a hospital bed with

Larry and Bud beside her. She'd been found in her apartment covered in blood, just as Marla had been found in hers. As night approaches, she tells the doctors that the things that lurk in the dark are coming for her, but, as they've done before, they put this all down to a psychotic episode she's having. The faces of the dead are not quite human here (there's a fantastic description of a shark-mouthed creature) and in the end Winter appears. Amy has misplaced her guide, but she must still leave everything behind in the real world. After finding Marla, she repeats the "I'm not real" speech we heard right at the start and accepts her fate.

The effective ending sees Larry quitting because he thinks Amy and Marla have been killed by the cult, while Amy pays a visit to Bud and initiates him into the Deaders. Taking off her sunglasses in an action that mimics Marla, Bud sees that she has no eyes now, just dark, gaping holes.

Similar to *Ring* (Gore Verbinski, 2002), with its video mystery and determined news reporter as central protagonist, the *Deader* script would have made a decent movie in its own right. Stevens' initial idea draws on concepts explored in films like *Flatliners* (Joel Schumacher, 1990) and *Jacob's Ladder*, but it does so in a unique way. The screenplay, however, after being acquired by Dimension, was then selected as having potential for a *Hellraiser* movie. It was handed over to Tim Day, co-writer of *Hellseeker*, for him to insert the mythos elements. He would also cut some of the other more expensive or extraneous bits.

To this end, the character of Larry is the first to go. His presence serves only to hint at a possible relationship with Amy, which goes against the grain of her character, anyway. By taking him out, the *Hellraiser* Amy becomes more of a loner, who rarely asks anyone for help. Thus, Joey becomes not an informant she has used before but one of the Deaders himself, whom Marla directs her to. In actual fact this tightens up at least part of the script and reinforces the investigation side of it. The "baby table" sequence and other Nightworld hallucinations were all removed, replaced by flashbacks Amy keeps having of childhood revolving around her father. Day tied the abuse aspect in to the stabbing scene, by having Amy use a very similar weapon on her Dad: the personal demons Winter must force her to remember before she can become a Deader (which results in another recurring line: "Fear is where we go to learn"). Therefore, although it is still Marla who stabs Amy, the reporter finds no knife now in the woman's apartment. It is instead a replica of the one she herself used to kill her father that winds up in her back.

A pre-credits scene showing Amy actually inside the crack den was also added, which says more about her character than dark clothes ever could. This is someone who will go that extra mile for a story, someone willing to brave the seedy underbelly of society and won't stop until she's uncovered the enigma of the Deaders. Two shifts in location were also required. The first made the paper English because the majority of actors used for these scenes would be of this nationality — necessitating a name change to *London Underground*. Because the star had to be American, her new job is explained away in a conversation with her editor (now named Charles), who refers to her having been sacked from the *New York Post*, though Amy prefers to call it "reassigned." This has the added effect of bolstering her bad girl image. In addition, Day connected the dots between Amy and Charles by simply having a photograph in his office of the two of them together on an assignment in the past, hinting at a long-term history.

The second shift in territory reflected the movie's budget. Dimension knew that it would be much cheaper to shoot the film in Romania than in either the UK or the U.S.— so cheap, in fact, that they decided to shoot *Hellraisers 7* and *8* back to back over there. So, rather than filming in Bucharest and pretending they were in the lower East Side of Manhattan — where Stevens' script was initially set — the home of the Deaders was changed to Romania where, according to Charles, "All the Eurotrash kids looking for a good time are heading these days." If nothing else, it would open up the *Hellraiser* world again beyond the confines of Britain or New York. Romania is also steeped in horror genre history, having direct links with Dracula and vampires in general.

Day's other principal task would prove much harder. *Deader* arrived with a fully fledged mythology of its own, so the problem was how to integrate the already established *Hellraiser* components. The notion was put forward that Winter should somehow be connected to the maker of the box. In fact, it was in the script right up until almost shooting that Winter's great-grandfather was the creator of the Lament Configuration. It was Doug Bradley who pointed out that Lemarchand had done this in both the original Barker novella and in the complex storyline of *Bloodline*. In the finished film, Winter's association with that particular family is left extremely vague.

When talking to Amy, he claims the box is a "family heirloom" that belongs to him. As Pinhead gives his — now almost compulsory — summing up speech during the finale, he says, "It seems that evil does run in the family. Your lineage is that of a craftsman. A maker of toys. You should have stayed in the family business." It is obvious that Winter cannot be little Jack; for one thing, he is the wrong age (Jack would only be in his teens). For another, Winter dies without — to our knowledge — leaving any children behind to carry on the bloodline which would eventually culminate in Paul Merchant's birth. More likely is the possibility that he is a cousin of Jack's or perhaps even a brother of John's we weren't aware of. (After all, Jack is shown already building things with his Meccano, whereas Winter is involved in another game entirely.) That none of this is clarified reflects the haste with which the change was made.

Another factor that wasn't quite thought through was Winter's new motivation for the Deaders. Tantalizing though the thought of building a force to fight the Cenobites is — indeed, it was even used in the *Hellraiser* comic series for "The Harrowers" plotline (see chapter 33) — it jars when coupled with the original Deader idea. In Stevens' incarnation, Winter represents the Nightworld and unreality, in direct opposition to the light or Dayworld. In *Hellraiser* there can be only one source of darkness, that of the Cenobites.

In contrast to the Stevens written character, Winter wears white (trousers, T-shirt and coat) like an angel and pits himself against Pinhead. Yet the world in which he lives is very similar to the Hell we know: dark and clandestine, stone walls and shadowy corridors. Also, the methods he uses are questionable, to say the least, as he recruits his group from the hedonistic thrill seekers of Romania's backstreets. He even repeats Pinhead's line, "Don't think for a second you're not in danger." The struggle over Amy's soul — she being the only one who can both open the box and become a Deader — is inventive, but it is not fully explained why Winter should want her to do this. If he is of Lemarchand's line, then surely the last thing he'd want is for *anyone* to open the box? In Day's script Amy has already done this by the time she meets Winter, an encounter with chains and Pinhead in her apartment her reward for finding the box at Marla's. Indeed, the prising of the box from Marla's dead finger's is a retread of Amy reaching for the package: two suspense scenes for the price of one.

Both the Deader and Hellraiser strands work perfectly on their own, but do conflict somewhat with each other. This was something Stevens contended when he saw a copy of the finished shooting script. (As a requirement of the Writer's Guild, when there is more than one writer involved in a screenplay, a copy must be sent to all participants past and present.) He told *The Hellbound Web* via e-mail in 2003 that he'd had no contact whatsoever with Day or the makers of the final movie. "I haven't spoken to anyone at Dimension in years," he said. "I simply cannot be enthusiastic about the process that transformed my script, which had nothing whatsoever to do with *Hellraiser* or the *Hellraiser* universe, into a direct-to-video *Hellraiser* movie."[9] Director Bota diplomatically said, "Neil Marshall Stevens had really brilliantly written a story in dialogue, but once it was changed along the way into a *Hellraiser* sequel, there were several scenes which really did not work anymore within the mythology."[10]

So, this was the script the makers had and, barring changes on the way such as the inclusion of underground tunnels after a scouting trip to Romania (Bota found the perfect Deader den — World War II Army bunkers on the outskirts of Bucharest), this would remain pretty close to the finished film. As mentioned, Dimension wanted to shoot two *Hellraiser* sequels back-to-back in Romania, which would mean extremely short schedules — an incredible twenty-five days for *Deader* — and possible problems when trying to hire Bradley again. In his book, *Behind the Mask of the Horror Actor*, Bradley tells readers how Dimension wanted to book him for both movies, but only pay for one.[11] Luckily, all came to an agreement and the role was once again secure in Bradley's capable hands. For his part, he was particularly happy to be involved again because it meant for the first time in the series' history he'd be working with the same director twice and wouldn't have to go through the motions of explaining the character.

For the daunting part of Amy Klein, the makers chose another experienced genre actress, something they'd later be very thankful for. Born in 1967 in Brookfield, Connecticut, Kari Wuhrer began studying acting at thirteen, as well as singing at every opportunity (she was the youngest member of the band Freudian Slip). RADA trained, when she was old enough she moved to New York and applied for as many auditions as she could. Ford's Model Talent Division signed her up and she appeared in a number of commercials on TV Her first film was *Fire with Fire* (Duncan Gibbins, 1986), but almost immediately afterwards she landed a job as an MTV VJ, co-hosting *Remote Control*. When she returned to movies, it was for the 1990 comedy *The Adventures of Ford Fairlane* (Renny Harlin, 1990) and *Beastmaster 2: Through the Portal of Time* (Sylvio Tabet, 1991). She also found time to star as Abigail in the *Swamp Thing* TV series (1990).

Parts followed in such films as *Beyond Desire* (Dominique Othenin-Girard, 1996) and Stephen King's *Thinner* (Tom Holland, 1996), but it

An unused Cenobite: Spike (courtesy Gary J. Tunnicliffe).

was on television again that her next big break came, playing Maggie Beckett on the sci-fi parallel universe show, *Sliders*, from 1997 onwards. Just before taking the role of Amy, Wuhrer had starred in the big budget Hollywood creature feature, *Eight Legged Freaks* (Ellory Elkayem, 2002), alongside David Arquette. The film actually had its Romanian premiere during filming of *Deader*. She had also just executive produced her first feature in 2001, coincidentally entitled *Spider's Web* (Paul Levine). Said Wuhrer afterwards about the experience, "The pace of making this movie, it was extreme. It was the longest day imaginable on a film set that we could get away with ... and yeah, I was in every scene, start to finish, and it was grueling."[12]

For the enigmatic role of Winter, Wales-born Paul Rhys was also perfect casting. The intense actor's first film was 1986's *Absolute Beginners* (Julien Temple), followed quickly by TV roles in an adaptation of *My Family and Other Animals* (1987), *Tumbledown* (1989) and *Opium Eaters* (1990), as well as a part as Sydney Chaplin in *Chaplin* (Richard Attenborough, 1992). The television work continued for over a decade with productions such as *The Healer* (1992), *The Haunting of Helen Walker* (1995), *King Lear* (1998), *I Saw You* (2000) and the new version of *Randall and Hopkirk (Deceased)* (2000) with Vic Reeves and Bob Mortimer. But it was in the lavishly superb adaptation of Alan Moore's graphic novel, *From Hell* (Albert & Allen Hughes, 2001), that he really shone with a career best performance as Dr. Ferral, one of the suspects in Johnny Depp's Jack the Ripper investigation.

Londoner Georgina Rylance took on the difficult part of Marla, now more European-looking than Asian. Another TV actress, she had been a regular as Anna in the series *As If* (2002), in addition to securing roles in *Manchild* (2002) and the U.S. fantasy program *Dinotopia* (2002). Georgina had one of the toughest tests of the shoot, to lean forward and hold still while pretending to be dead on the toilet, the process of which actually hurt her back during takes. She was joined by Northampton-born Marc Warren as Joey, whose energetic, spontaneous performance caused some headaches when it came to editing, as no two takes were the same. Warren had enjoyed a long and varied acting career that encompassed everything from the BBC's *Casualty* medical series (1991) to the Spielberg produced *Band of Brothers* (2001) on television, and *Bring Me the Head of Mavis Davis* (John Henderson, 1997) and *f2point8* (Paul Hills, 2002) in the cinematic realm. He would definitely add a much-needed humorous slant and his last line, "For fuck's sake!" after Pinhead runs him through with a chain, is one of the most memorable in the entire franchise.

Another Englishman, Simon Kutz, was hired to play Amy's boss, Charles. Kuntz's admirable credits included *Four Weddings and a Funeral* (Mike Newell, 1994), Disney's *The Parent Trap* (Nancy Meyers, 1998) and homegrown horror chiller *The Bunker* (Rob Green, 2001). A regular also on British TV, Kuntz brought a requisite charm and ruthlessness to the role of Charles that would lead some to believe he was in league with the Cenobites themselves, especially after Amy's line: "You know there's something vaguely demonic about you, Charles." The other woman in his life, secretary Betty, would be portrayed by veteran actress Linda Marlowe.

The majority of other actors in *Deader* would be drawn from Romanian stock. The Landlord, for instance, Costi Barbulescu; Young Amy, Maria Pintea; Amy's father, Daniel Chirea; Anna, Madalina Constantin; Subway Cops, Mircea Constantinescu and Marius Ratiu; the Deader Guide who shows Amy the way to their hideout, Nike Phanzu; and the Young Girl who paints in the asylum, Daria Enescu in addition to the numerous extras needed for scenes like the subway carriage lair. Many of these actors couldn't speak a word of English and had to learn the lines parrot-fashion, particularly impressive when you consider the inflections they managed to achieve. But this would expose one of the largest problems the U.S. director faced, the language barrier with a Romanian crew.

As hardworking as they were — though in Hollywood terms they were being paid relatively little, their Romanian wage was a cut above the average worker there — Bota would find it difficult to communicate his meaning on occasion. This would become particularly apparent when dealing with major crew members like cinematographer Vivi Dragan Vasile [*Ultima noapte a singuratatii* (Virgil Calotescu, 1976) and *Dark Angel: The Ascent* (Linda Hassani, 1994)]. As we saw in previous chapters, Bota is an experienced DP himself and even wondered whether or not to hire a cinematographer at all for *Hellseeker*. But he was actually looking forward to working with a foreign DP of this caliber. And the majority of the time there was very little problem working with the translator on set. "It was just the fine detail and explaining of things. I think he was more traditional, so things like odd camera movements and odd lighting decisions didn't come as easily to him. I think he was thinking he was doing an American movie, and I was thinking I was doing a European movie. He wanted to add lights, I wanted to subtract light and, given the language difficulties, there were times we definitely clashed."[13] In addition, Bota had difficulty securing some of the locations he'd set his heart on when scouting. For example, the director wanted to film in one of the old, run-down subway stations for the scenes with Joey and Winter, but instead the Romanians had arranged for him to shoot in a new station that hadn't even opened yet.

Bota did have some recognizable faces around him, though, like Gary Tunnicliffe, who was not just handling the make-up effects this time, but was also directing the second unit filming (his are the close-up shots at the start in the crack den). Tunnicliffe also turned his hand to acting, for a memorable exchange with Wuhrer in the *London Underground* office during the title sequence: he's the one who asks Amy to show him what's she's learnt while she's been undercover. Tunnicliffe's expertise was especially useful when filming the finale, where the chains jet out of the walls and hook into Winter, pulling him apart in the same gruesome way they did Frank in the original. "Although it looks as though we have many pieces of wall, we actually only use one wall section and we just make a different hole, blast one chain through, then take it out, patch it up, and then just blast another section.... But from different angles, shot high and low, at different frame rates, faster speed, slower speed, it'll look like the hooks and chains are bursting from all over the place."[14] Perhaps the fact that one producer of *Deader* was special effects maestro Stan Winston (who created the monsters for *Aliens* and *Jurassic Park*) made him raise the bar even higher for this outing.

Bota would also receive quite a bit of help from the other producer, Ron Schmidt, who had previously worked on Wes Craven's interpretation of *Dracula* in 2000 (Patrick Lussier) and, of course, *Hellseeker*. Said Bota, "He's just a great guy to be working with because he's just so determined to get you what you need, and I really felt like I had a lot of support."[15] Schmidt made the transition of working in Romania much smoother and generally the shoot was an enjoyable, if tough one — and particularly emotionally draining for Wuhrer.

Perhaps because of how well they got on, two of the best scenes emerged from Bota and Wuhrer working almost in isolation. The first was filmed in breaks during other scenes, it is the section where Amy squeezes herself down a corridor and the walls close in on her. The sense of claustrophobia is palpable here and Wuhrer's acting is superb, as it is in the bathroom scene after she is stabbed. Bota had always been nervous about filming this because he feared it was one of those scenes that read well in the script but would be difficult to interpret on celluloid. He needn't have worried. "Everybody was tired," recalls Wuhrer.

"I had been in and out of bloodstained clothes all day. It was cold, I'm constantly wet and having to be dried off, it was freezing and we just said let's go for it! So he's [Bota] got the camera on his shoulder.... We locked eyes and we knew if we didn't fully commit ... And we just started filming and I went for stuff and he followed me, and there wasn't any set choreography, it was all motivated by emotion.... I followed his leads and there was the silent communication. It was brilliant."[16] The outcome was an extremely distressing scene.

In post-production, *House on Haunted Hill* (William Malone, 1999) editor Anthony Adler had his work cut out for him but did a great job of splicing together the footage and adding even more tension. Visual effects supervisor Jamison Goei included touches like the chains springing out of the box and hooking Amy's face, lightning crackling around the box itself, the Cenobites' entrance at the end, and the Deaders being skewered by Pinhead's chains. German composer Henning Lohner (who provided additional music for *The Ring*) could then also lay down the soundtrack. Bota had been petitioning Dimension to buy the rights to Young's signature themes from *Hellraiser*, which he wanted to use at key points, like when Pinhead first appears, but Lohner's themes do a fair impersonation without breaking that copyright. And his theme for the titles and credits provide a terrific sense of melancholy.

But one mystery remains, even after Amy has solved the puzzle of the Lament Configuration and the Deaders. That is why Dimension chose to hold back on releasing the movie until the summer of 2005. With *Hellseeker* making its appearance in 2002 at the same time *Deader* was being filmed, a release the following year would have helped to keep *Hellraiser* in the public eye. It would be a riddle that would not only haunt this movie, but the eighth *Hellraiser* film as well.

27

Fear Is Where We Go to Learn

Deadly Addictions

The first theme of *Deader* is signaled within moments of the film's opening. In a pre-title sequence we're shown close-ups of a spoon with heroin boiling on it, needles to one side (a different kind of pinprick than customary in *Hellraiser*), a bottle on bare floorboards—and then we pan across to witness the aftermath of this addiction spree: the first crackhead, face down, cigarette smoking away in his hand. All but one of the major addictions is covered here, and to reinforce the last one we settle on a woman lighting up. As we saw in *Hell on Earth*, there's a definite link between smoking and being damned in *Hellraiser* lore, so when Amy wakes and the first thing she does is take a drag on her cigarette — and chain smoke her way through the entire movie — we know she won't make it through the picture unscathed.

Yet her determining addiction has nothing to do with narcotics. The drugs available here do not interest her, they are merely a means by which she can satisfy her thirst for a good story. After checking her dictaphone and taking her pictures, she slips quietly out of the den. "You want any of this?" one druggie asks when she's at the door. "No thanks," Amy replies, "I got what I need." And the proof of this comes when she picks up a copy of the *London Underground* in their office and it has her story on the front. A simple byline is her high, and like Joey before her in *Hellraiser III* she will go to any lengths to get that elusive credit. Editor Charles knows this and by involving her in the Deader story he's supplying Amy with what she really desires. Charles is her dealer, getting her hooked and then using her to find him a good story. Indeed, it is insinuated that he might have been the one who started her on this road in the first place: the pair definitely have a reporting history together, judging by the black and white picture he keeps on his shelf. "Back in the trenches together, just like old times," he says. "Don't get all sentimental on me," is Amy's reply.

The difference between the pair is that he has distanced himself from the front lines. He delegates now, mainly because he doesn't have the same urges Amy does. This is highlighted in his speech after he bails her out at the police station. "Why'd you give me this story, Charles?" she asks. Charles answers, "Who else would have taken it? Either they're going to think it's bullshit, or they're going to be too afraid. But Amy Klein ... For the average person the hunger for knowledge is like the hunger for food. We want to know just enough to take the edge off our appetite. Then we're satisfied, and we stop. But you are a glutton. You can't help overeating." He gets her to do his eating for him, so he doesn't suffer from what he calls mental indigestion. "I take them [people] as they come and use them as they pass by," he finishes. It is something borne out when Amy vanishes at the end and we see him hooking another female reporter on this particular stimulant.

In his own way, Charles *is* like the Cenobites; they provide the ultimate in pleasure and pain for those who have become weary of what the real world has to offer. Like Pinhead with Frank, or Julia with Channard, he gives Amy only what she truly wants, regardless of the cost. It is why Amy states that there's "something vaguely demonic" about him. He, in turn, informs her that the word demon comes from the Greek word for knowledge.

In their own way, the Deaders are also addicted. As Pinhead says at the end, Winter was tempted to live beyond death, and, turning to the Deaders: "This world. It obviously disappoints you all. That is why you chose to begin this journey." Even Joey, who is addicted not to drugs but to sex (his carriage filled with naked flesh, a woman there orally pleasuring him as Amy tries to have a conversation) has embraced the Deader way of life. The ultimate addiction for these people is to blur the perimeters of reality and fantasy, to reject the solid and declare that they are "not real." Except for Winter. For him, there is also the added attraction of power and cultist leadership. In this environment he becomes like a prophet or even a messiah — Surely the most tempting addiction of all.

A Matter of Life and Death

In its standpoint on life and death, *Deader* comes down firmly on the side of the deceased. All the members of the cult have taken their own life, some with a gun to the head like Katya (formerly Sheila in Stevens' script), or by hanging, like Marla. They proudly display their wounds to Amy when she stumbles into their lair. Slashed wrists are held up for her to see, knife wounds worn like badges of honor or some bizarre rite of passage. But this is a slightly different kind of death. As Marla points out to Amy after she's been stabbed, neither of them should be walking around: "Why aren't you dead? Why aren't I? Because when it's dark enough there's no such thing. There's no difference between being dead and being alive." Theirs is a resurrected existence, one where you can jump in front of speeding trains and still survive, or bleed profusely but never let your wounds fell you.

The "Deaders" in *Zombie 3* resemble the zombies of Fulci but are different in certain ways.

In looks, these Deaders bear

more of a resemblance to the zombies of George A. Romero's *Night of the Living Dead* (1968), *Dawn of the Dead* (1978) and *Day of the Dead* (1985), or Lucio Fulci's *Zombie Flesh Eaters* (1979), *City of the Living Dead* (1980) and *The Beyond* (1981). Their milky white eyes have no color, the decaying flesh peeling away from cheeks or chins to reveal the bone. The main difference, of course, is that, far from shambling along looking for brains to devour, the Deaders operate at a similar capacity to when they were alive. They walk and talk normally, and some even appear completely human, those who totally accept that death is not the end. This isn't the first time zombies have been linked to the *Hellraiser* series. In his book, *Zombies* (1992), Andrew Black makes a case for seeing both Frank and the Cenobites as zombies: all resurrected flesh, all living beyond death. "If *Hellraiser* is indicative of the standard of forthcoming zombie films," he states, "then the future of the genre seems assured."[1]

But in spirit the Deaders have much more in common with ill-fated Brandon Lee's Eric Draven from *The Crow* (Alex Proyas, 1994). Sheer emotional will brings him back for revenge upon those who murdered him and his girlfriend. In the case of Draven it is love that spurs him on, in the case of the Deaders devotion to Winter's doctrines. But it can be no coincidence that a black crow does appear twice in the film, the very first time on the grainy video Amy watches as Winter brings back Katya from the grave. And how does he do this? By kissing her, just as he does with the unidentified male Deader when Amy arrives in the underground room. In a reversal of the typical *Hellraiser* motif, a kiss brings life rather than death. There is no betrayal, apart from that of the natural order of things.

When we first encounter Amy she looks dead. She's on the couch in the crack den, head back, hardly breathing. She has surrounded herself with the nearly dead as well. The bodies she steps over to get out appear just as lifeless as those on Joey's train carriage the final time we see them. In the script, she's described as wearing black (which is the standard color of funerals) and having a pale face (just like a corpse); this is something that Wuhrer pulls off well in the movie. In essence, Amy is dead right from the beginning; she simply doesn't realize it yet. "I just want to go home," she tells Marla. "Amy, you are home," Marla enlightens her. The question is not *if* she will die, then, but what will happen to her soul? Both Winter and Pinhead wish to claim it, and the balance changes throughout the film. Twice we see Amy ascending stairs at the start, in the office and at Marla's home, suggesting she might end up safe or in some sort of Heaven. But both times she finds herself in danger after these ascensions: Charles sends her on the assignment and she finds Marla's body and the box in her flat.

It is after this point, and after she has opened the Lament Configuration, that we see her descending: into the subway to find Joey, into the Deader's dungeon, and then down into the subway again. This would lead us to believe that her soul is well and truly doomed. In the end, the sacrifice she makes of killing herself — falling backwards martyr-style with arms outstretched — saves her from both of these fates. Neither Winter nor Pinhead can really possess her soul now that she has made the choice herself — now that she has accepted death in its true form.

Stabbed in the Back

Trust issues imbue *Deader*, or more correctly the *loss* of trust. The most horrendous loss of trust there can ever be is that between a parent and child. And this, as we see piece by piece, is what happened to Amy as a little girl. The very first images, those black and white flashbacks of the checkered floor (once more hinting at the colossal chess game being played behind the scenes), and a corridor leading to a door (recalling Joseph Thorne's flashbacks from *Inferno*), presage the revelations to come. The confined space where Amy hides to get away from her abusive father parallels the scene in which she becomes stuck in the gap between the walls when looking for the Deaders, just before being stabbed by the hooded figure.

The flashbacks again herald a stabbing, this time in the back while she lies in bed, tying the physical to the mental. Amy was stabbed in the back by her father (figuratively, although one fears when he turns Amy onto her stomach on the table that he might be doing this literally, only not with a knife). As she thinks about the events, facing her demons, the knife in the back manifests itself and her blood flows freely like the memories.

It is not until she remembers fully in the hospital corridor — obviously her mindscape, complete with checkered floor — that the wound starts to bleed again and the implication is clear. But it is *what* she recalls that is important: Amy stabbing her father in the stomach — penetrating him, as he has done her — and killing him. In the flashback we see the adult Amy take the place of her younger self in a floral dress, and we know she has confronted her fear so that she can move on to the denouement. "Why is it that you feel no pain?" Pinhead asked her when she accused him of doing this to her. At the time, she felt no pain because she'd buried the memories so deep they couldn't possibly hurt her. The more blood she loses, the more the past comes flooding back.

The way this happens is through photographic images. The scenes in that crack den that Amy takes pictures of are now frozen black and white moments in time, as is the picture of her and Charles that we zoom in on at the end. (The camera dissolves blocking out Charles and finding Amy's face, her eyes; this was her story, after all.) Her memories are just moving monochrome representations of a childhood she'd rather forget, opened up by the various keys in the movie: the one that opens the Deader gate, the Lament Configuration that opens the pathway to Hell, and the opening of the cupboard door where young Amy hides.

Finally, there is the trust the Deaders place in Winter, who ultimately betrays them all. Without their knowledge, they are being used in his war against the Cenobites; Winter is amassing troops for the final push. But in the end he has sealed all their fates. One can therefore state in no uncertain terms that their trust in him was completely misplaced.

28

DEADER, LIKE ME?

With a mixture of anticipation and excitement (remember the film had a two and a half year build-up), *Hellraiser: Deader* was finally released on DVD in June 2005. Dave Davis of Chud.com was one of the first to review it, saying, "Director Rick Bota has done a few movies in the series, and he seems to be getting the hang of it, judging by the murk and mayhem of *Deader*. Of course, it's only just superficially a *Hellraiser* movie — it feels like an original horror script was refurbished to incorporate Pinhead and the pain aficionados." Which, of course, it was.

John J. Puccio of *DVDTown* said: "The *Hellraiser* series has always been about grotesque imagery, mostly of death and dying, and this entry is no exception. But the editing and direction leave a lot to be desired, with too many important plot details blithely skipped over."

The Film Journal's Rick Curnutte, Jr., was more optimistic in his assessment: "Though none of the subsequent films have captured the sexual potency of the first film or the fantastic allegory of the second, *Deader* returns, at least in spirit, to the more organic tones of the earlier installments." This positivism was echoed by *Slasherpool*'s reviewer AnthroFred, who even stated: "It's really a shame that they started going DVD with the *Hellraiser* movies because this movie is definitely the best since the first *Hellraiser* movie and I think that this might have done pretty well at the box office."

Tony Whitt of *Now Playing Magazine* commented, "Perhaps it's my own lower expectations, then, but *Deader* turned out to be a pleasant surprise. It hasn't got the gravitas of the first two movies, the flash of the third, nor even the plot twists of the fourth, but it's still a deeply scary, deeply disturbing little movie."

To conclude, *Pop Matter*'s associate music editor, Tim O'Neil, summed up thus: "For about the first two thirds of its running time, it creates a deliciously evil atmosphere of dread and dismay. Kari Wuhrer's performance as a desperate reporter being dragged further into the grips of hallucinatory madness while investigating a strange death-defying cult leader is especially good. Her intensity, especially during extended scenes dealing with her own death and bloody rebirth, is far more evocative than any B-movie has the right to expect."

29

HELL OF A WORLD

But, as we know, *Deader* wasn't the only *Hellraiser* movie to be made in Romania at that time, although it was the only script Rick Bota and the crew took there with them. Throughout early stages of filming for the seventh movie in 2002, there was an initial idea for a script revolving around a party in an old house. But there were also a considerable amount of historical flashbacks involved — one venturing to Nazi Germany — and so the producers decided it would prove too complicated and too expensive to make. With shooting on *Deader* continuing apace and no film as such waiting to be made when it finished, the net was once again cast to find a *Hellraiser* story. Joel Soisson, who wrote *Trick or Treat* (Charles Martin Smith, 1986) and *Mimic 2* (Jean de Segonzac, 2001) and produced the *Prophecy* series, had written a short treatment called "Dark Camp Breathe."

"It began mostly as a way of jotting down what I thought my own worst nightmare was," said Soisson upon watching the finished film.[1] This turned out to be implanted memories through drug-induced suggestion and being buried alive. The story came across the desk of Nick Phillips, executive producer on *Deader* and the eighth film. "I thought it was just great in and of itself," he enthused. "And in trying to find some use for it, we obviously decided to try to integrate it with the *Hellraiser* mythology."[2] With time fast running out, Bota contacted Carl Dupré, who had been one of the writers on *Hellseeker*. Dupré had to work fast and turned the treatment into a script within two weeks. In this he played around with the *Hellraiser* mythology, thinking outside the box to create an Internet gaming ring called Hellworld that would entice the players to come to a *Hellraiser* party, thereby utilizing the Gothic-looking house in Bucharest that would have been the location for the movie in its original form. The writer did leave some of the scenes vague, though, in particular the murder sequences, so that others could have their say. Once *Deader* had completed shooting, Bota and the producers retreated to their hotel to bat around ideas. Bota had only one week's preparation time (where usually a director would enjoy about five). But soon the moment had arrived and the shoot was about to begin.

The makers had to think on their feet in terms of casting as well. But Bradley was already over there and two of the other slots virtually filled themselves. Khary Payton had just starred in Dimension's *Dracula II: Ascension* (Patrick Lussier, 2003), so he was fresh in their minds when it came time to fill the role of Derrick. He also came with the added bonus of having had his head cut off in that film, so they could use this prop again for his death in *Hellworld*. Speaking about the movie Payton said, "Hellworld is like candyland without the candy. It's a state of mind ... All hell breaks loose again. And why wouldn't it? It's *Hellraiser*."[3] Payton, who had also featured in TV shows like *Walker, Texas Ranger* and *Imagine That*, would bring a welcome spark of energy to the whole proceedings.

Newcomer Anna Tolputt had already auditioned for the part of Marla in *Deader* and impressed Bota. The young English actress wasn't quite right for that part, but when the role of Allison came up she would prove perfect. With just the right hint of "Goth"—and resembling Thora Birch in *The Hole* (Nick Hamm, 2001)—Anna would have one of the most horrific deaths of any *Hellraiser* film, being bled dry in the Sacrificial Chair with two spinning razor-sharp wheels.[4] She would also have to be buried in make-up for the chase scene around the house and for her final death scene in the coffin where she has clawed out her own throat.

Born in 1983, Henry Cavill grew up in Jersey on the Channel Islands. He became interested in theatre acting at boarding school, and this in turn eventually led to film work. His first appearance on the big screen was playing Thomas Aprea in *Laguna* (Dennis Berry, 2001) and this was swiftly followed by a role in the major Hollywood swasherbuckler, *The Count of Monte Cristo* (Kevin Reynolds, 2002), alongside Guy Pearce and Richard Harris. He also appeared on British television in *The Inspector Lynley Mysteries* and *Goodbye, Mr. Chips* (both 2002). With his dark good looks there is little wonder he only just missed out on playing Superman, but for the role of Mike in *Hellworld* Cavill would also display a distinctly comic sensibility that would lighten the mood in between the darker parts of the film.

Writer of *Hellworld*, Carl Dupré, on the steps of the Host's house (courtesy David Robinson).

The other male lead was a role filled by Canadian Christopher Jacot. He had a number of TV and film credits to his name by the time he was cast in *Hellworld*, including *Twice in a Lifetime*, *The Famous Jet Jackson* and *MythQuest* on the small screen, and *Get Over It* (Tommy O'Haver, 2001) with Colin Hanks (son of Tom) and Kirsten Dunst, and *The Bay of Love and Sorrows* (Tim Southam, 2002) in the cinema. He would bring just the right balance of brooding teen angst and vulnerable hero qualities to Jake, best friend of the boy who dies at the start of the film because he was playing "Hellworld." "He gave a performance filled with despair and anger," said Bota about the young actor.[5]

For the key role of Chelsea, those casting turned to up-and-coming starlet Katheryn Winnick, who was born and raised in Etobicoke and could speak only Ukranian until the age of eight. Winnick studied acting in New York and had made a name for herself in TV shows like *Student Bodies*, *PSI Factor: Chronicles of the Paranormal* and *Relic Hunter*, and had also starred in *Two Weeks Notice* (Marc Lawrence, 2002) with Hugh Grant and Sandra Bullock. Winnick was one of the hopefuls of 2002's *The It Factor* which proclaimed her to be one of the next talents to have "it." When the makers found out that not only did she have the looks, but also holds a third-degree black belt in Tae Kwon Do, a second-degree black belt in Karate, and is a licensed bodyguard, they quickly wrote in a couple of scenes that would show this off (namely when someone tries to pick her up at the party and when she roundhouse kicks The Host near the climax of the movie). "You know, I think the actual footage of it looks like a double," said the actress of that last scene, "because my hair was in my face. But no, Mom, that's me. I did it!"[6] Since making *Hellworld* Winnick has gone on to star as Ivana Trump in the biopic *Trump Unauthorized*. "It's the untold version," she says. "It's not Donald's version."[7]

Playing the Uniformed Cop who comes to check out Chelsea's phone call was a face familiar to British audiences. Victor McGuire had starred for many years as Jack Boswell in the sitcom *Bread* from the mid 1980s onwards, and then in another successful comedy as time-traveling Nicholas Lyndhurst's pal, Ron Wheatcroft, for *Goodnight, Sweetheart* (1993–1999). Movie audiences might recognize him from *Lock, Stock and Two Smoking Barrels* (Guy Ritchie, 1998) and *Thunderpants* (Peter Hewitt, 2002). For someone who knows him from these UK roles it is a little strange to see him with a New York accent, but he masters it quite well.

David Robinson would join him as Cop #2, under some very unusual circumstances. David, from Cheshire, England, won a competition to find "Britain's Scariest Person." "The competition's not been held since, so I guess I still am!" said David. "The prize was for a walk-on part in a horror movie and I was thrilled when it was eventually arranged to be a *Hellraiser* movie.... The first scene I shot is right near the end of the movie where we pull Chelsea from the coffin."[8] David was absolutely delighted at his prize, being a massive *Hellraiser* fan (which was coincidentally what the whole film was about). After chatting with Gary Tunnicliffe, the pair became friends and David now runs his Web site (*www.garyjtunnicliffe.com*). It's to be hoped it won't be David's last appearance on-screen as he does a very good job.

Like Andrew Robinson in *Hellraiser*, the film's biggest coup would be securing the services of Lance Henriksen. A true Hollywood veteran, Henriksen was born in New York in 1940 and studied at the Actors Studio before securing parts in off-Broadway plays. In the '70s he starred in such classics as *Dog Day Afternoon* (Sidney Lumet, 1975) with Al Pacino, Spielberg's *Close Encounters of the Third Kind* (1977) and the second outing for the demon child in *Damien: Omen II* (Don Taylor, 1978). In the '80s he enjoyed even more success when he was almost cast as The Terminator in James Cameron's futuristic thriller, and his eventual role of Detective Vukovich led to a part in Cameron's next movie, *Aliens* (1986). It was this that really catapulted the actor to fame, playing the heroic android Bishop—a franchise role that he would reprise for two of the later films (including 2004's prequel *Aliens vs. Predators* directed by Paul W. Anderson). Parts in Kathryn Bigelow's savvy vampire movie, *Near Dark* (1987), *The Pit and the Pendulum* (Stuart Gordon, 1990) and John Woo's first U.S. film, *Hard Target* (1993), came next. But it was the spin-off from the highly acclaimed *X-Files*, *Millennium*— also created by Chris Carter—that gave Henriksen his second most famous role: that of ex–FBI profiler Frank Black (1996–1999). Nor was Henriksen a stranger to haunted buildings like the one in *Hellworld*, having starred in *House III: The Horror Show* (James Isaac) in 1989.

His involvement in the film came after Bota bumped into him in a restaurant in Romania on the director's first day there; Henriksen was just finishing up duties there on *Mimic 3: Sentinel* (J.T. Petty, 2003). Bota told him how much he admired his work and that he really wanted to use him in something. There were no parts appropriate in *Deader* but

Henriksen told Bota to send him something to look at. This turned out to be *Hellworld*, with Dupré being in the fortunate position of writing the part of The Host with Henriksen in mind. When the actor read the script back in America, he was so excited by it he got on another plane and flew back to Romania. "I was very happy and very fortunate to have Lance Henriksen step into the role of The Host,"[9] said Bota, who immediately put him to work when he got there, digging the holes that the teens would eventually find themselves in. Professional that he is, Henriksen also made a request of the make-up department that they glue his ears back so he would look more feral—like a wolf or a Doberman.

As with *Deader* there would also be some peripheral members of the cast who were sourced from Romania itself. To begin with, there were the two girls actually from the train carriage scene with Joey in the previous film, who would now stand in for Gratuitous Titshot Girl and Sister Ursala. Ursala (Catalina Alexandru) would be required not only to strip this time but also to play a ghost nun who seduces Jake and sleeps with him in an attic room of the house. The police officer victim who gets staked in the mouth by Pinhead (Costi Mirica) and the smoothie who tries to pick up Chelsea (not credited) couldn't speak a word of English and had to have their lines dubbed over. Someone else who didn't get to say much, but wasn't Romanian, was writer Dupré himself, who turns up as a barman in one scene, following in a tradition set by Peter Atkins back in *Hellraiser III: Hell on Earth*.

Crew-wise, Gary Tunnicliffe was a given, although he did find time to go back home briefly between shoots. In early drafts of the script there was something called the Hydro baby, which would come from inside a jar and run around attacking people à la Chucky. Bota asked Tunnicliffe to design this, but the cost of operating it would have been prohibitive. They then thought about a CGI one, which would have fallen—as always—under the remit of Jamison Goei's visual effects department. In the end, it was decided to just fill what came to be known as the The Specimen Lab set (meant to be the basement of the house) with lots of Area 51-type deformed babies in jars. Tunnicliffe was also responsible for rounding up as much *Hellraiser* paraphernalia as he could for The Host's "museum," such as boxes, chains, and the Cenobite tarot cards. Other than that, it was business as usual, with the effects maestro going to work on the cast and generally piling on the gore, whether it be on hand during Tolputt's Sacrifice Chair scene or lying just below Winnick to pump spurting blood out of the wound when she is stabbed by mistake. "Actually, all the cast were great," said Gary. "We did a lot of prosthetics stuff to them and beat them up all quite badly at various points in this, everything from burying them in the ground in the freezing cold to having dirt on them, and they were all real troupers."[10] The cast were no less complimentary of him, Winnick stating, "Gary was a hoot!"[11] and Payton saying, "God gave him a gift, and it was to bloody up the world!"[12]

Tunnicliffe was also in charge of the Cenobite make-up again, which included Doug Bradley's distinctive look and the return of Chatterer and Bound, albeit in a slightly different form. Bound—now called Banded—was male this time and responsible for raising one of the teen victims up on a meat hook, taking the scene from *Texas Chainsaw Massacre* just that little bit further. The Cenobites would be played on this occasion by a combination of Tunnicliffe himself, Mike Regan and Snowy Highfield. But Tunnicliffe could also be seen right at the very end, when the coffins are discovered, with notepad in hand standing next to a police car—a character he maintains, with tongue in cheek, is the reporter from *Deader* who talks to Amy at the start, the only character apart from Pinhead to make it into both movies. He also handled the second unit direction, including various inserts to the film.

Most of Goei's postproduction contributions to *Hellworld* were more subtle but had no less an impact on the overall film — the white mask, for instance, which suddenly takes on a hideous appearance during Mike's fellatio scene, the extra blood spurts for Allison's death, and the removal of the floor when trying to give the appearance of a whole room full of dead partygoers hanging from hooks and chains. But his tour de force would be the death of The Host, the Cenobites slicing him in pieces with blades on the end of chains — a homage to Bishop being ripped apart by the Alien Queen in *Aliens*. And the cinematographer on this shoot was another Romanian technician, Gabriel Kosuth, and the aim this time was to go for an American feel rather than European, because the movie is supposed to be set in the U.S. The DP's previous credits included 1992's *Filmare/Filmage*, which Kosuth also directed, and *The Secret Kingdom* (David Schmoeller, 1998).

The music score would come from Lars Anderson, who had worked on *Anacardium* (Scott Thomas, 2001) and the James Bond video game, *Nightfire* (2002). Anderson would provide some haunting piano music to match the tone of the ghost-house completely (in particular when Jake and Sister Ursala make love). But the thumping rock soundtrack would be mainly the department of music supervisor Melanie Miller, who brought in stacks of music from bands that the production could afford. The result was even more tracks than *Hell on Earth* boasted, such as some standouts from Bosshouse like "It Ends," "Haunted," "Bug Spray" and the number that ends the movie with perfect irony, "Look Who's Standing Tall." Other tracks included "91" by Skipngonaked, "Stay With Me (Unlikely)" and "Frozen" by Celldweller, "1 Man" by Sons of Poseidon, "Glass Procedure" by CIRRUS, "Berlin Wall" by Stumbling Mumbler and "I Funk Therefore I Am" by Sonicanimation.

Once more, the shoot was a fast and furious one (twenty to twenty-four days), fun but exhausting. *Hellworld* was shot on location at the big house — with rooms fitted out by production designer Christian Niculescu — and in its grounds, although for the forest shots the crew would have to move about thirty-five miles down the road outside the main part of town. Some interior scenes were filmed in The Writer's House, the basement of the university hospital and on set (the attic where Chelsea puts her hand through the floorboards, for example). Bota was used to communicating through translators now, but still found it delayed things sometimes. The main problem, however, was the climate. When the clothing for the cast was chosen it was September and still moderately warm. Even when the shoot began in October, the weather held off, allowing Winnick to shoot the scenes where she runs to the car in only her cut-off red top with little difficulty. But by the end of the shoot in December, temperatures for the outside filming had dropped to something like -12° Celsius. A warm trailer had to be standing by between takes for Winnick now, and the steam you see coming from actors' mouths is very genuine, indeed. As Doug Bradley commented, "There was no getting round the fact that standing in those temperatures was like plunging my head in a bucket of ice."[13] The upshot was Winnick losing her voice at one point and her double catching pneumonia. "It was so cold," reiterated Winnick, "it was to a point where my lips would freeze and I couldn't get my words out."[14]

Shooting of the scene where Adam — also a Romanian who could speak no English (Stelian Urian) — has to set fire to himself had to take place in the open air, too, which was a bit of a problem as he was supposed to be digging a grave in his basement. This required the construction of a three-walled set out in a field, and the borrowing of a fire-suit from *Mimic 3* which had to be filmed in long shot when ablaze. But it was all worth it, as this resulted in one of the best and most harrowing scenes in the entire movie.

When a rough cut was ready and brought back to the States, Clive Barker was invited to take a look and again made some notes for Bota. This included teasing out the story of what's really happening to the teens with quick inserts of them in the coffins during the hallucinatory scenes, and the appearance of two nuns at the start to foreshadow Sister Ursala's story. This would mean that The Host's exposition-heavy explanation at the end would be set up nicely, and Bota worked hard on the editing of this to give it more movement. More inserts were filmed the following spring, such as some sunny landscape shots, but by mid 2003 the movie was completed, although as we have already noted it was not released until 2005. What audiences were given then was a self-referential horror movie, an up-to-date, hip and young *Hellraiser*, made in the post *Scream* (Wes Craven, 1996) era. Henriksen had himself just starred in the third installment of that particular trilogy (Craven, 2000). But was there more beneath the surface gloss than met the eye at first glance?

30

WELCOME TO THE PARTY

A Better Place

The main story of *Hellworld* is based on two crucial, interlinked concepts, of equal importance. The first of these — exactly like *Deader*— is given away in the first scene. We hear the sounds of digging even before we see the initial shot of Adam, on his own, working away at the soil. He is literally digging his own grave, but it is the fact that he is alone that is significant — not just physically, but mentally. (We even discover later that his father abandoned him: "I don't even think he's got a dad," says Derrick, "I think he made it all up.") When the group go to his funeral, they discuss how they should have seen it coming but didn't, how they couldn't get through to him. It forms a massive part of the plot, spawning the guilt complex they — especially Chelsea and Jake — have about the suicide. "Suppose we're in Hell because we belong here," Chelsea says to Jake when she's trapped in the attic. "For what?" asks Jake. "For not saving Adam," she elucidates. "From who?" Jake says, still not understanding. "From himself. From Hellworld … We knew what Hellworld was doing to Adam but we kept on playing it." It is vital to note that when she makes this key speech, apart from the mobile phone — which we will come to in a moment — Chelsea is also quite alone. And like the birds she finds there (in direct contrast to the ones flying from the trees at the beginning) she is trapped.

So, indisputably, the first theme we must take into consideration is that of isolation, including enforced isolation. Each one of the characters is killed alone, first Allison who comes across a door with a Keep Out sign on the front of it, which she naturally opens. Inside she finds the Sacrifice Chair, which she sits in, then she bleeds to death as the spinning blades enter her chest. Derrick drops his inhaler on the dance floor and it is kicked down a grate, but he traces it down to the Specimen Room and retrieves it. Lying on a gurney, recovering from his asthma attack, he is then beheaded by Pinhead. Mike, meanwhile, is lured down there by the dark mystery woman whom he has hooked up with at the party — only for her to shut him in the room on his own. He then faces a painful death on the hook, killed by the Banded Cenobite. The tightly knit clump of teens are systematically separated and then murdered, all alone except for their killers. But then, when the ending reveals that they are actually suffering from chemical induced hallucinations, we realize that not even their killer was with them at the end — and in effect they killed themselves, dying in complete isolation buried inside wooden coffins in the grounds of the house (which itself is seemingly cut off completely from civilization).

Chelsea and Jake are split up as well, the former following the ghost of Adam to a room and then getting locked inside, the latter trailing Sister Ursala to her upstairs bedroom. This leads inevitably to them dealing with nightmare scenarios on their own, Chelsea — when she is finally released — encountering first The Host in the back of her car, then Pinhead in the middle of the wooded grounds. Jake has already experienced the most telling scene linked to isolation, when he tries to engage partygoers in conversation only for them all to ignore him: "Hey, how did you get into Hellworld? ... Is

David Robinson with The Host, Lance Henriksen (courtesy David Robinson).

this a joke, hey ... Hey!" Soisson's original idea here was to have Jake turn them around one by one but still be presented with their backs. The chilling effect we get instead sees Jake turn briefly before leaving and witness the entire population of the room hanging dead from hooks and chains.

To do this to the five teens is the greatest act of revenge one could imagine. We do not see that they have any family, indeed they in essence form a family unit themselves, apart from Jake who has made it his mission to distance himself from the rest of the group. "This isn't a reunion, I never was one of you guys and never will be." But his words ring false. Like Adam, they are the only family he has. But the one who is the most alone of all is The Host. Not even revealing his name, he makes his dramatic entrance on his own, and throughout the film appears to have no allies, except possibly the Cenobites. Yet we discover that this isn't so, that he was the father who left Adam behind, regrets it and has come to take revenge on them all — something that leaves a bitter taste in all of their mouths. "You son of a bitch," shouts Jake, "you were never there for your own son. Your son spent his life waiting for a father who never came home.... That kid took sixteen years of loneliness to his grave and now you wanna come back and get revenge on *us*?" The last scene with The Host has him sitting in a hotel room, drinking and smoking, totally alone once more and looking at old photos of his son, the placement of a recent picture over the top of Adam as a child signifying that he wishes he could get that time back again. He is just as guilt-ridden as Adam's friends, except he has just cause to be. In a way, when he then opens the puzzle box and the Cenobites carve him up, they are doing him a favor, putting him out of his misery.

We cannot end this section without talking about the most dramatic example of isolation in the whole movie: that of being buried. A famous fear of Poe's, the idea of being buried alive and waking up in a coffin is something that chills us all to the marrow. But for the protagonists of *Hellworld* this fear becomes fact, when they are placed in the earth at the back of the house by The Host, with pipes for air so they won't die too quickly. Even Adam, burned and dead, makes an attempt to climb out of his coffin in the church at the start (albeit in Chelsea's dream). Or is it possibly a way of communicating with her? This brings us to our second major theme in the film.

Can you hear me?

Communication, and more specifically the inability to communicate effectively, is another fundamental theme on which *Hellworld* is based. Adam is a prime example of this in his ghost-like form, when he appears to Chelsea throughout the course of the movie. The first time, we have just discussed, but then he leads her to a room which locks on its own — possibly to keep her safe from what is happening in the rest of the house — and reaches through the floorboards in the attic to grab hold of her later on. It could be argued that the reason these attempts at communication from beyond the grave fail or are perceived as malicious stem from the fact that they have manifested themselves in Chelsea's own imagination. She is, after all, buried inside a coffin and not really experiencing any of this in the real world. As The Host says: "Your own guilt-ridden subconscious even threw Adam in there." However, he does communicate towards the end in order to save Jake and Chelsea's lives, calling the police from her own cell phone back in the house. Like the old-fashioned radio and the television in *Hell on Earth*, more modern means are now employed so that the dead can make contact with the living, and the crane shot of Chelsea looking up at the window to see Adam there confirms that it has worked this time.

Jake, too, believes that he has been in contact with Adam through electronic means. When he enters The Host's study, the computer is switched on and he sees a picture on the screen of the two of them together. A line of writing then appears on that screen telling him, "It's just a game," reiterating what they have all been saying about Hellworld. This mode of communication, though, is not to be trusted, as it was the way in which they were all lured here in the first place. Mike, Allison and Derrick are all shown solving an online Lament Configuration which asks "Dare you enter Hell?" for the fifth Annual Hellworld Party at the Leviathan House. Jake's bait is much more subtle; he meets what he thinks is a girl in a Hellworld chat room and agrees to meet her at the party. Unwittingly, he has told The Host everything he needs to know about the mythos in order to set up the whole charade. "I take my hat off to you. I couldn't have done it without you, Jake," he says smirking.

Returning to mobile phones for a moment, apart from when Adam uses it at the end, these are no more reliable as a method of communication. Each guest is given one with a specific number on it, as well as a mask (another way of isolating one's true self). "If you wish to engage in the pleasures that only flesh can bring," The Host tells them, "you pick a tasty morsel and dial that number." But right away Derrick has trouble getting through to Mike when testing it: "Can you hear me now?" he asks twice. Allison uses hers as a joke to distract Derrick when he is chatting up two girls, but it is no joke when it is used later to relay her screams to Chelsea after she has been murdered. If anything, a sort of ESP tells Chelsea something is wrong and she goes up to the room where Allison is — there is no way she could have heard her screams over the music of the party — but she finds it locked. Mike's use of the mobile gets him into trouble as well, when he contacts Mystery Girl 9364 and says, "I'd love to see your puzzle box.... Wanna dance?" She shakes her head and he reads her thoughts in a way only horny teenagers can. "Wanna party?" he asks, which garners the correct response. But this path will lead to his demise in the Specimen Room.

Chelsea, too, finds her phone useless when she attempts to contact the police. She gets through but the operator can hardly hear her. When the police do arrive, she bangs on the window to try and attract their attention, failing miserably. Once more she rings them, but even talking with the officer in charge doesn't get her anywhere; he cannot see her in spite of the fact he's looking up and right at her. "Definitely on drugs," he concludes, and he is right, but Chelsea did not take these herself. "I'm rerouting you to dispatch," he tells her and effectively ends the call. Chelsea had similar luck with Mike, just prior to this. In the middle of receiving oral sex from Lady 9364, he isn't interested in her plight. "Oh, so now you want me...?" Handing the phone to the mystery woman, she switches it off. The mobiles are then used to keep the only survivors off balance. The Host calls Chelsea and pretends to be Jake in trouble to get her back to the house. Jake sees a reflection of Chatterer and stabs the figure, only to discover it is Chelsea instead, although a call to his mobile from the real Chelsea reveals that his mind is being played with.

In reality, one mobile has been left in each of the coffins—and is a way by which the group can be manipulated with subliminal messages from The Host, as well as to contact each other when they think they are in danger. Finally, a cell is used one last time by The Host after he has been killed in the hotel room. Just when Jake and Chelsea think they have come through the nightmare, and they are driving back home, with Jake keeping his promise that they would live to see another sunrise, her phone goes off. She answers it and The Host appears briefly in the back seat. Perhaps it is an after-effect of the drugs they have been on, or maybe it is The Host himself using the device from "the other side."

We cannot ignore two other means of communication. The first has been used in every single *Hellraiser* film to date, and will no doubt be used in any to come. It is the puzzle box itself. A communication conduit to Hell, it reaches out to the Cenobites and tells them when another victim is ready. The second is the very process of playing the film, by which all these ideas are communicated to audiences around the world, to fans of the *Hellraiser* series.

Get Your Mythology Right, Buddy

More so than even *Hellseeker*, *Hellworld* refers to other films in the series and even utilizes the mythology in a completely different way. Its deliberately self-referential tone is one of the things that marks this film apart from any other *Hellraiser* that has gone before it. Right from the start we are immersed in *Hellraiser* lore. When Mike shows up at Chelsea's apartment we're led to believe that The Chatterer is making an early appearance, perhaps in a hallucinatory sequence à la *Inferno* or *Hellseeker*. But he is only wearing a mask that he has picked up for $100 from the Internet (and like many that are actually freely available in the real world). Chelsea then reminds us that in their cinematic world, like ours, "Cenobites don't exist, and even if they did, I never opened the Lament Configuration." During the movie, Chelsea is our constant commentator on the mythos, and our constant reminder that none of this is real: "The props are cool," she tells The Host, "but this is just an old house, Lemarchand is a character from some scary story, the puzzle box a myth and Hellworld? Just a game."

It is Chelsea who misdirects us into thinking that the rules will be the same for this sequel as they were in previous ones. When The Host takes a victim, Pinhead is never far behind, leading both us as an audience and Chelsea to reach the same conclusion. "You're going to rip off your face and morph into some franchise icon, right? Gimme a break." This is our first signal that things might well be different this time, and actually The Host is *not* Pinhead. He is someone who also doesn't believe in *Hellraiser*, and is simply using it to get his revenge. Far from *being* Pinhead, he is one of the souls our Lead Cenobite collects at the finale. Just as Chelsea has started to believe the whole mythos might be real, The Host — in complete reversal — goes from being the biggest *Hellraiser* aficionado alive, to not believing a word of it. He even opens the box, thinking it to be nothing more than a replica like the one he gave to Jake to drug him (the Invitation Box, which pierces Jake's thumb). This proves his ultimate undoing.

To quote Gary Tunnicliffe again, this is "A fan film for fans of the films."[1] References abound, from the attic set which could so easily have housed Frank, to the statues of Jesus that Julia and Kirsty came across all those years ago in Lodovico Street. The Internet site the group access could be any of a dozen *Hellraiser* fan sites on the net that really do exist, and Pinhead's famous lines waft through the air as they manipulate the digital Lament Configuration. Many young *Hellraiser* fans will recognize themselves in the characters of Chelsea, Mike, Derrick (sporting his fetching Pinhead T-shirt) and Allison. But there is one difference between fans of this franchise and *Space Voyage*, as Chelsea calls it (a thinly veiled reference surely to another popular franchise), fearing that the party might be like some sort of convention where people dress up as aliens. As Allison puts it so succinctly: "Hellraisers *know* how to party!" And if the *Hellraiser* house — the ultimate fan party location, at 86 Hellbound Drive — is anything to go by, how can anybody disagree? "I've died and gone to Hell," says Derrick when he sees the huge spinning box and the throngs of people dancing to the music, before reminding us again that we are in actual fact watching a horror film: "Gratuitous tit shot," he states when he sees a bare-breasted woman coming down the stairs. The audience knows it, and the makers know that they do, too, therefore they can play with the conventions to entertain. Although The Host treads a fine line, providing critics with a line to savage the film with if they so desired. "It's like a bad horror movie, isn't it?" he says to Chelsea.

Yet in among all these references to previous films, *Hellworld* also attempts to weave in some mythology of its own, adding to the already multilayered *Hellraiser* history. As The Host takes them down into the basement, he clues them in as a resident expert on the Leviathan House. He claims it was Phillip Lemarchand's second greatest architectural achievement after the Lament Configuration, originally a convent commissioned by the church.[2] "And for decades it stood as such. Then came the convent's final Mother Superior, Sister Ursala, a nun whose vows were shattered by an obsession for a shiny puzzle box and the unholy pleasures seated inside of it. Sometime during the blizzard of 1808 some hundred and eighty women vanished from this house without a trace. Ursala was the only one they found, only she wasn't all there. You might say she went to pieces.... Years later the house was renovated and became a lock up for the criminally insane." Or, as Derrick sniggers: "From nuns to nuts." Apparently drawing quite heavily on the *Nightmare on Elm Street* mythology, where a nun was trapped in a mental asylum and raped by a hundred maniacs, this nonetheless remains in keeping with *Hellraiser*'s and Pinhead's ongoing discord with the church and with religion, further compounded by all the imagery at the start.

31

WORLD IN ACTION

Hellraiser: Hellworld was released on DVD 6 September 2005, just three months after *Deader*. Generally speaking, the critics took this movie for what it was—completely different to what had gone before in the series, but using familiar horror tropes to cater to fans of the genre as a whole. *Arrow in the Head's* online review said: "I entered *Hellraiser: Hellworld* ready to have an 'okay' time and to my big surprise ... I had a freaking blast!" The review continued: "Overall, this flick was a F*cking-A good time! It knew what it was and wasn't ashamed of it!"

John J. Puccio of *DVD Town* drew attention to the franchise aspects of the movie: "You've seen the movies. You've read the books. You've even collected the action figures. Now, play the game!" He went on to talk about the more explicit nature of the material: "The sex and nudity are purely gratuitous and have nothing to do with the plot. The violence is mainly what we came for, but the filmmakers know that viewers expect sex and nudity and violence to go together, and, as I've said, the filmmakers are intent on providing viewers with everything they expect."

The Cenobites are part of the mythology that *Hellworld* openly references (courtesy Gary J. Tunnicliffe).

One of the most detailed reviews came from a familiar name to any horror fan, that of writer Staci Layne Wilson, who wrote about the film for horror.com and got what the movie was really all about: "The setting, characters, and killings are all standard horror stuff on the surface, but director Rick Bota (channeling a meth-addled William Castle) and screenwriter Carl V. Dupré (doing his best Mario *Bay of Blood* Bava) brought their A game with inventive little twists and shocks all throughout the gory proceedings." She was also pleased to see Henriksen in the film, saying, "The screen is owned by Henriksen as The Host (and his character is leaps and bounds better than another host he played in a 2003 disappointment called *The Invitation*) Best Host line: 'If you need anything ... scream.'" And she was impressed by the rest of the cast, especially the feisty heroine, who follows in the best tradition of Kirsty and Joey: "Chelsea (Katheryn Winnick) is also a lot of fun to watch as she's put through the wringer, making many narrow escapes."

But *Deader* and *Hellworld* were not the only *Hellraiser* films to be made in recent years. There was one more, a short movie that examines what the last days of the Cenobites might be like and features Pinhead as you've never seen him before.

32

NO MORE SOULS

Filmed in the space of a weekend, on a small set at his Two Hours in the Dark, Inc., effects workshops in Canoga Park, California, Gary J. Tunnicliffe's short *Hellraiser* film is certainly quite impressive. Shot for a budget of $2,400, twelve hundred of which was spent hiring a high definition camera from World Wide Broadcast Services, Inc., *No More Souls: One Last Slice of Sensation* imagines an alternate future for Pinhead to the one shown in *Bloodline*. Here humanity has destroyed itself in a nuclear war and in one fell swoop both Heaven and Hell are filled to the brim with four billion human souls. During the first millennium the souls were processed in Hell, but of course once they had run out there were no more souls to harvest. Tunnicliffe studied the instruction manual on the camera and visited a cinematography chat room to ask questions before the shoot.

He also gathered together friends and colleagues to help with the film, which he had written himself and would produce, direct and stand in as DP and production designer. Executive producing the short were Claire-Jane Vranian and Michael Jay Regan (who would play Chatterer again for this production). Regan would also help with the set construction along with Steven Lawrence (who was playing Bound) and Blake Bolger (who doubled as the Prosthetics assistant). And when it came to putting everything together in postproduction, Tunnicliffe found assistance in the form of Kirk Morri as post production supervisor, Patrick Lussier (who edited all the *Scream* films for Dimension) and Lisa Romano as editors, with sound design from Jonathan Miller and music by *Deader*'s Henning Lohner. And there was certainly no shortage of special effects people on hand to deal with this side of the film.

Perhaps the most intriguing aspect of *No More Souls*' shoot was the fact that Tunnicliffe played an old version of Pinhead, making him only the second person to appear in the famous make-up in the series' history. In a final dedication on the film, Tunnicliffe writes: "For Doug ... For creating the wonderful character that budget decreed I mimic ... Please forgive me." With cataracts in his eyes and a general world-weariness, this more thick-set version of Pinhead is possibly what the character would look like after centuries had passed by; no longer enjoying the sport, he simply sits on what looks like a plain wooden chair or throne, the monarch of a long dead kingdom.

The movie itself begins with a pan across scorched earth with skulls half buried in the sand. These simple images accompany the almost Shakespearian monologue that Pinhead gives us: "In the end it was just two sins that proved deadly for the world, greed and lust. And when the leading superpowers saw the end was nigh they chose to cut off the nose of humanity to spite the face of mankind." We then descend into that earth, traveling below to Hell, which would suggest a more traditional one than we have seen before. Except we pan down to see Pinhead sitting, bored and tired amidst the hanging chains and stone walls. He continues to relate the story: "The years have passed silently, taking with them my will, and my hunger. For what is there to wait for? Another 65 million years until I can know the eternal delight of an experience where hurt and ecstasy become one. Too much time to wait for such a fleeting sensation."

Believing his once loyal troops will turn on him eventually anyway, Pinhead opens the Lament Configuration and gives them one last soul to gorge upon: his own. The final scenes show Chatterer and Bound appearing in a flash of blue light and attacking Pinhead, his mouth now smeared with blood. We then cut to Chatterer nailing something onto the now-familiar Torture Pillar, and when he steps away we see it is the stretched skin of Pinhead's face, not alive as it was at the end of *Hellbound*, but flat and lifeless.

Lasting only about five minutes in total, the film has a deep impact beyond its running time and deserves its place in the *Hellraiser* canon, simply for the audacity of the ending. For here, Pinhead not only dies, but the whole of Hell has been utterly defeated by what it coveted in the first place. Leviathan has been hoist by its own petard. But, as we will see in the final chapter Tunnicliffe wasn't the only one planning Pinhead's final exit. *No More Souls* appeared as part of the *Deader* package on DVD in 2005, tucked away as a hidden "Easter Egg" which could be accessed by selecting Special Features on the main menu, scrolling down to More at the bottom and selecting that, then moving down the second page, so that Play is highlighted, and pressing the down button once more on the DVD remote. Nothing appears to be highlighted now, but by pressing the Right button the Lament Configuration lights up and the film plays. A puzzle worthy of *Hellraiser* in its own right.

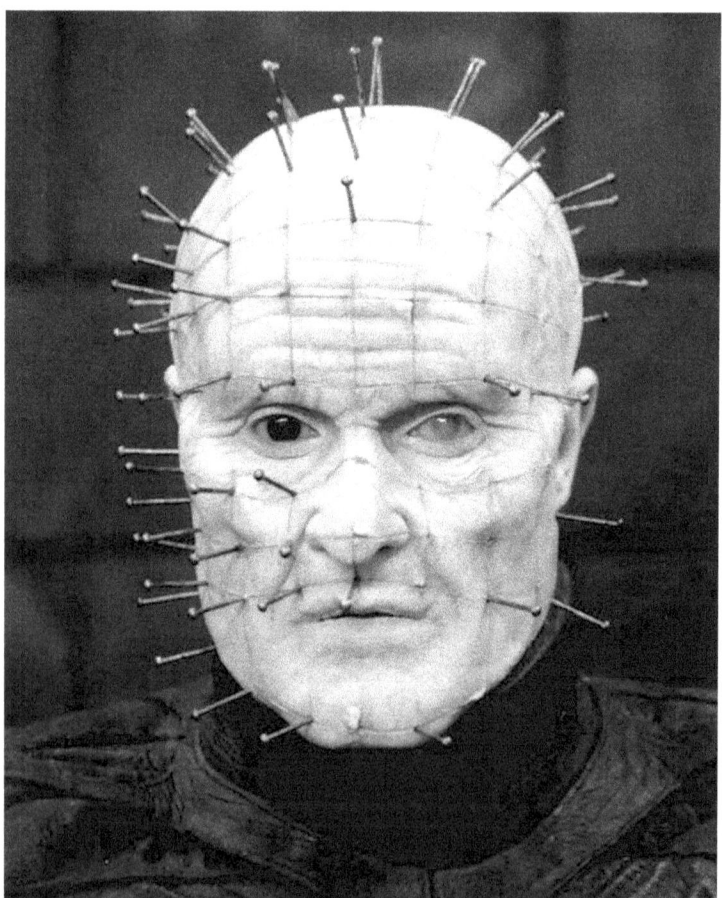

Gary as an old and weary Pinhead in *No More Souls* (courtesy Gary J. Tunnicliffe).

33

COMICS FROM HELL

In addition to the cinematic outings of the Cenobites and their puzzle box, an official graphic interpretation of the mythos appeared from 1989 to 1993 and spawned its own spin-offs and sequels, often more cerebral and ambitious than its filmic counterparts. Published by Marvel's Epic Imprint and launched as a quarterly, Book 1 of the comic series—actually more a 64-page book with a spine than a comic—boasted an eye-catching John Bolton rendering of Pinhead on the cover, and introductions by editor Daniel Chichester and Clive Barker. In his foreword, Chichester discloses that the possibility of a horror comic from Epic had long been a possibility, but they were waiting for the right subject matter: "We were ... convinced that to use the medium to its fullest potential *today* would require us to overcome the pitfalls of so many horror comics of the recent past, the ones where the stories always ended with a clichéd 'twist' of 'And she woke up the next morning to find that her husband—in the bed next to her—HAD REALLY BEEN DEAD FOR THE PAST SIX YEARS!'"[1]

He found this in *Hellraiser*, but knew that a straightforward adaptation wouldn't do the title any justice. Hence, right from the start, the aim of the comic series was to set stories in the same universe, exploring possibilities only hinted at in the movies. Barker used his space to expound upon the curious nature of a creation becoming public property: "The little bastard movie I made's got a life of its own. Who'd have thought it? Who'd have *ever* thought?"[2] He was to remain a consultant on the series, though, and he had final approval over everything.

As for the stories themselves, writer Erik Saltzgaber and Bolton came up with a brilliant medieval tale called "The Canons of Pain," in which a Lament Configuration is discovered in the Holy Land and brought back to England, thus extending *Hellraiser*'s back-history even further. "Dead Man's Hand," written by Sholly Fisch and illustrated by Dan Spiegle, was set in another historical period, the Wild West, and centered on a Guardian gambling in a saloon with the puzzle box. By winning, the cowboy he's playing against doesn't get to see what's inside. In "The Warm Red" Jan Strnad created in Maureen a character to rival Julia, wonderfully rendered by Bernie Wrightson. Out to cheat a lonely man out of his land and make herself a fortune in the process, Maureen uses her feminine charms, little realizing that the man has struck up another deal with a Cenobite. There's a final gripping twist, however, which sees Maureen once again taking control of the situation and teaming up with the demon. Finally, "Dance of the Fetus" by Ted McKeever, was the most poignant entry in this first volume. Presented with virtually no dialogue, it told of what happened to a woman's unborn child after she agrees to go to Hell. ("This just won't do," says the Cenobite to the fetus. "There are regulations. I mean, what would it be like if we could just take anyone?")

Cover of Check Books *Best of Hellraiser* collection, volume 1 (courtesy Checker Books).

This initial collection set the tone for the volumes to come, and also introduced us to some new Cenobites, such as Face — who we later discovered was an actor before Hell took him, and who now wears the skin masks of his victims ("To Prepare a Face" *Hellraiser Book 4*, 1990). Other fan favorites would join him over the comings months, like the stick thin Hunger (introduced in a superb story called "Diver's Hands" in Book 2 about the relationship between a patient suffering from leprosy and his caregiver) and former Vietnam vet Atkins (from "Tunnel of Love" in Book 6), weapons master in Leviathan's ranks. And while fresh Cenobites were utilized, Pinhead and his original cohorts were far from absent in these pages. The range of ideas was also impressive in those fledgling volumes, covering everything from virtual reality torture in "The Threshold" (Book 2), to the impact of the Cenobites on 1920s Paris avant-garde in "The Blood of a Poet" (Book 3), and a link to Jack the Ripper in "Under the Knife" (Book 7). The Lament Configuration itself was ripe for reinvention, too, as we saw the various guises it could take. In "Glitter and Go" (Book 5), for example, people cast themselves from the rooftops of an office building like lemmings in the hopes they would fall through the dimensional portal, while in "Demons to Some, Angels to Others" (Book 7), it takes the form of a rod puzzle wielded by a minister. ("If thou desirest glory enough, then it shall be given unto you to solve.")

In its first couple of years, the title attracted some of the best writers and artists working in the industry, as well as old friends of the *Hellraiser* series. Peter Atkins penned Book 3's standout "Songs of Metal and Flesh," about a blind musician who eventually plays the Devil's music to get into Hell, lavishly illustrated by Dave Dorman and Lurene Haines. Erstwhile Chatterer Nicholas Vince joined in for Volume 4 and wrote "Cenobite!" about one person's journey to become a demon, featuring artwork by John Van Fleet. By this time, Marc McLaurin had taken over as editor and was instrumental in steering the series towards a bimonthly production schedule and introducing a longer multilayered story arc called "The Devil's Brigade." Speaking in an interview with *Fangoria* he said, "The anthology is firmly entrenched, and each issue will still have at least one self-contained story. But I've found that many of our readers appreciate a sense of continuity, so we're aiming for stronger, more detailed storylines and stretching them from issue to issue."[3]

This storyline, written in part by Chichester, saw a selection of Cenobites, including Pinhead, Atkins, Face, Abigor (a dominatrix-esque warrior Cenobite), and Balberith (Hell's Librarian), each set a task to influence events on Earth. Their targets were a pair of police detectives, a woman on the verge of curing AIDS, a priest, a politician in an apartheid divided country, and a spokesperson for the homeless, all of whom stood at the crossroads between chaos and order at the pivotal "Time of Configuration" (an infernal equinox foretold by the Flagellum, who reads her own entrails to discover the truth before calling the Cenobites to arms). This lengthy and multifaceted tale ran over nineteen parts—including a prelude and epilogue—up until Book 16 of the series, and was definitely one of the highlights of the comic incarnation.

By the conclusion of this arc, *Hellraiser* had already started to produce its own spin-off publications. Summer, spring and Christmas specials were only to be expected, the latter displaying a Kevin (*Nemesis the Warlock*) O'Neill picture of Pinhead as Santa Claus on the cover. The last of these specials, though, in 1994 was actually written by Larry Wachowski, now famous for the *Matrix* trilogy which he co-wrote and directed with his brother. Indeed, Wachowski had contributed a story previously to Book 9 of the regular anthology called "Closets" which has some delicious hints of things to come. (A character asks in true Oracle fashion, "Would you like a candy?" and a child is found inside a cupboard with its mouth stitched up, just as Neo's mouth is sealed over in the first *Matrix* film.) But nothing could have been as eagerly anticipated as Chichester's two-part *Jihad* from 1991. Epic had already been running its own *Nightbreed* comic parallel to the *Hellraiser* one, which had itself been fleshing out that other Barker universe with new characters and situations. In *Jihad* these two universes spectacularly collided, positing a tantalizing theory that the Nightbreed were the chaotic yang to the Cenobites' ordered yin.

Talking about this project to *Dread* magazine, Chichester explained: "We're going on the theory that the Nightbreed and the Cenobites have a history, although the Nightbreed don't necessarily know about this history. At this point in time, with the Nightbreed being released back into the world after being driven out of Midian, they are a massive chaotic force.... Hell has got to deal with this in order to get on with their war against mankind."[4]

In the story, the Breed's Peloquin becomes a central character and even has to take over when Boone is killed. Pinhead finds himself stranded behind enemy lines after members of his own army turn on him, forcing him to form an uneasy alliance with the Nightbreed. The body of Boone must then join with the god Baphomet in order to defeat the rogue Cenobites. The story ends with a promise of another round of the war to come as Pinhead states: "Unity against a common threat was a necessary evil — not a pardon, but a stay." Excellent visuals by Paul Johnson, in particular the two-panel battle scenes, helped to give this release an almost cinematic feel.

More text-based was *Clive Barker's Book of the Damned*, a biannual companion to the comics. The first — also 1991 — contained scraps of information about one man's encounter with a "Prophet of Doom" on Michigan Avenue, who reveals to him that the events in the *Hellraiser* films are real. The contents of a canvas bag the prophet gives him include written extracts about the Guardians of the Box, the genesis of the Revelation Puzzle, extracts from *Of Hell* (written by Wachowski, which formed the basis of his Spring Special story), notes on the tarot High Priestess card based on the Female Cenobite from *Hellraiser* and *Hellbound*, the origins of Abigor, and a love story involving Pinhead: the only time he broke Leviathan's rules. The whole book had a distinctly post modern feel to it, its self-referential flavor embodied by a mock cover of *Domination Magazine*. A showcase for the writers and for artists to do full page work, the *Book of the Damned* ran to four volumes, the third of which pre-empted *Bloodline* by giving readers the journal of Lemarchand, the maker of the puzzle box. Far from being a simple toymaker, he was presented here as being of noble birth, someone who delves into the areas of the occult and bases his plans on a box built by Albertus Magnus.

Book 17 of the *Hellraiser* anthologies (1992) marked the start of yet another serial, this one created by Barker himself. In an introduction he told readers: "Pinhead and his cohorts have wandered through these tales with the arrogant air of creatures who are wise to every trick humanity has up its sleeve ... never, that I can remember, has a soul they have taken to Leviathan's corridors returned to the land of the living. After all, who would dare those infernal depths, policed as they are by the Cenobitical clan? The Harrowers, that's who."[5] The Harrowers (the name of which itself comes from Dante) in question were nicely set up by a backstory in the previous issue about a goddess called Morté Mámme.

She fought the Cenobites thousands of years ago using specially trained humans, but all were captured and buried alive. "Resurrection," written by Anna Miller, Malcolm Smith and Fred Vicarel — based on the Barker story — introduced the replacements: New York tattooist and biker Ron Ringwood; escaped convict Vera Wyshak; Winston Gage and his cat Zinc; twins Lavinia and Lucinda; Native American Marty Sevenbirds; and former professor Dublin Morse. Each were drawn to the location of the former Harrowers' defeat, then given special weapons by the goddess to combat the Cenobites (Dublin could turn invisible, for instance, while Vera's spittle was like acid to them) and free trapped human souls. This intriguing premise had real potential, and Alex Ross's illustrations were breathtaking. Unfortunately, when the team moved to their own, slimmer, publication in December 1993, the plotlines deteriorated into nonsense about setting Cleopatra free and the spirit of Marc Antony taking over a stone statue and rampaging through the streets of New York. More interesting was the downfall of Dublin, who sacrificed his place with the Harrowers to make his own Faustian pact and free his twin brother from Hell.

The Harrowers were not the only characters to get their own title, though. In a shrewd move, Epic gave Leviathan's favorite son a six part comic series which ran from Dec 1993 to May 1994. It wasn't the first time Pinhead's name had been on the front cover, but on the last occasion a month previously he'd had to share it with Pat Mills and Kevin O'Neill's superhero-hunting creation, Marshall Law, a tongue in cheek crossover which had Law and Pinhead slugging it out in the corridors of Hell. Now, in Chichester's spotlight story, Pinhead was sent back through time to inhabit various incarnations of himself and heal a rift that threatened to destroy them all. But as an act of revenge for keeping him in Hell, Ludovico Maria Sinistrari sabotaged his time machine. The result was that Pinhead not only had to contend with The Aggregate, a creature made up from the present-day remains of Leviathan's victims, but also the consciousness of whichever incarnation he had jumped into. While it was fun to see Pinhead as the likes of a Sioux warrior in 1879, a Monsignor from the Vatican in 1728 Paris, and a Mayan in 627 A.D., the artwork on occasion let the *Quantum Leap*-style plot down.

Its parent series went out on a high with Book 20, after McLaurin had left to oversee the spin-off Barker titles (which also included *Ectokid* and *SaintSinner*). This also coincided with a drop in page count to 48 pages. David Wohl took over as editor for this final issue, but this at least gave collectors a story from *Sandman* creator Neil Gaiman, working with his old friend Dave McKean. (The pair have recently gone on to make a film together, *MirrorMask*, 2005.) "Wordsworth" used the clever notion of a crossword puzzle as a Lament Configuration, and the experimental layout of the pages meant that this was one of the most remarkable stories they had ever published. Though *Hellraiser* should have continued much longer, its narrative influence can still be seen in the movies from the early 1990s onwards, and they are now, thankfully, being re-released in superb bumper collected "best of" books from Checker, the first of which included the classic stories such as "Like Flies to Wanton Boys," "Dead Things Rot" and the first two tales of "The Harrowing."

# 34

Further Explorations

So now that we are coming to the end of our examination of the *Hellraiser* mythology in all its forms, what does the future hold for the series? A few tantalizing glimpses of new projects have been afforded us, but whether they will actually become a reality someday is yet to be seen.

Helloween

Prior to the success of *Freddy vs. Jason* (Ronny Yu, 2003) the prospect of Pinhead and Michael Myers from *Halloween* sharing the screen seemed remote. Dave Parker (*Masters of Horror*) had apparently already suggested these ideas in the mid–'90s and had been turned down on both scores: "I had pitched, unsuccessfully, *Freddy vs. Jason* to a guy named Ross Hammer at Sean Cunningham's company around '94 or early '95. After that didn't go well, I started to think about what other franchises were at other studios. It was a no-brainer to see that Dimension had both the *Halloween* and *Hellraiser* franchises, so I put together a trailer using footage from the *Halloween* movies, including *Halloween* 6 which was just getting ready to come out, and the *Hellraiser* movies one through four."[1] He added in a later interview, "The (original) story takes place when people try to destroy the Myers house and they find the box hidden between the walls. Of course, they open it and Pinhead shows up, and it's Halloween and it's the Myers house, so Michael shows up because there are people there and Pinhead recognizes that Michael is Sam Hain because he can feel it, which begins this whole battle in the real world. And of course, the third act takes them all to Hell."[2]

Naturally, when everybody saw that two icons of horror cinema *could* be pitted against each other and make quite a lot of money in the process, *Helloween* suddenly became a distinct possibility. Doug Bradley told the *Brownsville Herald* in late 2003: "At this point, in fact, Dimension Films are planning a Hellraiser/Halloween crossover.... They are hoping to have it out by Halloween next year. That would be pretty fast, but that's their plan." This came not long after an "official" poll was taken on the Halloween Movies site to gauge fan reaction to the idea. Rumors started flying not long afterwards, but it appeared that Clive Barker would be writing the film and the original *Halloween* director, John Carpenter, would be at the helm.

Sadly, as we know, the movie didn't make it to theaters in 2004. Bradley, speaking to Mike Hodge in the summer of that year, said, "It looked like a fascinating, mouth-watering prospect. And then it stopped dead in its tracks.... As far as I know, that's where it stays.

Fans at Horrorfind were showing me a recent *USA Today* which said Dimension were currently developing the movie — but that, or suggestions that it may be an animated film, is news to me."³ It certainly would have been an interesting film, one which would have delved into the mythos of both franchises. There's always the possibility with *any* idea that it might still be made and so all we, as students of *Hellraiser* lore, can do is watch and wait. At time of writing, though, plans for a ninth film in the *Halloween* series are going ahead, possibly with the title of *The Bloodline of Michael Myers*.⁴

Tortured Souls

Another movie that has stalled but could still come out in the future is *Tortured Souls*, based on a toy range that Barker developed for the ever-popular McFarlane line. While not specifically *Hellraiser* related the figures did bear an uncanny resemblance to their Cenobite cousins, but would came with their own fully fledged mythology. Launched in 2001 at the New York Toy Fair, these were then sent out to studios by Barker with a pitch for a film he would write and direct, his first feature since *Lord of Illusions*. In November *The Hollywood Reporter* and *Variety* both conveyed that Universal had bought the rights with the intentions of creating a franchise based on the toys.

Clive Barker then worked on the script for the next couple of years, which would once again see a female lead venturing into a demon-dwelling land, this time called Primordium, a place of horror, darkness and monsters. He told Fangoria.com in January 2004, "I'm turning in the script in four weeks, and if Universal likes it, they're prepared to go into production right away. I've taken the Tortured Souls toys and really expanded their universe, so it'll be different than what fans are expecting."⁵ There it stayed for the rest of 2004, until Universal let the lease lapse and it passed over to a sub-company of theirs called Rogue. As Barker was so busy producing movies for other directors, doing the paintings for his *Abarat* books, putting together material for his new art book, *Visions of Heaven and Hell* (2005), and writing *The Scarlet Gospels* (which we will come to in a moment) he didn't really have time to commit to directing the feature now anyway. Again, this is one project that might well come about, but it could be some time before it does.

Hellevision

In December 2004, *Variety* reported that *Hellraiser* was bound for television screens as an hour-long weekly series. The people behind the proposed project were Panacea Entertainment, Park Avenue Entertainment and Blueprint Entertainment. While Dimension still owned the rights to the filmic versions of Hellraiser, the executive producer on the show, Eric Gardner, had represented the property since Larry Kuppin reacquired the New World film library from Ronald Perelman in 1991. Kuppin was also slated to be involved as an executive producer on the series, which would apparently revolve around a tabloid journalist stumbling upon a plot hatched between Pinhead and a rich software magnate.

Doug Bradley was to be approached and a pilot was about to be written, seemingly putting paid to rumors that UK TV station Channel Four would be doing a *Hellraiser* anthology series. "The mythology of the character and the series has been worked out slowly over the years," Kuppin said. "Pinhead is one of the most branded characters in the horror genre.

There are all kinds of psychological angles to be explored, along with a good scare."[6] If any franchise was ripe for transference to the small screen it must surely be the *Hellraiser* saga, as the comic book incarnation had shown. Its flexibility would allow tales to be told without any possibility of running out of locations, characters or ideas. At the time of writing Doug Bradley had not heard any further news about this venture,[7] but the promise of a *Hellraiser* television series — if done properly — is definitely something to look forward to.

Scarlet Gospels

Finally, we ourselves come full circle, as does the series' creator himself, Clive Barker. While Barker does not retain the cinematic rights to *Hellraiser* or the characters, he does still own the literary rights following the publication of *The Hellbound Heart*. He has long been promising his readers a return to his horror roots with another collection of fiction to match the *Books of Blood*. And as part of this collection, he has been working on a novella which features two of his most famous creations, Pinhead and Harry D'Amour. Little is known about the plot yet, although by the time this book is published *The Scarlet Gospels* should be out and wowing readers everywhere. But one thing we do know is the outcome of the battle between Barker's detective and the Crown Prince of Hell. "I want to finish the story and finish it on my terms, rather than the movies' terms," he told *SFX* on his return to British shores to publicize the second *Abarat* book. "People don't have much of a clue as to the mythology of the Lament Configuration. How the box works. Who the hell the guy with pins in his face is! But more important than just filling in mythological detail, for me, is to bring an end to Pinhead's life that is not arbitrary and feels consistent with what I tried to do in the earlier movies."[8]

Box of Pleasures by Steelgohst (courtesy Steelgohst).

The Future

At this moment in time, *Hellraiser*'s popularity is again high. The company NECA acquired the coveted rights to produce a dedicated line of reproduction toys, figures and other items, which they started to do in 2003 (for full details of their range visit http://www.hellraiserthemovie.com) under the guidance of the director of product development, Randy Falk. This would include seven-inch figures of all the characters, from Pinhead to Skinless Julia, plus terrific eighteen-inch motion activated Pinheads and Chatterers, replica puzzle boxes and even Pinhead busts.

Places like the Prop Store of London (http://www.propstore.com) run by Stephen Lane are still selling original memorabilia from the films, with a one of a kind Giant Hero Puzzle box from *Hellbound* fetching up to $9,429. Though obviously they sell much more affordable items, this just goes to show the collectability of material from the movies. And this can also be seen in the items The Haunted Studios have on offer (http://www.hauntedstudios.com), from rare photos, to props, to lifemasks based on stars from the films. While the Pyramid Gallery (http://www.pyramid-gallery.com) have an entire range of exquisitely rendered puzzle boxes for sale "based on the lost designs of Lemarchand," Cleverwood (www.cleverwood.com) and the Puzzle Box Shop (www.HellraiserPuzzleBox.com) offer replica boxes, some of which open up, a particular request of *Hellraiser* supporters.

Fan sites like the Hellbound Web (http://www.cenobite.com) offer not only a wealth of material on the subject, but also a place for like-minded damned souls to congregate on message boards; it even offers a showcase for artwork like some of the digital work of Eric Gross. In addition, Anchor Bay released their Puzzle Box set of the first three movies on DVD with lots of extras just in time for Christmas 2004, prompting a rather unusual ad campaign which featured Pinhead as Santa's Little Helper. With the twentieth anniversary of the original film fast approaching the popularity of *Hellraiser* can only increase.

As for the future of the cinematic interpretations, *DVD Exclusive* reported that, after splitting with Disney and Miramax, Bob and Harvey Weinstein and Dimension have retained the rights to this line of films. "*Hellraiser* boasts a particularly flexible story structure that makes for endless sequel possibilities," said Dimension vice president Nick Phillips.[9] Whether any of these will be a movie of Barker's novella still remains to be seen, but when asked in that same *SFX* interview about the

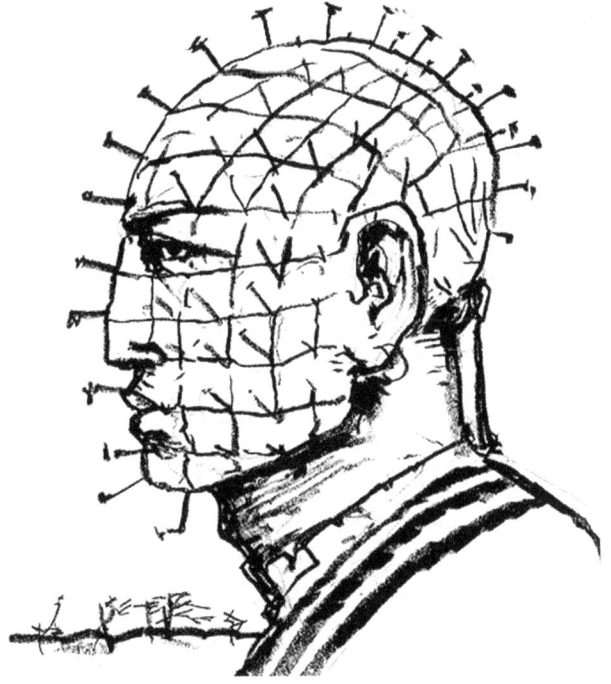

A recent sketch of Pinhead by Clive Barker (courtesy Clive Barker).

possibility that someone, somewhere might turn his "Pinhead vs. D'Amour" story into a motion picture, Barker laughed: "Yeah, that *had* occurred to me."[10]

But we'll finish this book with his thoughts about the original. "I can imagine that at some point, somebody will decide to remake the first *Hellraiser* picture, as they have with *The Texas Chainsaw Massacre*. There would arguably be some cool things about that, but I won't have anything to do with it.... The mythology has been kind to me and I've thoroughly enjoyed it, which is another reason why I want to bring it to a respectful end."[11]

And it is here that we must end our own journey. I hope you've enjoyed this trip through Hell, as much as I've enjoyed being your guide. The pleasure, I can assure you, was all mine. But no tears please. It's a waste of good suffering.

Chapter Notes

Preface

1. Stephen King's *Maximum Overdrive* was unpopular with both critics and audiences. *Variety* claimed: "King, making his directorial debut from his own script, fails to create a convincing enough environment to make the kind of nonsense he's offering here believable or fun." Speaking to Gary Wood in *Cinefantastique,* February 1991, the author admitted himself: "I didn't do a very good job of directing it.... What some guys take six years to learn, I learned in about ten weeks. The result was a picture that was just terrible."

2. *Hellraiser* made it to number sixteen in *Total Film*'s "25 Scariest Movies Ever" list, beating *The Texas Chainsaw Massacre, Friday the 13th* and *Night of the Living Dead* (December 1999, no. 35, p. 56). It reached number 28 in *Shivers* magazine's Top 50 Horror Film Awards (September 1996, no. 33, p. 13) and was listed as one of the Greatest Horror Movies Ever in *Empire*'s Special Collector's Edition Definitive Guide.

3. Kim Newman, ed., *The BFI Companion to Horror* (London: Cassell, 1996), 31.

4. Steve Chibnall and Julian Petley, *British Horror Cinema* (London: Rutledge, 2002), 4.

5. The term "auteur" dates back to the 1920s, when French film theorists used it to describe a director who wrote his own scripts, as opposed to those who made scenario-led movies where the scripts were commissioned. In the 1950s, critics from the film magazine *Cahiers du Cinéma*— including André Bazin — related the auteur theory to a director's style, misé en scene or filmic signature, so it could encompass both filmmakers who wrote their own scripts and those who worked within a more Hollywood studio-based structure. Clive Barker could be considered an auteur not only because he wrote the script for *Hellraiser* but because the film bears his artistic stamp.

6. Bob Keen speaking in the documentary featurette *Hellraiser: Resurrection* (Seraphim Films, 2000) U.S. DVD.

Chapter 1

1. Douglas E. Winter, *The Dark Fantastic* (London: HarperCollins, 2001), 10.

2. Nigel Floyd, "Slime Time," *Time Out* (September 2–9, 1987). Published as "Hellraiser" in *Clive Barker's Shadows in Eden,* edited by Stephen Jones (Lancaster, Pennsylvania: Underwood-Miller, 1991), 313.

3. *South Bank Show: Clive Barker* (London Weekend Television, 1994).

4. Clive Barker, *Incarnations: Three Plays* (London: HarperCollins, 1996), 281.

5. *Clive Barker's Books of Blood,* Vol. 1 (London: Sphere, 1984), 26.

6. Michael A. Morrison, "Monsters, Miracles and Revelations: Clive Barker's Tales of Transformation," in *Clive Barker's Shadows in Eden*, edited by Stephen Jones, 175.

7. *Clive Barker's Books of Blood,* Vol. 4 (London: Sphere, 1985), 48.

8. *The Dark Fantastic*, 147.

9. Douglas E. Winter, "Give Me B-Movies or Give Me Death!" Published in *Faces of Fear* (1985) and reprinted in *Clive Barker's Shadows in Eden*, edited by Stephen Jones, 28.

10. Stanley Waiter, "Catching Up with Clive Barker," in Anthony Timpone, ed., *Fangoria: Masters of the Dark* (New York: Harper Prism, 1997), 124. Waiter's interview with Barker was originally featured in *Fangoria* magazine (May 1986).

11. Philip Nutman, "Gangsters vs. Mutants," published in *Fangoria* (1991) and reprinted in *Clive Barker's Shadows in Eden*, edited by Stephen Jones, 271.

12. Alan Jones, "Rawhead Rex," *Cinefantastique* 7, no. 5 (December 1987).

13. Ibid.

14. In his review for *Starburst* magazine (no. 103, March 1987) Alan Jones described Rex as "looking suspiciously like a freaked-out member of Sigue Sigue Sputnik."

15. Stanley Waiter, "Catching up with Clive Barker," in Anthony Timpone, ed., *Fangoria: Masters*

of the Dark, 126. Waiter's interview with Barker was originally featured in *Fangoria* magazine (May 1986).

16. Bradley would finally get to play the derelict later in the series, for *Hellraiser: Hellseeker* (Rick Bota, 2002).

17. *Hellraiser* Boxed Set, released by Anchor Bay, 2004. Supplementary Disc: *The Forbidden Interviews.*

18. George R.R. Martin, ed., *Night Visions* (London: Arrow, 1987), 202.

19. Ibid., 205.

20. Ibid., 280.

21. Ibid., 205.

22. Barker quoted from the "In the Picture" section of *Sight and Sound* 56, no. 4 (Autumn 1987), 234.

23. George R. R. Martin, ed., *Night Visions,* 291.

24. Ibid., 236.

25. Ibid., 209.

26. Ibid., 234.

27. Phil Nutman, "Hammering Our *Hellraiser,*" in Anthony Timpone, ed., *Fangoria: Masters of the Dark,* 136. Nutman's article was riginally featured in *Fangoria* magazine (March 1987).

28. The documentary featurette *Hellraiser: Resurrection,* U.S. DVD.

29. Audio Commentary for U.S. *Hellraiser* Laserdisc.

30. U.S. *Hellraiser* Laserdisc.

31. Simon Bamford, interview by Nick Vince in *Pandemonium: Further Explorations into the Worlds of Clive Barker,* edited by Michael Brown (New York: Eclipse Books, 1991), 88.

32. Nick Vince, interview by Diane Keating, 1991.

33. Doug Bradley, *Behind the Mask of the Horror Actor* (London: Titan Books, 1996/2004), 209.

34. The documentary featurette *Hellraiser: Resurrection.* U.S. DVD.

35. There were concerns at one point that the title *Hellraiser* wouldn't prove palatable to some in the American South. One of the other suggested titles came from a production coordinator called Claire St. John, who thought *What a Woman Would Do for a Good Fuck* best summed up the story.

36. *The Hellraiser Chronicles,* ed. Stephen Jones (London: Titan, 1992), 7.

37. Douglas E. Winter, "The Heights and Depths of *Hellraiser,*" in Anthony Timpone, ed., *Fangoria: Masters of the Dark,* 146.

38. *Films and Filming,* no. 389 (February 1987), 23.

39. *Hellraiser* Boxed Set: Anchor Bay, 2004. Supplementary Disc: *The Forbidden Interviews.*

40. U.S. *Hellraiser* Laserdisc, commentary by Clive Barker.

41. In the Picture, *Sight and Sound* 56, no. 4 (Autumn 1987), 234.

42. U.S. *Hellraiser* Laserdisc, commentary by Clive Barker.

Chapter 2

1. Clive Barker, "The Tragical History of Dr. Faustus," in *Horror: 100 Best Books,* eds. Stephen Jones and Kim Newman (New York: Carroll & Graff, 1988/2000).

2. *Hellraiser* screenplay, 21.

3. Brigid Cherry, Brian Robb and Andrew Wilson, "*Weaveworld,*" in *Nexus,* no. 4 (November-December, 1987).

4. *Hellraiser,* screenplay, 3–4.

5. George R.R. Martin, ed., *Night Visions* (London: Arrow, 1987), 202.

6. Audio Commentary for U.S. *Hellraiser* DVD.

7. Most recently in "Under the Skin," *Hellraiser* DVD Extra. Henrik Ibsen (1828–1906), born in Skien, Norway, was noted for social problem plays like *A Doll's House* (1879).

8. Gary Hoppenstand, "The Secret Self," in *Pandemonium,* ed. Michael Brown (New York: Eclipse Books, 1991), 94–5.

9. Edgar Allan Poe, *The Selected Works of Edgar Allan Poe* (Ann Arbor, Michigan: Mundus, 2002), 486.

10. *Hellraiser* Boxed Set, Supplementary Disc: *Salomé* Interviews.

11. Iconography is the collective term for visual motifs and style in a film. This includes dress codes and conventions (such as pin-stripe suits for gangster movies). Because it is a visual medium, color also plays a role in signification, and historical examples include the traditional black slinky dress for the femme fatale of film noir, and the lighter colors of the lawman hero in westerns.

12. Carol Clover, *Men, Women and Chainsaws* (London: BFI, 1992), 39. See also Vera Dika's informative essay, "The Stalker Film," from *American Horrors,* edited by Gregory A. Waller (Champaign: University of Illinois Press, 1988).

13. *Hellraiser,* script, 54C (amended 3 November 1986).

14. Martin, ed., *Night Visions,* 213.

15. "Under the Skin: Doug Bradley on *Hellraiser.*" *Hellraiser* Boxed Set.

Chapter 3

1. Clive Barker Speaking at UCLA, February 25, 1987.

2. The Marquis de Sade (Donatien Alphonse François de Sade, 1740–1814) was possibly the most infamous writer in French history. His published work gave rise to the term sadism — the enjoyment of cruelty, often with a sexual bent. Arrested after many scandals and condemned to twenty-seven years in various prisons, he wrote sexually explicit material, including *Les Journées de Sodome* (*The 120 Days of Sodom* 1782–85), *Justine* (1791), and a ten-volume novel *Les Crimes de L'Amour* (*Crimes of Passion,* 1800).

3. George R.R. Martin, ed., *Night Visions* (London: Arrow, 1987), 205.
4. The documentary featurette *Hellraiser: Resurrection*. U.S. DVD.
5. *Fear in the Dark*, TV Documentary (1991).
6. "Doug Bradley: Pinned Down," in *Hellbreed*, no. 2 (June 1995), 21.
7. The documentary featurette *Hellraiser: Resurrection*. U.S. DVD.
8. *The Hellraiser Chronicles*, 80.
9. *Hellraiser: Resurrection*. U.S. DVD.
10. Doug Bradley, *Behind the Mask of the Horror Actor* (London: Titan Books, 1996/2004), 211.

Chapter 4

1. "*Hellraiser*: Barker's Box of Delights," interview by Nigel Floyd in *Samhain* no. 4 (July/August 1987), 6.
2. *Hellraiser: Resurrection*. U.S. DVD.
3. Clive Barker, ed., *The Essential Clive Barker* (London: HarperCollins, 1999), 16.
4. George Christy, "The Great Life," *The Hollywood Reporter*, November 17, 1987.
5. Douglas E. Winter, "Give Me B-Movies or Give Me Death!" Published in *Faces of Fear* (1985) and reprinted in *Clive Barker's Shadows in Eden*, 30.
6. *Fear in the Dark*.
7. Douglas E. Winter, "Raising Hell with Clive Barker," in *Rod Serling's The Twilight Zone Magazine* 7, no. 5 (December 1987).

Chapter 5

1. Kim Newman, "*Hellraiser* Review," *Monthly Film Bulletin* 54, no. 644 (September 1987), 276.
2. http://www.groovymovie.info and http://www.ironworks.demon.co.uk

Chapter 6

1. Alan Jones, "*Hellbound: Hellraiser II*," *Cinefantastique* 19, no. 1 (January 2, 1989).
2. Ibid.
3. Peter Atkins, "A Dog's Tail," in *Shadows in Eden*, ed. Stephen Jones (Lancaster, Pennsylvania: Underwood-Miller 1991), 115.
4. Ibid.
5. *South Bank Show: Clive Barker* (London Weekend Television, 1994).
6. Ibid.
7. Michael Brown, ed., *Pandemonium* (New York: Eclipse Books, 1991), 38.
8. Edwin Pouncey, "Go Straight to Hell," *New Musical Express* (April 2, 1988).
9. *Hellbound: Lost in the Labyrinth* Documentary. *Hellraiser* Boxed Set released by Anchor Bay, 2004.
10. Ibid.
11. *Hellbound: Hellraiser II*, Audio Commentary. *Hellraiser* Boxed Set.
12. *Dread*, no.1, 1991, 11.
13. *Hellbound: Lost in the Labyrinth* Documentary. *Hellraiser* Boxed Set.
14. On-set Interview: *Hellraiser* Boxed Set.
15. *Hellbound*, second draft screenplay (November 1, 1987), 74.
16. Ibid., 96.
17. Stephen Jones, ed., *Clive Barker's A–Z of Horror* (London: BBC Books, 1997), 202.
18. On-set Interview: *Hellraiser* Boxed Set.
19. Ibid.
20. Doug Bradley, *Behind the Mask of the Horror Actor* (London: Titan Books, 1996/2004), 245.
21. *Samhain*, no. 9 (June/July 1988), 6.
22. *Hellbound: Lost in the Labyrinth* Documentary. *Hellraiser* Boxed Set.
23. Michael Brown, ed., *Pandemonium*, 85.
24. John Skipp and Craig Spector, Pinewood Studios, March 1989.
25. *Hellbound: Hellraiser II*, Audio Commentary. *Hellraiser* Boxed Set.
26. Dave Hughes, "Clive Barker in the Flesh," *Skeleton Crew*, no. III/IV (1988).
27. Source: http://www.the-numbers.com/movies/series/
28. Bob Strauss, "Director Conjures Up His Hades," *Chicago Sun-Times*, December 25, 1988.

Chapter 7

1. When asked to write about his favorite horror movie, Peter Atkins chose the film *Orphée* for PS Publishing's 2005 book, *Cinema Macabre*, edited by Mark Morris. N.B. Paul Kane wrote about *Hellraiser*.
2. *Samhain*, no. 11 (October/November 1988), 12.
3. *Hellbound: Hellraiser II*, 2004 DVD release, audio commentary with Peter Atkins and Tony Randel.
4. "Keeping Company with Cannibal Witches," *Daily Telegraph*, January 6, 1990.
5. Ansel Dibell, *Plot* (London: Robinson, 1988), 102.

Chapter Eight

1. Aleister Crowley (1875–1947) was an English magician and occultist who described himself as The Beast of the Apocalypse. He practiced rites of sex magic and blood sacrifice, but despite his excesses some consider him one of the most brilliant magicians of modern times. *Dictionary of the Occult* (London: Brockhampton Press, 1996).
2. *Hellbound: Hellraiser II*, Audio Commentary. *Hellraiser* Boxed Set.
3. Ibid.

Chapter 9

1. The *Bible* Revelations 19:20.
2. Ibid., 20:10.
3. Ibid., 21:8.
4. The *Bible,* Revelations 20:3, 17:8, 9:1; Romans 10:7; Psalms 69:15; Numbers 16:31–34; Isaiah.5:14; Ezekiel 16:20.
5. The *Bible,* Revelations 14:9–11.
6. The *Bible*. Matthew 8:12.
7. Stuart Gordon, *The Paranormal: An Illustrated Encyclopaedia* (London: Headline, 1992), 88.
8. *Dictionary of the Occult* (Geddes and Grosset, 1996), 54.
9. Nicholas Vince, "Look See." Online at www.cenobite.com.
10. Doug Bradley, *Behind the Mask of the Horror Actor* (London: Titan, 1996/2004), 216.
11. William Wilson Goodson, Jr., "The Origin of Pinhead," *Cinefantastique* 22, no. 6 (June 1992), 26.

Chapter 10

1. *Samhain,* no. 12 (December 1988/January 1989), 25.
2. Ibid., 26.
3. Ibid.
4. Ibid.
5. *Hellbound: Hellraiser II,* Audio Commentary. *Hellraiser* Boxed Set released by Anchor Bay, 2004.
6. *Films and Filming,* no. 416 (June 1989), 38.
7. *Gorezone,* no. 5 (January 1989).
8. *Daily News,* December 28, 1988.
9. Ibid., December 23, 1988.
10. *Variety,* September 14, 1988, 27.
11. *Monthly Film Bulletin* 56, no. 666 (July 1989), 206.
12. Dave Hughes, "Clive Barker in the Flesh," *Skeleton Crew,* no. III/IV (1988).
13. *Monstroid,* no. 3 (Spring 1993), 8.

Chapter 11

1. Douglas E. Winter, *The Dark Fantastic* (London: HarperCollins, 2001), 325
2. "*Hellraiser III* & Me," Clive Barker interview by Alan Jones, *Shivers,* no. 5, (February 1993), 25
3. "Hell Writer," Peter Atkins interview by Alan Jones, *The Dark Side* (March 1992), 15.
4. *Under the Skin: Doug Bradley on Hellraiser III: Hell on Earth*. *Hellraiser* Boxed Set released by Anchor Bay, 2004.
5. "Hell Writer," Peter Atkins interview, 15.
6. *Hellraiser III: Hell on Earth,* script by Peter Atkins, first draft (May 1991, revised May 29, 1991), 10.
7. Ibid., 30.
8. Ibid., 54.
9. Ibid., 84.
10. Ibid., 85.
11. Ibid., 89.
12. Ibid., 96.
13. Ibid., 100.
14. Ibid., 102.
15. Ibid.,104.
16. Philip Nutman, "Welcome to Club Dead," *Fangoria,* no. 110 (March 1992), 38.
17. Alan Jones, "Hickox Raises Hell," *The Dark Side* (March 1992), 22.
18. Nutman, "Welcome to Club Dead," 40.
19. Jones, "Hickox Raises Hell," 23.
20. "*Hellraiser III* & Me," Clive Barker interview by Alan Jones, *Shivers,* no. 5, (February 1993), 25.
21. *Raising Hell on Earth* Documentary. *Hellraiser* Boxed Set.
22. Jones, "Hickox Raises Hell," 23.
23. *Raising Hell on Earth* Documentary.
24. "*Hellraiser III: Hell on Earth,*" *Cinefantastique* 22, no. 6 (June 1992), 27.
25. *Raising Hell on Earth* Documentary.
26. Nutman, "Welcome to Club Dead," 38.
27. *Hellraiser III,* Audio Commentary. *Hellraiser* Boxed Set.
28. *Raising Hell on Earth* Documentary.
29. *Hellraiser III,* Sound Track Notes.
30. *Under the Skin: Doug Bradley on Hellraiser III: Hell on Earth.*
31. Nutman, "Welcome to Club Dead," 36.
32. Steve Biodrowski, "*Waxwork II,*" *Cinefantastique* 22, no. 6 (June 1992), 49.
33. Alan Jones, "Pinhead Unbound," *Shivers,* no. 1 (June 1992), 18.
34. *Hellraiser III,* Audio Commentary. *Hellraiser* Boxed Set.
35. Doug Bradley, "Pinhead's Progress," *Fangoria,* no. 112 (May 1992), 28.
36. Nutman, "Welcome to Club Dead," 40.
37. Jones, "Hickox Raises Hell," 26.
38. "*Hellraiser III* & Me," 26.
39. In the interview Barker says initially this was $3 million. *Fangoria* and *Starburst* reported that the final budget was $5 million, which would include the reshoots.
40. "*Hellraiser III* & Me," 26.
41. Ibid.
42. Ibid.

Chapter 12

1. *Hellraiser III,* Audio Commentary. Boxed Set released by Anchor Bay, 2004.
2. Simon Bacal, "Directing *Hellraiser III,*" *Starburst* 15, no. 3 (November 1992), 17.
3. *Hellraiser III: Hell on Earth,* script by Peter Atkins, first draft (May 1991, revised May 29), 13.
4. *Hellbound*'s director, Tony Randel, had a particular interest in shortwave radio himself. At

the age of 12 he was given a ham radio license, which in the U.S. requires you to learn Morse code, so in his first four or five films he always included his call sign in the background.

5. Simon Bacal, "Directing *Hellraiser III*," *Starburst* 15, no. 3, (November 1992), 17.

6. Lewis Carroll (1832–1898) was born Charles Lutwidge Dodgson near Warrington, England. Reportedly a shy person with a stammer, he much preferred the company of children to adults and his interest in games led to his writing the Alice Adventures.

7. Lewis Carroll, *Alice in Wonderland* and *Through the Looking Glass* (1865 and 1871), (New York: Quality Paperback Book Club, 1994), ix.

8. Ibid., 180–181.

Chapter 13

1. Doug Bradley, *Behind the Mask of the Horror Actor* (London: Titan, 1996/2004), 252–253.

2. Alan Jones, "Pinhead Unbound," *Shivers*, no. 1 (June 1992), 16.

3. Simon Bacal, "Directing *Hellraiser III*," *Starburst* 15, no. 3, (November 1992).

4. Jones, "Pinhead Unbound," 17.

Chapter 14

1. *Hellraiser* Boxed Set Booklet released by Anchor Bay, 2004.

2. *The Dark Side* (November 1992), 39.

3. *Monstroid*, no. 2 (Winter 1992–1993), 24.

4. Source: http://www.the-numbers.com/movies/series/

5. Mentioned in the foreword of this book and in conversation with the author at the British Fantasy Open Night, 2 September 2005.

Chapter 15

1. Anthony C. Ferrante, "To Hell and Back," *Fangoria*, no. 141 (April 1995), 42.

2. George R.R. Martin, ed., *Night Visions* (London: Arrow, 1987), 202.

3. *Hellraiser: Bloodline* script (sixth draft), 1995, 1.

4. Ibid., 2.
5. Ibid., 3.
6. Ibid., 4.
7. Ibid., 5.
8. Ibid., 9.
9. Ibid.
10. Ibid., 13.
11. Ibid., 18.
12. Ibid., 21.
13. Ibid., 27.
14. Ibid., 40.
15. Ibid., 48.

16. Ibid., 63.
17. Ibid., 46.
18. Nick Joy, "Doug Bradley, Hell to Pay," *Shivers*, no. 57 (September 1998), 35.
19. Joe Mauceri, "Raising Hell Again," *Shivers*, no. 14 (January 1995), 8.
20. Ibid., 9.
21. *Fangoria*, no. 141 (April 1995), 44.
22. Simon Bacal, "Raising Hell," *Sci Fi Universe*, no. 5 (February/March 1995).
23. *Fangoria*, no. 141, 45.
24. Bacal, "Raising Hell."
25. David Howe, "Sex, Death and Pinhead," *Shivers*, no. 21 (September 1995), 40.
26. Ibid., 41.
27. Ibid., 42.
28. *Fangoria*, no.141, 45.
29. Ibid., 69
30. *Shivers*, no. 57 (September 1998).
31. *Fangoria*, no. 141, 43.
32. Mauceri, "Raising Hell Again," 10.
33. "Pins and Needles," interview by Chris Fullwood. *Firelight Shocks*, no. 4 (September 2002).
34. Michael Beeler, "*Hellraiser IV: Bloodline*," *Cinefantastique* 27, no. 2 (November 1995).
35. Ibid.
36. Ibid.
37. *Firelight Shocks*, no. 4 (September 2002).
38. The Alan Smithee credit originated in 1967 after Don Siegel replaced Robert Totten as director on *Death of a Gunfighter* 25 days into the shoot, and both were unhappy about the way the finished film turned out. Since then it has been used for films such as the extended version of *Dune* (1984)—cinematically released under director David Lynch's name—*Stitches* (1985), *Ghost Fever* (1987) and *The Shrimp on the Barbie* (1990).
39. Jay Stevenson, "Hellraiser," *Imagi-Movies* 1, no. 2 (Winter 1993/1994).
40. Source: http://www.the-numbers.com/movies/series/
41. David Hughes, "Truly, Bradley, Creepily," *Fangoria*, no. 175 (August 1998).
42. Ibid.
43. Anthony C. Ferrante, "To Surrender Hell," *Fangoria*, no. 151 (April 1996).

Chapter 16

1. *Reputations*, dir. Tim Kirby, BBC 2 (1999).
2. *Hellraiser: Bloodline* script (sixth draft), 4.

Chapter 17

1. *Hellraiser: Bloodline* U.S. Press Kit (March 1996).
2. *Hellraiser: Bloodline* script, 72.

Chapter 18

1. *Shivers,* no. 39 (March 1997), 16.
2. Ibid., 17.
3. *Lost Souls* Web site (1996).
4. Nick Joy, "Doug Bradley Hell to Pay," *Shivers,* no. 57 (September 1998), 35.
5. AOL online appearance, 16 July 1996.

Chapter 19

1. Nick Joy, "Doug Bradley, Hell to Pay," *Shivers,* no. 57 (September 1998), 36.
2. Anthony C. Ferrante, "Things to Do in Denver When You're Pinhead," *Fangoria,* no. 198 (November 2000), 31.
3. Ibid.
4. Doug Bradley, *Behind the Mask of the Horror Actor* (London: Titan, 1996/2004), 265.
5. Ibid., 266.
6. Chris Fullwood, "Pins and Needles," *Firelight Shocks,* no. 4 (September 2002).
7. *Fangoria,* no.198 (November 2000), 28.
8. Ibid.
9. Ibid., 31.
10. The Dominion online appearance, 8 March 1999.
11. Gary Tunnicliffe interview by Mark Adams, *The Hellbound Web* (2003).
12. *Fangoria,* no. 198 (November 2000), 30.
13. Scott Derrickson interview by Mark Adams, *The Hellbound Web* (2002).
14. Philip Nutman, "Pinhead Turns 100," *Fangoria,* no. 198 (November 2000), 29.
15. Ibid.
16. *Fangoria,* no. 198 (November 2000), 30–31.

Chapter 20

1. Scott Derrickson interview by Mark Adams, *The Hellbound Web* (2002).
2. The documentary featurette *Hellraiser: Resurrection.* U.S. DVD.
3. Ibid.

Chapter 21

1. Scott Derrickson interview by Mark Adams, *The Hellbound Web* (2002).
2. Christ Fullwood, "Pins and Needles," *Firelight Shocks,* no. 4 (September 2002).
3. At American Cinemateque First Festival of Fantasy, Horror and Science Fiction, Los Angelos, CA, 25 Aug 2000 (Fandom.com).
4. Interview by Craig Fohr in *Lost Souls* Newsletter (September/December 2000). Interview took place 25 August 2000.
5. Lucius Gore, "*Hellraiser 5* Director Responds to Clive Barker," e-mail to *Esplatter,* 2 September 2000 (Fandom.com).

Chapter 22

1. Scott Collura, "Going To Hell," *Cinescape,* no. 66/67 (November/December 2002).
2. *Hellraiser: Hellseeker* DVD, Audio Commentary.
3. Ibid.
4. Carl V. Dupré and Tim Day, *Hellraiser: Hellseeker* script, 4.
5. [The Arrow], "The Arrow Interviews," http://www.joblo.com/arrow (October 2001).
6. *Hellraiser: Hellseeker,* Audio Commentary.
7. Mark Adams, interview for *Hellbound Web* (2003).
8. *Hellraiser: Hellseeker Effects* DVD Extra.
9. *Hellraiser: Hellseeker* DVD, Audio Commentary.
10. *Hellraiser: Hellseeker* script, 12.
11. *Hellraiser: Hellseeker* DVD, Audio Commentary.
12. *Hellraiser: Hellseeker* script, 2.
13. Kier-la Janisse, "Monster Invasion: Hellseeker," *Fangoria,* no. 215 (August 2002), 8.
14. *Hellraiser: Hellseeker* DVD, Audio Commentary.
15. *Fangoria,* no. 215 (August 2002), 8.

Chapter 23

1. Carl V. Dupré and Tim Day, *Hellraiser: Hellseeker* script, 79.
2. Ibid., 40.

Chapter 24

1. Carl V. Dupré and Tim Day, *Hellraiser: Hellseeker* script, 81.
2. Ibid.

Chapter 26

1. Neal Marshall Stevens, *Deader* script, 1.
2. Ibid., 2.
3. Ibid., 5.
4. Ibid., 27–28.
5. Ibid., 32.
6. Ibid., 52.
7. Ibid., 68.
8. Ibid., 72.
9. *The Hellbound Web* (2003).
10. *The Making of Deader* Documentary, DVD (2005).
11. Doug Bradley, *Behind the Mask of the Horror Actor* (London: Titan Books, 1996/2004), 276.
12. *The Making of Deader.*
13. Ibid.
14. *Hellraiser: Deader: Practical Effects* Documentary, DVD.
15. *Hellraiser: Deader,* Audio Commentary.
16. *The Making of Deader.*

Chapter 27

1. Andrew Black, *Zombies* (United Kingdom: A. G. Black, 1992), 82.

Chapter 29

1. *Hellraiser: Hellworld,* Audio Commentary.
2. Ibid.
3. *Making of Hellworld* DVD, Bonus Featurette.
4. According to Gary Tunnicliffe the Sacrifice Chair was actually inspired by a medical procedure involving bleeding a patient, used to treat George Washington just before his death.
5. *Hellraiser: Hellworld,* Audio Commentary.
6. *Making of Hellworld* DVD, Bonus Featurette.
7. http://www.toromagazine.ca/current/toro_woman.html.
8. E-mail to the author, 16 September 2005.
9. *Making of Hellworld* DVD, Bonus Featurette.
10. *Hellraiser: Hellworld,* Audio Commentary.
11. *Making of Hellworld* DVD, Bonus Featurette.
12. Ibid.
13. Doug Bradley, *Behind the Mask of the Horror Actor* (London: Titan Books, 1996/2004), 279.
14. *Making of Hellworld* DVD, Bonus Featurette.

Chapter 30

1. *Hellraiser: Hellworld,* Audio Commentary.
2. This would appear to contradict *Bloodline*'s account of Lemarchand's history. Indeed, the painting of him in the Leviathan house shows him more as an older man and an aristocrat. But all this can be forgiven when we remember that The Host is not really the authority he claims to be, but rather is playing the role based on information he was able to pick up along the way. There is nothing to say that the Leviathan House was even designed by Lemarchand at all; more likely it was simply an appropriate house for his needs.

Chapter 33

1. *Hellraiser,* Book 1 (Epic Comics), 2.
2. Ibid., 3.
3. *Fangoria,* no. 105 (August 1991), 43.
4. *Dread,* no. 1 (1992), 6.
5. *Hellraiser,* Book 17 (Epic Comics), 2.

Chapter 34

1. Ryan Rotten, "Michael, Meet Pinhead," *Creature Corner,* 20 August 2003.
2. "Dave Parker Talks Director's Cut and *Hellraiser* vs. *Halloween,*" Fangoria.com, 8 October 2003.
3. Kevin Garcia, "Pinhead Terrorizes Brownsville," *The Brownsville Herald,* October 23, 2003.
4. According to Moviehole.net.
5. "Clive Barker Update on Tortured Souls," Fangoria.com, 29 January 2004 (full text online at http://www.fangoria.com).
6. http://www.movieweb.com/news/news.php?id=6233.
7. Meeting with the author, 2 September 2005.
8. Jason Arnopp, "Hellboy," *SFX,* no. 123 (November 2004), 59.
9. Eliza Gallo, "Weinsteins Work Out DVD Details, Retain Rights to *Hellraiser, Halloween* Franchises," July 11, 2005 (full report at http://www.dvdexclusive.com/article.asp?articleID=2257).
10. Jason Arnopp, "Hellboy," *SFX,* no. 123 (November 2004), 59.
11. Ibid.

Bibliography

Books/Scripts

Atkins, Peter. *Hellbound,* Second draft screenplay. Nov. 1, 1987.
_____. *Hellraiser III: Hell on Earth,* Script, first draft. May 1991. Revised May 29, 1991.
_____. "A Dog's Tail." *Clive Barker's Shadows in Eden.* Edited by Stephen Jones. Lancaster, Pennsylvania: Underwood-Miller, 1991.
_____. *Clive Barker Presents Hellraiser III: Hell on Earth.* New York: Marvel Epic, 1992.
_____. *Hellraiser: Bloodline,* Script, sixth draft.
Barker, Clive. *Clive Barker's Books of Blood.* Vol. 1. London: Sphere, 1984.
_____. *Clive Barker's Books of Blood.* Vol. 2. London: Sphere, 1984.
_____. *Clive Barker's Books of Blood.* Vol. 3. London: Sphere, 1984.
_____. *Clive Barker's Books of Blood.* Vol. 4. London: Sphere, 1985.
_____. *Clive Barker's Books of Blood.* Vol. 5. London: Sphere, 1985.
_____. *Clive Barker's Books of Blood.* Vol. 6. London: Sphere, 1985.
_____. *Weaveworld.* London: Collins, 1987.
_____. *Cabal.* London: Fontana/Collins, 1988.
_____. *The Damnation Game.* London: Sphere, 1986.
_____. *Hellraiser* Screenplay.
_____. *The Great and Secret Show.* London: Fontana/Collins, 1989.
_____. *Clive Barker's Nightbreed: The Making of the Film.* London: Fontana/Collins, 1990.
_____. *Imajica.* London: HarperCollins, 1991.
_____. *Incarnations: Three Plays by Clive Barker.* London: HarperCollins, 1996.
_____. *Galilee.* London: HarperCollins, 1998.
Barker, Clive, ed. *The Essential Clive Barker, Selected Fictions.* London: HarperCollins, 1999.
Barker, Clive. *Abarat.* London: HarperCollins, 2002.
Black, Andrew. *Zombies.* United Kingdom: A. G. Black, 1992.
Boot, Andy. *Fragments of Fear: An Illustrated History of British Horror Films.* New York: Creation Books, 1996.
Bordwell, David, and Kristin Thompson. *Film Art: An Introduction.* New York: McGraw-Hill, 1979/1990.
_____. *Film History: An Introduction.* New York: McGraw-Hill, 1994.
Bradley, Doug. *Behind the Mask of the Horror Actor.* London: Titan Books, 1996/2004.
Brown, Michael, ed. *Pandemonium: Further Explorations into the Worlds of Clive Barker.* New York: Eclipse Books, 1991.
Carroll, Lewis. *Alice in Wonderland* and *Through the Looking Glass* (1865 and 1871). New York: Quality Paperback Book Club, 1994.
Carroll, Noel. *The Philosophy of Horror.* London: Routledge, 1990.
Chibnall, Steve, and Julian Petley. *British Horror Cinema.* London: Rutledge, 2002.
Chichester, Daniel G., Mark McLaurin and David Wohl.eds. *Clive Barker's Hellraiser.* Books 1–20. New York: Marvel Epic, 1989–1993.
Chichester, Daniel G. *Jihad.* Books 1 & 2. New York: Marvel Epic, 1991.
Chichester, Daniel G., Mark McLaurin and David Wohl, series eds. *Clive Barker's Collected Best Hellraiser.* Vols. 1–3. Ohio: Checker Books, 2002–2004.
Clover, Carol. *Men, Women and Chainsaws.* London: BFI, 1992.
Daning, Tom, Mark McLaurin and David Wohl, eds. *Clive Barker's Hellraiser Spring Slaughter.* New York: Marvel Epic, 1994.
Dibell, Ansen. *Plot.* London: Robinson, 1988.
Dictionary of the Occult. London: Brockhampton Press, 1996.
Dika, Vera. "The Stalker Film 1978–81." In *American Horrors.* Edited by Gregory A. WallerUniversity of Illinois Press, 1987.

Dupré, Carl V., and Tim Day. *Hellraiser: Hellseeker*. Script. 2000.
Dyson, Jeremy. *Bright Darkness: The Lost Art of the Supernatural Horror Film*. London: Cassell, 1997.
Eyles, Allen, Robert Adkinson and Nicholas Fry, eds. *House of Horror: The Complete Hammer Films Story*. New York: Creation Books, 1973/1994.
Fischer, Dennis. *Horror Film Directors 1931–1990*. Jefferson, North Carolina: McFarland, 1991.
Floyd, Nigel. "Slime Time." In *Time Out*, September 2–9, 1987. Published as "Hellraiser" in *Clive Barker's Shadows in Eden*. Edited by Stephen Jones. Pennsylvania: Underwood Miller, 1991.
Frayling, Christopher. *Nightmare:The Birth of Horror*. London: BBC Books, 1996.
Gerard, Noel. *Christopher Lee: Prince of Darkness*. France: Nostalgia Archives, 1991.
Gordon, Stuart. *The Paranormal: An Illustrated Encyclopaedia*. London: Headline,1992.
Grant, Barry K., ed. *Planks of Reason: Essays on the Horror Film*. Metuchen, New Jersey: Scarecrow Press, 1984.
Grimm, J.L.C., and W.C. Grimm. *Grimm's Fairy Tales*. Hertfordshire: Wordsworth, 1993.
Hardy, Phil, ed. *The Aurum Film Encyclopedia: Horror*. London: Aurum Press, 1996.
Harkavy, Michael D, editor-in-chief. *The New Webster's International Encyclopedia*. Florida: Trident, 1996.
Hayward, Susan. *Key Concepts in Cinema Studies*. London: Routledge, 1996.
Hodge, Nicola, and Libby Anson. *The A–Z of Art*. London: Carlton/BCA, 1996.
Hoppenstand, Gary. "The Secret Self." In *Pandemonium: Further Explorations Into the Worlds of Clive Barker*. Edited by Michael Brown. New York: Eclipse, 1991.
H.R. Giger Arh. Germany: Taschen, 1991.
Jancovich, Mark. *Horror*. London: B.T. Batsford, 1992.
_____. *The Horror Film Reader (In Focus)*. London: Routledge, 2003.
Jones, Stephen, ed. *Clive Barker's Shadows in Eden*. Pennsylvania: Underwood Miller, 1991.
_____, ed. *The Hellraiser Chronicles*. London: Titan, 1992.
_____, ed. *Clive Barker's A–Z of Horror*. London: BBC Books. 1997.
Jones, Stephen, and Kim Newman, eds. *Horror: 100 Best Books*. New York: Carroll & Graf, 1988/2000.
Karney, Robyn, editor-in-chief. *Chronicle of the Cinema: 100 Years of the Movies*. London: Dorling Kindersley, 1995.
Katz, Ephraim. *The Macmillan International Film Encyclopedia (New Edition)*. London: Macmillan/HarperCollins, 1994/1996.
Lloyd, Ann. *The Films of Stephen King*. London: Brown Books, 1993.
Magnusson, Magnus, ed. *Chambers Biographical Dictionary*. Edinburgh: W&R Chambers, 1993.
Martin, George R.R., ed. *Night Visions*. London: Arrow, 1987.
Maxford, Howard. *The A–Z of Horror Films*. London: B.T. Batsford, 1996.
McCarty, John, ed. *The Fearmakers*. New York: St. Martin's, 1994.
McLaurin, Mark, ed. *Clive Barker's Hellraiser Summer Special*. New York: Marvel Epic, 1992.
McLaurin, Mark, and David Wohl, eds. *Clive Barker's Hellraiser Dark Holiday Special: Christmas*. New York: Marvel Epic, 1992.
_____, eds. *Clive Barker's Book of the Damned*. Vols. I–IV. New York: Marvel Epic, 1991–1993.
Michel, Jean-Claude. *Fantasy Film Memory: Lucio Fulci, Italy's Gore Master*. France: F.F.M., 1990.
Morris, Mark, ed. *Cinema Macabre*. Hornsea: P.S. Publishing, 2005.
Morrison, Michael A. "Monsters, Miracles and Revelations." In *Clive Barker's Shadows in Eden*. Edited by Stephen Jones. Pennsylvania: Underwood Miller, 1991.
Neale, Steve. *Genre and Hollywood*. London: Routledge, 2000.
Newman, Kim, ed. *The BFI Companion to Horror*. London: Cassell, 1996.
Niles, Steve, adaptation. *The Yattering and Jack*. London: Eclipse, 1993.
_____, adaptation. *Rawhead Rex*. London: Eclipse, 1994.
Nutman, Philip. "Gangsters vs. Mutants." In *Clive Barker's Shadows in Eden*. Edited by Stephen Jones. Pennsylvania: Underwood Miller, 1991.
Piranesi's Prisons: A Perspective. Sheffield: Graves Art Gallery, 1988.
Poe, Edgar Allan. *The Selected Works of Edgar Allan Poe*. Ann Arbor, Michigan: Mundus, 2002.
Salisbury, Mark, and Alan Hedgcock. *Behind the Mask:The Secrets of Hollywood's Monster Makers*. London: Titan, 1994.
Sinyard, Neil. *Classic Movies*. London: Chancellor Press, 1985/1993.

Stevens, Neal M. *Deader*. Script. 2001 or 2002 (?).
Timpone, Anthony, ed. *Fangoria: Masters of the Dark*. New York: HarperPrism, 1997.
Walker, John, ed. *Halliwell's Film and Video Guide*. London: HarperCollins, 2002.
Waller, Gregory A., ed. *American Horrors*. Champaign: University of Illinois Press, 1987.
Winter, Douglas E. "Give Me B-Movies or Give Me Death." In *Faces of Fear* 1985 reprinted in *Clive Barker's Shadows in Eden*. Edited by Stephen Jones. Pennsylvania: Underwood-Miller, 1991.
_____. "The Heights and Depths of *Hellraiser*." In *Fangoria: Masters of the Dark*. Edited by Anthony Timpone. New York: HarperPrism, 1997.
_____. *The Dark Fantastic*. London: HarperCollins, 2001.
Wollen, Peter. "The Auteur Theory." In *Signs and Meaning in the Cinema*. London: Secker and Warberg, 1967 & 1972.

Articles/Interviews/Magazines

Abery, James. "The Strange History of Frankenstein." *Shivers*, no.13 (December 1994).
Adams, Mark. "Scott Derrickson Interview" for *The Hellbound Web* (2002). http://www.cenobite.com
_____. "Gary Tunnicliffe Interview" for *The Hellbound Web* (2003). http://www.cenobite.com
Arnopp, Jason. "Hellboy." Clive Barker Interview. *SFX* 123 (November 2004).
Atkins, Peter. "Children of the Fire." *The Hellbound Web*. http://www.cenobite.com
Bacal, Simon. "Directing *Hellraiser III*." *Starburst* 15, no. 3 (November 1992).
_____. "Sweet Talking Guy." Clive Barker Interview. *Shivers* 1, no. 4 (December 1992).
_____. "Raising Hell." *Sci Fi Universe*, no. 5 (February/March 1995).
Barker, Clive. Speaking at UCLA, 25 February 1987.
_____. The Dominion: Online appearance, 8 March 1999.
Barnabas (transcription). "Q&A Session with Clive Barker and Peter Atkins," 9 April 2000. http://www.clivebarker.com
_____. (transcription) "Clive Barker and Ashley Laurence at the Egyptian Theatre," 25 August 2000. http://www.clivebarker.com
Beeler, Michael. "Lord of Illusions." Clive Barker Interview. *Cinefantastique* 26, no. 5 (August 1995).
_____. "Hellraiser IV: Bloodline." *Cinefantastique* 27, no. 2 (November 1995).
Biodrowski, Steve. "Waxwork II: Lost in Time." *Cinefantastique* 22, no. 6 (June 1992).
Bradley, Doug. "Pinhead's Progress." *Fangoria* 112 (May 1992).
Braund, Simon, production ed. *Special Collectors' Edition, Empire: The Greatest Horror Movies Ever*. 2000.
Brown, Michael. *Dread*, nos. 1–6. Phantom Press, 1992.
Bryce, Allan. "Life after *Hellraiser*." Interview with Clive Barker. *The Dark Side* (March 1992).
Buscombe, Edward. "Ideas of Authorship." *Screen* 14, no. 3 (Autumn 1973).
Cherry, Brigid, Brian Robb and Andrew Wilson. "Weaveworld." *Nexus*, no. 4 (November–December 1987).
Cherry, Brigid. "Screaming for Release: The Role of the Female Archetype in Horror Films." *Samhain*, no. 8 (March/April 1988).
Christy, George. "The Great Life." *The Hollywood Reporter*, November 17, 1987.
Collura, Scott. "Going To Hell." *Cinescape*, nos. 66/67 (November / December 2002).
Daning, Tom and David Wohl, eds. *Pinhead*, nos.1–6. New York: Marvel Epic, 1993–1994.
"Dave Parker Talks Director's Cut and *Hellraiser vs. Halloween*." http://www.Fangoria.com, 8 October 2003
Ebert, Roger. "Hellbound: Hellraiser II." *Daily News*, December 28, 1988.
Ferrante, Anthony C. "To Hell and Back." *Fangoria* 141 (April 1995).
_____. "To Surrender Hell." *Fangoria* 151 (April 1996).
_____. "Things To Do in Denver When You're Pinhead." *Fangoria* 198 (November 2000).
Floyd, Nigel. "*Hellraiser*: Barker's Box of Delights." Interview with Clive Barker. *Samhain*, no. 4 (July/August 1987).
_____. "Nightmare Movies at the 36th London Film Festival." *The Dark Side*, November 1992.
_____. "The *SFX* Interview: Clive Barker." *SFX* 16 (September 1996).
"From Dog Days to Bloodlines." Peter Atkins Interview on the *Lost Souls* Web site. http://www.clivebarker.com
Fullwood, Chris. "Pins and Needles." Interview with Doug Bradley. *Firelight Shocks*, no. 4 (September 2002).
Garcia, Kevin. "Pinhead Terrorizes Brownsville." Interview with Doug Bradley. *The Brownsville Herald*, October 23, 2003.

Goodson, Jr., William W. "*Hellraiser III: Hell on Earth.*" *Cinefantastique* 22, no. 6 (June 1992).

_____. "The Origin of Pinhead." *Cinefantastique* 22, no. 6 (June 1992).

Gregory, Jon. *Hellraiser*. Vol. 1 (1992).

Griffiths, Richard, and Nigel Floyd. "The Horror Strand." *Monstroid* 2 (Winter 1992-1993).

Gullidge, John, and John Martin. "Beyond the Limits." *Samhain*, no. 8 (March/April 1988).

_____. "Be Flayed ... Be Very Flayed." Interview with Geoff Portass. *Samhain*, no. 9 (June/July 1988).

Guran, Paula. "Peter Atkins Interview." November 2000.http://www.horroronline.com

"Hellbound: Hellraiser II." *Variety* 14 (September 1988).

"Hellbound: Hellraiser II." *Monthly Film Bulletin*, 56, no. 666 (July 1989).

Hellraiser: Bloodline. U.S. Press Kit (March 1996).

Howe, David. "Sex, Death and Pinhead." *Shivers*, no. 21 (September 1995).

_____. "Sex, Death and Pinhead, Part 2." *Shivers* 22 (October 1995).

Hughes, David. "Clive Barker in the Flesh." *Skeleton Crew*, no. III/IV (1988).

_____. "The Road to Hell." Interview with Clive Barker. *State* 1, no. 3 (December 1992-January 1993).

_____. "Truly, Bradley, Creepily." *Fangoria*, no. 175 (August 1998).

James, Gareth. "Time to Flay." Interview with Peter Atkins. *Monstroid*, no. 3 (Spring 1993).

Janisse, Kier-la. "Monster Invasion: *Hellseeker*." *Fangoria*, no. 215 (August 2002).

Jones, Alan. "Rawhead Rex." *Starburst*, no. 103 (March 1987).

_____. "Rawhead Rex." *Cinefantastique* 7, no. 5 (December 1987).

_____. "Hellbound: Hellraiser II." *Cinefantastique* 19, no. 1/2 (January 1989).

_____. "Hell Writer." Interview with Peter Atkins. *The Dark Side* (March 1992).

_____. "Hickox Raises Hell." *The Dark Side*, March 1992.

_____. "Pinhead Unbound." *Shivers*, no. 1 (June 1992).

_____. "*Hellraiser III* & Me." Interview with Clive Barker. *Shivers*, no. 5 (February 1993).

Joy, Nick. "Doug Bradley: Hell to Pay." *Shivers*, no. 57 (September 1998).

"Keeping Company with Cannibal Witches." *Daily Telegraph*, January 6, 1990.

Labbe, Rodney A. "To Hell with Comics.'" Interview with Marcus McLaurin and D.G. Chichester. *Fangoria*, no. 105 (August 1991).

Martin, John. "Hellwriter." Interview with Peter Atkins. *Samhain*, no. 10 (August/September 1988).

_____. "The Scouse that Dripped Blood." Interview with Peter Atkins. *Samhain*, no. 11 (October/November 1988).

Martin, John, and Jeremy Clarke. "The Grand Old Puke of Yorks: *Hellbound*, the Case For and Against." *Samhain*, no. 12 (December1988/January 1989).

Mauceri, Joe. "Raising Hell Again." *Shivers*, no. 14 (January 1995).

McLaurin, Mark, and Mike Lackey, eds. *Clive Barker's The Harrowers: Raiders of the Abyss*, nos.1–6. New York: Marvel Epic, 1993–1994.

Miller, David. "Top 50 Horror Film Awards: *Hellraiser*." *Shivers*, no. 33 (September 1996).

Mills, Pat. *Pinhead vs. Marshall Law*. New York: Marvel Epic, 1993.

Newman, Kim. "*Hellraiser*." *Monthly Film Bulletin*, 54, no. 644 (September 1987).

_____. "In the Picture." *Sight and Sound* 56, no. 4 (Autumn 1987).

_____. "*Hellraiser III: Hell on Earth*." *Sight and Sound* 3, no. 2 (February 1993).

Nicholls, Stan. "Making a Pact with the Popcorn Eaters." Interview with Peter Atkins. *The Dark Side*, March 1993.

Nutman, Philip. "Welcome to Club Dead." *Fangoria*, no. 110 (March 1992).

_____. "Pinhead Turns 100." *Fangoria*, no.198 (November 2000).

_____. "The Dark Backward." Interview with Clive Barker. Excerpted from *Fangoria*, no. 200. http://www.fangoria.com

Phantom of the Movies. "Hellbound: Hellraiser II." *Daily News*, December 23, 1988.

Pouncey, Edwin. "Go Straight to Hell." *New Musical Express*, April 2, 1988.

Pulleine, Tim. "*Hellraiser*." *Films and Filming*, no. 389 (February 1987).

Rotten, Ryan. "Michael, Meet Pinhead." *Creature Corner* 20 (August 2003).

Shapiro, Marc. "Hellbound: Hellraiser II." *Gorezone*, no. 5 (January 1989).

_____. "Clive Barker's Lord of Illusions. *Shivers*, no. 13 (December 1994).

Slater, Mandy. "Just for the Hell of It." Interview with Peter Atkins. *SFX*, no. 39 (June 1998).

Stevenson, Jay. "*Hellraiser*." *Imagi-Movies*, 1, no. 2 (Winter 1993/1994).

Strauss, Bob. "Director Conjures Up His Hades." *Chicago Sun-Times,* December 25, 1988.

Stroby, W.C. "Boundless Imajination." Interview with Clive Barker. *Fangoria,* no. 109 (January 1992).

Sutton, Martin. "*Hellbound: Hellraiser II.*" *Films and Filming,* no. 416 (June 1989).

Tomlinson, Anthony. "*Hellraiser* Bloodline." *Shivers,* no. 39 (March 1997.

_____. "Hellraiser IV — Tracing the Bloodline" in *Shivers* Issue 50, February 1998.

"The 25 Scariest Movies Ever." *Total Film* # 35, December 1999

Vince, Nicholas. "Doug Bradley: Pinned Down." *Hellbreed,* no. 2 (June 1995).

_____. "Doug Bradley: Pin-Points. *Hellbreed,* no. 3 (July 1995).

_____. "Look See." *The Hellbound Web.* http://www.cenobite.com.

Winter, Douglas E. "Raising Hell with Clive Barker." *Rod Serling's The Twilight Zone Magazine* 7, no. 5 (December 1987).

Other Sources

Documentaries/Commentaries

Fear in the Dark. Dir: Dominic Murphy (1991).

Hellbound: Hellraiser II, Audio commentaries (2004).

Hellbound: Lost in the Labyrinth, Documentary. *Hellraiser* Boxed Set: Anchor Bay, 2004.

Hellraiser: Audio Commentary (2001).

Hellraiser: Deader Audio Commentary (2005).

Hellraiser: Hellseeker, Audio Commentary (2001).

Hellraiser: Hellseeker Effects, DVD Extra (2001).

Hellraiser: Hellworld, Audio Commentary (2005).

Hellraiser: Resurrection, U.S. DVD (2001).

Hellraiser III, Audio Commentary (2004).

Hellraiser III: Hell on Earth, Anthony Hickox Interview. *Hellraiser* Boxed Set: Anchor Bay, 2004.

Making of Deader, DVD Documentary (2005).

Making of Hellworld, DVD Bonus Featurette (2005).

Raising Hell on Earth Documentary. *Hellraiser* Boxed Set: Anchor Bay, 2004.

Reputations: Hitchcock. Dir. Tim Kirby, BBC 2 (1999).

Salome & The Forbidden. Hellraiser Boxed Set: Anchor Bay, 2004.

South Bank Show: Clive Barker. London Weekend Television, 1994.

Under the Skin: Doug Bradley on Hellraiser, Hellbound & Hellraiser III: Hell on Earth. Hellraiser Boxed Set: Anchor Bay, 2004.

Web Sites

http://www.bible.org
http://www.biblegateway.com
http://www.biblestudents.net/studies/doctrine/biblehell.htm
http://www.biblestudy.org
"Development Hell." http://alansmithee.5u.com/smithee/bloodline/Hell1.html
Escher Web site. http://www.mcescher.com
http://www.fandom.com
http://www.fangoria.com
http://www.finalfrontier.org.uk/hell.htm
http://www.groovymovie.info
http://www.hammerfilms.com
Hellbound Web site, http://www.cenobite.com
Internet Movie Database, http://www.imdb.com
http://www.ironworks.demon.co.uk
http://www.joblo.com/arrow
Lost Souls Web site, http://www.clivebarker.com
http://www.movieweb.com/news/news.php?id=6233
Revelations Web site, http://www.clivebarker.dial.pipex.com
Review References, http://www.rottentomatoes.com
http://www.toromagazine.ca/current/toro_woman.html
"Weinsteins Work Out DVD Details." Retain rights to *Hellraiser, Halloween* franchises By Eliza Gallo, 11 July 2005. Full report at www.dvdexclusive.com/article.asp?articleID=2257
Wikipedia.wikipedia.org/wiki/Main Page

INDEX

Abaddon 89
Abarat 35, 225, 226
Adam (*Hellworld*) 208, 210–212
"The Age of Desire" 11
Alice 59, 125
Alien 15, 52, 87, 116, 155–156
Aliens 59, 73, 92, 155–156, 163, 197, 206, 208
All Quiet on the Western Front 115
Allison (*Hellworld*) 205, 208, 210, 212, 214
An American Werewolf in London 14
Anchor Bay 227
Angelique (*Bloodline*) 133–139, 141–142, 145–153, 155
Apocalypse Now 114
Argento, Dario 13, 21–22, 37
Argenziano, Carmen 164
Armored Saint 107
Army of Darkness: The Medieval Dead 130
Asmodeus 89
Atkins, Peter 9, 18, 53–61, 63, 65–67, 72, 75–76, 80, 87, 92–98, 100, 106–108, 110, 119, 120, 126, 128, 130–135, 137, 140–143, 148, 150, 155, 158–159, 162, 165–166, 207, 221

Bamford, Simon 22, 57, 62, 95
Barbie Cenobite 101, 106, 110, 116, 124
Barker, Clive 1–3 5- 7, 9–11, 13–16, 18, 20–32, 34–35, 40–43, 45–46, 48, 50–55, 57–59, 63, 65–67, 75, 77, 84, 87–88, 90–91, 93, 95–97, 99, 103, 107, 111, 113, 121, 124, 130–132, 136–137, 139–143, 157–158, 160, 162, 169, 172–173, 177, 180, 189, 194, 208, 219, 222–228
Barrese, Sasha 163–164
Beauty and the Beast (1946) 46
Bedazzled 24, 89
Beelzebub 89
Behemoth 89

Belial 89
Bernhardt, Kevin 104–105
Bernie (*Inferno*) 163–4, 167, 169–170, 172
The Beyond 201
The Bible 22, 35, 39, 84, 87–89, 110
Blade Runner 168
Blake, William 46, 86
Blue Velvet 32, 161, 169
Boardman, Paul Harris 160, 164, 166, 174
The Books of Blood 10–11, 13, 15, 48, 90, 226
Boorman, Imogen 59
Born on the Fourth of July 114
Bosch, Hieronymous 46, 86
Bota, Rick 175–180, 187, 190, 195, 197–198, 203–209, 216
Bound Cenobite 178, 207, 218
Bradley, Doug 1–3, 7, 9–10, 16, 18, 22–23, 39, 42–44, 57, 60–62, 90–91, 95–97, 99, 104–105, 107–108, 110, 115, 119, 126–127, 130–131, 136–137, 139, 140–143, 155, 158–162, 165–166, 173–174, 176, 180, 183, 194–195, 204, 207–208, 224–226
The Brain That Wouldn't Die 80
The Bride of Frankenstein 80
British Board of Film Classification 50
Bruce Almighty 117
Buchanan, Mike 21, 57, 61
Buffy the Vampire Slayer 5, 107, 163
Butterball Cenobite 22, 34, 43, 57, 90, 124

Cabal 11, 34, 75, 95, 162
Camerahead Cenobite 105, 110, 116, 143
Campbell, Ramsey 13, 18
Candyman 11, 111, 113, 130
Candyman 2: Farewell to the Flesh 136, 142
Carnival of Souls 87
Carpenter, Ken 105

Carroll, Lewis 59, 125
Cavill, Henry 205
C.D. Cenobite 101, 105, 110, 116, 122, 124, 143
Cenobites 1, 10–11, 18, 20–22, 27, 29–31, 33–34, 37–41, 43–44, 48, 54, 56–59, 62, 67, 69, 71, 74, 76, 87, 90–91, 93, 98, 100–101, 106–107, 110, 116–117, 119, 124–125, 127, 135–136, 139, 143, 145–148, 153, 156, 159, 161, 164, 170, 172, 178, 183, 194, 196, 198, 200–202, 207–208, 211, 213, 216, 219, 221–223
Channard, Dr. 57–58, 60–63, 65, 67–80, 82–83, 90–94, 97, 99, 115, 121, 125, 127, 135, 183, 185–187, 200
Chapman, Sean 21, 57, 104
Chappelle, Joe 141–142
Charles (*Deader*) 193–194, 196, 199, 200–202
Chatter Beast 135–136, 139, 143, 147, 156
Chatterer Cenobite 22, 34, 43, 57, 62, 71, 90, 124, 135, 141, 207, 213, 217–218, 221, 227
Chelsea (*Hellworld*) 205–208, 210–214, 216
Chevalier, Catherine 60, 95
Chichester, Daniel 219, 221–223
Children of the Corn 159
Child's Play 136
The China Syndrome 117
Cinderella 76
City of the Living Dead 201
Cocteau, Jean 45–46, 66, 71, 125
"Confessions of a Pornographer's Shroud" 11
Constantine 87
Corman, Roger 21, 55
Cotton, Frank 10–11, 16, 18, 20–23, 25, 27–35, 37–38, 40, 45–46, 48–50, 55–58, 60, 67–71, 73–79, 88, 90, 92, 98–99, 104, 123, 128, 146, 156, 161, 175–176, 187, 197, 200–201, 214
Cotton, Julia 11, 20–22, 27–35,

243

37–39, 46, 49–50, 54–60, 62–63, 67–80, 82–83, 89–90, 93, 99, 123–124, 146, 149, 200, 214, 219, 227
Cotton, Kirsty 16, 18, 20–21, 23–24, 30–35, 37–40, 48, 54–59, 61–62, 64, 67–76, 78, 82–83, 87–88, 92–93, 99–100, 104, 121–125, 128–129, 135, 143, 146, 150, 152, 159, 175–177, 179, 182–185, 187–190, 214, 216
Cotton, Larry 20, 22, 24, 28–30, 32–35, 37–39, 45, 57–58, 67–68, 73, 75, 124, 149, 152, 176, 187
Cranham, Kenneth 60, 62, 65
Cronenberg, David 13, 48, 95, 121, 153, 181
Cronos 136
The Crow 201
Cube 5
The Curse of Frankenstein 79

The Damnation Game 11, 13, 34
D'Amour, Harry 136, 226, 228
Dangerous Liaisons 155
Dante, Alighieri 85–87, 89, 116, 159, 161, 222
Dante's Inferno 85, 87
Daphne (*Inferno*) 163, 167–168, 170–171
Darkness Falling 160
Dawn of the Dead 105, 201
Day, Tim 175–176, 189, 193–195
Day of the Dead 201
The Deaders 192–194, 198, 200–202
Deep Space Nine 104
Demon(s) 6, 11, 27, 29, 35, 38–40, 42–43, 68, 71, 75, 84–86, 88–91, 113, 115, 121, 128, 133–135, 141, 145–146, 148, 150, 152–154, 158–159, 161, 164, 173, 181, 193, 200, 202, 206, 219, 221, 225
Derelict (Keeper of the Box) 35, 106, 133–134,
Derrick (*Hellworld*) 204, 210, 212, 214
Derrickson, Scott 160–162, 164–166, 169, 173–174
The Devil 7, 10, 13, 27, 37–38, 84, 88–90, 100, 116, 121, 177, 179, 221
The Devil Rides Out 89
The Devil's Assistant 87
The Devil's Rain 89
Dimension 110, 159–162, 166, 174–175, 178, 191, 193, 195, 198, 204, 217, 224–225, 227
Dr. Cyclops 80
Dr. Jekyll and Mr Hyde 9, 77–80, 103, 125
The Dog Company 9–10, 21–23, 40, 53–54

Doré, Gustave 86, 116
Dormere, Dr. Allison (*Hellseeker*) 177–178, 181–182, 184
Dracula 9, 42, 110, 127, 194, 197, 204
Dracula Has Risen from the Grave 127
Dracula — Prince of Darkness 127
Dracula 2000 197
Dread Magazine 56, 222
Dukes, David 14–15
Dupré, Carl V. 175–176, 189, 204, 207, 216,

EDIFLEX 110
The Elephant Man 101
Elysium Configuration 134, 136, 144, 145, 147–149, 153–154
The Engineer 20, 24, 34, 50, 143, 159, 161, 169
Englund, Robert 42
Entertaining Mr. Sloane 101
Escher, Maurits 87
E.T. 44
Event Horizon 5
Evil Dead 45, 51
The Exorcist 5, 24, 35
Exorcist III 100
Eyes Without a Face (Les Yeux Sans Visage) 82

Falk, Randy 227
The Fall of the House of Usher 34
Fangoria magazine 2, 13, 15, 108, 110, 126, 139, 173, 221, 225
Farrell, Terry 104, 113, 117, 130
Farscape 5
Faustus 16, 27, 77
The Fearless Vampire Killers 102
Female Cenobite 22, 30, 34, 40, 43, 56–57, 59, 69, 90, 124, 143, 187, 222
Figg, Christopher 21–22, 53–55, 57, 63, 95
Film futures 53, 95–96
Film noir 13, 61, 80, 161, 167–168
Fisher, Daniel "Doc" 105
Flash Gordon 123
The Fly (1986) 48
The Forbidden (film) 16, 18, 38, 54
"The Forbidden" (story) 11, 111
Frankenstein 9, 42, 63, 77–80, 102, 154–155, 192
Friday the 13th 31
Friday the 13th: The Final Chapter 136
From Beyond 136
Fulci, Lucio 201

Gaiman, Neil 223
Galligan, Zach 102, 108
The Gate 87

Giger, H.R. 87
Givens, Detective 178, 182, 184
Goei, Jamison 164, 176, 178, 184, 198, 207–208
Goya 46
Grand Guignol 10, 48
The Great and Secret Show 35, 75
Gregory, Dr. (*Inferno*) 161–162, 167, 170–171
Gremlins 102
Groundhog Day 168
Gwen (*Hellseeker*) 177, 181–185

Halloween 31, 142, 224–225
Halloween: The Curse of Michael Myers 141
Hammer 6, 31, 42, 79–80, 101, 127, 155
Hardie, Steve 106, 116, 166
Harnos, Christine 139
The Harrowers 194, 222–223
Harryhausen, Ray 16, 48
Hayward, Rachel 177
Hell 1, 5, 9, 11, 15, 27, 30, 35, 37–39, 42–43, 52–55, 57–60, 62, 64–65, 67–71, 73–76, 79, 84–92, 94, 96, 100–101, 107, 110, 114–116, 119, 121, 123–124, 129–135, 141–144, 146–147–148, 150–151, 153, 155, 159, 161, 169, 171, 173, 179, 182–183, 185, 187, 194, 202, 204, 210, 212–214, 217–219, 221–224, 226, 228
The Hellbound Heart 15, 18, 20, 38, 41, 43, 132, 175, 226
Hellbound: Hellraiser II 1, 5, 20, 29, 33, 53, 55–58, 60, 62–67, 69–72, 76, 80, 82–84, 87, 89–95, 97, 100, 107, 121, 123–124, 126–127, 130, 132, 143, 146, 152, 173, 183, 185, 187, 218, 222, 227
The Hellbound Web 169, 195, 227
Hellboy 5
Helloween 224
Hellraiser 5–7, 9, 10–11, 13–16, 18, 20–24, 26–27, 29, 31–32, 34–35, 37, 39–46, 48, 50–55, 57, 59–60, 62–65, 67, 71–72, 74–75, 77, 84, 90–91, 95–96, 98–100, 103, 104, 107, 113–114, 121–122, 124, 126–131, 136–138, 140–141, 143, 146, 149–151, 153, 156–162, 164–166, 171–176, 179–180, 185–190, 193–195, 198–199, 201, 203–207, 209, 213–219, 221–228
Hellraiser (TV show) 225
Hellraiser: Bloodline 98, 131–132, 136–139, 141–143, 145–146, 148, 152–153, 155, 157–158–159, 164–165, 169, 170, 173–174, 186, 194, 217, 222
Hellraiser: Deader 191, 193–201, 203–207, 210, 215–218

Hellraiser: Hellfire 159
Hellraiser: Hellseeker 80, 169, 175–177, 181, 183–187, 189–190, 193, 197–198, 204, 213
Hellraiser: Hellworld 193, 204–208, 210–216
Hellraiser: Inferno 95, 148, 160, 162–164, 166–175, 177–179, 181, 186, 190–191, 202, 213
Hellraiser III: Hell on Earth 1, 95–98, 100–101, 103–104, 107–108, 110, 113–115, 116, 121–124, 126–132, 134, 137, 139–140, 143, 146, 150, 173, 186–187, 199, 207–208, 212
"Hell's Event" 11
Henriksen, Lance 59, 206–207, 209, 216
Hickox, Anthony 101–108, 110–111, 113, 116, 121, 123–124, 126, 130, 132, 175,
Higgins, Clare 21, 29, 57, 59
Hill, Clayton 105
Hines, Robert 30
The History of the Devil 10
Hitchcock, Alfred 13, 31, 45, 93, 145
Hope, William 59, 92
Hopkins, Anthony 42
Horror 1, 3, 5–6, 9, 11, 13–14, 20–22, 24–25, 31, 34–35, 37, 39–40, 42–45, 48, 51–53, 55, 59–60, 63, 65, 71, 75, 79, 82, 84, 93, 95, 101–102, 110–111, 113–117, 126–127, 130–131, 136–139, 141, 143, 152, 154–155, 157, 159, 163, 174, 181, 189, 191, 194–196, 203, 206, 209, 214–216, 219, 224–226
The Host 206–209, 211–214, 216

I Monster 79
"In the Flesh" 11
L'inferno 87
"The Inhuman Condition" 11
Invaders from Mars 31, 55
Invasion of the Body Snatchers 31
The Invisible Man 80
Invitation Box 214
Island of Dr Moreau 80

Jacob's Ladder 161, 171, 181, 193
Jacot, Christopher 205
"Jacqueline Ess: Her Will and Testament" 11
Jacques (*Bloodline*) 133–134, 138, 141, 142, 146, 150–152
Jake (*Hellworld*) 205, 207–208, 210–214
Jihad (Hellraiser/Nightbreed crossover) 222
Joel, Deborah (Skinless Julia) 60
Joey (*Hellraiser: Deader*) 191–193, 196–197, 200–201, 207
Jones, Alan 63, 110

Jones, Paul 106, 108
Jones, Stephen 24, 159
Judge Dredd 99, 163
Jurassic Park 111, 197

Keen, Bob 6–7, 21, 23, 43, 45, 62, 95, 102, 106–107, 139
King, Stephen 5, 51, 163, 195
Kirby, Grace 22, 59
Kiss, the *Hellraiser* 16, 30, 32, 37, 62, 71, 74–75, 79, 82, 100, 133, 148–150, 191, 201
Klein, Amy (*Deader*) 191–202, 207
Krueger, Freddy 24, 31, 42, 59, 126, 132, 138, 224
Kuppin, Lawrence 96, 103, 105–106, 110–111, 225
Kutz, Simon 196
Kyle (*Hellbound*) 59, 61, 67–68, 70–71, 73–74, 76, 78, 82

Lament Configuration 1, 16, 35, 63, 68, 71, 76, 78, 93, 96, 98, 101, 107, 115, 119, 121, 125, 132, 134–135, 146–148, 151, 156, 159, 161, 172, 182, 184, 194, 198, 201–202, 212–214, 218–219, 221, 223, 226
Lange, Detective 178, 180–182, 184
Laurence, Ashley 21–22, 57, 73, 104, 176, 179, 189
Lawrence of Arabia 101
Lecter, Hannibal 42, 61, 128
Lee, Christopher 42, 79, 110, 127
Lemarchand, Phillip 18, 132–138, 142–149, 150–152, 155, 171, 194, 213–214, 222, 227
Leviathan 62, 64, 69–70, 72, 74, 76, 79, 89–91, 115, 119, 121, 129, 141, 147, 151, 153, 159, 187, 212, 214, 218, 221–223
Licht, Daniel 143
L'Isle, Duc de 133–134, 138, 144, 147–148, 151–152, 154
Little Red Riding Hood 75
Lodovico Street 20, 29–30, 37, 39, 57, 67, 73, 78, 124, 214
Lohner, Henning 198, 217
Look Back in Anger 31
Lord of Illusions 136, 141, 225
Lord of the Rings 62
Lost Highway 161, 163
Lovecraft, H.P. 80, 90, 136, 176
Lucas, George 44
Lynch, David 32, 40, 101, 161, 163, 165, 169

MacInnes, Angus 59
Malahide, Dr 54, 56–58
The Maltese Falcon 167
The Man Who Could Cheat Death 80
La Manoir du Diable 89

Marden, Richard 24, 50, 63
Marla (*Deader*) 191–194, 196, 200–201, 205
Marlowe, Christopher 16, 27, 77
Marlowe, Linda 196
Marquis de Sade 40, 154
Marshall, Paula 104, 110
The Masque of Red Death 34, 133
The Matrix Reloaded/Revolutions 5, 182, 221–222
Maximum Overdrive 5
McGuire, Victor 206
McKean, Dave 223
McLaurin, Marc 221, 223
Memento 168
Merchant, John 134, 137–138, 142–153, 147–153, 169, 194
Merchant, Paul 135–137, 141, 144–145, 147–153, 156, 194
Meyers, Kim 138
"The Midnight Meat Train" 10
Mike (*Hellworld*) 205, 208, 210, 212–214
Miller, Jonathan 217
Miller, Randy 107
Milton, John 77, 89
Minos 70, 135–136, 139, 141, 147–148, 150, 152–153, 155–156
The Minotaur 70, 135
Miramax 110–111, 113, 132, 136, 140–141, 143, 158–160, 227
Mirrors 64, 66–67, 71–73, 75, 78–79, 91, 125, 135, 147, 150–153, 182–183, 185–186
Monroe, J.P. 98–101, 104–107, 110, 116, 119–120, 122–125, 127–130
Morri, Kirk 165, 217
Mortoff, Lawrence 106
Motion Picture Association of America 50
Motorhead 107, 113
Mountview 22
The Mummy 20, 31, 80, 97
The Mutations 80
Myers, Michael 31, 141, 158, 224–225

Nenonen, Tony 162, 167, 169–171
New World 21–24, 26, 28, 32, 44–45, 48, 51, 53, 55–58, 60, 63, 65, 95–96, 98, 225
Night of the Living Dead 5, 31, 137, 201
Night Visions 18
Nightbreed 11, 13, 34, 95–97, 106, 162, 222
Nightlives 10
A Nightmare on Elm Street 24–25, 31, 51, 126, 132, 136, 214
A Nightmare on Elm Street Part 2: Freddy's Revenge 138
1984 183
No More Souls 164, 217–218

The Omen 35, 165
Orphée 66, 71, 121, 125
Orpheus 46, 66–70, 79
Osbourne, Ozzy 107

Pandora's Box 35
Paradise Lost 77, 89,
Parker, Oliver 21, 23, 57, 60, 95
Parmagi, Mr. (*Inferno*) 163, 167, 169
Pavlou, George 13, 15
Payton, Khary 204, 207
Peeping Tom 31
Phillips, Nick 204, 227
Pillar of Souls 108, 119, 120, 123, 128, 132
Pinhead 1, 7, 9, 18, 20, 23, 39, 40–44, 56–57, 59, 63, 68–69, 71, 76, 78, 80, 82, 87, 90–94, 97–101, 104–105, 108, 110–111, 113–116, 119–120, 122–131, 134–139, 141–143, 145–153, 157–161, 165–167, 169–171, 173–174, 176, 182–188, 194, 196, 198, 200–203, 207, 210–211, 214, 216–219, 221–228
Piper, Kelly 14
Piranesi, Giovanni Battista 87
Platoon 114
Poe, Edgar Allan 9, 21, 34, 45, 211
Poltergeist 121
Portass, Geoff 7, 21, 62, 108, 139
Psycho 13, 31, 93, 163
Puritan Passions 89
Puzzle Box 2, 9, 11, 16, 18, 20, 27, 30–31, 35, 39–40, 43–44, 54, 58, 68, 73, 76, 87, 91, 100–101, 115, 119, 124–125, 129, 132–136, 138, 142, 144, 146, 148–149, 156, 161, 163, 168–169, 171, 174–176, 182, 185, 187–188, 194, 198, 201, 207, 211, 213, 214, 219, 222, 224, 226–227
Pyramid Gallery 120, 123, 185, 227

Rais, Gilles de 18, 154
Ramsey, Bruce 137, 152
Randel, Tony 24, 55–58, 60, 63, 65, 72, 80, 92–93, 95, 98, 101, 113, 130, 143
Rawhead Rex 13–15, 50
Re-animator 45, 80
Red Dwarf 156
Redmond, Sarah-Jane 177
Regan, Mike 164, 178, 207, 217
Remar, James 162
Rhys, Paul 196
Rimmer (*Bloodline*) 135, 139, 141, 143–145, 147, 150–151, 156
Rimmer, Phil 15–16
The Ring 164, 198
Ripley (The *Alien* series) 22, 73, 156

Robinson, Andrew 22–23, 29, 57–58, 60, 68
Robinson, David 206
Robocop 156
Rock-A-Bye-Baby 102
The Rocky Horror Picture Show 102
Rogers, Michael 178
Romero, George A. 5, 50, 105, 201
Rosemary's Baby 31, 55
Rule of Three 75–76, 144
Russell, Ken 63
Rylance, Georgina 196

Sadler, Nicholas 163
Sage (*Hellseeker*) 177, 181, 184–186
Salome 16, 30
Satan 77, 88, 89
The Satanic Rites of Dracula 127
Saturn 3 155
Savini, Tom 137
Scanners 48
The Scarlet Gospels 7, 225–226
The Scarlet Pimpernel 155
Schmidt, Ron 197
Scott, Ridley 15, 128, 168
Se7en 161, 168
Sheffer, Craig 95, 162
Silence of the Lambs 61, 161, 168
"Skins of the Fathers" 11
Smith, Michael Marshall 159
Smith, Oliver 23, 57, 60
Snow White 75
Soisson, Joel 204, 211
Spawn 87
Spencer, Elliott 98, 100, 104, 107–108, 111, 114–116, 119, 121, 124–125, 127–130, 146, 152–153, 156, 187
Spielberg, Steven 15, 21, 44, 111, 196, 206
Stannyar Isoryar Doktora Dzehila i Mistera Khaida 79–80
Star Trek: Deep Space Nine 104
Star Trek: The Next Generation 5, 156
Star Wars 44, 59
Steve (*Hellraiser*) 30, 32, 34, 35, 37, 59, 68
Stevens, Neal Marshall 191, 193–195, 200
Stitch Cenobite 178
Summerskill, Joey (*Hell on Earth*) 98–101, 104–106, 110–111, 114–117, 119–125, 127–130, 132, 146, 150, 187, 216
Sundown: The Vampire in Retreat 102, 105–106
Superman 117, 177, 205
The Surgeon 133, 178, 182

Tales from the Crypt 136, 165, 175, 179
A Taste of Honey 31

Tawny (*Hellseeker*) 177–178, 182, 185
Taylor, William S 178
"The Telltale Heart" 45
The Terminator 156, 206
Terminator 2: Judgement Day 111, 156, 164
Terri (*Hell on Earth*) 98–100, 104, 114, 116, 119–120, 123–125, 129
The Texas Chainsaw Massacre 31, 207, 228
Theatre of Blood 101
Thompson, Jody 177
Thorne, Joseph (*Inferno*) 160–165, 167–173, 175, 177, 202
Tiffany (*Hellbound*) 55–60, 68–76, 78, 83, 87, 92–93, 123, 146
Tillitt, James 60
The Time Machine 144
Tolputt, Anna 205, 207
Torso Chatterer 164
Tortured Souls 7, 225
Trans Atlantic Entertainment 96, 108
Trevor (*Hellseeker*) 175–188
Trick or Treat 136, 204
Tunnicliffe, Gary 1–7, 139, 141, 164, 166, 178–179, 197, 206–207, 214, 217–218
Turturro, Nicholas 162
Twin Peaks 161, 165, 169
The Twins 135–136, 139, 152–153

Underworld (a.k.a *Transmutations*) 13–15, 21
The Unholy 89, 102
Urban Legend 160
Ursala, Sister (*Hellworld*) 207, 208, 209, 210, 214
The Usual Suspects 161, 169

The Vampires of Summer 54
Vargas, Valentina 138–139, 141
Variety 51, 93, 130, 157, 225
Vasile, Vivi Dragan 197
Vesalius 9, 18, 45
Videodrome 121, 181
Vidgeon, Robin 6, 21, 45, 50, 57, 62, 65, 106
Vince, Nick 22, 57, 62–63, 90, 95, 221
Vorhees, Jason 31, 98, 158, 224

Warlock: The Armageddon 105
Warren, Marc 196
Waxwork 102, 105, 121, 125
Waxwork II: Lost in Time 101–106, 108, 175
Weaver, Sigourney 22, 59, 156
Weaveworld 35, 53, 75
Webster, John 48
Weinstein, Bob 110–111, 141, 160, 169, 227
Weinstein, Harvey 141, 227

Werzowa, Walter 165
Wilde, Barbie 59
Wildgoose, Jane 40–41
Winnick, Katheryn 205–208, 216
Winston, Stan 197
Winter (*Deader*) 191–194, 196–197, 200–202
Winters, Dean 176–178

Wire Twins 164, 169
The Witches of Eastwick 89
The Wizard of Oz 182
Wuhrer, Kari 195–197, 201, 203

X-Files 5, 177, 206

Yagher, Kevin 136–143, 157, 175

"The Yattering and Jack" 11, 90
Young, Christopher 24, 26, 45, 55, 63, 65, 107, 143, 179, 198
Yuzna, Brian 137

Zilva, Karen de 177
Zombie Flesh Eaters 201
Zulu Dawn 101

www.ingramcontent.com/pod-product-compliance
Ingram Content Group UK Ltd.
Pitfield, Milton Keynes, MK11 3LW, UK
UKHW051540291225
9797UKWH00040BB/759